CCCC

Bibliography of Composition and Rhetoric

1993

Gail E. Hawisher
Cynthia L. Selfe
Editors

Sibylle Gruber
Margaret F. Sweany
Associate Editors

Conference on College Composition and Communication,
A Conference of the National Council of Teachers of English

Southern Illinois University Press
Carbondale and Edwardsville

ISSN 1046–0675
ISBN 0–8093–1993–4
ISBN 0–8093–1994–2 pbk.

The paper used in this publication meets the minimum requirements of
American National Standard for Information Sciences—Permanence of
Paper for Printed Library Materials, ANSI Z39.48-1984. ∞

This volume is dedicated to the staff at Southern Illinois University Press—Curtis L. Clark, Susan H. Wilson, Robyn Laur Clark, and Stephen W. Smith—for their extensive support and persistent hard work. They continue to be invaluable to us; indeed, the care that they bring to the Bibliography makes it a far better publication than we could possibly produce without them. We are grateful to be working with such first-rate professionals, and we thank them for their expertise and thoughtful advice.

Contents

Preface

Gail E. Hawisher
Cynthia L. Selfe

Each year the CCCC Bibliography changes in subtle and not so subtle ways as the field of composition and rhetoric itself changes and expands its field of vision. For this 1993 volume, we have compiled 2054 entries that, for the most part, are not so different from the texts collected and annotated in former years. Entries include topics with which rhetoricians and compositionists have always concerned themselves—topics related to issues of theory, practice, and research in all areas of writing studies. At the same time, however, we note that the 1993 Bibliography, with well over two thousand entries, is the largest edition we have worked with so far and that many more of its titles deal with the relationship of composition and rhetoric to critical theory, gender issues, and cultural studies.

This volume also stands out from previous editions in that it includes a new section on electronic discussion groups or listservs. Such discussion groups have become increasingly popular among writing professionals in recent years, beginning with Michael Spitzer's first electronic conference for English professionals,

the "Fifth C." Founded in December of 1984, Spitzer's national electronic conference continued for three years and had its roots in the CCCC organization. Because Spitzer got his idea for starting the conference when he attended CCCC's special interest group of the "Fifth C," and because he saw the asynchronous online group as a place to continue discussions begun at the SIG, he named the electronic conference the "Fifth C." Between December 1984, and August 1987, about 100 people joined and participated in the conference before the monies from the grant ran out. According to Spitzer, "Discussion topics ranged from inquiries and responses regarding specific software packages to practical advice on setting up computer classrooms, to teaching strategies for use in classrooms with one computer or twenty computers, to a scholarly discussion of artificial intelligence and its impact on writing instruction and software" (Spitzer, email correspondence, September 28, 1993). Today while several such discussion groups continue to focus on computers and composition studies (e.g., Megabyte University), many others focus on the subspecialties that mark the larger field of composition and rhetoric (e.g., writing centers, writing across the curriculum, technical communication, English as a second language, etc.).

We believe these listservs can be important resources for writing professionals and have tried to find a way to include them within the Bibliography. Thus we have added a new category, Section 6: Listservs, as a place where readers will find entries that describe the Internet's various electronic discussion groups on composition and rhetoric. We have also included with the entries instructions as to how readers may join the various groups.

The largest and oldest ongoing list among them is Megabyte University (MBU), founded by Fred Kemp, after the 1989 CCCC Convention. Kemp, like Spitzer before him, wanted to create an electronic space where the spirited CCCC conversations might continue, conversations that now include almost 600 MBU participants. Since that time, the 21 other discussion groups included in Section 6 have been very successful, yet we know of no single place where a systematic listing of such electronic forums devoted to composition and rhetoric can be found. This section of the Bibliography is intended to provide just such a place. We welcome suggestions and advice from readers as to the usefulness of the new section.

We have made one other change in our method of collecting annotations that is not evident in the Bibliography itself but that we hope will move us closer to an online edition. Contributing bibliographers this year submitted a list of keywords pertinent to their entries, keywords that we will eventually use for building a future electronic edition of the Bibliography. Much of our time this year will be spent as editors working with a CCCC task force to explore the possibilities for such online distribution.

As the 1993 edition of the CCCC Bibliography goes to press, we thank the many contributing bibliographers for their support, advice, and overall invaluable assistance. We are also, as always, indebted to our associate editors, Sibylle Gruber and Margaret F. Sweany. Without their keen intelligence and painstaking attempts to work with us and the Bibliography, there would be no Bibliography as we know it. In many subtle and not so subtle ways, they continue to work their magic on the Bibliography, and for that we thank them.

Guidelines for Users of the *CCCC Bibliography*

Erika Lindemann

The CCCC Bibliography of Composition and Rhetoric, published by the Conference on College Composition and Communication, offers teachers and researchers an annual classified listing of scholarship on written English and its teaching. The bibliography lists each work only once, but it descriptively annotates all citations, cross-references them when appropriate, and indexes all authors and editors. A group of contributing bibliographers, listed on pages xv to xvi, prepared the citations and annotations for all entries appearing in this volume.

SCOPE OF THE BIBLIOGRAPHY

The CCCC Bibliography includes works that treat written communication (whether the writing people do is in English or some other language), the processes whereby human beings compose and understand written messages, and methods of teaching people to communicate effectively in writing. The Bibliography lists entries in six major categories (see the Contents for a more complete description of these categories):

Section 1. Bibliographies and Checklists
Section 2. Theory and Research
Section 3. Teacher Education, Administration, and Social Roles
Section 4. Curriculum
Section 5. Testing, Measurement, and Evaluation
Section 6. Listservs

The Bibliography makes few restrictions on the format, medium, or purpose of the works it includes, so long as the subject of the work falls into one of the six categories described in the preceding list. It lists published works—books, articles, monographs, published collections (of essays, conference presentations, or working papers), bibliographies and other reference works, films, microforms, videotapes, and sound recordings—and, new in 1993, electronic discussion groups of listservs. It includes citations for unpublished doctoral dissertations appearing in Dissertation Abstracts International. It also includes review articles that discuss several works, define movements or trends, or survey an individual's contribution to the discipline. It excludes masters theses, textbooks, computer software, and works written in a language other than English.

SOURCES

The CCCC Bibliography cites works from four major sources.

Periodicals. Journals publishing articles on composition and its teaching are the source for at least 1000 entries. Each journal is identified by an abbreviation; an alphabetical list of Journal Abbreviations begins on page xvii. With few exceptions, the contributing bibliographers preparing entries for journal articles examined the material firsthand.

Publishers. A second source of materials are commercial publishers and university presses. These publishers, whose participation in the bibliography project is voluntary, provided contributing bibliographers with written information for the books listed in this volume. Often, contributing bibliographers were unable to examine books firsthand and had to rely on these materials for their entries.

This volume also includes scholarly essay collections, books that bring together essays, articles, or papers by several authors. The Bibliography annotates these collections, but does not annotate each essay. All authors contributing to the collection are included in the annotation and listed in the Name Index.

Dissertation Abstracts International (DAI). DAI represents a third source for citations. Not all degree-granting institutions list their unpublished doctoral dissertations in DAI, and as a rule, the contributing bibliographers have not examined these dissertations firsthand. The citations in this volume serve only to direct readers to abstracts in DAI. Users will want to consult the DAI abstracts for additional information, including who supervised the degree

candidate's work and which institution granted the degree.

Resources in Education (RIE). A fourth source of materials in the CCCC Bibliography is the Educational Resources Information Center (ERIC), a federally funded document retrieval system coordinated by sixteen clearinghouses.

ERIC indexes its materials in two reference works. Journal articles appear in Cumulative Index to Journals in Education (CIJE). Resources in Education (RIE), on the other hand, indexes documents in the ERIC microfiche collection, available in 2600 regional libraries or directly from ERIC. These documents, frequently published elsewhere, include government documents, research and project reports, bibliographies, and conference papers. Documents indexed in RIE receive a six-digit "ED" number (e.g., ERIC ED 305 701) and are cross-referenced under various subject headings or "descriptors."

Some documents may be listed in RIE and may become available through ERIC several years after they were written. For convenience and to ensure comprehensiveness, the CCCC Bibliography reports ERIC documents cited in RIE during the years covered in the current volume; that is, this volume cites ERIC documents listed in RIE in 1993, even though the works themselves may have an earlier "date of publication." Also as a convenience, each ERIC entry includes the six-digit "ED" number.

Contributing bibliographers working with ERIC materials have developed the following criteria for determining what documents to include in this volume:

Substantiveness. Substantive documents of general value to college composition teachers and researchers are included. Representative publications are curriculum guides, federal government final reports, and technical reports from various publication series, such as those published, for example, by the Center for the Study of Writing and Literacy and the Center for the Study of Reading.

Relevance. Documents that seem to represent concerns of high interest to researchers are included. Topics related to first-year composition, computers and literacy, and gender studies, for example, represent concerns of greater relevance than the teaching of handwriting.

Inclusiveness. Relevant papers on composition and rhetoric available in ERIC and delivered at the annual meetings of the Conference on College Composition and Communication (CCCC) and the National Council of Teachers of English (NCTE—Fall and Spring conventions) are included. Papers delivered at other regional and national meetings—for example, meetings of the American Educational Research Association (AERA), the International Reading Association (IRA), and the Modern Language Association (MLA)—have also been selected for inclusion on the basis of their substantiveness and relevance.

Reference value. Items for which the ERIC microfiche system might provide unique access are included. Representative of entries meeting this criterion would be books or collections of articles no longer available from their original publishers.

Alternate access. Many professional organizations regularly make copies of book and monograph publications available as ERIC microfiche. And many papers presented as reports or conference talks and available in ERIC are later published as monographs or as articles in journals. When such information is available, the entry in this volume will include ERIC ED numbers to indicate an alternate source of access to the document. However, users of this volume should keep in mind that, although a book in ERIC reflects the exact contents of the published work, an article in ERIC is a manuscript that may see substantial revision before it is published.

The following criteria determine which items cited in RIE are excluded from this volume:

Local interest. ERIC documents concerned with composition and rhetoric but judged to be primarily of local interest are excluded. For example, this volume omits annual evaluation reports of writing programs in local schools.

Availability. Publications of commercial publishers and other organizations that are listed in RIE and assigned an ERIC ED number but are not available through the ERIC microfiche system are omitted.

Users of the CCCC Bibliography may wish to supplement this resource by consulting RIE or various computer-assisted retrieval systems that access ERIC documents. Copies of most documents indexed in RIE can be purchased in paper or microform from the ERIC system. ERIC clearinghouses also make available free or inexpensive guides to special topics of interest to rhetoric and composition teachers and researchers. Order forms and current addresses for these clearinghouses appear at the back of each monthly issue of RIE.

A few entries in this volume show publication dates earlier than 1993. By and large, these materials have two sources. They represent articles published in 1993 but appearing in journals showing earlier volume numbers, or they represent materials accessioned by ERIC clearinghouses in 1993 but originally published earlier.

The items listed in the annual bibliography are not housed in any single location or owned by any single individual. The CCCC Bibliography lists and describes these materials but does not provide users of the bibliography any additional means of retrieving them. However, librarians can be extremely helpful in finding copies of particular works to examine firsthand. Some materials may be available through interlibrary loan, OCLC and on-line catalogues, ERIC and other information retrieval systems, or state and university libraries. To locate materials cited in this volume, ask your librarian to help you.

CONTRIBUTING BIBLIOGRAPHERS

The reliability and usefulness of these annual volumes depend primarily on a large group of contributing bibliographers. Contributing bibliographers accept responsibility for compiling accurate entries in their areas of expertise, for preparing brief, descriptive annotations for each entry, for determining where each entry will appear within one of the five sections of the Bibliography, for cross-referencing entries when appropriate, and for submitting completed entries by a specified deadline.

To ensure consistency, contributing bibliographers receive a Handbook for Contributing Bibliographers to guide them in their work and fill out a printed form for each entry. Contributing bibliographers agree to serve a three-year term and, thereafter, may request reappointment for another two-year term. In return for their valuable service to the profession, they receive a copy of each annual volume they have had a substantial hand in preparing. Graduate students, teachers, researchers, or other individuals who wish to become contributing bibliographers may write to the editors.

ANNOTATIONS

Annotations accompany all entries in this volume. They describe the document's contents and are intended to help users determine the document's usefulness. Annotations are brief and, insofar as the English language allows, are meant to be descriptive, not evaluative. They explain what the work is about but leave readers free to judge for themselves the work's merits. Most annotations fall into one of three cate-

gories: they present the document's thesis, main argument, or major research finding; they describe the work's major organizational divisions; or they indicate the purpose or scope of the work.

CROSS-REFERENCES AND INDEXES

This volume cites and annotates each document only once, in one of the five major sections of the Bibliography. Every entry, however, receives an "entry number" so that cross-references to other sections are possible. Cross-references are necessary because much scholarship in composition and rhetoric is interdisciplinary. Cross-references appear as a listing of entry numbers preceded by "See also," found at the end of each subsection of the Bibliography.

The Subject Index lists most of the topics discussed in the works cited in this volume. Consulting the Subject Index may help users locate sections and subsections of the Bibliography that contain large numbers of entries addressing the same topic.

The Name Index lists all authors, editors, and contributors to publications cited in this volume.

Contributing Bibliographers

Valentina M. Abordonado
Elizabeth H. Addison
James C. Addison, Jr.
Clara Alexander
Melanie Angle
Ken Autrey
Kim Ballard
Linda Bannister
John Barber
Larry Beason
Karla Beckner
Carole Bencich
Lamar Bennett
Cynthia A. Berrie
Pam Besser
Renee Betz
Roberta Binkley
Edward Black
Bill Bolin
Virginia A. Book
Kerry Bostwiek
Diana Bowling
Kirk Branch
Barrett M. Briggs
Lady Falls Brown

Mary Louise Buley-Meissner
Kathryn M. Burton
Gaunjun Cai
Carol Callahan
Dan Callahan
Barbara L. Cambridge
Jim Cihlar
Shelley Circle
Carol Lea Clark
Gregory Clark
Irene Lurkis Clark
Michael Cody
Juanita Comfort
Louise Rodriquez Connal
Leni Cook
Elizabeth J. Cooper
Patricia Coward
Christopher Custer
Donald A. Daiker
Thomas E. Dasher
Ken Davis
Bonnie Devet
George Dillon
William Dodd
Ray V. Drake

James Michael Dubinsky
Ann Hill Duin
Leslie A. Dupont
Elizabeth Ervin
Chuck Etheridge
Timothy J. Evans
Marisa Farnum
Julia K. Ferganchick-Neufang
Janis Forman
Mark K. Fulk
Richard Fulkerson
T. Clifford Gardiner
Traci Gardner
Lisa Gerrard
Laura L. Gilligan
Joan I. Glazer
Judith Goleman
Alice Anne Goodwin-Davey
Perry M. Gordon
Patricia Goubil-Gambrell
Jane Greer
Stephen Hahn
Marcia Peoples Halio
Klaus Haltmayer
Liz Hamp-Lyons

Kathy Haney
Jim Hanlon
Kristine Hansen
Serena Hansen
James S. Harper
Myrna Harrienger
Gary Layne Hatch
Nancy Hayward
Cozette K. Heller
Edwina Helton
Alexandra Rowe Henry
Douglas Hesse
John Heyda
Dixie Elise Hickman
Betsy Hilbert
Elizabeth Hodges
Deborah H. Holdstein
Sylvia A. Holladay
Alice Horning
Rebecca Moore Howard
Elizabeth Huettman
Sue Yin Hum
Zita Ingham
Sherrie Inness
Rebecca Innocent
Dee James
Sandra Jamieson
Jack Jobst
Johndan Johnson-Eilola
Marian E. Jones
Jonathan Kandell
Patricia Kedzerski
Deborah P. Kehoe
Marty Kelley
Joyce Kinkead
James Kinney
Karla Kitalong
Renee L. Kuperman
Lisa Langstraat
Joan Latchaw
Greg Lau
Janice M. Lauer
Keith Lawrence
Cynthia Lewiecki-Wilson

Kenneth J. Lindblom
Erika Lindemann
Margaret Lindgren
Linda E. Lister
Joan Livingston-Webber
Patty Long
Kim Brian Lovejoy
Joyce MacAllister
Beryl C. Martinson
Lisa D. Mason
Sandra McBride
Allison McCormack
James McDonald
Robert L. McDonald
Dana Gulling Mead
Edwin Meek
Vincent P. Mikkelsen
Emily P. Miller
Theresa Moore
Charles Moran
Max Morenberg
Marie Wilson Nelson
Ed Nolte
Joe O'Connor
Terence Odlin
Robert Oldham
Suzanne C. Padgett
Peggy B. Parris
Bill Pedersen
Barry Pegg
Chere L. Peguesse
Michael A. Pemberton
Elizabeth F. Penfield
Virginia Perdue
Sheila Petruccelli
Alice Philbin
Virginia G. Polanski
James Postema
M. Karen Powers-Stubbs
John W. Presley
Margaret Procter
Jasna Randic
Frances Jeanne Ranney
D. R. Ransdell

David H. Roberts
M. J. Robinson
Dawn Rodrigues
Carolynn J. Root
Diana Royer
Christine G. Russell
Sala L. Sanders
Peter Sands
Lew Sayers
Judith A. Scheffler
Erica Scott
Celene Seymour
Nancy W. Shankle
Cynthia Miecznikowski Sheard
Dorothy Sheldon
Joyce A. Simutis
Barbara M. Sitko
Penelope Smith
Linda Stine
James Strickland
Gail Stygall
Patricia Sullivan
Bernard Susser
Wendy Swyt
Josephine K. Tarvers
Barr Taylor
Marcia Taylor
Nathaniel Teich
Patricia Terry
Laura Thomas
Charlotte Thralls
Nan Uber
Marilyn V. Urion
Billie J. Wahlstrom
Cynthia Walker
Keith Walters
John Warnock
Wendy K. Warren
Jaqueline Wheeler
William J. Williamson
David E. Wilson
William C. Wolff
George Q. Xu
Kathleen Blake Yancey

Journal Abbreviations

AA	American Anthropologist	Arg	Argumentation
AAF	Adult Assessment Forum	AS	American Speech
AAHE	AAHE Bulletin	ASch	The American Scholar
ACE	The ACE Newsletter	ATA	Advanced Composition Forum
ACEN	Assembly for Computers in English Newsletter	BABC	Bulletin of the Association for Business Communication
ADEB	The Association of Departments of English Bulletin	BEdF	Business Education Forum
AdEd	Adult Education	B&L	Brain and Language
AdLBEd	Adult Literacy and Basic Education	Boundary	Boundary 2: A Journal of Postmodern Literature and Culture
A&EQ	Anthropology and Education Quarterly		
AERJ	American Educational Research Journal	CACJ	Computer-Assisted Composition Journal
AJS	American Journal of Semiotics	CalE	California English
AM	Academic Medicine: Journal of the Association of American Medical Colleges	CALS	Carleton Papers in Applied Language Studies
		C&C	Computers and Composition
AmE	American Ethnologist	CCC	College Composition and Communication
AmP	American Psychologist		
Annals	Annals of the American Academy of Political and Social Sciences	CCR	Community College Review
		CCrit	Cultural Critique
		CE	College English
ArEB	Arizona English Bulletin	CEA	CEA Critic

CEAF	CEA Forum
CEd	Communication Education
CHE	Chronicle of Higher Education
CHum	Computers and Humanities
C&I	Cognition and Instruction
CJL	Canadian Journal of Linguistics
CLAJ	College Languages Association Journal
Cognition	Cognition
CollL	College Literature
CollM	Collegiate Microcomputer
CollT	College Teaching
ComM	Communication Monographs
CompC	Composition Chronicle
CompEd	Computers and Education
CompQ	Composition Quarterly
ComQ	Communication Quarterly
ComR	Communication Research
ComS	Communication Studies
Configura-tions	Configurations: Journal of Literature, Science and Technology
CPsy	Cognitive Psychology
CritI	Critical Inquiry
CSc	Cognitive Science
Daedalus	Daedalus: Journal of the American Academy of Arts and Sciences
DAI	Dissertation Abstracts International
Dialogue	Dialogue: A Journal for Writing Specialists
DP	Developmental Psychology
DPr	Discourse Processes
D&S	Discourse and Society
EdEPA	Educational Evaluation and Policy Analysis
EdM	Educational Measurement: Issues and Practice
EdPsy	Educational Psychologist
EdTech	Educational Technology
EDUCOM	Educom Review
EEd	English Education
EES	Explorations in Ethnic Studies
EJ	English Journal
ELQ	English Leadership Quarterly
ELTJ	English Language Teaching Journal

EnEd	Engineering Education
EngR	English Record
EnT	English Today
EQ	English Quarterly
ERQ	Educational Research Quarterly
ESP	English for Specific Purposes
ET	English in Texas
ETC	ETC.: A Review of General Semantics
ExEx	Exercise Exchange
FEN	Freshman English News
FLA	Foreign Language Annals
Focuses	Focuses: A Journal Linking Composition Programs and Writing Center Practice
FSt	Feminist Studies
GaR	Georgia Review
HCI	Human-Computer Interaction
HCR	Human Communication Research
HD	Human Development
HER	Harvard Education Review
HT	History Teacher
Hypermedia	Hypermedia
IDJ	Information Design Journal
IEEE	IEEE Transactions on Professional Communication
IHE	Innovative Higher Education
IL	Informal Logic
IlEB	Illinois English Bulletin
IndE	Indiana English
Inland	Inland: A Journal for Teachers of English Language Arts
Intelligence	Intelligence
IPM	Information Processing and Management
IRAL	International Review of Applied Linguistics in Language Teaching
Issues	Issues in Writing
JAC	Journal of Advanced Composition
JACET	JACET Bulletin
JAF	Journal of American Folklore
JALT	JALT Journal

JBC	Journal of Business Communication
JBS	Journal of Black Studies
JBTC	Iowa State Journal of Business and Technical Communication
JBW	Journal of Basic Writing
JC	Journal of Communication
JCBI	Journal of Computer-Based Instruction
JCE	Journal of Chemical Education
JCS	Journal of Curriculum Studies
JCST	Journal of College Science Teaching
JDEd	Journal of Developmental Education
JEd	Journal of Education
JEdM	Journal of Educational Measurement
JEdM&H	Journal of Educational Multimedia and Hypermedia
JEdPsy	Journal of Educational Psychology
JEdR	Journal of Educational Research
JEngL	Journal of English Linguistics
JEPG	Journal of Experimental Psychology: General
JEPH	Journal of Experimental Psychology: Human Perception and Performance
JEPL	Journal of Experimental Psychology: Learning, Memory, Cognition
JFR	Journal of Folklore Research
JGE	JGE: The Journal of General Education
JGTAD	The Journal of Graduate Teaching Assistant Development
JL	Journal of Linguistics
JLD	Journal of Learning Disabilities
JMEd	Journal of Medical Education
JMemC	Journal of Memory and Cognition: Learning, Memory, Cognition
JMemL	Journal of Memory and Language
JNT	Journal of Narrative Technique
JOC	Journal of Organizational Computing
JourEd	Journalism Educator
JPsy	Journal of Psychology
JPsyR	Journal of Psycholinguistic Research
JR	Journal of Reading
JRB	Journal of Reading Behavior: A Journal of Literacy
JRDEd	Journal of Research and Development in Education
JSLW	Journal of Second Language Writing
JT	Journal of Thought
JTEd	Journal of Teacher Education
JTW	Journal of Teaching Writing
JTWC	Journal of Technical Writing and Communication
Lang&S	Language and Style
LangS	Language Sciences
LangT	Language Testing
Language	Language: Journal of the Linguistic Society of America
L&E	Linguistics and Education: An International Research Journal
Leaflet	The Leaflet
Learning	Learning
Linguistics	Linguistics
L&M	Literature and Medicine
L&S	Language and Speech
LSoc	Language in Society
M&C	Memory and Cognition
MCQ	Managment and Communication Quarterly
MEd	Medical Education
MissQ	Mississippi Quarterly
MLJ	The Modern Language Journal
MLQ	Modern Language Quarterly
MLS	Modern Language Studies
M&M	Media and Methods
MSE	Massachusetts Studies in English
MT	Mathematics Teacher
Multimedia	Multimedia
MultiR	Multicultural Review
NYRB	The New York Review of Books
OralHR	Oral History Review
PC	The Professional Communicator
Perspectives	Perspectives
PhiDK	Phi Delta Kappan

PhS	Philosophical Studies	Signs	Signs
P&L	Philosophy and Literature	SLang	Studies in Language
PMLA	Publication of the Modern Language Association	SNNTS	Studies in the Novel
		SocStSc	Social Studies of Science
PMS	Perceptual and Motor Skills	StHum	Studies in the Humanities
PoT	Poetics Today	STHV	Science, Technology and Human Values
PPR	Philosophy and Phenomenological Research		
		Style	Style
PR	Partisan Review	SubStance	SubStance
P&R	Philosophy and Rhetoric		
Pre/Text	Pre/Text	TC	Technical Communication
PsyR	Psychological Review	TCQ	Technical Communication Quarterly
PsyT	Psychology Today		
		TESOLQ	Teachers of English of Speakers of Other Languages Quarterly
QJS	Quarterly Journal of Speech		
QNWP/ CSW	The Quarterly for the National Writing Project and the Center for the Study of Writing	TETYC	Teaching English in the Two-Year College
		TEXT	TEXT: An Interdisciplinaly Journal for the Study of Discourse
QRD	Quarterly Review of Doublespeak		
		TWM	Teachers and Writers Magazine
Raritan	Raritan		
Reader	Reader: Essays in Reader-Oriented Theory, Criticism, And Pedagogy	UEJ	Utah English Journal
RER	Review of Educational Research	Videography	Videography
RHE	Research in Higher Education	VLang	Visible Language
Rhetorica	Rhetorica	V&R	Visions and Revisions
RIE	Resources in Education		
RMR	Rocky Mountain Review of Language and Literature	WAC	Writing Across the Curriculum
RR	Rhetoric Review	WC	Written Communication
RRQ	Reading Research Quarterly	WCJ	Writing Center Journal
RSQ	Rhetoric Society Quarterly	W&D	Work and Days
RTDE	Research and Teaching in Developmental Education	WE	Writing on the Edge
		WI	The Writing Instructor
RTE	Research in the Teaching of English	WJC	Western Journal of Communication
R&W	Reading and Writing: An Interdisciplinary Journal	WLN	The Writing Lab Newsletter
		WLWE	World Literature Written in English
SAF	Studies in American Fiction	WN	The Writing Notebook
ScAm	Scientific American	WPA	Journal of the Council of Writing Program Administrators
SCJ	Southern Communication Journal	Writer	The Writer
SFS	Science Fiction Studies	WS	Women's Studies

Abbreviations in Entries

AACSB	American Assembly of Collegiate Schools of Business
ABC	American Business Conference
ACTFL	American Council on the Teaching of Foreign Languages
AI	Artificial Intelligence
AP	Advanced Placement
APA	American Psychological Association
CAI	Computer-Assisted Instruction
CAM	Categories, Agreement, and Morphology
CAT	Classroom Assessment Technique
CCP	Certified Claims Professional
CD-ROM	Compact Disc Read-Only Memory
CEO	Coded Elaborative Outlines
CIDWT	Computerized Inventory of Developmental Writing Traits
CIG	Construction-Based Interpretative Grammar
CLC	Classic Learning Core
CMC	Computer-Mediated Communication
CSF	Critical Success Factor
CSLI	Center for the Study of Language and Information
DNA	Deoxyribonucleic Acid
ENFI	Electronic Network for Interaction
ERIC	Educational Resources Information Center
ERIC/FLL	ERIC Clearinghouse on Language and Linguistics
ERIC/RCS	ERIC Clearinghouse on Reading and Communication Skills
ESL	English as a Second Language
ESOL	English to Speakers of Other Languages
FIPSE	Fund for the Improvement of Postsecondary Education
FL	Foreign Language
GB-theory	Govenrment-Binding Theory
GDSS	Group Decision Support systems
G.I. Bill	Veterans Benefits Act, Public Law 345, 1994
GPA	Grade Point Average
GTA	Graduate Teaching Assistant

ID	Instructional Design	PC	Politically Correct
IRF	Intermittent Reinforcement	RMS	Readability Measuring System
JRG	Journal Response Groups	Rx	Remote Exchange
L1	First Language	SAL	Structured Assembly Language
L2	Second Language	SESD	Space Electronic Security
LD	Learning Disabled		Division
LSU	Louisiana State University	SGML	Structured General Markup
MIT	Michigan Institute of		Language
	Technology	SLA	Second Language Acquisition
MLA	Modern Language Association	SRL	Self-Regulated Learning
MX	Missile, Experimental	SVEN	Survey of Vancouver English
NCTE	National Council of Teachers	TA	Teaching Assistant
	of English	TOEFL	Teaching of English as a
NES	Non-English Speaking		Foreign Language
NNS	Nonnative Speakers	UCLA	Univerity of California, Los
NS	Native Speakers		Angeles
OED	Oxford English Dictionary	USC	University of South Carolina
PAPE	Priority and Performance	WPA	Writing Program Administrator
	Evaluation		

CCCC

Bibliography of Composition and Rhetoric

1993

1

Bibliographies and Checklists

1 BIBLIOGRAPHIES AND CHECKLISTS

1. Albrecht, Lisa. "Bibliography: Jewish/Palestinian Middle East Peace Perspectives (with a Focus on Feminist Activist Work)." *MultiR* 2 (December 1993): 16–21.

Presents a bibliography of books, periodicals and essays about the Israeli-Palestinian conflict (especially about women) and contains a syllabus for a course using these texts.

2. Azzolina, David S. "Roundup of Recent Releases on the Gay and Lesbian Experience." *MultiR* 2 (December 1993): 22–27.

Presents an annotated list of nonfiction texts on gay and lesbian issues.

3. Azzolina, David S. "Boundaries of Identity: Cultural Regionalism and the American West." *MultiR* 2 (March 1993): 22–27.

Argues that if we understand our regional perspectives, we can raise larger questions about our culture. Contains an annotated bibliography of works on the West.

4. *Bibliographic Guide to Conference Publications: 1992.* G. K. Hall Bibliographic Guides. Boston, MA: G. K. Hall, 1993. 1000+ pages

Lists conference publications catalogued during the year by The Research Libraries of the New York Public Library, with additional entries from LC MARC tapes. Annually indexes some 26,000 private and government conferences, and collections of papers. Covers all disciplines, countries, and languages.

5. *Bibliographic Guide to Education: 1992.* Boston, MA: G. K. Hall, 1993. 600+ pages

Lists material recorded on the OCLC tapes of Columbia University Teachers College during the year, with additional entries from the New York Public Library for selected publications. Covers all aspects of education. Presents a supplement to the 1970 Dictionary Catalog of the Teachers College Library.

6. Conru, Paula M., Vickie W. Lewelling, and Whitney Stewart. *Speaking of Language: An International Directory of Language Service Organizations*. Language in Education: Theory and Practice.: ERIC Clearinghouse on Languages and Linguistics, 1993. 191 pages

    Provides detailed information on over 130 language service providers. Presents a guide to resources and services related to language study and teaching.

7. Denner, Michael. "Writing to Learn." Focused Access to Selected Topics (FAST) Bib No. 66, 1993. ERIC ED 356 484. 5 pages

    Annotates 31 ERIC documents and journal articles published between 1987 and 1992 concerning the "Writing-to-Learn" movement.

8. Dickinson, Patricia. "Gender Issues in Language and Writing." Focused Access to Selected Topics (FAST) Bib No.63, 1993. ERIC ED 356 486. 5 pages

    Focuses on gender issues in language and writing. Annotates 23 ERIC documents and journal articles published between 1987 and 1991.

9. Gottleib, Stephen S. "Legal Language: How It's Taught and Used." *CompC* 6 (February 1993): 9–10.

    Provides an annotated ERIC bibliography on law-related writing.

10. Greenberg, Reva M. *Education for Older Adult Learning: A Selected, Annotated Bibliography*. New York: Praeger Press, 1993. 219 pages

    Cites over 700 publications, computer programs, and other materials relevant to educating older adults.

11. Greene, Beth G. "New from ERIC/REC." *CompC* 6 (November 1993): 12–13.

    Provides an annotated bibliography of student writing samples and grading protocols in the ERIC database.

12. Harmon, Joseph E., and David R. Hamrin. "Bibliography on Communicating Technical Research Information." *IEEE* 36 (March 1993): 2–6.

    Provides an annotated list of articles and book chapters which offers advice to writers of technical reports.

13. Johnson, Glenderlyn. "Selected African-American Bibliography." *MultiR* 2 (March 1993): 47.

    Presents fifteen annotated selections of standard and best-selling works in African-American studies.

14. Jorn, Linda A. "A Selected Annotated Bibliography on Collaboration in Technical Communication." *TCQ* 2 (Winter 1993): 105–15.

    Includes selected items from scholarly and popular presses. Covers material from 1985–93.

15. Larson, Richard L., and A. L. Saks. "Annotated Bibliography of Research in the Teaching of English." *RTE* 27 (December 1993): 432–37.

    The authors provide selected annotated entries for recent literature in areas of curriculum, language, literature, teacher education, and writing.

16. Lobdell, James E., and Sandra R. Schecter. "Video Resources for the Teaching of Literacy: An Annotated Bibliography." Center for the Study of Writing, 1993. 33. 17 pages

    Lists available video resources in literacy education, indicating types of audience and specific problems each resource addresses.

17. McCoy, Ralph E. *Freedom of the Press: An Annotated Bibliography: Second Supplement, 1978–1992*. Carbondale, IL: Southern Illinois University Press, 1994. 576 pages

    Updates his two earlier works. Provides descriptive annotations of a variety of sources relating to freedom of the press in the English-speaking world, including works on pornography. McCoy's broad definitions of "press" encompasses printed and electronic media and performances. Includes a detailed, cross-referenced subject index.

18. Sensenbaugh, Roger. "Spelling Instruction and the Use of Word Lists." *CompC* 6 (April 1993): 8–9.

Presents an annotated ERIC bibliography on spelling instruction.

19. Sensenbaugh, Roger. "Teaching Business Communication Skills: A Bibliography." *BABC* 56 (December 1993): 52–55.

Provides an annotated bibliography of conference papers, books, curriculum guides, and conference proceedings.

20. Strickland, James. "An Annotated Bibliography of Representative Software for Writers." *C&C* 10 (November 1993): 25–36.

Provides brief overviews and purchase information for 45 writing-related software programs.

21. Walsh, Kathleen, and Philip Kenholz. "Annotated Bibliography of Manitoba Literacy Products." ERIC Clearinghouse, Indiana University, Bloomington, IN, April 1991. ERIC ED 357 660. 28 pages

Lists 178 items of literacy learning materials, curricula documents, reference documents, and source materials developed in Manitoba, Canada.

22. Weintraub, Sam. *Annual Summary of Investigations Relating to Reading, July 1, 1991 to June 30, 1992.* Newark, DE: International Reading Association, 1993. 222 pages

Summarizes reading research published in periodicals, books, conference proceedings, and other publications. Uses categories such as Teacher Preparation and Practice, Sociology of Reading, Physiology and Psychology of Reading, Teaching of Reading, and Reading of Atypical Learners. Includes journal listings and author index.

23. Wolff, William C. "Annotated Bibliography of Scholarship on Writing Centers and Related Topics, 1992." *Focuses* 6 (Summer 1993): 27–54.

Provides an annotated bibliography of 78 entries on writing centers and 50 entries on issues related to writing centers.

2

Theory and Research

2.1 RHETORICAL THEORY, DISCOURSE THEORY, AND COMPOSING

24. Alam, Monirul. "The Use of Arabic in the Composing Processes of Arab University Students Writing in English." *DAI* 54 (October 1993): 1338A.

Provides a qualitative study of Kuwaiti students' use of Arabic (L1) while composing texts in English (L2). Finds that they use Arabic as aid to composing.

25. Allen, James Edward. "Discerning Communities: Uniting Theory and Practice in the Social Epistemic Composition." *DAI* 53 (February 1993): 2718A.

Surveys concepts of social epistemic rhetoric; explores how the paradigm of discourse community helps to redefine the traditional rhetorical concept of audience. Develops a model for a course which draws on concepts and methods of contemporary and classical rhetorical theory.

26. Anderson, Charles W. *Prescribing the Life of the Mind: An Essay on the Purposes of the University, the Aims of Liberal Education, the Competence of Citizens, and the Cultivation of Practical Reason.* Madison, WI: University of Wisconsin Press, 1993. 190 pages

Argues in favor of making teaching critical thinking skills a core element of university education to unify competing departments and schools of thought.

27. Appel, Edward C. "Implications and Importance of the Negative in Burke's Dramatistic Philosophy of Language." *ComQ* 41 (Winter 1993): 51–65.

Examines the role of the negative in Burke's dramatistic philosophy of language.

28. Ascher, Carol, Louise DeSalvo, and Sara Ruddick. *Between Women: Biographers, Novelists, Critics, Teachers, and Artists Write about Their Work on Women.* 2d ed. New York, NY: Routledge, 1993. 500 pages

Investigates the "complex relationships between writers, teachers, and artists and the women who have moved, shaped and inspired them."

29. Atkinson, Paul. "Ethnography or Fiction: A Response to Whaley [*L&E* 5 (1993)]." *L&E* 5 (1993): 53–60.

Questions Whaley's reading of Myerhoff and his choice of model which he uses to critique scholarship.

30. Atwill, William D. "Through Plexiglass Darkly: Loss of Agency in Joan Didion's *Salvador.*" *Reader* 29 (Spring 1993): 1–7.

Examines the importance of using the brand name "Cherokee Chief." Draws connections between the persecution of Native Americans and those terrorized in El Salvador.

31. Avant, Gayle R. "Understanding Cultural Differences." *ETC* 50 (Winter 1993/1994): 449–60.

Points out that many Norwegians try to understand human behavior through the concept of Janteloven—the notion that the human mind seeks ways of understanding general patterns of human behavior. The article notes that generalizations can be oversimplified and misleading.

32. Barton, Ellen L. "Evidentials, Argumentation, and Epistemological Stance." *CE* 55 (November 1993): 745–69.

Discourse analysis of academic and student writing to reveal that student writing is rewarded for reproducing the "contrastive and competitive epistemological stance" of academic writing.

33. Baumlin, James S., and Tita French Baumlin, eds. *Ethos: New Essays in Rhetorical and Critical Theory.* Southern Methodist University Studies in Composition and Rhetoric. Dallas, TX: Southern Methodist University Press, 1993. 408 pages

The 16 contributors present an alternative history of *ethos*, expanding the canon and locating competing cultural traditions of *ethos* and ethical argument.

Essayists: Alcorn, Marshall W., Jr.; Baumlin, James S.; Baumlin, Tita French; Brooke, Robert; Corder, Jim W.; Davis, Robert Con; Enos, Richard Leo; Gross, David S.; Hirst, Russel; Hughes, Joseph J.; Jarratt, Susan C.; Kinneavy, James L.; Miller, Keith D.; Reynolds, Nedra; Schnakenberg, Karen Rossi; Short, Bryan C.; Sipiora, Phillip; Swearingen, C. Jan; Vitanza, Victor J.; Warshauer, Susan C.

34. Beach, Richard. *A Teacher's Introduction to Reader-Response Theories.* Urbana, IL: NCTE, 1993. 209 pages

Presents an historical overview of textual theories studying readers' knowledge of literary conventions; experiential theories, involving readers' personal experiences; theories focusing on readers' psychological involvement in texts; theories examining social contexts; and theories studying cultural contexts for readings.

35. Beach, Richard, and Chris Anson. "Stance and Intertextuality in Written Discourse." *L&E* 4 (1992): 335–57.

Examines aspects of intertextuality by looking at dialogue journals to analyze the role of cultural meanings inherent in writers' and readers' ideological stances.

36. Beauvais, Paul Jude. "Postmodernism and the Ideology of Form: The Narrative Logic of Joan Didion's *Democracy.*" *JNT* 23 (Winter, 1993): 16–30.

Uses Didion's novel to illustrate that postmodern consciousness ("ideology of form"), which is a set of esthetic and ideological demands, necessitates her metafictional technique.

37. Beck, Robert J., and Denis Wood. "The Dialogic Socialization of Aggression in a Family's Court of Reason and Inquiry." *DPr* 16 (July-September 1993): 341–62.

The authors analyze accounts of children who had been in fights. They point out that parents focused on intentions behind the actions narrated.

38. Benton, Stephen L., Kenneth A. Kiewra, Joleen M. Whitfill, and Rayne Dennison. "Encoding and External-Storage Effects on Writing Processes." *JEdPsy* 85 (June 1993): 267–80.

Discusses a study in which students wrote compare/contrast essays after taking notes of a videotaped lecture. Points out that composing processes improved when students refer to notes taken and reviewed.

39. Berg, Jonathan. "The Point of Interpreting Arguments." *IL* 14 (Spring/Fall 1992): 119–30.

Argues that an argument needs to be interpreted before it can be evaluated for its cogency.

40. Berkenkotter, Carol. "A 'Rhetoric for Naturalistic Inquiry' and the Question of Genre." *RTE* 27 (October 1993): 293–304.

Examines the meaning of naturalistic inquiry. Explores how genre functions in different disciplines.

41. Berkenkotter, Carol, and Thomas N. Huckin. "Rethinking Genre from a Sociocognitive Perspective." *WC* 10 (October 1993): 475–509.

The authors define "genre" as dynamic, situated "intellectual scaffolds," involving both form and content and reproducing a discourse community's norms even while helping to constitute them.

42. Berkman, Deborah B. "The Relationship of Family Environment to Writing Anxiety in College Students." *DAI* 53 (April 1993): 3474A.

Questions the correlation between family environment and the presence of writing anxiety. Stresses the importance of qualitative and quantitative methods.

43. Berman, Sanford I. "Irving J. Lee: A Teacher for Our Times." *ETC* 50 (Spring 1993): 27–35.

Argues most education is telling. Training involves setting up exercises for a person to perform. Learning comes at the point of performance.

44. Berry, Ellen E. "Guest Editor's Introduction: Institutional Paradoxes of the Book Review." *W&D* 11 (Spring 1993): 7–11.

Contends that book reviews are politically charged kinds of writing which should be examined more closely.

45. Bertelsen, Dale A. "Sophistry, Epistemology, and the Media Context [response to Muir, *P&R* 26 (1993)]." *P&R* 26 (1993): 296–301.

Suggests that Muir fails to consider debate as media-bound; argues that shifting cultural conditions and media contexts dictate the efficacy of an educational model.

46. Berthoff, Ann E. "What Works? How Do We Know?" *JBW* 12 (Fall 1993): 3–17.

Proposes that writing instruction promotes lively, substantial responses when teachers honor the connection between purposes and procedures. Explains language as meaning-making process.

47. Berube, Janet Lyon. "Feminist Polemics and the Manifesto's 'Hostile Hand.'" *DAI* 53 (February 1993): 2809A.

Dicusses feminist theory in relation to the manifesto; argues that manifestoes create audiences through the rhetoric of exclusivity; suggests that manifestoes, more than "plain talk," function along lines of militarism and exclusivity. Evaluates manifestoes by Holzer and Haraway.

48. Bialostosky, Don. "Toward a Rhetoric for English Department Curricular Debates." *ADE* 105 (Fall 1993): 20–22.

Applies Aristotle's three types of rhetoric to discussions of curriculum change and argues for deliberative—not epideictic—discourse as most productive.

49. Bishop, Wendy. *Writing from the Tips of Our Tongues: Writers, Tutors, and Talk*. Indiana, PA: Peer Tutoring in Writing Conference, October 1992. ERIC ED 350 629. 24 pages

> Discusses a long-term collaborative poetry project which investigates the role of talk and voice in writing. Concludes that writing is best taught in a class that includes time for talk, thus allowing freeing of the writer's inner voice and an opportunity to share ideas with others.

50. Bizzell, Patricia. "A Response to 'Fish Tales: A Conversation with "The Contemporary Sophist"' [response to Olson, *JAC* 12 (Fall 1992)]." *JAC* 13 (Winter 1993): 241–44.

> Interprets Fish's assumption that theories have "no yield." Agrees that students cannot be taught academic discourse from a meta-discursive position.

51. Blair, Kristine L. *Isocratean Discourse Theory and Neo-Sophistic Pedagogy: Implications for the Composition Classroom.* Cincinnati, OH: Conference on College Composition and Communication, March 1992. ERIC ED 352 672. 12 pages

> Argues that the most useful discourse is the one with a social end. Bases her argument on Isocrates' educational theory which favors social interaction through language.

52. Bleich, David. "Feminist Philosophy and Some Humanists' Attitudes toward the Teaching of Writing." *JAC* 13 (Winter 1993): 135–53.

> Argues that selected feminist critiques of philosophical adversativeness and of Descartes provide an appropriate model for communicative writing. Frames his article by the writing across the curriculum debate at Rochester.

53. Bobbitt, David A. "The Rhetoric of Redemption: A Development of Kenneth Burke's Theory of Guilt-Purification-Redemption and Its Application to Martin Luther King, Jr.'s 'I Have a Dream' Speech." *DAI* 53 (March 1993): 3043A.

> Presents the exposition and development of Kenneth Burke's theory of guilt-purification-redemption as applied through a critical analysis of King's speech.

54. Bohner, Gerd, and Norbert Schwartz. "Mood States Influence the Production of Persuasive Arguments." *ComR* 20 (October 1993): 696–722.

> Validates the hypothesis that happy individuals produce more original and more persuasive arguments, especially when asked to advocate an unfamiliar position.

55. Bole, Thomas James, III. "Plato and Aristotle in Agreement: the Neoplatonist Commentaries on Aristotle's 'Categories.'" *DAI* 54 (October 1993): 1391A.

> Argues that if Aristotle's blatantly anti-Platonist "Categories" could be shown as being in harmony with Plato's philosophy, his other works could be more easily accommodated.

56. Bolin, Bill. "Encouraging Students to (Continue to) Share Authority in the Classroom: A Response to Patricia Bizzell." *JBW* 12 (Fall 1993): 77–85.

> Argues against composition pedagogy which coerces students into accepting teachers' political views. Suggests strategies for productive exchange and development of ideas in basic writing classes.

57. Bolin, William Jay. "Critical Pedagogy and the Student-Centered Classroom: Multicultural Approaches to Writing Courses." *DAI* 54 (October 1993): 1337A.

> Argues for a social epistemic approach to college-level writing classes and assignments. Maintains that such an approach would grant greater recognition to students' own contributions to knowledge creation within the academy.

58. Bowers, John, and Kate Iwi. "The Discursive Construction of Society." *D&S* 4 (1993): 357–93.

> Analyzes how "society" is used as a rhetorical device in participants' discourse.

59. Bracci, Sharon Blinn, and Mary Garrett. "Aristotelian Topoi as a Cross-Cultural Analytical Tool." *P&R* 26 (Spring 1993): 93–112.

Explores an exemplar of Chinese literature, the *Intrigues of the Warring States*; determines that its argumentation echoes the Aristotelian topoi.

60. Bruce, Bertram C. "The Discourses of Inquiry: Pedagogical Challenges and Responses." Center for the Study of Reading, Urbana, IL, 1993. ERIC ED 357 396. 26 pages

Identifies epistemological, rhetorical, ideological, and community membership functions of discourse. Relates them to pedagogical approaches.

61. Brueggemann, Brenda Jo. "Context and Cognition in the Composing Processes of Two Deaf Student Writers." *DAI* 54 (July 1993): 159A.

Suggests that deaf student writers may benefit most when writing and literacy acquisition is taught as an interactive, bilingual, and bicultural process.

62. Brummett, Barry, ed. *Landmark Essays on Kenneth Burke*. Landmark Essays. Davis, CA: Hermagoras Press, 1993. 250 pages

Presents essays on Burke from 1948 to 1992. The articles are categorized into overviews and surveys, critical and philosophical issues, and politics and intervention.
Essayists: Blankenship, Jane; Booth, Wayne; Brummett, Barry; Chesebro, James W.; Conduit, Celeste; Duncan, Hugh Dalziel; Gregg, Richard B.; Griffin, Leland; Hyman, Stanley Edgar; Lentricchia, Frank; Murphy, Edward; Memerov, Howard; Nichols, Marie Hochmuth; Overington, Michael; Rosenwasser, Marie; Rueckert, William.

63. Brydon, Anne. "The Eye of the Guest: Icelandic Nationalist Discourse and the Whaling Issue." *DAI* 54 (July 1993): 225A.

Argues that the national self is constructed through discourses articulating space and constructing it as the locus for social action.

64. Buley-Meissner, Mary Louise. "Reclaiming Personal Knowledge: Investigations of Identity, Difference, and Community in College Education." *CE* 55 (February 1993): 211–21.

Reviews four texts written by teacher-researchers which illustrate that "practice must lead to theory because only practice is intimately connected with students' individual lives."

65. Butler, Judith. *Bodies That Matter*. New York: Routledge, 1993. 256 pages

Offers a reformulation of the materiality of bodies; examines how the power of heterosexual hegemony forms the "matter" of bodies, sex, and gender. Argues that power operates to constrain "sex" from the start, delimiting what counts as a viable sex.

66. Bybee, Michael D. "Logic in Rhetoric—and Vice Versa." *P&R* 26 (1993): 169–90.

Explores interrelationships between recent reviews of rhetorical and logical principles. Explains how each discussion can revise the other in actual practice.

67. Campbell, John Angus. "Reply to Gaonkar and Fuller [*SCJ* 58 (Summer 1993)]." *SCJ* 58 (Summer 1993): 312–18.

Focuses on Gaonkar's major claim about the thinness of rhetorical theory and Campbell's sins of intention, and on Fuller's objections to rhetoric as strategy.

68. Cariello, Matthew Michael. "Writing under the Influence: Modelling in a College Writing Classroom." *DAI* 54 (August 1993): 444A.

Looks at both model and modelled texts to elicit their compositional similarities and differences.

69. Chesebro, James W. *Extensions of the Burkean System*. Studies in Rhetoric and

Communication. Tuscaloosa, AL: University of Alabama Press, 1993. 350 pages

Examines Burke's theory of human communication. Includes one of his previously unpublished essay.

70. Chinn, Sarah, Mario DiGangi, and Patrick Horrigan. "A Talk with Eve Kosofsky Sedgwick." *Pre/Text* 13 (Fall/Winter 1992): 79–95.

Sedgwick explains how she rhetorically defines herself as queer even though she is heterosexual.

71. Christianson, Gale E. *Writing Lives Is the Devil: Essays of a Biographer at Work.* Hamden, CT: Shoe String Press, 1993. 240 pages

Presents 13 personal essays to explore the process of writing a biography. Traces the process from the beginnings of research through publication.

72. Chu, Godwin C., and Yanan Ju. *The Great Wall in Ruins: Communication and Cultural Change.* Albany, NY: State University of New York Press, 1993. 366 pages

Examines changing cultural values in China, focusing on data from the port city of Shanghai and the rural county of Qingpu.

73. Cintron, Ralph. "Wearing a Pith Helmet at a Sly Angle: Or, Can Writing Researchers Do Ethnography in a Postmodern Era?" *WC* 10 (June 1993): 371–412.

Accuses writing researchers of ignoring the postmodern crisis of representation in their reliance on realistic ethnographic accounts such as Heath's *Ways with Words.*

74. Clark, Carol Lea. "Imagining Texas: The Creation in Nineteenth-Century Newspapers and Periodicals of a Rhetoric of Texas." *DAI* 54 (October 1993): 1361A.

Argues that Texas rhetoric can be described as individualistic, heroic, prideful, exotic, as a verbal map, code, or system of thinking. Suggests that it borrowed images of "garden," "wilderness," "heroism," and "otherness."

75. Coe, Richard M. *'Prophesying after the Event': The Archeology and Ecology of Genre.* San Diego, CA: Conference on College Composition and Communication, March/April 1993. ERIC ED 357 345. 10 pages

Sees genre as social process in symbolic action. Argues that genres exist in context, and textual structures should be treated as artifacts from which implicit strategies should be resurrected and related to context. Discusses how to teach genres.

76. Cohen, Sande. *Academia and the Luster of Capital.* Minneapolis, MN: University of Minnesota Press, 1993. 184 pages

Examines ideas as "commodities" in the academic marketplace, using contemporary critical thought from philosophers such as Baudrillard and Lyotard.

77. Cook, William W. "Writing in the Spaces Left." *CCC* 44 (February 1993): 9–25.

Argues that a "willful deconstructive" reading of nineteenth-century African American texts reveals resistance and agency of marginalized voices.

78. Courage, Richard. "The Interaction of Public and Private Literacies." *CCC* 44 (December 1993): 484–96.

Suggests that rethinking the interactions between public and private literacies can help composition theorists to avoid making "a dichotomous choice" between students' language and academic literacy.

79. Couture, Barbara. "Against Relativism: Restoring Truth in Writing." *JAC* 13 (Winter 1993): 111–34.

Argues that rhetorical relativists such as Jasper Neel engage in ideological historicism, support an essentialist view about truth, and a fundamentalist view of human progress.

80. Cox, Brenda Haulbrooks. "Gender and Composing in Academic Discourse." *DAI* 54 (August 1993): 499A.

Proposes a theory of feminine rhetoric and pedagogy intended to expand the range of discourse development for all learners, regardless of gender.

81. Craig, Christopher P. *Form as Argument in Cicero's Speeches: A Study of Dilemma.* Atlanta, GA: Scholars Press, 1993. 266 pages

Focuses on how the Roman orator used his listeners' knowledge of rhetoric to influence their perceptions of his arguments.

82. Crosswhite, James. "Being Unreasonable: Perelman and the Problem of Fallacies." *Arg* 7 (1993): 385–402.

Describes how Perelman's rhetoric treats fallacies as exposing competing conceptions of universality and of what it is to be human.

83. D'Angelo, Frank J. "Organizing Texts: Some Classical and Modern Perspectives." *Focuses* 6 (Summer 1993): 3–15.

Proposes a theory of discourse structure based on classical and modern sources consisting of a matrix of tropes in varied relationships.

84. Dasenbrock, Reed Way. "The Myth of the Subjective and of the Subject in Composition Studies." *JAC* 13 (Winter 1993): 21–32.

Criticizes inherent inconsistencies in both Emersonian expressivism and European social constructionism. Proposes analytic philosophy of David Davidson as corrective.

85. Davidson, Phebe. *Speculations on the Presence of Ear in Writing.* 1993. ERIC ED 358 448. 19 pages

Discusses the importance of composition instructors recognizing difference as well as connection between speech and writing. Argues that each coexists with and creates the other.

86. Davis, James S., and James D. Marshall, eds. *Ways of Knowing: Research and Practice in the Teaching of Writing.* Iowa City, IA: Iowa Council of Teachers of English, 1988. 177 pages

Fifteen essays examine divergent perspectives of composition teachers/researchers. The contributors discuss higher education, research design, the need for interdisciplinary studies, assessment, clarifying reading/writing issues, changing views of literacy, secondary classroom practices, responding to writing, writing to learn in social studies, middle-school classrooms, elementary student conferences, writing curricula, and future trends.

Essayists: Applebee, Arthur N.; Britton, James; Conney, Myrna; Davis, James S.; Handlen, Tom; Hanzelka, Richard; Henke, Linda; Hillocks, George, Jr.; Kelly, Marilyn; Langer, Judith A.; Lloyd-Jones, Richard; Lyons, David; Lyons, William Cleo; Mapes, Lola; Marshall, James D.; Peters, Bill; Schubert, Barbara; Squire, James R.; Steinbrink, Carolyn.

87. Davson-Galle, Peter. "Arguing, Arguments, and Deep Disagreements." *IL* 14 (Spring/Fall 1992): 147–56.

Agrees that certain sorts of "deep disagreements" can be rationally unresolvable, even over quite limited issues.

88. Dean, Judy. "Spaces for Difference: Discourse Ethics and Feminist Theory." *DAI* 54 (July 1993): 299A.

Examines intersecting concerns of feminist theory and discourse ethics; argues for the ability of discursive universalism to include the concerns of women.

89. De Beaugrande, Robert. "Discourse Analysis and Literary Theory: Closing the Gap." *JAC* 13 (Fall 1993): 423–48.

Calls for an integrated, discourse-centered approach to the entire educational experience which places the language program in the position of training for discourse skills.

90. Dehart, Jean Laura. "A Rhetorical Analysis of the Perpetuation of an Educational Crisis: 1980–1989." *DAI* 53 (March 1993): 3042A.

Examines rhetorical strategies used in public discourse to depict a crisis in education. Posits that the 1980 to 1989 crisis was rhetorically constructed and perpetuated.

91. Delgado-Gaitan, Concha. "Researching Change and Changing the Researcher." *HER* 63 (Winter 1993): 389–411.

Describes the effects of participant observation on the researcher and on the subject community during a study of Mexican-American literacy.

92. Denton, Robert Frederick. "Time's Signatures: Narrative Theory and the Iterative Moment of *Walden*." *DAI* 53 (April 1993): 3428A.

Claims that criticism of iterative narrative ignores difference and textual heterogeneity. Argues that critics of *Walden* overlook the relationship between a thematical privileging of the present and iterative writing.

93. Detweiler, Jane A., Keith S. Lloyd, and Margaret M. Strain. *Forms of (Re)sil(i)ence: Engaging Unsaid Resistances in Disciplinary Discourses.* San Diego, CA: Conference on College Composition and Communication, March/April 1993. ERIC ED 358 484. 34 pages

Explores formal and theoretical possibilities through the use of feminist inquiry/criticism.

94. Devitt, Amy J. "Generalizing about Genre: New Conceptions of an Old Concept." *CCC* 44 (December 1993): 573–86.

Argues that recent conceptions of genre as "dynamic patterning of human experience" can serve as the basis for a unified theory of writing.

95. Dickinson, David K., and Allysa McCabe. "Beyond Two-Handed Reasoning: Commentary on Egan's Work [*L&E* 5 (1993)]." *L&E* 5 (1993): 187–94.

Though generally sympathetic to Egan's arguments, the authors focus on the notion of binary oppositions for the sake of theo-

retical clarification. They see this aspect of his thinking to promise significant negative impacts on teaching.

96. Dickson, Richard E. "Ramism and the Rhetorical Tradition." *DAI* 54 (August 1993): 439A.

Establishes a historical link between Ramism and the "doctrine of mechanical correctness" in modern composition pedagogy.

97. Dobrin, Sidney I. "Turning the Tables: An (Inter)view with Gary A. Olson." *CompSt* 21 (Fall 1993): 32–45.

Olson, known for his scholarly interviews, answers questions about his own writing.

98. Douglass, David Anderson. "Edward Clarke's 'Sex in Education': A Study in Rhetorical Form." *DAI* 53 (June 1993): 4128A.

Demonstrates through close textual analysis that Clarke's work also merits rhetorical significance as an exemplar of a hybrid rhetorical form.

99. Dow, Bonnie J., and Mari Boor Tonn. "'Feminine Style' and Political Judgment in the Rhetoric of Ann Richards." *QJS* 79 (August 1993): 286–302.

Offers an alternative perspective on feminine style which reflects the conditions of female existence in the public sphere.

100. Downing, David. "Response to 'Provocation on the Politics of Book Reviews.'" *W&D* 11 (Spring 1993): 27–33.

Argues that book reviews which undergo the same editorial scrutiny as articles are effective as acts of resistance.

101. Drew, Paul, and John Heritage, eds. *Talk at Work: Interaction in Institutional Settings.* New York: Cambridge University Press, 1993. 580 pages

Fifteen essays analyze oral interactions between professionals and clients. They explore theories used for this kind of discourse, examine specific activities of questioning and answering, and show how their interplay illuminates the structure of social institutions such as psychiatry, law, and the media.

Essayists: Atkinson, J. Maxwell; Bergmann, Jörg; Button, Graham; Clayman, Steven E.; Drew, Paul; Greatbatch, David; Gumperz, John J.; Heath, Christian; Heritage, John; Jefferson, Gail; Lee, John R. E.; Levinson, Stephen C.; Maynard, Douglas M.; Schegloff, Emmanuel A.; Sefi, Sue; Zimmerman, Don H.

102. Dugan, Jeanne Marie. "*Kyrion* and *Glotta*: The Tradition of Usage as Rhetorical Means." *DAI* 53 (January 1993): 2355A.

Argues that usage should be placed within a rhetorical context so that traditional rhetorical and stylistic concerns can guide usage decisions.

103. Dummit, Virginia R. "Restoring the People: The Fluid Net of Language." *DAI* 54 (August 1993): 706A.

Studies similarities between certain literary works of twentieth century American women and oral narratives.

104. Duncan, James S., and David Ley, eds. *Place/Culture/Representation.* New York: Routledge, 1993. 352 pages

The contributors show that writing becomes a means of revealing the author as well as presenting a supposed geographical reality. They discuss authorial power, discourses of the other, texts and textuality, landscape metaphor, the sites of power-knowledge relations, and notions of community and sense of place.

105. Dunlap, David Douglas. "The Conception of Audience in Perelman and Isocrates: Locating the Ideal in the Real." *Arg* 7 (1993): 461–74.

Contrasts two theoretical notions of ideal audience.

106. During, Simon, ed. *The Cultural Studies Reader.* New York: Routledge, 1993. 496 pages

The collection provides an introduction to cultural studies, offering a selection of essays by writers such as Barthes, Adorno, Lyotard, Stuart Hall, and Gayatri Spivak. It encompasses topics from sports to postmodernism, museums, supermarkets, gay and lesbian writing, and rock and roll.

Essayists: Adorno, Theodor; Ang, Ien; Barthes, Roland; Bourdieu, Pierre; Chow, Rey; Clifford, James; de Certeau, Michel; de Lauretis, Teresa; Delcourt, Xavier; Dyer, Richard; Forgacs, David; Foucault, Michel; Gunew, Sneja; Hall, Stuart; Hebdige, Dick; Horkheimer, Max; Lyotard, Jean-François; Mattelart, Armand; Mattelart, Michele; Morris, Meaghan; Radway, Janice; Rosaldo, Renato; Ross, Andrew; Sedgwick, Eve Kosofsky; Soja, Edward; Spivak, Gayatri Chakravorty; Stallybrass, Peter; Straw, Will; Wallace, Michele; West, Cornel; White, Allon; Williams, Raymond.

107. Egan, Kieran. "Narrative and Learning: A Voyage of Implications." *L&E* 5 (1993): 119–26.

Points out that learning theories which shape teaching and curriculum are drawn from studies of nonnarrative tasks. Argues that learning theories based on studies of narrative tasks are superior to current theories.

108. Egan, Kieran. "Response to Comments on 'Narrative and Learning: A Voyage of Implications.'" *L&E* 5 (1993): 219–24.

Responds to nine critiques of his essay.

109. Elbow, Peter. "The Uses of Binary Thinking." *JAC* 13 (Winter 1993): 51–78.

Defends the value of binary thinking which privileges contradictories such as creating/criticizing, teaching/research, doubting/believing, and theory/practice.

110. Enos, Theresa. *'Verbal Atom Cracking': Burke and a Rhetoric of Reading.* San Diego, CA: Conference on College Composition and Communication, March/April 1993. ERIC ED 357 379. 7 pages

Approaches esoteric discourse by looking for opposites, searching for identifiable cues to the writer's motives, achieving textual identification, and ordering sets of terms.

111. Erlandson, David A., Edward L. Harris, Barbara L. Skipper, and Steve D. Harris. *Doing Naturalistic Inquiry: A Guide to Methods.* Thousand Oaks, CA: Sage, 1993. 224 pages

The authors provide an action-based guide to naturalistic research methods. They argue that this method is applicable to naturalistic writing research.

112. ESSE Inaugural Conference. *English Studies in Transition.* Papers from the ESSE Inaugural Conference. New York: Routledge, 1993. 352 pages

Collects papers offered at the Inaugural Conference of the European Society for the Study of English held at the University of East Anglia in September, 1991. Topics covered are the canon, nationalism in postcolonial literature, poetics of language, and the representation of women

113. Etter-Lewis, Gwendolyn. *My Soul Is My Own: Oral Narratives of African American Women in the Professions.* New York, NY: Routledge, 1993. 192 pages

Presents the lives of early twentieth-century African American women (college educated in the 1920s and 1930s) and analyzes the context in which these women lived. Challenges long-held assumptions about African American women.

114. Evans, Rick. "Learning 'Schooled Literacy': The Literate Life Histories of Mainstream Student Readers and Writers." *DPr* 16 (July/September 1993): 317–40.

Points out that students distinguish between story reading, school reading, and leisure reading, and make similar distinctions with writing. Finds that they want high grades in their school writing.

115. Ewald, Helen Rothschild. "Waiting for Answerability: Bakhtin and Composition Studies." *CCC* 44 (October 1993): 331–48.

Argues that scholars and teachers of composition have to consider "specific and situational responses to ethical issues."

116. Fahnestock, Jeanne. "Genre and Rhetorical Craft." *RTE* 27 (October 1993): 265–71.

Defines "genre" and argues that it should be taught explicitly.

117. Faigley, Lester. *Fragments of Rationality: Postmodernity and the Subject of Composition.* The Pittsburgh Series in Composition, Literacy and Culture, edited by David Bartholomae and Jean Ferguson Carr. Pittsburgh, PA: University of Pittsburgh Press, 1993. 296 pages

Draws on the work of Foucault, Lyotard, and other postmodern analysts to address the debate about the "self" the student writer is asked to occupy, the "modernist" goal of producing a rational coherent student subject, and the writing instructor's unconscious imposition of elite values and expectations in evaluating student work.

118. Fairclough, Norman. "Critical Discourse Analysis and the Marketization of Public Discourse: The Universities." *D&S* 4 (1993): 133–68.

Explains one approach of discourse analysis for discursive aspects of marketization of public discourse (specifically in British higher education) and argues for the value of critical discourse analysis as a method of research and resource for social struggle.

119. Farmer, Frank, and Alan W. France. "Two Comments on 'Is Expressivism Dead?' [response to Fishman and McCarthy, *CE* 54 (October 1992)]." *CE* 55 (September 1993): 548–52.

Farmer criticizes Fishman's omission of origins and unclear ideological borders; France suggests Fishman deemphasized students "material situation," and calls for "principled critical intervention."

120. Farrell, Thomas B. *Norms of Rhetorical Culture*. New Haven, CT: Yale University Press, 1993. 416 pages

Challenges the notion that rhetoric is antithetical to reason. Includes interpretations of Aristotle's *Rhetoric* and of rhetorical concepts in such contemporary texts as Vaclav Havel's inaugural address, Betty Friedan's *Feminine Mystique*, and transcripts of the McCarthy hearings.

121. Fesmire, Alice Ann. "Transitions as Speech Acts." *JTWC* 23 (1993): 115–28.

Analyzes transitions in terms of their illocutionary and perlocutionary effects; offers recommendations for improving handbook explanations of effective transitions.

122. Fielding, Ian Robert. "Assessing Value Argument: The United States Military's Policy of Discriminating on the Basis of Sexual Orientation." *DAI* 53 (January 1993): 2160A.

Analyzes value arguments presented by the United States Army defending discrimination on the basis of sexual orientation. Judges arguments to be weak.

123. Fincher-Kiefer, Rebecca. "The Role of Predictive Inferences in Situation Model Construction." *DPr* 16 (January/June 1993): 99–124.

Argues that readers construct representations of text at more than one level, with situational representations enabling predictions to be made, and propositional representations providing fallback information.

124. Fishman, Stephen M. "Explicating Our Tacit Tradition: John Dewey and Composition Studies." *CCC* 44 (October 1993): 315–30.

Suggests that three Deweyan principles may have influenced some composition theorists. Concludes that these principles

can assist in the future development of composition pedagogy.

125. Flaschenriem, Barbara Lynn. "Seeing Double: Amatory Rhetoric and Gender in *Sappho*, the *Anacreontea*, and *Propertius*." *DAI* 54 (December 1993): 2138A.

Examines how amatory texts represent the self and human interaction, and how they address political and social issues.

126. Flinders, David J., and Geoffrey E. Mills, eds. *Theory and Concepts in Qualitative Research: Perspectives from the Field*. New York: Teachers College Press, 1993. 264 pages

The contributors focus on the roles and uses of theory in qualitative research. They define the issues, look at theory at work, and discuss theory in perspective. *Essayists:* Becker, Howard S.; Flinders, David J.; Greene, Jennifer C.; Henstrand, Joyce L.; Mathison, Sandra; Mills, Geoffrey E.; Munro, Petra; St. Maurice, Henry; Schwandt, Thomas A.; Smith, John K.; Smith, Louis M.; Stringer, Ernest T.; Thornton, Stephen J.

127. Fontaine, Sheryl I., and Susan Hunter, eds. *Writing Ourselves into the Story: Unheard Voices from Composition Studies*. Carbondale, IL: Southern Illinois University Press, 1993. 400 pages

The editors organize 23 essays into four categories: the invisible pedagogue of the discipline, the model of power that dominates composition, the ever-present but seldom heard student voice, and other voices excluded from professional development in composition studies. *Essayists:* Anson, Chris M.; Bishop, Wendy; Bloom, Lynn Z; Buckler, Patricia Prandini; Clark, Carol Lea; Dickson, Marcia; Fairgrieve, Jean; Fontaine, Sheryl I.; Franklin, Kay; Frost, Clare A.; Green, Lois E.; Greenwood, Claudia M.; Gunner, Jeanne; Hatch, Gary Layne; Hunter, Susan; McConnel, Frances Ruhlen; McCracken, Nancy Mellin; Nist, Elizabeth A.; Papoulis, Irene; Pemberton, Michael A.; Raines, Helon Howell; Robbins, Susan Pepper; Sloane, Sarah; Tuell, Cynthia; Walters, Margaret Bennett; Young, Thomas E.

128. Foss, Karen, and Stephen Littlejohn. *Teaching and Learning Rhetorical and Communication Theory*. Albuquerque, NM: Western States Communication Association, February 1993. ERIC ED 358 490. 17 pages

The authors maintain that despite differences in their contents, communication and rhetorical theory courses share similar teaching and learning processes. They point out that among chief issues facing future teachers in these disciplines are integrating the two theoretical backgrounds, a multicultural agenda, and student readiness to deal with abstract concepts.

129. Fraisse, Genevive, and Michelle Perrot, eds. *A History of Women in the West, Volume IV: Emerging Feminism from Revolution to World War*. Cambridge, MA: Harvard University Press, 1993. 660 pages

The essayists point out that despite the subordination of women to men during the early twentieth century, they emerged as a collective force in the political arena.

130. Fraker, Charles F. "*Oppositio* in Geoffrey of Vinsauf and Its Background." *Rhetorica* 10 (Winter 1993): 63–86.

Demonstrates that Vinsauf's reinvention of *oppositio* and *digressio* followed the practice of grammarians, not the rhetorical tradition.

131. France, Alan W. "Assigning Places: Introductory Composition as a Cultural Discourse." *CE* 55 (October 1993): 593–609.

Argues against expressivist pedagogies in favor of structuralist criticism and cultural materialism.

132. Frankenberg, Ruth. *White Women, Race Matters: The Social Construction of White-*ness. Minneapolis, MN: University of Minnesota Press, 1993. 289 pages

Reads race in white women's lives through "life history interviews" of several women; "views white women's lives as sites both for the reproduction of racism and for challenges to it."

133. Freedman, Aviva. "Show and Tell? The Role of Explicit Teaching in the Learning of New Genres." *RTE* 27 (October 1993): 222–51.

Defines explicit teaching of genre. Argues that such instruction is rarely useful. Calls for more research on this topic.

134. Freedman, Aviva. "Situating Genre: A Rejoinder." *RTE* 27 (October 1993): 272–81.

Discusses different views on the importance of teaching genre explicitly in classrooms.

135. Frisk, Philip. *Black English and the Henry Higgins Project: Avoiding Disempowering Interventions into "Black English."* Seattle, WA: Conference on College Composition and Communication, March 1989. ERIC ED 348 673. 19 pages

Analyzes the discourse of African-American students in a first-year composition class and discusses how Freire's "domesticating education" negatively impacts on student interaction.

136. Frow, John, and Meaghan Morris, eds. *Australian Cultural Studies: A Reader*. Champaign, IL: University of Illinois Press, 1993. 304 pages

The contributors address topics such as ethnographic audience research, cultural policy studies, popular consumption, "bad" aboriginal art, landscape in feature films, and the intersections of tourism with history and memory.

Essayists: Ballantine, Kevin; Bennett, Tony; Cunningham, Stuart; Gibson, Ross; Grace, Helen; Gunew, Sneja; Hartley, John; Martin, Adrian; Michaels, Eric; Morris, Meaghan; Nightingale, Virginia; O'Regan,

Tom; Perera, Suvendrini; Sanders, Noel; Stern, Lesley; Turner, Graeme; Wark, McKenzie.

137. Fuller, Steve. *Philosophy, Rhetoric, and the End of Knowledge: The Coming of Science and Technology Studies*. Rhetoric of the Human Sciences, edited by John Lyne, Donald N. McCloskey, and John S. Nelson. Madison, WI: University of Wisconsin Press, 1993. 421 pages

Advocates knowledge as rhetorica; suggests that the methods and conclusions of Science and Technology Studies be used to break down interdisciplinary barriers; responds to critics such as Stanley Fish.

138. Fuller, Steve. " 'Rhetoric of Science': A Doubly Vexed Expression [response to Gaonkar, *SCJ* 58 (Summer 1993)]." *SCJ* 58 (Summer 1993): 306–311.

Suggests that rhetoricians of science position themselves increasingly as rhetorical agents interested in not merely interpreting but in changing the practices of their audiences.

139. Gaillet, Lynee Lewis. *Learning from Our Predecessors: The Work of Fred Newton Scott and George Jardine*. San Diego, CA: Conference on College Composition and Communication, March/April 1993. ERIC ED 357 372. 21 pages

Maintains that the works of Fred Newton Scott and George Jardine prefigured the composition theories developed since the mid-twentieth century. Argues that studying them would be beneficial to contemporary developments in composition studies.

140. Gale, Frederic G. "Don't Know Much about Automobiles: Fish's Anti-Theory Theory [response to Olson, *JAC* 12 (Fall 1992)]." *JAC* 13 (Winter 1993): 250–52.

Argues that Fish fails to distinguish between critical theory and less specialized theories such as theories of the classroom.

141. Gale, Irene Frances. "Toward a Dialogic Pedagogy: An Interactive Model of Composition Instruction." *DAI* 53 (May 1993): 3828A.

Examines current uses of dialogism in composition and proposes a comprehensive theory of dialogic pedagogy for composition.

142. Gaonkar, Dilip Parameshwar. "The Idea of Rhetoric in the Rhetoric of Science." *SCJ* 58 (Summer 1993): 258–95.

Presents a three-part essay which examines rhetoric as hermeneutics, as a discursive formation, and as an inventional strategy. Discusses the politics of identity and the humanist paradigm.

143. Garcia Moreno, Beatriz Teresa. "Contextualist Thought and Architecture." *DAI* 53 (March 1993): 3019A.

Analyzes contextualist thought and the construction of knowledge.

144. Garner, Ana Christina. "The Disaster News Story: The Reader, the Content, and the Construction of Meaning." *DAI* 53 (January 1993): 2141A.

Uses intensive interviews to demonstrate the information derived by twenty-four readers of accounts of an airplane crash.

145. Garrett, Mary M. "*Pathos* Reconsidered from the Perspective of Classical Chinese Rhetorics." *QJS* 79 (Feburary 1993): 19–39.

Reconsiders *pathos* through a look at classical Chinese rhetoric, and concludes that full integration of *pathos* in Western rhetorical theory is necessary to render it fully human.

146. Gebhardt, Richard C. "Forms of Scholarly Publication: Some Trends and Some Risks." *Focuses* 6 (Winter 1993): 93–96.

Asks scholars and editors to be sensitive to clashes between innovative or personal types of articles and traditional scholarship.

147. Gere, Anne Ruggles, ed. *Into the Field: Sites of Composition Studies*. New York: Modern Language Association of America, 1993. 222 pages

Collects 13 essays that challenge the characterization of composition studies as an applied field and that consider its relationship to hermeneutics and other philsophical and theoretical traditions. Concludes with a forum in which contributors raise questions about one another's essays.
Essayists: Berlin, James A.; Bleich, David; Dillon, George; Gates, Rosemary; Gere, Anne Ruggles; Gleason, Barbara; Halden-Sullivan, Judith; Murphy, Richard J., Jr.; Owens, Derek; Papoulis, Irene; Schildgen, Brenda Deen; Spellmeyer, Kurt; Trimbur, John.

148. Gibbs, Raymond W., Jr., Darin L. Buchalter, Jessica F. Moise, and William T. Farrar, IV. "Literal Meaning and Figurative Language." *DPr* 16 (October/December 1993): 387–403.

The authors point out that individuals conceive of literal meaning as conventional meaning, subject-matter meaning, nonmetaphorical meaning, truth-conditional meaning, and context-free meaning.

149. Gibson, Timothy R. "Towards a Discourse Theory of Abstracts and Abstracting." *DAI* 53 (March 1993): 3193A.

Investigates the extent to which certain linguistic variables affect the perceived success of an abstract.

150. Gibson, Walker. "In Praise of the Sophists." *CE* 55 (March 1993): 284–90.

Argues that the Sophistic view of reality has practical consequences for teachers of writing.

151. Gilbert, David. *Ethnography as a Composition Research Genre: Establishing a Methodological Center for Assessing Writing Programs*. Louisville, KY: National Council of Teachers of English, November 1992. ERIC ED 356 482. 9 pages

Argues that a traditional ethnographic approach to composition research is more efficient, pragmatic, and utilitarian.

152. Giora, Rachel. "On the Function of Analogies in Informative Texts" *DPr* 16 (October/December 1993): 591–611.

Suggests that conventional views of the facilitative role of analogies are mistaken; argues that analogies are redundant in texts that clearly show their topic and information structure.

153. Glenn, Cheryl. "Medieval Literacy Outside the Academy: Popular Practice and Individual Technique." *CCC* 44 (December 1993): 497–508.

Uses *The Book of Margery Kempe* to explain certain features of medieval English popular literacy.

154. Goetsch, James Robert, Jr. "Vico's Axioms: A Study of the Methodology of the 'Scienza Nuova' in the Light of Aristotle's 'Rhetoric.'" *DAI* 54 (October 1993): 1393A.

Argues that Vico's axioms reject deductive orientation of new sciences; Vico's new science requires reconstruction of basic language of science which are rooted not in logic but in Aristotle's doctrine of topics.

155. Goggin, Maureen Daly, and Elenore Long. "A Tincture of Philosophy, a Tincture of Hope: The Portrayal of Isocrates in Plato's *Phaedrus*." *RR* 11 (Spring 1993): 301–24.

The authors argue that the figure of Isocrates represents the possibility of reform in rhetoric.

156. Golden, Richard M., and David E. Rumelhart. "A Parallel Distributed Processing Model of Story Comprehension and Recall." *DPr* 16 (January/June 1993): 203–37.

The authors define comprehension as inferences to determine the most probable causal chains of a story, while they see recall as reconstructing the memory trace representing the causal chain.

157. Goodnight, G. Thomas. "A 'New Rhetoric' for a 'New Dialectic?' Prolegomena to a Responsible Public Argument." *Arg* 7 (1993): 329–42.

Offers a rhetoric of situated public discourse in which interlocutors are obligated both to argue effectively and to hold open norms of communicative reason.

158. Gorden, Ellen J. "Legislating Identity: Language, Citizenship, and Education in Lithuania." *DAI* 54 (September 1993): 1077A.

Examines the role of language in formation and preservation of national identity.

159. Graves, Heather Brodie. "Regrinding the Lens of Gender: Problematizing 'Writing as a Woman.'" *WC* 10 (April 1993): 139–63.

Suggests that theories of gendered writing may be essentialist, overlooking other factors in writers' histories. Notes opposite gender characteristics in writings by Kenneth Burke and Julia Kristeva.

160. Griffin, Cindy L. "Women as Communicators: Mary Daly's Hagography as Rhetoric." *ComM* 60 (June 1993): 158–77.

Uses Daly's writings to develop a theory of women as communicators. Reveals a rhetorical foreground that silences women and an alternative background where women are active.

161. Griffin, Cindy Lee. "A Feminist Reconception of Form: A Case Study of Mary Wollstonecraft's Three Polemical Works." *DAI* 53 (March 1993): 3044A.

Concludes that much of Wollstonecraft's work is feminist. Calls for a reevaluation of rhetorical form to account for rhetoric of individuals or minority groups.

162. Groff, Marsha A. "Personality Types, Writing Strategies, and College Basic Writers: Four Case Studies." *DAI* 53 (February 1993): 2787A.

Investigates the relationship between personality type and writing strategies.

163. Gross, Alan G. "Experiment as Text: The Limits of Literary Analysis." *RR* 11 (Spring 1993): 290–300.

Argues that a rhetorical approach to understanding the reports generated in experimental science is preferable to a literary analysis of them.

164. Gross, Alan G. "Rhetorical Imperialism in Science." *CE* 55 (January 1993): 82–87.

Reviews three texts which illustrate the influence of rhetorical analysis on the history of science. Speculates on how scientific practice can influence rhetorical and literary theory.

165. Gross, Alan G. "What If We're Not Producing Knowledge? Critical Reflections on the Rhetorical Criticisms of Science [response to Gaonkar, *SCJ* 58 (Summer 1993)]." *SCJ* 58 (Summer 1993): 301–5.

Responds to Gaonkar's attack on the Aristotelian vocabulary of criticism and the 'Aristotelian ideology' of agent-centered persuasion.

166. Guthrie, James. "Commentary: Little Words." *JTWC* 23 (1993): 233–37.

Points out that the misuse of little words such as "the," "this," "with," "is," "have," and "then" is usually the reader's first evidence that communication has gone wrong.

167. Hagen, Peter Lawrence. "The Rhetorical Effectiveness of Verbal Irony." *DAI* 53 (June 1993): 4129A.

Argues that irony is a rhetorically effective use of language. Points out that this effectiveness can be explained in terms of form.

168. Harms, Dawson C. "Alternative Configurations of Invention: Process, Disruption, and Play." *DAI* 53 (April 1993): 3464A.

Explores writing process pedagogy's conceptualization and representation of invention; focuses on disruptive tensions. Suggests alternative conceptions of invention.

169. Harrington, Henry R. "The Jouissance of English Department Politics: A Tale of Shem and Shaun." *ADE* 105 (Fall 1993): 23–27.

Uses composition to exemplify departmental psychodynamics; applies Lacan's terms to argue for a reflective interpretation of what it means to be an English Department.

170. Harrington, Thea Anne. "Self-Writing and Self-Knowledge: The Figure of Autobiography in Hegel, Woolf, Kristeva, and Proust." *DAI* 54 (December 1993): 2141A.

Looks at how self-writing and self-knowledge intertwine; questions the status of autobiography.

171. Hassett, Michael J. *Constructing an Ethical Writer for the Postmodern Scene*. San Diego, CA: Conference on College Composition and Communication, March/April 1993. ERIC ED 357 343. 10 pages

An ethical postmodern writer will attempt to write in a way that invites readers into the text's space as a full partner in making meaning.

172. Hatch, Jill A., Charles A. Hill, and John R. Hayes. "When the Messenger Is the Message: Readers' Impressions of Writers' Personalities." *WC* 10 (October 1993): 569–98.

The authors point out that readers of 61 college admissions essays consistently agreed in their sense of writers' *ethos*. The results of a smaller intervention study suggest that revising texts can change readers' negative impressions.

173. Haynes-Burton, Cynthia. "Interview with Victor J. Vitanza." *CompSt* 21 (Spring 1993): 49–65.

In this question and answer interview, Vitanza resists codification and focuses on identity issues.

174. He, Weiyun. "Reconstructing Institutions through Talk: A Discourse Study of Academic Counseling Encounters." *DAI* 54 (September 1993): 915A.

Uses conversation analysis, functional systematic linguistics, and ethnography to discover that content is embodied in rather than outside of institutional discourse.

175. Heilker, Paul. "Rehabilitating the Essay: An Alternative Form for Composition Instruction." *DAI* 53 (February 1993): 2720A.

Asserts that current composition practices are inadequate. Looks at the expanding essay form as a means to ameliorate deficiencies.

176. Heller, Carol Elizabeth. "The Multiple Functions of the Tenderloin Women Writers Workshop: Community in the Making." *DAI* 53 (April 1993): 3491A.

Examines social and personal contextual elements that influence the lives and literary products of the participants.

177. Helmers, Marguerite H. "Constructing Students in the Rhetoric of Practice." *ADE* 105 (Fall 1993): 32–36.

Surveys published "testimonials" in composition studies; finds conflict between student-centered *ethos* and a stock representation of "student" that calls for further inquiry into an apparent paradox.

178. Helmers, Marguerite H. "The Constitution of Students: Genre and Representation in the Composition Testimonial." *DAI* 53 (January 1993): 2280A.

Draws on articles published between 1967–91 in *College Composition and Communication* to explore testimonials which are stories about teaching practice.

179. Hendrickson, Aletha Staunton. "The Rhetoric of Intimidation: A Study in the Rhetoric of Institutional Power." *DAI* 54 (November 1993): 1785A.

Looks at rhetorical and linguistic features of three rhetor/audience relationships.

180. Herndl, Carl G. "Teaching Discourse and Reproducing Culture: A Critique of Research and Pedagogy in Professional and Nonacademic Writing." *CCC* 44 (October 1993): 349–63.

Suggests ways to join professional writing research and pedagogy with theories of resistance and radical pedagogy.

181. Herrick, James A. "Rhetoric, Ethics, and Virtue." *ComS* 43 (Fall 1992): 133–49.

Concludes that rhetorical virtues can be identified and incorporated into both moral judgments about rhetorical practice and an ethically guided pedagogy of communication.

182. Higgins, Lorraine Denise. "Argument as Construction: A Framework and Method." *DAI* 54 (October 1993): 1148A.

Offers a synthesis of classical rhetoric, field theory, cognitive theory, and research on writing to understand the process by which written arguments are constructed. Suggests that current argument theory does little to specify the means by which situational and personal resources are used.

183. Higgins, Mary Anne. "Toward a Critical Rhetoric: A Case Study of Farm Crisis Rhetoric from 1981—1985." *DAI* 53 (February 1993): 2600A.

Employs McKerrow's theory and praxis of a critical rhetoric to analyze texts that portray the rhetoric of the farm crisis.

184. Hill, Martin Dominic. "A Proposed Expository Device to Enhance the Coherence of Reported Research." *DAI* 54 (September 1993): 1649B.

Uses Kintsch's theory of discourse comprehension to introduce to research reports, summarize research problems, and reveal variables and rationales.

185. Hirsch, David A. "De-Familiarizations, De-Monstrations." *Pre/Text* 13 (Fall/Winter 1992): 53–65.

Examines current conflicting rhetorical constructions of homosexuality through Mary Shelley's *Frankenstein*.

186. Hochman, Will. *The Legacy of Richard Hugo in the Composition Classroom*. San Diego, CA: Conference on College Composition and Communication, March/April 1993. ERIC ED 358 455. 18 pages

Describes Richard Hugo's thinking about creative writing and his perception that creative writing can help develop self-discovery, metacognition, and emotional honesty for all writers.

187. Hocks, Elaine D. "Dialectic in a New Key: A Lacanian Dialogue with the Theories of Coleridge, Polanyi, and Bakhtin as They Pertain to Composition." *DAI* 53 (May 1993): 3919A.

Proposes conceptual parallels between three theorists and reexamines their work in terms of Lacan's rhetorical and psychoanalytic theory.

188. Hoger, Elizabeth Anne. "Writing in the Discipline of Music: Rhetorical Parameters in Writing about Music Criticism." *DAI* 54 (July 1993): 159A.

Concentrates on musician's metacritical statements concerned with writing about music.

189. Hollis, Karen. "Literacy Theory, Teaching Composition, and Feminist Response." *Pre/Text* 13 (Spring/Summer 1992): 104–15.

Argues that process-centered writing practices fail to address questions of critical literacy. Suggests feminist pedagogies as a way to create new classroom dynamics.

190. Holtrop, Stephen Dean. "Instructional Scaffolding in Context: Three Case Studies of Writing Instruction." *DAI* 53 (May 1993): 3828A.

Explores the nature of instructional contexts for learning to write in process writing teachers' classrooms.

191. Horne, Dee Alysion. "The Role of the Journal in the Creative Writing Processes of Virginia Woolf, Elizabeth Smart, and Sylvia Plath." *DAI* 53 (May 1993): 3894A.

Shows that the journal is a creative tool which aids writers in search of voice and form.

192. Horne, Janet S. "Rorty's Circumvention of Argument: Redescribing Rhetoric." *SCJ* 58 (Spring 1993): 169–81.

Focuses on redescription as the critical function of tropological rhetoric and as a means of social and political action.

193. Hourigan, Maureen Marmion. "Literacy as Social Exchange: The Influence of Class, Gender, and Culture on Academic Discourse." *DAI* 53 (January 1993): 2347A.

Argues that radical pedagogies often ignore students who are marginalized by race or ethnicity.

194. Hudelson, Sarah J., and Judith Wells Lindfors, eds. *Delicate Balances: Collaborative Research in Language Education*. Urbana, IL: NCTE, 1993. 148 pages

Nine essays describe eight different collaborative research projects; they illustrate a variety of relationships between researchers, explore how the collaboration influenced methods, scope, and results of research, and evaluate some of the strengths and limits of collaborative research. *Essayists:* Alvermann, Donna E.; Boyde, Chris; Buchanan, Judith; Crafton, Linda K.; Edelsky, Carole; Fecho, Bob; Lytle, Susan L.; Mackinson, JoAnn; Mangiola, Leslie; Olson, James; Pease-Alvarez, Lucinda; Peyton, Joy Kreeft; Porter, Carol; Samway, Katharine; Schultz, Katherine; Taylor, Dorothy; Umpleby, Richard.

195. Hurlbert, C. Mark, and Michael Blitz. "The Institution('s) Lives!" *Pre/Text* 13 (Spring/Summer 1992): 59–78.

The authors argue that through institutional rhetoric the production and conservation of information/knowledge remains an exclusive domain. They maintain that educators must work to alter institutional ideologies.

196. Hutcheon, Linda. "Peer Review and Its Discourse." *W&D* 11 (Spring 1993): 41–45.

Suggests that those who act as academic peer reviewers are under review themselves even as they critique others.

197. Ingham, Zita. *Rhetoric of Writing Instruction: Learning from Creative Writing "How-To" Books*. Laramie, WY: Wyoming Conference on English, June 1993. ERIC ED 358 453. 9 pages

Maintains that assumptions made by writers of "how-to" books on creative writing differ from those made by writers of composition texts. Points out that "how-to" books are rich in varied personas, creativity, art, and detail. Argues that composition texts should follow suit.

198. Jackson, Jennifer Ann. "Contemporary Fictions, Social Texts: Don Dellilo's 'White Noise,' 'Libra,' and 'Mao II' as Postmodern Cultural Rhetorics." *DAI* 53 (January 1993): 2370A.

Argues that rhetoricians should be more aware of postmodern cultural rhetorics that question representation, subjectivity, and the possibility of social change.

199. James, Stanlie M., and Abena P. A. Busia, eds. *Theorizing Black Feminisms: The Visionary Pragmatism of Black Women*. New York: Routledge, 1993. 288 pages

The book presents a compilation of the latest work from Black women in the academy. The contributors write from the shared belief that Black women are not simply the victims of various oppressions but are also visionary and pragmatic agents of change. *Essayists:* Barbee, Evelyn; Brewer, Rose; Clarke, Cheryl; Cole, Johnetta; Courville, Cindy; Guy-Sheftall, Beverly; Little, Marilyn; McKay, Nellie; Ogundipe, O'molara; Obbo, Christine; Ross, Loretta.

200. Jandreau, Steven Michael. "Sentence Meaning and Discourse Meaning." *DAI* 54 (July 1993): 725A.

Concludes that we need to redraw the boundaries between sentence processing and text processing, and that we need to recognize the complexities of discourse processing and the differences in strategy across ability levels.

201. Jankowski, Katherine Anne. "The Battle of Ideologies: A Struggle for Ownership in the Deaf Community." *DAI* 53 (January 1993): 2160A.

Employs a Foucauldian approach to address how rhetoric shapes the empowerment of the cultural identity of the deaf social movement.

202. Jenkins, Ruth Y. "The Intersection of Gender and Culture in the Teaching of Writing." *CollT* 41 (Winter 1993): 19–24.

Examines theoretical and pedagogical implications of alternative rhetorical patterns from a feminist perspective to supplement a traditional linear argument.

203. Jennings, Gladness Gayle. "Storytales: Performed Features of Conversational Story Telling between Ministers." *DAI* 53 (April 1993): 3409A.

Studies the performed features of speakers and listeners during conversational story telling among ministers.

204. Johnston, Dennithorne. "Dynamite." *ETC* 50 (Spring 1993): 20–24.

Notes that one can't possibly anticipate real world happenings. Points out that readers with low memory span tend to eschew open-ended interpretations.

205. Johnston, Paul. "Success, Ghosts and Things." *ETC* 50 (Fall 1993): 168–72.

Explains that although things and people from the past do not exist as they once did, we carry powerful images of them in us.

206. Jonsberg, Sara Dalmas. "Writing to Rehearse Alternative Discourse: Choice and Desire in Teen Pregnancy." *DAI* 53 (April 1993): 3435A.

Examines discourse alternatives as a means of providing teenage girls with an understanding of societal sexism and its power in identity formation.

207. Jordan, Jon Richard. "A Functional Analysis of Public Discourse." *DAI* 53 (February 1993): 2787A.

Reviews linguistic approaches to language criticism. Uses a functional approach to public discourse that distinguishes between "marked" and "unmarked" expressions. Sorts out various genres of public discourse.

208. Kamberelis, George, and Karla Dannette Scott. "Other People's Voices: The Coarticulation of Texts and Subjectivities." *L&E* 4 (1992): 359–403.

The authors argue that conceptualizing writing and voice as historical, intertextual, social, and political necessitates a literacy pedagogy which casts writing and interpreting texts as practices of discourse analysis and social and political negotiation.

209. Kamimski, Theresa. "From Personal to Public: Women's Liberation and the Print Media in the United States, 1968–1974." *DAI* 53 (January 1993): 2517A.

Analyzes women's liberation rhetoric as it appeared in liberationist publications and the subsequent interpretation of that rhetoric by the popular print media.

210. Kaplan, Carey, and Ellen Cronan Rose. "Strange Bedfellows: Feminist Collaboration." *Signs* 18 (Spring 1993): 547–61.

Describes authors' long-distance collaborations; they adopt a lesbian metaphor to describe their collaborative processes.

211. Karmiloff-Smith, Annette, Hilary Johnson, Julia Grant, Marie-Claude Jones, Yara-Natasha Karmiliff, Jon Bartrip, and Pat Cuckle. "From Sentential to Discourse Functions: Detection and Explanation of Speech Repairs by Children and Adults." *DPr* 16 (October/December 1993): 565–89.

The authors maintain that both adults and children can detect and repair problems involving discourse although they explain these problems less satisfactorily than they do lexical or referential problems.

212. Katz, Steven B. "Aristotle's Rhetoric, Hitler's Program, and the Ideological Problem of *Praxis*, Power, and Professional Discourse." *JBTC* 7 (January 1993): 37–62.

Explores *praxis* and *phronesis* as sociological and ideological dimensions of deliberative technical rhetoric.

213. Keith, William. "Rhetorical Criticism and the Rhetoric of Science: Introduction." *SCJ* 58 (Summer 1993): 255–57.

Introduces a special issue devoted to a critique of Dilip Parameshwar Gaonkar's "The Idea of Rhetoric in the Rhetoric of Science."

214. Kelvin, Patricia Rosemary. "Classical Rhetoric and Contemporary Composition at Work: A Study of Editorialists and Their Writing." *DAI* 53 (February 1993): 2788A.

Suggests that newspaper editorialists provide a better model for college student writers than literary essayists.

215. Kent, Thomas. "Language Philosophy, Writing and Reading: A Conversation with Donald Davidson." *JAC* 13 (Winter 1993): 1–20.

Discusses "externalism," "triangulation," "charity," and the fact-value distinction with the British anti-foundationalist, analytic philosopher Donald Davidson. The interviewer sees Davidson's views as correctives to some interpretations of social constructionism.

216. Kirsch, Gesa E. *Women Writing the Academy: Audience, Authority, and Transformation*. Carbondale, IL: Southern Illinois University Press, 1993. 168 pages

Explores, through extensive interviews with 35 women from five different disciplines and four academic ranks, experiences of women writers in academia.

Brings together findings on audience, authority, and gender in professional writing.

217. Koch, Kevin James. "Gertrude Buck and the Emergence of a Transactional Theory of Language." *DAI* 53 (January 1993): 2350A.

Examines the roots of modern and contemporary language theory in turn-of-the-century writings of Gertrude Buck, with special emphasis on composition and literary theory.

218. Kreitler, Shulamith, and Hans Kreitler. "Meaning Effects of Context." *DPr* 16 (October/December 1993): 429–49.

The article establishes that although context may leave meanings unaffected, it can also narrow, transform, or create new meanings. Experimental results support interactive theories of metaphor.

219. Kress, Gunther. "Against Arbitrariness: The Social Production of the Sign as a Foundational Issue in Critical Discourse Analysis." *D&S* 4 (1993): 169–91.

Argues that critical discourse analysis needs to be aware of the social significance of the texts selected for analysis.

220. Kunkel, Kathryn. "Diversity of English and the Multicultural Classroom." *DAI* 54 (September 1993): 909A.

Describes attempts to enforce language conformity in Hawaii and mainland universities. Provides a theoretical foundation for basic writing in multicultural classrooms.

221. Kutash, Emilie. "Anaxagoras and the Rhetoric of Plato's Middle Dialogue Theory of Forms." *P&R* 26 (Spring 1993): 134–62.

Proposes that Plato appropriated tropes from Anaxagorean physics and put them to new use for philosophy in order to produce new signifying matrices from an old coinage.

222. Lacy, Michael G. "Toward a Rhetorical Conception of Civil Racism." *DAI* 53 (February 1993): 2600A.

Suggests a broad spectrum of racism ranging from traditional racism produced in closed rhetorical communities to civil racism found in every-day polite contexts.

223. Ladidtka, James N. "Undecidability: An Ethics of Language, Judgment, Power, and Voice in the Discourses of Feminism, Postmodernity, and Teaching." *DAI* 53 (March 1993): 3189A.

Argues that teaching practice informed by feminism nurtures students' agency. Maintains that deconstructing gendered discourse roles responds to the ethical imperative of otherness.

224. Langstraat, Lisa R. *Dissonance and Difference: Invention Strategies for a Feminist Composition Classroom*. Louisville, KY: National Council of Teachers of English, November 1990. ERIC ED 354 535. 13 pages

Advocates a feminist composition classroom with inventive strategies that heighten students' awareness of social, political, and economic factors which make writing and reading a gendered activity.

225. Larsen, Elizabeth. "Re-Inventing Invention: Alexander Gerard and *An Essay on Genius*." *Rhetorica* 11 (Spring 1993): 181–98.

Argues that Gerard's associationist essay transformed *inventio* instead of abandoning it.

226. Lauer, Janice M. "A Response to 'The History of Composition: Reclaiming Our Lost Generations' [Varnum, *JAC* 12 (Winter 1992)]." *JAC* 13 (Winter 1993): 252–54.

Criticizes Varnum for misunderstanding and misquoting a speech given by the author.

227. Laurence, Patricia, Peter Rondinone, Barbara Gleason, Thomas J. Farrell, Paul Hunter, and Min-Zhan Lu. "Symposium on Basic Writing Conflict and Struggle, and the Legend of Mina Shaughnessey." *CE* 55 (December 1993): 879–903.

The authors examine the politicization of composition theories; they analyze Lu's

"conflict and struggle" position and assess Shaughnessey's work in a historical perspective. They also evaluate student-teacher "power relationship" debates.

228. Lazar, Michelle M. "Equalizing Gender Relations: A Case of Double-Talk." *D&S* 4 (1993): 443–65.

Argues that some educational ads in Singapore work to maintain the social inequality between the sexes.

229. Lee, Irving. "Why Discussions Go Astray." *ETC* 50 (Spring 1993): 41–53.

Argues that breakdowns in discussions often occur because people fail to understand one another, when a speaker identifies so thoroughly with an issue that criticism of the issue is viewed as a personal attack.

230. Leff, Michael. "The Idea of Rhetoric as Interpretive Practice: A Humanist's Response to Gaonkar [*SCJ* 58 (Summer 1993)]." *SCJ* 58 (Summer 1993): 296–300.

Focuses on Gaonkar's binary contrast between the productive/performative function of classical rhetoric and the theoretical/interpretive function of contemporary rhetoric.

231. Leibold, Nora Collins. "Interactive Linguistic Strategies in Campaign Rhetoric: Their Use and Function." *DAI* 54 (August 1993): 504A.

Demonstrates that the presence of *ethos*, *pathos*, and *logos* in connection with a claim-backing model appeals to speakers in nonpropositional political speeches.

232. Lemon, Hallie S. *Portfolio Units in a Process Classroom*. Oxford, OH: Miami University "New Directions in Portfolio Assessment" Conference, October 1992. ERIC ED 354 517. 18 pages

Describes a Western Illinois University teacher who had resisted using portfolios in a writing classroom, and who developed a shorter portfolio unit to incorporate the best aspects without many of the disadvantages of portfolios.

233. Leonard, Rebecca, and Don C. Locke. "Communication Stereotypes: Is Interracial Communication Possible?" *JBS* 23 (March 1993): 332–43.

Studies 12 communication traits most frequently attributed to African Americans by white students and to whites by African American students.

234. Livingston-Webber, Joan. "Self-Sponsored Writing, Genre, Intertext, and Writing Quality." *DAI* 53 (March 1993): 3190A.

Foregrounds the role of genre and intertextuality in religious writings of two women.

235. Lofty, John Sylvester. *Time to Write: The Influence of Time and Culture on Learning to Write*. Albany, NY: State University of New York Press, 1993. 292 pages

Uses voices and writings of students in a small school to dramatize students' encounters with school-based cultures of time and literacy. Reviews industrial models of schooling and time order of process-oriented writing instruction.

236. Looser, Devoney. "Composing as an 'Essentialist'? New Directions for Feminist Composition Theories." *RR* 11 (Spring 1993): 54–69.

Discusses whether feminist composition theory must necessarily presuppose cultural and historical assumptions about the label "woman."

237. Lorentz, Robert L., James W. Carland, and Jo Ann C. Carland. "The Résumé: What Value Is There in References?" *JTWC* 23 (1993): 371–77.

An empirical investigation of personnel managers in Fortune 500 companies concludes that résumés should not include references but should indicate readiness to supply references on request.

238. Lury, Celia. *Cultural Rights: Technology, Legality and Personality*. New York: Routledge, 1993. 256 pages

Uses Walter Benjamin's thesis about the effects of mechanical reproduction to examine "originality" and "authenticity" in postmodern culture. Looks at the histories of print, broadcasting, and information technology.

239. Mack, Nancy, and James Thomas Zebroski. "Remedial Critical Consciousness?" *Pre/Text* 13 (Spring/Summer 1992): 82–101.

The authors argue that theory shouldn't be separated from everyday life, particularly from class issues. They fear that critical consciousness will become hegemonic practice that reinforces the status quo.

240. Magliano, Joseph P., William B. Baggett, Brenda K. Johnson, and Arthur C. Graesser. "The Time Course of Generating Causal Antecedent and Causal Consequence Inference." *DPr* 16 (January/June 1993): 35–53.

The authors argue that lexical decision tasks indicate that causal antecedent inferences are generated online while causal consequences are not.

241. Malinowitz, Harriet. "Construing and Constructing Knowledge as a Lesbian or Gay Student Writer." *Pre/Text* 13 (Fall/Winter 1992): 37–52.

Argues that homosexual students face a double bind in assignments that call for self-reflection or personal experiences.

242. Marback, Richard Carl. "Daemons, Idols, Phantasms: The Rhetoric of Marsilio Ficino." *DAI* 53 (February 1993): 2849A.

Demonstrates Ficino's position on rhetoric through a reading of his commentaries on the *Phaedrus*, *Sophist*, and *Symposium*, arguing for a "magical" art of rhetoric.

243. Martin, Thaddeus D. "A Semiotic Phenomenology of the Will-to-Communicate in the Philosophy of Karl Jaspers." *DAI* 53 (February 1993): 2602A

Explores themes of communication, philosophy, and communicology through Jasper's will-to-communicate philosophy.

244. Martinez, Timothy Ailes. "Power and Presidential Discourse: An Analysis of Discursive Power and the Formation of Human Subjects." *DAI* 53 (May 1993): 4069A.

Analyzes discourses of presidents Wilson, F. D. Roosevelt, and Reagan; focuses on relationships among subjectivity, technology, and capitalism in the formation of metaphors.

245. Matthews, David Gray. "Jim Corbett and the Sanctuary Movement: Defining a Social Movement's Rhetorical Situation." *DAI* 54 (November 1993): 1596A.

Analyzes Corbett's rhetorical strategy of definition and how this influenced a social movement. Focuses on a close reading of a wide variety of Corbett's writings.

246. McClure, Kevin Robert. "The Denominational Ministry Strategy: A Rhetorical Study of the Public Sphere." *DAI* 53 (June 1993): 4130A.

Explores the influence exerted upon discourse in the public speaking sphere by religious and economic institutions.

247. McComiskey, Bruce. *Neo-Sophistic Rhetorical Theory: Sophistic Precedents for Contemporary Epistemic Rhetoric*. Cincinnati, OH: Conference on College Composition and Communication, March 1992. ERIC ED 349 556. 20 pages

Investigates the view of rhetorical epistemic called "neo-sophistic" and discusses the value of "neglected" sophists to present scholarly concerns.

248. McCullough, Mary Catherine. "Figuring Gender: British and American Women's Narratives of the 1890s." *DAI* 53 (April 1993): 3530A.

Examines the "New Woman Novel" as a new form of female identity, its "eroticized

essentialism" as an "enabling political strategy," and its contribution to the modern discourse of sexuality.

249. McKoon, Gail, Roger Ratcliff, Gregory Ward, and Richard Sproat. "Syntactic Prominence Effects on Discourse Processes." *JMemL* 32 (October 1993): 593–607.

Experiments indicate that the salience of parts of the discourse and the organization and context of the mental representations are influenced by surface syntax.

250. McKowski, Nancy. "A Postmodern Critique of the Modern Projects of Fredric Jameson and Patricia Bizzell." *JAC* 13 (Fall 1993): 329–44.

Redefines marxist/leftist voices in composition theory as academically conservative reactions against postmodernism, involuntarily in league with neo-conservativism.

251. McLaren, Peter, and Peter Leonard, eds. *Paulo Freire: A Critical Encounter*. New York: Routledge, 1992. 208 pages

The contributors to this book incorporate Freire's ideas into first world contexts. They address Freire's relation to feminist critique and his philosophical roots and evaluate his ideas from postmodernist and postcolonialist perspectives.

252. McNeill, David, and Elena T. Levy. "Cohesion and Gesture." *DPr* 16 (October/December 1993): 363–86.

The authors suggest that gestures work in tandem with speech to help track referents, to vary patterns of information, and to create closure.

253. McNenny, Geraldine, and Duane H. Roen. "Collaboration or Plagiarism—Cheating Is in the Eye of the Beholder." *Dialogue* 1 (Fall 1993): 6–27.

Explains how the notion of ideas as private property, which underlies university standards of academic honesty, actually defines most scholarly collaboration as plagiarism.

254. Melehy, Hassan. "Writing Cognito: Descartes, Montaigne, and the Institution of the Modern Subject." *DAI* 54 (September 1993): 924A.

Examines Descartes' construction of autonomous subject against threats posed by disjunctives in language such as those in Montaigne's *Essais*.

255. Milich, Barbara. "Pornology: Discourses on Pornography." *W&D* 11 (Spring 1993): 65–83.

Describes how ideas about state, textuality, and sexual ethics inform five ways of speaking publicly about pornography: conservative, radical-liberal, moderate, radical-feminist, and anti-censorship. Includes Venn diagrams.

256. Miller, J. Hillis. "Nietzsche in Basel: Writing Reading." *JAC* 13 (Fall 1993): 311–28.

Uses Nietzsche's early work to demonstrate a fundamental bond between reading and writing.

257. Miller, Richard Earl. "Representing the People: Theoretical and Pedagogical Disjunction in the Academy." *DAI* 54 (August 1993): 440A.

Advocates consideration of multicultural student populace as knowing and responding subjects rather than as objects for reform.

258. Miller, Susan. *Textual Carnivals: The Politics of Composition*. Carbondale, IL: Southern Illinois University Press, 1993. 288 pages

Provides a historical and political analysis of the status and context of composition teaching, research, and administration within university settings. Finds, through survey research and reflections on her own career, that composition's minimal political clout in universities is fostered by composition teachers themselves. Argues that an apologetic acceptance of compositions's service role should give way to increased intellectual rigor.

259. Mills, Sara. *Discourses in Difference: An Analysis*. New York: Routledge, 1993. 208 pages

Focuses on case studies of three women travellers—Alexandra David-Neel, Mary Kingsley, and Nina Mazuchelli—in the high colonial period. Uses theories of Edward Said, Louise Pratt, and Gayatri Spivak to assert that these women produced "alternative accounts of the imperial presence in colonial countries."

260. Mirskin, Jerry. "Writing as a Process of Valuing." *DAI* 54 (October 1993): 1337A.

Proposes a socio-cognitive model of writing based on social theories of G. H. Mead, M. M. Bakhtin, and L. S. Vygotsky. Combines a theoretical discussion of writing as "calling out" socially valued responses with a case study of one first-year student's writing processes.

261. Mishra, Rama K. "Planning in Writing: Evidence from Cognitive Test and Think-Aloud Protocols." *DAI* 53 (June 1993): 4257A.

Investigates the role of planning for good and poor writers using think-aloud protocols.

262. Mohan, Mary Leslie. *Organizational Communication and Cultural Vision: Approaches for Analysis*. Albany, NY: State University of New York Press, 1993. 202 pages

Studies contemporary theory and research in organizational culture.

263. Moore, Michael. "The Language Problem." *ETC* 50 (Winter 1993): 461–68.

Argues that human speech conceals more than it reveals. Includes a collection of quotations from authors that shows that concealment has been bemoaned from the time of St. Augustine to the present.

264. Moore, Patrick, and Chad Fitz. "Gestalt Theory and Instructional Design." *JTWC* 23 (1993): 137–57.

Applies six Gestalt principles to show the improvements when Gestalt theory is considered in instructional design.

265. Morley, David. "Active Audience Theory: Pendulums and Pitfalls." *JC* 43 (Autumn 1993): 13–19.

Reviews "problems and misdirections" in contemporary active audience theory.

266. Morrison, Margaret. "Laughing with Queers in My Eyes: Proposing 'Queer Rhetoric(s)' and Introducing a Queer Issue." *Pre/Text* 13 (Fall/Winter 1992): 11–36.

Argues that "queer" is a performative signifying practice. Introduces the special issue.

267. Morse, Janice M., ed. *Critical Issues in Qualitative Research Methods.* Thousand Oaks, CA: Sage, 1993. 360 pages

The contributors examine and critique current qualitative research methods. They apply their studies to ethnographic and phenomenological writing research. *Essayists:* Bottorff, Joan; Boyle, Joyceen; Carey, Martha Ann; Chapman, Linda; Cohen, Marlene Zichi; Dreher, Melanie; Hutchinson, Sally; Knafl, Kathleen A.; Leininger, Madeleine; Lipson, Juliene; May, Katharyn; Morse, Janice; Muecke, Marjorie; Omery, Anna; Peters, Jennifer; Ray, Marilyn; Sandelowski, Margarette; Sorfman, Bernard; Stern, Phyllis Noerager; Swanson, Janice; Thorn, Sally; Tripp-Reimer, Toni; Waterman, James.

268. Mortensen, Peter, and Gesa E. Kirsch. "On Authority in the Study of Writing." *CCC* 44 (December 1993): 556–72.

The authors question the perception of authority as a "stable and uniform term" and propose a dialogic model "informed by an 'ethic of care.'"

269. Morton, Donald. "Made to Serve: Patrolling the Borders of Dominant Intelligibilities." *W&D* 11 (Spring 1993): 35–40.

Claims that bringing together a "panel of 'experts'" to debate the politics of book reviewing only serves to reinforce the dominant political paradigm.

270. Moss, Roger. "The Rhetoric that Dare Not Speak Its Name." *Pre/Text* 13 (Fall/Winter 1992): 109–22.

Argues that because much of Wilde's writing relates to homosexuality, these aspects remained hidden in his texts. Claims that Wilde, in this respect, is a sophist.

271. Moxley, Joseph M. "Reinventing the Wheel or Teaching the Basics: College Writers' Knowledge of Argumentation." *CompSt* 21 (Fall 1993): 3–15.

Studies basic, first-year, and advanced composition students. Finds that advanced students can rank arguments by logic effectiveness and suggests that basic writers need instruction in argumentation.

272. Muir, Star A. "A Defense of the Ethics of Contemporary Debate." *P&R* 26 (1993): 277–95.

Argues that using academic debate as an educational tool promotes a morality consistent with the democratic ethic. Emphasizes that it encourages social values such as tolerance and fairness.

273. Murray, John D., Celia M. Klin, and Jerome L. Meyers. "Forward Inferences in Narrative Text." *JMemL* 43 (August 1993): 464–73.

The authors conclude that forward inferencing is triggered by breaks in causal coherence and by repetition of focal propositions.

274. Murray, Susan Allen. "The Role of Text Structure in Composing from Sources." *DAI* 53 (June 1993): 4258A.

Investigates the use of structural patterns in expository text as strategic tools for synthesizing and organizing information in a source-based composing task.

275. Musgrove, Laurence Emerson. "Composing Character in Rhetoric and Composition." *DAI* 53 (April 1993): 3464A.

Recommends a way of reading theories of rhetoric so that college composition teachers become more aware of how they discover, examine, and select teaching methods.

276. Nash, Jane Gradwohl, Gary M. Schumacher, and Bruce W. Carlson. "Writing from Sources: A Structure-Mapping Model." *JEdPsy* 85 (March 1993): 159–70.

The authors point out that adopting Gentner's model of analogical reasoning proved useful in "conceptualizing how writers use multiple sources" in writing comparison/contrast essays. They warn against overgeneralizing their results.

277. Neal, Maureen. "Social Constructionism and Expressionism: Contradictions and Connections." *CompSt* 21 (Spring 1993): 42–8.

Suggests that expressionism and social construction are not polar opposites. Points out that both are process-centered rather than product-centered.

278. Neale, Robert. *The Common Writer: Theory and Practice for Writers and Teachers.* New York: Oxford University Press, 1993. 160 pages

Acknowledges the gap between words and referents as related to metaphor, irony, and subjectivity. Clarifies issues such as correctness, ambiguity, and point of view. Analyzes the writing process in light of language history and the evolution of the alphabet. Summarizes developments in teaching writing. Includes practical exercises.

279. Neale, Robert. *Writers on Writing.* New York: Oxford University Press, 1993. 451 pages

Presents a study tool for writers wanting to refine their craft; presents advice and insights of 55 English language poets and prose writers on composing processes, problems, techniques, frustrations, and success stories. Topics range from the metaphysics to the daily grind of getting words on paper.

280. Near, Michael R. "Anticipating Alienation: *Beowulf* and the Intrusion of Literacy." *PMLA* 108 (March 1993): 320–32.

Argues that *Beowulf* presents writing as a means of social isolation and oral literacy as a mode of inclusion. Considers this depiction as a means to reveal community values.

281. New, William Sloan. "Linguistic Knowledge, Planning, and Expository Writing." *DAI* 54 (1993): 3880A.

Studies interactions between linguistic knowledge and planning ability when writing. Discusses how they affect writing abilities.

282. Nwoye, Onuigbo G. "Social Issues on Walls: Graffiti in University Lavatories." *D&S* 4 (1993): 419–42.

Argues that graffiti presents ways for a minority group to articulate social and political concerns.

283. Odell, Lee, ed. *Theory and Practice in the Teaching of Writing: Rethinking the Discipline.* Carbondale, IL: Southern Illinois University Press, 1993. 352 pages

The contributors explore specific sets of assumptions about knowledge, education, and writing and examine the basic relationships between theory and practice. *Essayists:* Corder, Jim W.; Hampton, Sally; Heath, Shirley Brice; Herrington, Anne J.; Hillocks, George, Jr.; Kaufer, David; Moss, Beverly J.; Odell, Lee; Peterson, Jane; Walters, Keith; Young, Richard.

284. Ok, Jong-Seok. "Korean and English Expository Prose: A Study in Constrastive Discourse." *DAI* 53 (June 1993): 4301A.

Reveals a sharp contrast in the structural organization of English and Korean.

285. Olson, Gary A. "Literary Theory, Philosophy of Science; and Persuasive Discourse: Thoughts from a Neo-Premodernist." *JAC* 13 (Fall 1993): 283–310.

Examines Toulmin's career efforts to "dismantle" Cartesian rationalism, and to establish a postmodern philosophical tradition to contend with poststructuralism.

286. Ong, Rory Jay. "The Practice of Rhetoric and the Struggle for Everyday Life: Toward a Genealogy of Resistant Formations of Discourse in the Margins." *DAI* 53 (January 1993): 2373A.

Explores his identity as an Asian American and theorizes about narratives generated in the margins. Discusses contradictory representations and questions of identity in relation to Protagoras and Vico.

287. Onyemenem, Anselm Nwanne. "African American Students' Critical Reflections on Expository Writing in California Colleges." *DAI* 54 (October 1993): 1267A.

Analyzes African-American students self-perceived skills and needs in first-year composition classes at a community college. Suggests that writing teachers frequently do not understand students' writing abilities.

288. Opalenik, Mary. "Recognizing and Providing an Audience for Female Voices." *EJ* 82 (November 1993): 61–62.

Points out that female students from patriarchal cultures need special attention to develop their own voices.

289. Osman, Mahamed Eltanir. "The Effects of Think-Ahead Questions and Prior Knowledge on Learning and Retention." *DAI* 53 (March 1993): 3096A.

Suggests that think-ahead questions improve higher-order learning and that a rationale and prior knowledge increase learning and retention.

290. Owens, Derek. *Resisting Writings (and the Boundaries of Composition)*. Southern Methodist University Studies in Composition and Rhetoric. Dallas, TX: Southern Methodist University Press, 1993. 212 pages

Calls for a more eclectic and culturally diverse embrace of innovative discourse philosophies. Proposes to overlap composition and poetics and to teach writing

from a discourse perspective which includes feminist, non-Eurocentric, and experimental perspectives.

291. Padgett, Donna M. "Instructional Applications of Protocol Analysis: An Exploratory Study." *DAI* 53 (May 1993): 3830A.

Argues that protocol analysis is appropriate for tutoring and for classroom demonstrations of a videotaped writer's processes.

292. Pajares, M. Frank, and Margaret Johnson. *Confidence and Competence in Writing: The Role of Self-Efficacy, Outcome Expectency, and Apprehension*. Atlanta, GA: American Educational Research Association, April 1993. ERIC ED 358 474. 26 pages

Discusses a study of writing self-efficacy, outcome expectations, apprehension, and the performance of 30 undergraduate students throughout one semester.

293. Papp, James Ralph. "Parody: Cognition, Rhetoric and Social History." *DAI* 54 (October 1993): 1347A.

Argues that in order to understand parody we must understand its cognitive purpose, rhetorical function, historical causes, and effects in social structures. Suggests that the cognitive purpose of parody includes development and survivability in Darwinian terms.

294. Papper, Carole Clark. "Personality Theory and Collaborative Writing Groups." *DAI* 53 (February 1993): 2788A.

Examines the role of personality type in the negotiation of writing-group roles and writing behaviors.

295. Parry-Giles, Trevor Stirling. "Public Issue Construction and Rhetorical Access: The 1985 Banning of 'Real Lives—at the Edge of the Union' in Great Britain." *DAI* 53 (May 1993): 3732A.

Explores how public issues are rhetorically constructed according to prevailing ideological commitments that demarcate parameters for public discussion.

296. Pearce, Richard. "The Practical Politics of Book Reviewing: From the Desk of a Book Review Editor." *W&D* 11 (Spring 1993): 23–25.

Stresses the dilemma of being a review editor of a journal. Questions the ability to present authors fairly and to control one's own political agenda.

297. Pemberton, Michael A. "Modeling Theory and Composing Process Models." *CCC* 44 (February 1993): 40–58.

Discusses the value of modeling theory for composition research and calls for making explicit the epistemological assumptions underlying composing process models.

298. Pennycook, Alastair. "The Cultural Politics of Teaching English in the World." *DAI* 53 (June 1993): 4239A.

Explores cultural and political implications of the global spread of English.

299. Penrose, Ann M., and Barbara M. Sitko, eds. *Hearing Ourselves Think: Cognitive Research in the College Writing Class.* Social and Cognitive Studies in Writing and Literacy. New York: Oxford University Press, 1993. 240 pages

The essayists discuss socio-cognitive processes in college classrooms and emphasize a move from research results to classroom action, thereby lining research and theory with practice. They note that students study reading/writing processes and contexts, incorporating their observations into principles for practice.
Essayists: Bowen, Betsy A.; Burnett, Rebecca E.; Greene, Stuart; Haas, Christina; Higgins, Lorraine; Nelson, Jeannie; Penrose, Ann M.; Schriver, Karen A.; Sitko, Barbara M.

300. Penticoff, Richard Roy. "Invoking the Social: Metaphors of Community in Composition Scholarship." *DAI* 54 (October 1993): 1338A.

Analyzes metaphors of community used by composition theorists such as Bruffee, Lunsford, Bartholomae, and Bizzell. Argues for a more complete analysis of interactions between writing and other social phenomena.

301. Perkins, Nancy S. "The Echoes Project: Five Case Studies of Students Writing Research Papers Using Primary Sources in a Collaborative Community." *DAI* 53 (June 1993): 4306A.

Presents patterns of community college students' researching and writing about local topics published for the local community.

302. Perloff, Marjorie. "On the Politics of Book Reviewing." *W&D* 11 (Spring 1993): 13–17.

Argues that writing book reviews counts for little in academia; offers suggestions for senior and junior faculty who wish to change this problem.

303. Perry, Donna. *Backtalk: Women Writers Speak Out.* New Brunswick, NJ: Rutgers University Press, 1993. 360 pages

Interviews contemporary women writers about getting started as writers, the influence of family and communities, writing as women, the responsibility of the writer to the community, and the role of literary tradition to their growth.

304. Prelli, Lawrence J. "Rhetorical Perspective and the Limits of Critique [response to Gaonkar, *SCJ* 58 (Summer 1993)]." *SCJ* 58 (Summer 1993): 319–27.

Argues that Gaonkar's critique is flawed because of the limits and frame of the analytical method.

305. Procter, David E. "Bridging Social Change through Mythic Regeneration." *ComS* 43 (Fall 1992): 171–81.

Analyzes the process by which myths explain changing social conditions while retaining national persona and socio-political order.

306. Proctor, Russell. "Communications Research." *ETC* 50 (Fall 1993): 201–20.

Examines how, when confronted by their reactions to a confrontative message, people can learn to accept responsibility.

307. Puckett, Thomas F. N. "Phenomenology of Communication and Culture: Michel Foucault's Thematics in the Televised Popular Discourse of *Star Trek*." *DAI* 53 (January 1993): 2162A.

Develops a general taxinomia of communication and culture using phenomenological research protocol and a theory of rupture.

308. Quinn, Arthur. *Figures of Speech: Sixty Ways to Turn a Phrase*. Davis, CA: Hermagoras Press, 1993. 103 pages

Presents a glossary of terms of interest to students of language, rhetoric, composition, and critical theory.

309. Raign, Kathryn Rosser. *Burke's Method of Dramatism and Its Use as a Tool for Teaching Developmental Writing*. Cincinnati, OH: Conference on College Composition and Communication, March 1992. ERIC ED 354 508. 17 pages

Proposes that Burke's pentad may provide a key for teachers to increase students' oral abilities as well as their basic writing skills.

310. Ramsey, Jarold. "Francis LaFlesche's 'The Song of Flying Crow' and the Limits of Ethnography." *Boundary* 19 (Fall 1992): 180–96.

Presents an eight-paragraph theme by LaFlesche (the "first American Indian anthropologist") as a unique and linguistically interesting personalization of "an ethnographic experience."

311. Ramsey, Ramsey Eric. "Listening to Heidegger on Rhetoric." *P&R* 26 (1993): 266–75.

Analyzes the relationship between Aristotle's *Rhetoric* and Heidegger's claims in relation to it. Explores the concept of listening-while-speaking as theory for approaching rhetorical situations.

312. Ratcliffe, Kristan. "A Rhetoric of Textual Feminism: (Re)reading the Emotional in Virginia Woolf's *Three Guineas*." *RR* 11 (Spring 1993): 400–16.

Defines textual feminism using Virginia Woolf's writing on women and language, Kenneth Burke's definition of rhetoric, Nelly Furman's concept of "textual feminism," and Karyln Kohrs Campbell's call for a feminist critique of discourses. Argues that textual feminism gives value to the emotional in discourse.

313. Reed, Joy Lynn H., and Diane Lemonnier Schallert. "The Nature of Involvement in Academic Discourse Tasks." *JEdPsy* 85 (June 1993): 253–66.

The authors conclude that the degree of engagement in reading, writing, and oral communication tasks is "influenced by cognitive and motivational/affective factors."

314. Reimer, Kathryn Meyer, and Bertram C. Bruce. "Building Teacher-Researcher Collaboration: Dilemmas and Strategies." Center for the Study of Reading, Urbana, IL, June 1993. Technical Report No. 577. ERIC ED 357 331. 13 pages

Examines some ethical dimensions of collaborative research.

315. Rhodes, Barbara C. "Learning through Writing: Teachers' Perceptions and Pedagogical Strategies in Three Academic Disciplines at a Community College." *DAI* 54 (July 1993): 68A.

Proposes that teachers' perceptions of writing and of themselves as writers determine their attitudes toward writing programs and their perceptions of student writing success.

316. Richter, Francine Kay Ramsey. "A Rhetorical Analysis of 'Goodbye to a River' for the Composition Classroom." *DAI* 54 (October 1993): 1271A.

Advocates using Graves' text for Rhetoric and composition classrooms because it is a rhetorical masterpiece which treats the river as a woman.

317. Rider, Janine. "Memory as Muse: Recomposing Memory in Rhetoric and Composition." *DAI* 53 (February 1993): 2789A.

Elevates the status of memory as a vital canon of contemporary rhetoric critical to the formation of both forms and ideas.

318. Rosenblatt, Louise M. "The Transactional Theory: Against Dualisms." *CE* 55 (April 1993): 377–86.

Addresses the connections between writing theory and critical theory; emphasizes pragmatist transactionalism and the resisting of contentious dichotomies.

319. Ross, Susan. "A Rhetorical Analysis of the Writings of Women Prisoners: A Thematic Examination." *DAI* 53 (December 1992): 1726A.

Analyzes the writings of life-sentenced women prisoners in a writing workshop for evidence that writing creates inner authority and empowerment.

320. Rossetti, Livio. " 'If We Link the Essence of Rhetoric with Deception': Vincenzo on Socrates and Rhetoric [response to Vincenzo, *P&R* 25 (1992)]." *P&R* 26 (1993): 311–21.

Suggests that Vincenzo misrepresents Socrates' dialogues by overlooking Socrates' rhetoric and by refusing to recognize the potential within rhetoric for deception.

321. Rouster, William J. "Social Construction, the Dominant Classes, and Cultural Criticism." *Pre/Text* 13 (Spring/Summer 1992): 118–30.

Believes that theory and practice are both needed in critical pedagogy. Offers teaching strategies designed to introduce students to issues of cultural criticism.

322. Rubin, Donnalee. *Gender Influences: Reading Student Texts, Studies in Writing and Rhetoric*. Carbondale, IL: Southern Illinois University Press, 1993. 175 pages

Discusses how gender perception and expectation can influence assessment decisions that seem neutral on the surface.

323. Russell, Charles G. "Who Controls Your Life?" *ETC* 50 (Spring 1993): 17–19.

Suggests that language shapes peoples' realities. Argues that if people want to be responsible for their feelings, they should recognize that others can affect their emotions.

324. Russell, David R. "Vygotsky, Dewey, and Externalism: Beyond the Student/Discipline Dichotomy." *JAC* 13 (Winter 1993): 173–97.

Maintains that externalists reject binaries such as mind/world and thus the need for a mediating third agency. Points out that externalism conflicts with both romantic and liberatory pedagogies.

325. Sarangi, Srikant K. "The Dynamics of Institutional Discourse: An Intercultural Perspective." *DAI* 53 (April 1993): 3514A.

Discusses encounters between Asian migrants and British bureaucrats. Suggests to recognize societal context and to study native and nonnative encounters like other discourse.

326. Sauer, Beverly, A. "Revisioning Sixteenth-Century Solutions to Twentieth-Century Problems in Herbert Hoover's Translation of Agricola's *De Re Metallica*." *JTWC* 23 (1993): 269–86.

Demonstrates how technical articles reflect the writer's political ideologies and how political arguments presented as purely technical debates shape the uses and construction of future technologies.

327. Scheurer, Erika. "Voices(s) and the Collaborative Essay: . . . Megaphones, Magnifying Glasses." *Focuses* 5 (Winter 1992): 90–102.

Holds that collaborative writing aids students to discover dialogue through personal development in continual transformation eliciting issues of authority, hierarchy, and personal voice.

328. Schiappa, Edward. "Arguing about Definitions." *Arg* 7 (1993): 403–17.

Describes Perelman's notion that definitions are rhetorical by showing how they direct discourse from "ought" claims to pseudo "is" claims.

329. Schiappa, Edward. "Burkean Tropes and Kuhnian Science." *JAC* 13 (Fall 1993): 401–20.

Constructs a language-centered perspective on social constructionism by juxtaposing Burkean philosophy of language with Kuhnian philosophy of science.

330. Schick, Ruth Sharon. "Gender Differences in Student Writing: A Cross-National Comparison." *DAI* 54 (October 1993): 1267A.

Integrates sociolinguistic and writing-achievement test data from Chile, Sweden, and the United States. Reveals that patterns of gender differences in writing are shaped by cultural, historical, and institutional practices and assumptions.

331. Schonberg, Jeffrey Brett. "Plato and Textual Authority: an Examination of Plato's Dominative Influence in Four Genres of Ethnography Leading to a Postplatonic, Rhetorical Model of Textual Authority." *DAI* 54 (July 1993): 160A.

Studies the connection between Plato's work and subsequent genres; offers a postplatonic model of textual authority which focuses on rhetorical choices made by readers.

332. Schratz, Michael J., ed. *Qualitative Voices in Educational Research*. Bristol, PA: Falmer Press, 1993. 206 pages

The contributors offer a critical insight into the scientific rationale and the methodological application of qualitative analysis. *Essayists:* Altrichirt, Herbert; Burgess, Robert G.; Garzia, Carlos Marcele; Huber, Günter L.; Larcher, Dietmar; Mehan, Hugh; Reinharz, Shulamit; Rudduck, Jean; Schratz, Michael; Spindler, George; Spindler, Louise; Walker, Rob.

333. Sebberson, David. "Composition, Philosophy, and Rhetoric: The 'Problem of Power.'" *JAC* 13 (Winter 1993): 199–216.

Critiques Phelp's *Composition as a Human Science* for not dealing with power. Considers Habermas' theory as a solution and suggests rereading Aristotle from a Habermasian perspective.

334. Seshadri-Crooks, Kalpana. "Post-Colonial Women and Cross-Cultural Negotiation in Feminist Theory (India)." *DAI* 53 (January 1993): 2573A.

Examines dominant feminist discourses between Euro/American and Third World post-colonial (South Asian) women on questions of cultural identity and political change.

335. Shapiro, Marilyn. *What Do We Teach and How Do We Teach It*? San Antonio, TX: College English Association Conference, April 1991. ERIC ED 348 689. 23 pages

Discusses the effects of some feminist critics' approach of composition with a preconceived feminist perspective. Argues for an introduction of narrative theory in pedagogy.

336. Shea, B. Christine. *Anecdotia Ad Nauseum: An Argument Analysis of D'Souza's 'Illiberal Education.'* Boise, ID: Annual Meeting of the Western States Communication Association, February 1992. ERIC ED 353 608. 27 pages

Points out that when examined as an argument from example, the book fails the cogency test and is not logically convincing.

337. Sheard, Cynthia Miecznikowski. "*Kairos* and Kenneth Burke." *CE* 55 (March 1993): 291–310.

Suggests that Burke shares a Sophistic conception of language as grounded in *kairos*.

338. Shepherd, Gregory J. "Communication as Influence: Definitional Exclusion." *ComS* 43 (Winter 1992): 204–19.

Argues for a definition that will include and affirm both masculine and feminine views. Points out pragmatic, theoretical, and research consequences.

339. Shi, Huifen. "The Relation between Freshman Writing Coherence and Cohesion, Functional Roles, and Cognitive Strategies." *DAI* 54 (September 1993): 910A.

Concludes that high-rated essays use implicit cohesive ties and planning strategies whereas low-rated essays depend more on conjunctions.

340. Shollar, Barbara. "Writing Ethnicity/Writing Modernity: Autobiographies by Jewish-American Women." *DAI* 53 (April 1993): 3531A.

Discusses the relationship of Jewish-American women's autobiographies to masculinist writings representing women within secular progressivism.

341. Sierra, Judy. "What Makes a Tale Tellable? Narrative and Memory Process." *DAI* 54 (September 1993): 1050A.

Tests whether conformity to the story grammar developed by pyschologists Mandler and Johnson explains the difference between "tellable" and "nontellable" tales.

342. Simonsen, Stephen. "Transfer of Learning between Reading and Writing: Models and Implications." *RRDE* 8 (1991): 1–6.

Provides an overview of a limited body of resarch on the transfer of learning between reading and writing in mature adults.

343. Smith, Kenneth A. "Contrasting Discourses in the Essays of Virginia Woolf, James Baldwin, Joan Didion, and E. B. White." *DAI* 53 (May 1993): 3896A.

Finds that the tension between social voices is an essential trait of the essays.

344. Smith, Louise Z. "Profession and Vocation: Trends in Publication." *Focuses* 6 (Winter 1993): 75–86.

Argues that theory wars distract English professionals from their vocation; offers a wish list for articles engaging in conversations about theory-and-pedagogy interaction.

345. Solsken, Judith W. "The Paradigm Misfit Blues." *RTE* 27 (October 1993): 316–25.

Discusses conventional paradigms and their shortfalls. Suggests that traditional paradigms must be critiqued.

346. Spano, Shawn. "John Locke and the Epistemological Foundations of Adam Smith's Rhetoric." *SCJ* 59 (Fall 1993): 15–26.

Examines the theoretical relationship linking Locke with Smith. Analyzes communication characteristics of Smith's rhetoric as well as the evolution of modern rhetorical theory.

347. Spellmeyer, Kurt. " 'Too Little Care': Language, Politics, and Embodiment in the Life World." *CE* 55 (March 1993): 265–83.

Suggests that writing teachers must assist students who struggle to decide who they have been and what they will become.

348. Spellmeyer, Kurt. "Writing and Truth: The Decline of Expertise and the Rebirth of Philosophy." *JAC* 13 (Winter 1993): 97–110.

Maintains that high modernists, unable to ground knowledge in experience, retreated to artificial systems, thus sacrificing experiential truth.

349. Sperling, Melanie. "The Social Nature of Written Text: A Research-Based Review and Summary of Conceptual Issues in the Teaching of Writing." National Council of Teachers of English, 1993. NCTE Concept Paper Series No. 8. ERIC ED 359 547. 66 pages

Analyzes the implications of research methods in various studies of writing; discusses social contexts of written communication, focusing particularly on how writing instruction adopts social modes of discourse; surveys "core" concepts of the most promising approaches.

350. Spicer, Edward H. "The Nations of a State." *Boundary* 19 (Fall 1992): 26–48.

Connects Native Americans with other subordinated peoples. Discusses languages (and attitudes toward them) as one cultural aspect separating the various nations within each state.

351. Stamm, Carol Anne. "Talk about Writing in Student-Student Content Conferences and Student-Teacher Editing Conferences." *DAI* 54 (October 1993): 1271A.

Investigates types and relative amounts of talk used by seventh-grade students and teachers in one-on-one writing conferences. Compares male and female students and between high- and low-achieving writers.

352. Stearney, Lynn M. "Private Expression in the Public Sphere: The Rhetoric of Contemporary Feminism and Its Implications for an Understanding of Public Discourse in Rhetorical Theory and Criticism." *DAI* 53 (November 1992): 1324A.

Argues that a public/private distinction has unnecessarily excluded material from the contemporary women's movement from rhetorical analysis; uses textual analysis to demonstrate a move from the individual to the political.

353. Stieve, Edwin. *Breaking Down Gender Barriers: Theories into Practice*. San Diego, CA: Conference on College Composition and Communication, March/April 1993. ERIC ED 358 535. 11 pages

Maintains that breaking down gender barriers includes an awareness of gender-specific modes of writing and interpreting text.

354. Stoffel, Judith A. "Affective Concerns and Cognitive Processes of Adult, Distance, Female College Students Writing Documented Papers." *DAI* 54 (October 1993): 1202A.

Examines adult, female students' self-reported comments on affective (positive/negative) and cognitive (strategies/needs) concerns while writing documented papers in a distance-writing situation.

355. Strain, Margaret. "Toward a Hermeneutic Model of Composition History: Robert Carlsen's 'The State of the Profession 1961–1962.'" *JAC* 13 (Winter 1993): 217–40.

Reads Carlsen's report in a historical context. Argues that composition's subordinate status allowed access to government monies. Points out that cultural attitudes toward science shaped composition.

356. Strange, Jeffrey John. "The Facts of Fiction: The Accommodation of Real-World Beliefs to Frabricated Accounts." *DAI* 54 (August 1993): 358A.

Shows that readers construct "referential contexts" and remember longer what is presented as historical fact rather than the product of the writer's imagination.

357. Sturrock, John. *The Language of Autobiography: Studies in the First Person Singular*. New York: Cambridge University Press, 1993. 322 pages

Analyzes the truth-claims of 20 literary autobiographies to show how artificial and self-conscious this form of writing is.

358. Subramanian, Ram, Robert G. Insley, and Rodney Blackwell. "Performance and Readability: A Comparison of Annual Reports of Profitable and Unprofitable Corporations." *JBC* 30 (January 1993): 49–62.

Presents a computer stylistic analysis of 60 annual reports which reveals a positive correlation between readability and performance.

359. Sullivan, Dale L. "The *Ethos* of Epideictic Encounter." *P&R* 26 (Spring 1993): 113–33.

Describes the importance of *ethos* to epideictic rhetoric and the characteristics of *ethos* appropriate to it. Defines epideictic *ethos* as the "consubstantial space which enfolds participants."

360. Swigart, Leigh. "Practice and Perception: Language Use and Attitudes in Dakar." *DAI* 54 (July 1993): 228A.

Focuses on ways in which Wolof/French bilinguals make choices about the languages available to them in their linguistic repertoire.

361. Talbot, Mary Margaret. "Language, Intertextuality and Subjectivity: Voices and the Construction of Consumer Feminism." *DAI* 53 (March 1993): 3198A.

Examines how discourse shapes women as feminine social subjects; uses intertextual coherence to analyze consumer features in a magazine.

362. Tannen, Deborah, ed. *Gender and Conversational Interaction*. New York: Oxford University Press, 1993. 352 pages

Looks at gender-related differences in conversational interactions. Sees male and female styles of language as reflective of different "cultural" practices. Challenges generalizations and explores the complexity of gender and language use. *Essayists:* Brown, Penelope; Clarke, Sandra; Drakich, Janice; Eckert, Penelope; Edelsky, Carol; Eder, Donna; Goodwin, Marjorie Harness; James, Deborah; Johnstone, Barbara; Sheldon, Amy; Tannen, Deborah.

363. Terry, Ralph B. "An Analysis of Certain Features of Discourse in the New Testament Book of I Corinthians." *DAI* 54 (November 1993): 1785A.

Establishes that all the problems addressed grew out of cultural traditions of the ancient Greek world which was in conflict with Christianity.

364. Thomas, Douglas. "Burke, Nietzsche, Lacan: Three Perspectives on the Rhetoric of Order." *QJS* 79 (August 1993): 336–55.

Examines the rhetorics of Burke, Nietzsche, and Lacan to demonstrate that rheto-

ric both produces and is produced by the way in which we order our world.

365. Thomas, Douglas Edward. "Toward a Nietzschean Theory of Rhetoric: The Valuative Interpretation of Discourse and the Reversal of Platonism." *DAI* 53 (December 1992): 1727A.

Reevaluates Nietzsche's work as fully developed theory of rhetoric; emphasizes the social construction of the world in language.

366. Thomas, Jeannie Banks. "Transgressing Language: Laughter and the Narratives of Women." *DAI* 53 (February 1993): 3018A.

Examines laughter as a paralinguistic feature to show that laughter fundamentally alters the signification of words in narratives.

367. Tompkins, Jane. "Postcards from the Edge." *JAC* 13 (Fall 1993): 448–57.

Recounts her first attempt to decentralize her classroom and discusses the trauma she experienced when handing classroom authority over to students.

368. Torell, Barbara A. Constantine. "Conversations with History: An Analysis of Leadership and Ideology.' . . . Mirroring the Present in the Past and the Past in the Present' (Hans-Georg Gadamer, 1976)." *DAI* 53 (March 1993): 3199A.

Examines presidential inaugural addresses and congressional narratives to show how ideology strengthens historical continuity and reinforces unification of the national community.

369. Towns, Cheryl Hofstetter. "Dumbo or Colleague? Our Professional Perceptions of Students." *CompSt* 21 (Spring 1993): 94–103.

Reviews three years of February issues of *CCC*, analyzing nouns used to refer to students.

370. Trimbur, John. "Articulation Theory and the Problem of Determination: A Reading of

Lives on the Boundary." *JAC* 13 (Winter 1993): 33–50.

Examines Rose's book from the perspective of Stuart Hall's articulation theory. Finds the book more problematic than it seems and sees it as a mixture of comforting success story and American literacy myth.

371. Trimbur, John. "'Fish Tales' and the Politics of Anti-Professionalism [response to Olson, *JAC* 12 (Fall 1992)]." *JAC* 13 (Winter 1993): 245–50.

Sees Fish's case for literature as profession as a useful corrective to two common images. Argues that we must rearticulate professionalism to redirect popular passions toward democratic culture.

372. Trimbur, John. "'In the Beginning Was the Sixties': A Conversation with Richard Ohman and John Trimbur." *Pre/Text* 13 (Spring/Summer 1992): 134–47.

Discusses Ohman's career as radical teacher-scholar. Offers a critique of the current state of the cultural left.

373. Truesdale, Laura Sanders. "Teacher as Researcher: Transforming Lives through Dialogue and Dialogue Journals in an Eighth-Grade Whole Language Curriculum." *DAI* 54 (October 1993): 1234A.

Studies five eighth graders' use of dialogue and dialogue journals in a reading class. Maintains that students were changed through such dialogic interactions and specified patterns of results.

374. Tulbert, Beth Lorene. "Effect of a Cognitive Strategy on the Writing Ability of College Students with Learning Disabilities." *DAI* 54 (July 1993): 147A.

Studies the effectiveness of cognitive writing strategy instruction on the written expression skills of college students with learning disabilities.

375. Turner, Ron, and Susan Fowler. "Dear Susan/Dear Ron: Time for a New Expository

Discourse Genre." *EQ* 26 (Fall 1993): 21–25.

Discusses expository writing theory and gender bias of traditional genres; suggests the use of letters as a new form of discourse.

376. van Dijk, Teun A. "Principles of Critical Discourse Analysis." *D&S* 4 (1993): 249–83.

Discusses principles of critical discourse analysis and the relationship between power and discourse.

377. van Eemeren, Frans H., Rob Grootendorst, Sally Jackson, and Scott Jacobs. *Reconstructing Argumentative Discourse*. Studies in Rhetoric and Communication, edited by E. Culpepper Clarke, Raymie E. McKerrow, and David Zarefsky. Tuscaloosa, AL: University of Alabama Press, 1993. 224 pages

Uses descriptive and normative perspectives to study argumentation in settings such as everyday conversation, religious disputes, and letters to the editor.

378. van Leeuwen, Theo. "Genre and Field in Critical Discourse Analysis: A Synopsis." *D&S* 4 (1993): 193–223.

Relates genre and field to discourse and discursive practice.

379. Verene, Donald Phillip. "The Limits of Argument: Argument and Autobiography." *P&R* 26 (Winter 1993): 1–8.

Argues that ancients are reread today as moderns which takes the form of an over-attraction to argument in philosophy.

380. Villanueva, Victor, Jr. *Bootstraps: From an American Academic of Color*. Urbana, IL: National Council of the Teachers of English, 1993. 151 pages

Uses diverse approaches to look at language, teaching, politics, cultural identity, and racism. Explores his own experiences, and critiques the intellectual framework of education and language studies in the United States.

381. Villanueva, Victor, Jr. "Hegemony: From an Organically Grown Traditional Intellectual." *Pre/Text* 13 (Spring/Summer 1992): 17–34.

Reviews Gramsci's political life and development of the hegemonic concept. Argues that Gramsci's educational scheme is rhetorical and amounts to a critical cultural literacy.

382. Vitanza, Victor J., ed. *PRE/TEXT: The First Decade*. The Pittsburgh Series in Composition, Literacy and Culture, edited by David Bartholomae and Jean Ferguson Carr. Pittsburgh, PA: University of Pittsburgh Press, 1993. 384 pages

Presents 12 essays selected and reprinted from the first 10 years of articles published in *PRE/TEXT*, a journal devoted to exploring and expanding the field of rhetoric and composition. Each essay is paired with a short commentary by its author. *Essayists:* Bartholomae, David; Bazerman, Charles; Berlin, James A.; Bizzell, Patricia; Covino, William; Crowley, Sharon; Halloran, S. Michael; Jarratt, Susan; Kameen, Paul; Mailloux, Steven; Phelps, Louise Wetherbee; Schilb, John; Swearingen, C. Jan; Vitanza, Victor J.

383. Voss, James F., Rebecca Fincher-Kiefer, Jennifer Wiley, and Laurie Ney Silfies. "On the Processing of Arguments." *Arg* 7 (1993): 165–81.

Describes a model of informal argument processing in which a claim activates an attitude, which then activates reasons and values.

384. Wagner-Martin, Linda. *Telling Women's Lives*. New Brunswick, NJ: Rutgers University Press, 1993. 200 pages

Discusses issues of writing women's biographies, including authorial stance, voice, biography as partial invention, responsibility of the writer, and stereotyping. Reviews life stories of famous and ordinary women.

385. Wald, Priscilla. "Terms of Assimilation: Legislating Subjectivity in the Emerging Nation." *Boundary* 19 (Fall 1992): 77–104.

Traces subjugation, dispossession, and disenfranchisement of Native Americans through examinations of subjective and nationalism-serving language in nineteenth-century political and legal narratives.

386. Walters, Frank D. "Isocrates and the Epistemic Return: Individual and Community in Classical and Modern Rhetoric." *JAC* 13 (Winter 1993): 155–72.

Argues that Isocrates made an epistemic move when he turned rhetoric from philosophy to politics. Points out that theorists such as Elbow, Murray, and Flower and Hayes similarly revalorize the individual as meaning maker.

387. Walters, Frank D. "Taxonomy and the Undoing of Language: Dialogic Form in the Universal Languages of the Seventeenth Century." *Style* 27 (Spring 1993): 1–16.

Argues that universal languages invented by seventeenth-century science and designed to override heteroglossia are impractical for communication.

388. Walton, Douglas N. "Alethic, Epistemic, and Dialectical Modes of Argument [response to Johnson, *P&R* 23 (1990)]." *P&R* 26 (1993): 302–10.

Criticizes Johnson's treatment of Hamblin's study of fallacies. Uses alethic, epistemic, and dialectical conceptions of argument to show the efficacy of Hamblin's model.

389. Walzer, Arthur, ed. *Rhetoric in the Vortex of Cultural Studies: Proceedings of the Fifth Biennial Conference*. St. Paul, MN: Rhetoric Society of America, 1993. 259 pages

Presents 21 papers and the keynote address presented at the May 1992 Rhetoric Society of America Conference in Minneapolis, MN. Also includes five responses to George A. Kennedy's translation of Artistotle's *On Rhetoric: A Theory of Civic Discourse.*

Essayists: Barthel, Brea; Beale, Walter H.; Bridwell-Bowles, Lillian; Campbell, Kermit; Consigny, Scott; De Vinne, Christine; Farrell, Thomas B.; Goldrick-Jones, Amanda; Hesse, Doug; Jaeger, Sharon Ann; Kallendorf, Craig; Kennedy, George A.; Lares, Jameela; Larson, Richard; Mao, LuMing R.; McClish, Glen; McComiskey, Bruce; McKowski, Nancy; Merrill, Yvonne; Miller, Bruce A.; Moore, Evelyn; Musgrove, Laurence E.; Ochs, Donovan J.; Poulakos, Takis; Schiappa, Edward; Taylor, Maureen; Waddell, Craig; Walzer, Arthur.

390. Welch, Nancy. "One Student's Many Voices: Reading, Writing, and Responding with Bakhtin." *JAC* 13 (Fall 1993): 493–502.

Uses a classroom approach which rejects form/content and personal/public dichotomies and advances the notion that writing is a "dynamic meeting of reflection and production."

391. Whaley, Terrence R. "Ethnography or Fiction: An Essay on Confounding Reader Response in Barbara Myerhoff's *Number Our Days.*" *L&E* 5 (1993): 38–51.

Argues that the recent trend to describe qualitative research reports as narrative and to liken its techniques to those employed by fictional writers may undermine researchers' credibility by deemphasizing the scientific aspects of the work.

392. Whaley, Terrence R. "Rejoinder: Fiction! At Least a Whisper Goes So [response to Atkinson, *L&E* 5 (1993)]." *L&E* 5 (1993): 61–69.

Suggests that while Atkinson and he agree on the seriousness with which ethnography should be pursued, Atkinson "too quickly dismisses the question of ethnography or fiction as false dichotomy."

393. Whang, In Sung. "A Structuralistic Narrative Analysis of Television Evening News

Coverage of the Homeless, 1985–1991." *DAI* 54 (November 1993): 1583A.

Examines reportage using narrative and semiotics theories, to determine how the homeless are differentiated and blamed for their own condition.

394. White, David A. *Rhetoric and Reality in Plato's Phaedrus.* SUNY Series in Ancient Greek Philosophy, edited by Anthony Preus. Albany, NY: State University of New York Press, 1993. 272 pages

Shows how the details of the myth and the accounts of interaction between lovers are based on a metaphysical structure. Discusses the connections between the metaphysical domain in Plato's thought and the more visible and vibrant areas of the psychology of eros and practical rhetoric.

395. Williams, Jerri Lynn. "The Rhetoric of *Ethos* in Business and Technical Writing Textbooks." *DAI* 54 (July 1993): 166A.

Uses the rhetoric of *ethos* and the concept of visual rhetoric to establish a rhetorical foundation for business and technical writing textbooks.

396. Williams, Joseph M., and Gregory G. Colomb. "The Case for Explicit Teaching: Why What You Don't Know Won't Help You." *RTE* 27 (October 1993): 252–64.

The authors argue that explicit teaching of genres in undergraduate and graduate writing courses is beneficial.

397. Wilson, Stephanie G., Mike Rinck, Timothy P. McNamara, Gordon H. Bower, and Daniel G. Morrow. "Mental Models and Narrative Comprehension: Some Qualifications." *JMemL* 43 (April 1993): 141–54.

The authors discuss how task demands and readers' goals influence structure and content of mental representations created during narrative comprehension.

398. Winsor, Dorothy. "Owning Corporate Texts." *JBTC* 7 (April 1993): 179–95.

Presents an ethnographic study that shows that technical writers invest in corporate texts as much as they do in personal ones.

399. Winterowd, W. Ross. "Where Is English—In the Garden or in the Agora?" *Focuses* 5 (Winter 1992): 65–89.

Reviews *Stories to Grow On*, edited by Julie M. Jensen, *The English Coalition Conference: Democracy through Language*, edited by Richard Lloyd Jones and Andrea Lunsford, and Peter Elbow's *What Is English*.

400. Wise, William Griffith. "The Effects of Revision Instruction on Eighth-Graders' Persuasive Writing." *DAI* 53 (May 1993): 3791A.

Examines the effects of small-group collaboration and direct instruction of revision strategies on eighth-grade students' persuasive essays.

401. Wiss, Kathryn A. "A Communication Analysis of Power in Small Claims Court: A Feminist Perspective." *DAI* 54 (August 1993): 373A.

Examines speech strategies used in public institutions. Discusses how power relations of race, gender, class, and ethnicity were maintained, challenged, or negotiated.

402. Wittmer, George Bolton. "Isocrates and the Rhetoric of Culture." *DAI* 53 (March 1993): 3048A.

Bases his argument on Aristotle's and Isocrates' views of rhetoric. Discusses the necesssity of teaching university students to apply their studies in cultural contexts.

403. Wonham, Henry Brunie. "The Rhetoric of Humor: Mark Twain and the Art of the Tall Tale." *DAI* 54 (October 1993): 1371A.

Argues that the tall tale's "text" functions as "pretext" for interpretive confrontation which lends the form significance as folk ritual capable of affirming community values against outsiders.

404. Wood, Julia T. *Who Cares? Women, Care, and Culture*. Carbondale, IL: Southern Illinois University Press, 1993. 208 pages

Examines caregiving roles and the personal, political, and social issues that surround the question of who cares. Argues that caring must be recognized and promoted as an activity that commands the respect and participation of all members of society—men and women alike.

405. Wood, Robert G. "The Dialectic Suppression of Feminist Thought in Radical Pedagogy." *JAC* 13 (Winter 1993): 79–95.

Points out that a dialectic search for critical consciousness contains an androcentric bias which can suppress the development of feminist thought in female students.

406. Woods, William Walker. "Rhetorical Theory Concerning the Making of a Writer in the Poetry of Charles Bukowski." *DAI* 54 (September 1993): 936A.

Maintains that Bukowski offers sound rhetorical theory in his poetry which can be applied to college composition courses.

407. Wright, Raymond E., and Sheldon Rosenberg. "Knowledge of Text Coherence and Expository Writing: A Developmental Study." *JEdPsy* 85 (March 1993): 152–58.

The authors suggest that "over a wide age range, knowledge of global coherence in expository essays . . . affects the ability to write coherent essays."

408. Zappen, James P. "Logic and the Rhetoric of John Stuart Mill." *P&R* 26 (1993): 191–200.

Explores Mill's *A System of Logic* and *On Liberty* and their relationship to inductive logic.

409. Zebroski, James Thomas. *Thinking through Theory: Vygotskian Perspectives on the Teaching of Writing*. Portsmouth, NH: Heinemann-Boynton/Cook, 1993. 368 pages

Sixteen essays explore the uses of "theory," as concept and as tool, in the teaching of postsecondary writing; the essays are informed mainly by Vygotsky, but also by the language studies of Volosinov, Bakhtin, and Lotman.

410. Zhao, Heping. "'Wen Xin Diao Long': An Early Chinese Rhetoric of Written Discourse." *DAI* 53 (March 1993): 3190A.

Reinterprets Wen Xin Diao Long and argues for the existence of a rhetorical treatise in ancient China. Challenges the notion that rhetoric has been an entirely Western phenomenon.

2.2   RHETORICAL HISTORY

411. Abbott, Don Paul. "Mayans' *Rhetorica* and the Search for a Spanish Rhetoric." *Rhetorica* 11 (Spring 1993): 157–80.

Discusses precedents for Mayans' eighteenth-century Spanish rhetoric. Demonstrates how it modified classical rhetoric into rhetoricized poetics, and hence became part of Spanish literature.

412. Adams, Katherine H. *A History of Professional Writing Instruction in American Colleges: Years of Acceptance, Growth and Doubt*. Southern Methodist University Studies in Composition and Rhetoric. Dallas, TX: Southern Methodist University Press, 1993. 208 pages

Uses archival evidence to examine common roots of courses in journalism, technical and business writing, advanced composition, and creative writing from their nineteenth-century beginnings to the present. Maintains that segmentation and separatism of writing department specialities lessens the vitality and usefulness of college writing instruction.

413. Altom, Tim. "Why We Use Big Words: A Historical Perspective." *TC* 40 (August 1993): 456–58.

Describes the historical influence of Latin on English and how it contributed to the belief that polysyllabic words are superior.

414. Arthur, Simon. "The Site of Crisis: Representation and the Assassination of JFK." *DAI* 54 (July 1993): 350A.

Examines the complex process by which history is constructed through forms of representation.

415. Azad, Usef. "The Government of Tongues: Common Usage and the 'Prescriptive' Tradition, 1650–1800." *DAI* 53 (January 1993): 2354A.

Argues that differences in discussions of usage are produced by different models of linguistic identity and progress, not by a prescriptive-descriptive opposition.

416. Bagnall, Roger S. "Writing, Teachers and Students in Graeco-Roman Egypt." *DAI* 54 (August 1993): 509A.

Studies how the writing of Greek was taught and learned in Graeco-Roman Egypt.

417. Binfield, Kevin. "Shelley and Radical Rhetoric." *DAI* 54 (October 1993): 1373.

Argues that Shelley's rhetoric is characterized by appeals to the future and to a benevolent essence; surveys rhetoric of early opposition writers and discusses the issue of community making.

418. Boyd, Richard. "Mechanical Correctness and Rhetoric in the Late Nineteenth-Century Composition Classroom." *RR* 11 (Spring 1993): 436–55.

Looks at cultural conditions in the United States that contributed to the dominance of the current-traditional model in the discipline.

419. Broadhead, Richard H. *Cultures of Letters: Scenes of Reading and Writing in Nineteenth-Century America*. Chicago, IL: University of Chicago Press, 1993. 245 pages

Discusses writers and readers in different nineteenth-century American literary worlds, including the culture of mass-produced reading matter, hierarchical high literary culture, and the culture of postemancipation black education.

420. Brody, Miriam. *Manly Writing: Gender, Rhetoric, and the Rise of Composition*. Carbondale, IL: Southern Illinois University Press, 1993. 272 pages

Points out that although language is not inherently gendered, so-called "masculine" writing has historically been valorized as plain, forceful, and truthful, while "feminine" writing has been disdained for its vagueness, ornateness, and deceitfulness. Employs critical-interpretive and historical analyses to explore rhetorical and ideological implications of gendered notions of language and imagery.

421. Casaregola, Vincent. *'Declassicizing' Ancient Rhetoric: Toward a Reconstructed Rhetoric of Oral Performance*. Cincinnati, OH: Conference on College Composition and Communication, March 1992. ERIC ED 348 695. 18 pages

Uses society's attachment to conventions of its print-based culture to explain why most contemporary scholars of composition discuss ancient rhetoric via written texts, not oral performance.

422. Cichocka, Helena. "The Study of Byzantine Rhetoric in Central and Eastern Europe: Selected Problems." *Rhetorica* 10 (Winter 1993): 43–50.

Surveys Central and Eastern European scholarship, places rhetoric in relation to poetics and literary theory, examines Byzantine rhetoric, and notes their formalistic character.

423. Clark, Gregory, and S. Michael Halloran, eds. *Oratorical Culture in Nineteenth-Century America: Transformations on the Theory and Practice of Rhetoric*. Carbondale, IL: Southern Illinois University Press, 1993. 304 pages

Nine essays explore nineteenth-century changes in theory and practice of rhetoric. The contributors illustrate how the moral authority of rhetoric was reconceived to meet changing cultural needs. Part 1 describes rhetoric at the beginning of the century. Part 2 illustrates cultural changes in rhetorical theory and practice.
Essayists: Antczak, Frederick J.; Clark, Gregory; Halloran, S. Michael; Hirst, Russel; Johnson, Nan; Peaden, Catherine; Reid, Ronald F.; Rouse, P. Joy; Siemers, Edith; Tonkovich, Nicole.

424. Condit, Celeste Michelle, and John Louis Lucaites. *Crafting Equality: America's Anglo-African Word*. Chicago, IL: University of Chicago Press, 1993. 356 pages

Draws on speeches, newspapers, and other forms of public discourse to study the changing meanings of equality in America from 1760 to the present. Argues that African-Americans have played a critical role in the processes of interaction and negotiation that have defined the concept.

425. Corbett, Edward P. J. *From Literary Critic to Rhetorician: A Professional Journey*. Cincinnati, OH: Conference on College Composition and Communication, March 1992. ERIC ED 358 482. 12 pages

Chronicles his professional career as context for changes in the discipline of rhetoric. Argues that there is growing sophistication and professionalism surrounding the teaching of composition as well as a continuing scholarly attention to the history of rhetoric and rhetorical theory.

426. Eldred, Janet Carey, and Peter Mortensen. "Gender and Writing Instruction in Early America: Lessons from Didactic Fiction." *RR* 11 (Spring 1993): 25–53.

The authors trace the history of literacy and writing instruction for women from colonial times to the early years of the United States.

427. Enos, Richard Leo. *Greek Rhetoric before Aristotle*. Prospect Heights, IL: Waveland Press, 1993. 159 pages

Examines the origins of rhetoric as an evolving consciousness about the relationship between thought and expression. Argues that the composition of Homeric literature and the evolution of prose writing through logography were integral events in the development of rhetoric.

428. Fraser, Veronica. "The Influence of the Venerable Bede on the Fourteenth-Century Occitan Treatise *Las Leys d'Amors.*" *Rhetorica* 10 (Winter 1993): 51–62.

Shows that Bede's *De schematibus et tropis* adds to Donatus and Cassiodorus and influences *Leys d'Amors'* treatment of tropes. Sees it as consistent with political and religious history.

429. Gaillet, Lynée Lewis. *A Foreshadowing of Modern Theories and Practices of Collaborative Learning: The Work of Scottish Rhetorician George Jardine*. Cincinnati, OH: Conference on College Composition and Communication, March 1992. ERIC ED 354 546. 20 pages

Traces collaborative learning in American college classrooms and the work of George Jardine, professor of logic and philosophy at the University of Glasgow, 1774–1826, and describes Jardine's pedagogical plan.

430. Gaillet, Lynée Lewis. "A Legacy of Basic Writing Instruction." *JBW* 12 (Fall 1993): 86–99.

Discusses George Jardine, a nineteenth-century Scottish rhetorician. Argues that his educational plan for beginning writers prefigures twentieth-century theories and practices, particularly those of Mina Schaughnessy.

431. Garza-Falcon-Sanchez, Leticia Magda. "The Chicano: A Literary Response to the Rhetoric of Dominance." *DAI* 54 (October 1993): 1350A.

Questions the history of dominance in the American West and Southwest; explicates several obscure literary works by people of Mexican descent as a vital response to history and to W. P. Webb's writing.

432. Glan, Gregory R. "Mirroring Ourselves? The Pedagogy of Early Grammar Texts." *RR* 11 (Spring 1993): 418–35.

Argues that a rule-based, teacher-centered approach to grammar instruction, popular in texts of the eighteenth century, still prevails as does a notion of students as "undeveloped and unable to work with a language without first learning its rules."

433. Handal, Saleem A. "St. Augustine, Chaucer, and 'Troilus and Criseyde': A Study of Medieval Communication and Performance." *DAI* 53 (December 1992): 1724A.

Traces the influence of Augustinian exegesis on Chaucer's views of God, life, and love. Connects these views with Kleinau and McHughes' vision of Interpreter's Theatre.

434. Hatch, Gary Layne. "Appropriations from Adam Smith in Hugh Blair's 'Lectures on Rhetoric and Belles Lettres.'" *DAI* 53 (February 1993): 2825A.

Discusses charges of plagiarism against Blair in the context of eighteenth-century attitudes toward plagiarism, authorship, and literary property.

435. Horner, Winifred Bryan. "Author's Response (to James Yawn's Review)." *Dialogue* 1 (Fall 1993): 83–85.

Notes that some of Yawn's points are valid; points out philosophical differences in their approaches to historiography.

436. Horner, Winifred Bryan. *Nineteenth-Century Scottish Rhetoric: The American Connection*. Carbondale, IL: Southern Illinois University Press, 1993. 212 pages

Uses ninteenth-century students' class notes to document changes in the content of logic, rhetoric, and *belles lettres* courses taught in Scottish universities. Argues that these changes help us understand the evolution of American current-traditional and belletristic composition courses.

437. Kaufer, David S., and Kathleen M. Carley. *Communication at a Distance: The Influence of Print on Sociocultural Organization and Change*. Hillsdale, NJ: Lawrence Erlbaum Associates, 1993. 488 pages

Examines the impact of print within larger socio-cultural context and across multiple historical contexts.

438. Kindrick, Robert L. *Henryson and the Medieval Arts of Rhetoric.* New York: Garland Publishing, 1993. 345 pages

Presents a critical study of fifteenth-century Scottish poet Robert Henryson. Describes his relationship to three medieval arts of rhetoric: the *ars praedicandi, ars poetriae,* and *ars dictaminis.*

439. Lattin, Bohn David. "The Irenic and Sermonic Nature of Erasmus's Rhetorical System." *DAI* 53 (February 1993): 2601A.

Suggests that rhetoric scholars have focused on Erasmus's contributions to literary style while largely ignoring the sermonic and irenic elements of his theory of rhetoric.

440. Leff, Michael. "The Uses of Artistotle's Rhetoric in Contemporary American Scholarship." *Arg* 7 (1993): 313–27.

Reviews issues of Aristotle's *Rhetoric* in the current dispute to argue that rhetoric has productive, practical, and theoretical aspects.

441. Lloyd-Jones, Richard. *The Right to Write: Some History.* Louisville, KY: National Council of Teachers of English, November 1990. ERIC ED 354 534. 7 pages

Points out that the documents prepared by the Commission on Composition in the early 1970s, "The Student's Right to Write," is useful to contemporary practitioners of writing instruction. Recapitulates that the report reflects a strong initiative arising in the 1970s to rethink beliefs and practices then prevalent in English teaching.

442. Lloyd-Jones, Richard. *Writing the Resolutions: An Institutional History.* San Diego, CA: Conference on College Composition and Communication, March/April 1993. ERIC ED 357 344. 16 pages

Recalls the production of the CCCC resolution and statement on the *Students' Right to Their Own Language*, discusses the responses to the resolution, and suggests two major moves as it is reinterpreted for the twenty-first century.

443. Miller, Thomas P. "John Witherspoon and Scottish Rhetoric and Moral Philosophy in America." *Rhetorica* 10 (Autumn 1992): 381–404.

Shows that Hutcheson and Witherspoon and their students redefined the classical relationship between rhetoric and moral philosophy, stressing a civic humanist perspective and political rhetoric.

444. Miller, Thomas P. "Teaching the Histories of Rhetoric as a Social Praxis." *RR* 12 (Fall 1993): 70–82.

Summarizes how the history of rhetoric is taught, and discusses how one may study rhetoric as a social praxis.

445. Moss, Jean Dietz. *Novelties in the Heavens: Rhetoric and Science in the Copernican Controversy.* Chicago: University of Chicago Press, 1993. 352 pages

Examines rhetoric as defined by sixteenth- and seventeenth-century participants in the Copernican controversy. Argues that the Copernican controversy marked revolution in rhetoric as well as in science. Describes argumentative strategies used by the participants and shows how persuasion is used in scientific debate.

446. Murphy, Michael. "After Progressivism: Modern Composition, Institutional Service, and Cultural Studies." *JAC* 13 (Fall 1993): 345–64.

Examines composition's origins in and institutional history of resistance to the progressivist notion of social utility in education.

447. Newfield, Christopher. "What Was Political Correctness? Race, the Right, and Managerial Democracy in the Humanities." *Critl* 19 (Winter 1993): 308–36.

Presents a brief history of PC wars analyzing the extent to which issues of university governance and matter of race were at its root.

448. *The New Rhetoric of Ramon Llull (1232–1316) Text and Translation of His Rethorica Nova.* Translated by Arthur Quinn. Davis, CA: Hermagoras Press, 1993. 100 pages

First edition and translation of the Majorcan lay theologican, preacher, and philosopher Ramon Llull who wrote 300 works in Latin, Arabic, and Catalan. The *Rethorica Nova* is divided into four parts: Order, Beauty, Knowledge, and Love.

449. Nissen, Hans J., Peter Damerow, and Robert K. Englund. *Archaic Bookkeeping: Early Writing and Techniques of Economic Administration in the Ancient Near East.* Chicago: University of Chicago Press, 1993. 224 pages

The authors collect current scholarship on the earliest writing system. They consider how the development of written records affected patterns of thought, concept of number, and administration of household economics.

450. Nystrand, Martin, Stuart Greene, and Jeffrey Wiemelt. "Where Did Composition Studies Come From? An Intellectual History." *WC* 10 (July 1993): 267–333.

The study traces epistemological bases underlying the development of composition studies as an interdisciplinary research field.

451. Ochs, Donovan J. *Consolatory Rhetoric: Grief, Symbol, and Ritual in the Greco-Roman Era.* Columbia, SC: University of South Carolina Press, 1993. 144 pages

Explores Greco-Roman funeral rituals to reveal how opposing symbols functioned rhetorically to comfort ancient communities. Draws on descriptions of funerals in literature, histories, archaeological evidence, art histories, and rhetorical treatises.

452. Olson, Lester. "An Ideological Rupture: Metaphorical Divergence in Loyalist Rhetoric during the American Revolution." *Rhetorica* 10 (Autumn 1992): 405–22.

Exemplifies the problem of metaphorical divergence using American Loyalists' rhetoric during the mid-1770s.

453. Ouditt, Sharon. *Fighting Forces: Female Identity and the First World War.* New York: Routledge, 1993. 192 pages

Argues that temporary powers of citizenship gained during the war were again exclusive to men after the armistice. Focuses on Jeanne Maitland, Virginia Woolf, Vera Brittian, and Rose Macaulay.

454. Peaden, Catherine Hobbs. "Condillac and the History of Rhetoric." *Rhetorica* 11 (Spring 1993): 135–56.

Argues that Condillac adds to Locke's work a developmental account of understanding, resulting in dual rhetorics—an aesthetic, expressive rhetoric and an empirical, referential rhetoric.

455. Petrucci, Armando. *Public Lettering: Script, Power, and Culture.* Translated by Linda Lappin. Chicago: University of Chicago Press, 1993. 256 pages

Reconstructs the history of public writing (inscriptions on buildings, commercial graphics, and signs) in Western culture; traces its social functions from the eleventh century through the modern period. Argues that writing is an instrument of public power.

456. Purcell, William M. "Eberhard the German and the Labyrinth of Learning: Grammar, Poesy, Rhetoric, and Pedagogy in *Laborintus*." *Rhetorica* 11 (Spring 1993): 95–118.

Demonstrates that Eberhard's *Laborintus*, the first printed *artes poetriae*, offers an allegorical account of grammar, poesy, and rhetoric. Points out that it contains Christian homilies as primers for teachers.

457. Pytlik, Betty P. *Teaching the Teacher of Writing: Whence and Whither*. San Diego, CA: Conference on College Composition and Communication, March/April 1993. ERIC ED 355 541. 13 pages

Documents the long-term effects of the G. I. Bill of 1944 on the field of teaching composition.

458. Rapple, Brendan A. "The Early Greek Sophists: Creators of the Liberal Curriculum." *JT* 28 (Fall/Winter 1993): 61–76.

Describes sophistic influences in today's liberal arts education, primarily the concept of being educated in a broad range of subjects.

459. Reynolds, John Frederick, ed. *Rhetorical Memory and Delivery: Classical Concepts for Contemporary Composition and Communication*. Hillsdale, NJ: Lawrence Erlbaum, 1993. 216 pages

Examines classical and contemporary interpretations of rhetorical memory and delivery.
Essayists: Allen, V.; Bolter, J. D.; Connors, R. J.; Crowley, S.; Dragga, S.; Gronbeck, B. E.; Helsley, S. I.; Horner, W. B.; Marc, D.; Middleton, J. I.; Reynolds, J. F.; Welch, K. E.

460. Rose, Amy. "A Good Woman Speaking Well: The Oratory of Frances E. Willard." *DAI* 53 (March 1993): 3047A.

Presents an oratorical biography of Frances E. Willard.

461. Rose, Mark. *Authors and Owners: The Invention of Copyright*. Cambridge, MA: Harvard University Press, 1993. 192 pages

Traces the conception of author as the creator and owner of a work to eighteenth-century Britain. Discusses current issues of intellectual property.

462. Sachs, Andrew Adam. "The Imperialist Style of Henry Cabot Lodge." *DAI* 53 (March 1993): 3046A.

Examines Lodge's rhetorical discourse as a key to understanding the late nineteenth-century debate over imperialism.

463. Sawaya, Francesca Josephine. "The Home Front: Domestic Nationalism and Regional Women's Writing, 1869–1913." *DAI* 53 (February 1993): 2817A.

Examines how three regional women writers deployed the conventional divisions between country and city, and domestic and industrial labor to prevent social conflict in America.

464. Schildgen, Brenda Deen. "Petrarch's Defense of Secular Letters, the Latin Fathers, and Ancient Roman Rhetoric." *Rhetorica* 11 (Spring 1993): 119–34.

Explains that Petrarch defended secular learning, drawing on classical rhetoric's epistolary form and Ciceronian debate.

465. Sheard, Cynthia Miecznikowski. "A New Sophistic: The First Sophists and Contemporary Rhetorical Theory." *DAI* 53 (January 1993): 2164A.

Shows that Sophistic rhetoric is a viable mode of critical inquiry that can promote real changes in the world.

466. Shelton, Donna Lea Skeen. "The Cycle and the Spiral: Rhetorical Strategies in Malory's 'Morte D'Arthur.'" *DAI* 53 (February 1993): 2808A.

Demonstrates the recursive nature of medieval structure through rhetoric, church litany, ritual, and the view of women.

467. Sizemore, Beverly A. "Literacy Identity and Literacy Practices in Iceland: Sociocultural and Sociocognitive Aspects." *DAI* 53 (May 1993): 3970A.

Examines the tradition of literacy in Iceland and its role in Icelandic society, culture, and national identity. Compares and contrasts literacy "practices" and literacy identity.

468. Solomon, William S., and Robert W. McChesney, eds. *Ruthless Criticism: New Per-*

spectives in U.S. Communication History. Minneapolis, MN: University of Minnesota Press, 1993. 389 pages

The essayists write on the history of print and broadcast media. Topics include the emergence of a black commercial press, images of women in nineteenth-century labor newspapers, depictions of childhood in early television, and the government's role in mass-communication research. *Essayists:* Allen, Holly; Baldasty, Gerald J.; Bernhard, Nancy E.; Bekker, Jon; Douglas, Susan J.; Kreiling, Albert; Meehan, Robert W.; Nerone, John C.; Simpson, Christopher; Solomon, William S.; Spigel, Lynn; Steiner, Linda; Warner, Michael.

469. Strohmayer, Ulf. "Of Meaning and Justification: Contributions to a Critique of Knowledge." *DAI* 53 (January 1993): 2501A.

Investigates the language of Kant, de Saussure, Husserl, Heidegger, and Gadamer. Argues that social science must abandon its claim to an *a priori* access to rationality.

470. Tebeaux, Elizabeth. "Technical Writing for Women of the English Renaissance: Technology, Literacy, and the Emergence of a Genre." *WC* 10 (April 1993): 164–99.

Tracks the growing literacy rates among English women (1500–1640) through an analysis of how-to texts published for them; notes emergent technical style in these texts.

471. Varnum, Robin R. "A Maverick Writing Course: English 1–2 at Amherst College, 1938–1968." *DAI* 53 (June 1993): 4232A.

Offers a description of English 1–2 at Amherst College to counter the assumption that nothing interesting happened in composition classrooms before 1960.

472. Vitanza, Victor J., ed. *Writing Histories of Rhetoric.* Carbondale, IL: Southern Illinois University Press, 1993. 384 pages

The collection presents a historiography of rhetoric that draws on classical, revisionary, and avant-garde rhetorical approaches to describe, contextualize, and interrogate revisionist writings of rhetorical history. Twelve scholars offer answers to two questions: "What does it mean to be a revisionist historian?" and "Who is the 'we' writing histories of rhetoric?" *Essayists:* Atwill, Janet M.; Berlin, James A.; Covino, William A.; Crowley, Sharon; Kellner, Hans; Poulakos, John; Poulakos, Takis; Schilb, John; Sutton, Jane; Welch, Kathleen Ethel; Worsham, Lynn; Vitanza, Victor J.

473. Walters, Frank D. "Scientific Method and Prose Style in the Early Royal Society." *JTWC* 23 (1993): 239–58.

Examines the proper method of scientific experimentation and writing style for communicating scientific knowledge in the Royal Society's first decade. Emphasizes the relevance to contemporary technical writing.

474. Warnick, Barbara. *The Sixth Canon: Belletristic Rhetorical Theory and Its French Antecedents.* Columbia, SC: University of South Carolina Press, 1993. 160 pages

Discusses the influence of Cartesian psycho-physiology and British empiricism on British rhetoricians of the late eighteenth century. Argues for an examination of texts by Bernard Lamy, François Fenelon, Charles Rollin, Hugh Blair, Adam Smith, and George Campbell in terms of psychological and aesthetics rather than the more traditional five-canon model.

475. Weidner, Heidemarie Z. *Members of Literary Societies Are Exempt from Rhetorical Exercises: Claiming Literary Societies for the History of Rhetoric and Composition.* Cincinnati, OH: Conference on College Composition and Communication, March 1992. ERIC ED 348 685. 14 pages

Posits the importance of literary societies to nineteenth-century rhetoric and composition instruction. Attributes the progress of nineteenth-century women for equality in higher education to their roles as instructors.

476. Whitson, Steve, and John Poulakos. "Nietzsche and the Aesthetics of Rhetoric." *QJS* 79 (May 1993): 131–45.

Steps away from epistemological rhetoric and argues that no discursive effort can escape its own rhetoricity, and that all discourse is based on aesthetic impulses.

477. Worthington, Ian. *A Historical Commentary on Dinarchus: Rhetoric and Conspiracy in Later Fourth-Century Athens.* Ann Arbor, MI: University of Michigan Press, 1993. 416 pages

Translates and studies three speeches by the Greek orator Dinarchus (ca. 360—292 B.C.). Uses his work to explore Athenian history during the last years of Alexander the Great.

478. Yawn, James. "Review of *Nineteenth-Century Scottish Rhetoric: The American Connection*, by Winifred Bryan Horner." *Dialogue* 1 (Fall 1993): 78–82.

Notes that Horner's projected audience is too specialized and the presentation of archival materials is incomplete for the purpose of making primary sources available to scholars.

479. Yusee, Azad. "The Government of Tongues: Common Usage and the 'Prescriptive' Tradition, 1650 to 1800." *DAI* 53 (January 1993): 2354A.

Discusses views of the prescriptive and descriptive nature of authority in the use of language.

2.3 POLITICAL, RELIGIOUS, AND JUDICIAL RHETORIC

480. Adams, Michael Jay. "Toward the Text: A Theory of Good Preaching Utilizing the Persuasive Elements of Communication, Rheto-

ric, and Advertising." *DAI* 53 (March 1993): 3041A.

Discusses rhetoric as a persuasive art implemented in preaching. Bases his argument on the theory that all language is value-laden.

481. Adee, Michael James. "American Civil Religion and the Presidential Rhetoric of Jimmy Carter." *DAI* 53 (March 1993): 3041A.

Discusses the function of a civil religion idiom in the presidential discourse of Jimmy Carter. Uses a rhetorical approach to civil religion.

482. Adler, Barbara Jean. "'They Are Us': Identification Strategies in the Rhetoric of Two Lutheran Church Organizations." *DAI* 54 (September 1993): 733A.

Compares and analyzes the rhetoric of a "conservative" Missouri Synod with a recently formed "liberal" Evangelical Lutheran Church; finds that rhetoric matches the existing social reality in both.

483. Allen, Craig. *Eisenhower and the Mass Media: Peace, Prosperity, and Prime-Time TV.* Chapel Hill, NC: University of North Carolina Press, 1993. 288 pages

Links Eisenhower's public popularity to his skillful use of television, including televised cabinet meetings, news conferences, and fireside chats.

484. Apple, Michael W. *Official Knowledge: Democratic Education in a Conservative Age.* New York: Routledge, 1993. 232 pages

Analyzes the effects of conservative beliefs and strategies on educational policy and practice. Looks at the conservative agenda's incursion into education through the curriculum, textbook adoption policies, and the efforts of the private and business sectors to centralize its interests within schools.

485. Armour, Ellen True. "Deconstruction and Feminist Theology: Toward Forging an Alliance with Derrida and Irigaray." *DAI* 54 (October 1993): 1417A.

Argues for an alliance between deconstruction and feminist theology. Shows how deconstruction can be useful to help feminist theology deal more adequately with differences.

486. Arrigo, Bruce A. "Madness, Language, and Law: A Semiotic Analysis of Current Civil Commitment Appellate Case Law." *DAI* 54 (November 1993): 1929A.

Describes language used by lawyers to discuss mental disorder.

487. Artz, Burton Lee. "Power and Communication in Nicaragua: A Dialectical Materialist Analysis." *DAI* 53 (May 1993): 3730A.

Uses dialectical materialist analysis to explore the relationship between rhetoric, social position, and communication during the 1979 Nicaraguan revolution.

488. Bloom, Jonathan D. "Brookwood Labor College and the Progressive Labor Network of the Interwar United States, 1921–1937." *DAI* 53 (February 1993): 2949A.

Discusses the importance of colleges in "workers education" programs; follows their progress as they came under the influence of socialist or communist parties, the New Deal, or universities.

489. Bostdorff, Denise M. *The Presidency and the Rhetoric of Foreign Crisis*. Columbia, SC: University of South Carolina Press, 1993. 352 pages

Examines president crisis management as a tool for accumulating and forfeiting political power. Presents case studies from six administratons to demonstrate the rhetoric of crisis and public response to it.

490. Bowers, Detine Lee. "A *Strange* Speech of an Estranged People: Theory and Practice of Antebellum African-American Freedom Day Orations." *DAI* 53 (March 1993): 3041A.

Uses Freedom Day oratory to argue that an Afrocentric ontology or interactive event cycle world view constitutes cyclical-regenerative organization, form, and content of oratory.

491. Braden, Waldo W. *Abraham Lincoln, Public Speaker*. Baton Rouge, LA: Louisiana State University Press, 1993. 119 pages

Studies the sixteenth president's speaking practices from 1854 through 1865. Analyzes his public roles as storyteller, lawyer, politician, debater, and advocate. Includes discussions of the Gettysburg Address and first and second inaugural addresses.

492. Branson, Susan Janney. "Politics and Gender: The Political Consciousness of Philadelphia Women in the 1790s." *DAI* 53 (January 1993): 2514A.

Examines women's political consciousness and place in political culture during the 1790s. Shows that women involved themselves in political events and controversies of the new nation.

493. Browne, Stephen H. "Contesting Political Oratory in Nineteenth-Century England." *ComS* 43 (Fall 1992): 191–202.

Examines conservative attacks on the language of reform. Identifies ways in which public argument serves as medium of social transformation.

494. Browne, Stephen H. *Edmund Burke and the Discourse of Virtue*. Studies in Rhetoric and Communication. Albany, NY: State University of New York Press, 1993. 143 pages

Describes the British statesman and orator's belief in virtue as a principle of civic action and responsibility. Treats six speeches from the 1770s to the 1790s.

495. Buckrop, Jacquelyn Jo. "Homelessness in America: An Analysis of the Rhetorical Relationship between Legitimacy and Guilt." *DAI* 53 (November 1992): 1322A.

Uses Burkean pentad analysis to Congressional hearings on homeless people to examine the terms "legitimacy" and "guilt."

Finds the terms both oppositional and appositional.

496. Bullmore, Michael Andrew. "St. Paul's Theology of Rhetorical Style: An Examination of 1 Corinthians 2.1–5 in the Light of First Century Graeco-Roman Rhetorical Culture." *DAI* 54 (November 1993): 1839A.

Examines St. Paul's preaching against the culture of the first century A.D. Corinthians, focusing on Paul's plain rhetoric as contrasted with the Corinthians' stylistic inventiveness.

497. Burns, Robert Earl. "What God Wants: A Content Analysis of American Presidential Civil Religion on the Man-Nature Relationship, 1961–1993. (Volumes I and II)." *DAI* 53 (March 1993): 3042A.

Claims that presidents express a perceived divine intent for environmental preservation in prosperous times but invoke an intent for development during recessionary conditions.

498. Byars, Terry Grant. "The Theatre of Religion: Jimmy Swaggart within American Myth Discourse." *DAI* 53 (March 1993): 3048A.

Explores how televangelist Jimmy Swaggart manipulates cultural myths to promote his own heroism.

499. Callahan, Linda F. "History: A Critical Scene within Jesse Jackson's Rhetorical Vision." *JBS* 24 (September 1993): 3–15.

Uses Bormann's fantasy theme criticism to analyze Jackson's rhetorical vision in his speeches, sermons, and articles between 1976 and 1986.

500. Calloway-Thomas, Carolyn, and John Louis Lucaites. *Martin Luther King, Jr., and the Sermonic Power of Public Discourse*. Studies in Rhetoric and Communication, edited by E. Culpepper Clarke, Raymie E. McKerrow, and David Zarefsky. Tuscaloosa, AL: University of Alabama Press, 1993. 240 pages

The authors analyze primary texts to demonstrate how King communicated his vision through sermonic discourse.

501. Cerutti, Steve Matthew. "Cicero's Accretive Style and Rhetorical Strategies in the *Exordia* of Select Judicial Speeches." *DAI* 53 (March 1993): 3190A.

Provides an analysis of Cicero's judicial speeches; explores how Cicero uses a variety of rhetorical strategies to fulfill the aims of the *exordium*.

502. Chilton, Paul, and Mikhail Ilyin. "Metaphor in Political Discourse: The Case of the 'Common European House.'" *D&S* 4 (1993): 7–31.

Proposes a model of political discourse as a kind of "conversation" and a framework for analyzing the metaphors of the "common European house."

503. Chiste, Katherine Beaty. "A Rhetorical Analysis of Political Discourse: The First Ministers' Conference on Aboriginal Constitutional Matters." *DAI* 53 (April 1993): 3670A.

Describes the origins of native peoples' "counter-discourse" in their relationship to the Canadian state.

504. Condit, Celeste Michelle, and John Louis Lucaites. "Malcolm X and the Limits of the Rhetoric of Revolutionary Dissent." *JBS* 23 (March 1993): 291–313.

Analyzes Malcolm X's revolutionary rhetoric to show the limits inherent in rhetoric itself.

505. Conklin, William E. "The Legal Language of Authority." *DAI* 54 (September 1993): 1116A.

Argues that legal language in a modern state is a secondary genre which represents the addressive experiences of victims who live through primary genres.

506. Corgan, Verna Corrine. "Stories of Justice: Controversial Judicial Opinions and the

Community." *DAI* 53 (February 1993): 2600A.

Examines opinions of trial judge Miles Welton Lord to discover how the judge attempted to create community through persuasive discourse.

507. Cunningham, Stanley B. "Sorting Out the Ethics of Propaganda." *ComS* 43 (Winter 1992): 233–45.

Argues that the neutrality counterthesis is increasingly associated with propaganda strategies and communication structures.

508. Dauber, Cori Elizabeth. *Cold War Analytical Structures and the Post Post-War World: A Critique of Deterence Theory.* New York: Praeger Publishers, 1993. 244 pages

Discusses nuclear strategic doctrine as a rhetorical method of persuasion.

509. Eaves, Michael Howard. "A Rhetorical Analysis of Davis Versus Davis: Merging Postmodern and Feminist Voices." *DAI* 54 (August 1993): 370A.

Uses an analysis of explicit change which incorporates Foucault and postmodern feminism to reconstruct Davis versus Davis, a case involving seven frozen embryos.

510. Elwood, William Norelli. "Critical Rhetoric and the Issue of Drug Control: A Rhetorical Commentary on Contemporary Discourse in the American War on Drugs." *DAI* 54 (July 1993): 26A.

Uses a postmodern orientation and critical rhetoric to analyze four types of texts in the "war on drugs." Concludes that discursive formation perpetuates the current state on drug control.

511. Fabiano, Theodore F., and F. Todd Goodson. "Political Rhetoric and the English Classroom." *EJ* 82 (December 1993): 50–52.

The authors conclude that political rhetoric helps students understand and interpret language that tries to persuade and provoke subjective responses.

512. Fergenson, Loraine. *Politics and the English Instructor: Using Political Literature to Teach Composition.* Pittsburgh, PA: College English Association, March 1992. ERIC ED 359 509. 14 pages

Discusses the use of political literature to teach composition, arguing that students are more motivated, write better, and are better prepared for the world outside the classroom.

513. Fetterman, David M., ed. *Speaking the Language of Power: Communication, Collaboration and Advocacy.* Bristol, PA: Falmer Press, 1993. 236 pages

The essayists discuss how ethnography can be used in the policy making process and to conduct qualitative evaluations.
Essayists: Bauer, Barbara Rylko; Brown, Mary Jo McGee; Christman, Jolley; Fetterman, David M.; Hess, G. Alfred, Jr.; Hopper, Kim; Langley, Bertney; de Abascal-Hildebrand, Mary Lopez; Maxwell, Joseph A.; Mertz, Ronald E.; Parker, Linda; Schensul, Jean J.; Simon, Elaine; van Willigen, John; Weeks, Margaret R.

514. Fliegelman, Jay. *Declaring Independence: Jefferson, Natural Language, and the Culture of Performance.* Stanford, CA: Stanford University Press, 1993. 296 pages

Sets the *Declaration of Independence* in its aesthetic, cultural, oratorical, and rhetorical context.

515. Fritzman, J. M. "Blumenberg and the Rationality of Rhetoric." *Rhetorica* 10 (Autumn 1992): 423–36.

Argues that Blumenberg's philosophical anthropology should be rejected but his notion of the rationality of rhetoric should be retained.

516. Garroute, Eva M. "Language and Cultural Authority: Nineteenth-Century Science and the Colonization of Religious Discourse." *DAI* 54 (November 1993): 1956A.

Proposes a generalizable model for understanding the way in which one ideology establishes dominance over another.

517. Germain, Richard G. *A Discourse on Disenchantment: Reflections on Politics and Technology*. SUNY Series in Political Theory. Albany, NY: State University of New York Press, 1993. 256 pages

Studies the ongoing debate over the status of the "disenchanted" world. Draws on the writings of various theorists on this and discusses the rift between mind and matter.

518. Giroux, Henry A., and Peter McLaren, eds. *Between Borders: Pedagogy and the Politics of Cultural Studies*. New York: Routledge, 1993. 256 pages

The essayists look at the relationship between pedagogy and media literacy, the intersection of critical pedagogy with issues concerning postmodernism, race, the politics of desire, and postcolonialism, and the question of representation with respect to the relationship between popular culture, the arts, and the state.

519. Glass, Matthew. *Citizens against the MX: Public Languages in the Nuclear Age*. Champaign, IL: University of Illinois Press, 1993. 216 pages

Discusses the coalition of ranchers, environmentalists, Mormons, and Native Americans organized in opposition to MX missile sites in Nevada and Utah. Uses the critical social theory of Jürgen Habermas to show how the coalition's political discourse differs from that of other anti-nuclear groups.

520. Greaves, Gail-Ann Gelisa. "An African-Centered Rhetorical Analysis of Selected Calypsoes of Political Commentary of Trinidad from 1988–1991." *DAI* 53 (March 1993): 3043A.

Uses rhetorical analysis to show that the calypso of political commentary incorporates many African-centered features to reinforce and crystallize the public's views.

521. Gregory, Wayne P. "Making the Secular Sacred: An Analysis of Linguistic Devices Used to Give Religious Perspective to Ordinary Events." *DAI* 53 (February 1993): 2792A.

Studies a religious community whose participants seek to create a different kind of social reality via a variety of linguistic devices.

522. Gudaitis, Teresa Mary. "Loaded Words, Loaded Topics, and Diversity of Language in Police Reports of Rape." *DAI* 54 (July 1993): 26A.

Analyzes "loaded" language in 60 rape reports; concludes that patrol officer reports are more positive than detectives'; finds greater diversity of language in "student" versus "prostitute" reports.

523. Gustafson, Thomas. *Representative Words: Politics, Literature, and the American Language, 1776–1865*. New York: Cambridge University Press, 1993. 481 pages

Relates the state of language to the American experiment in a representative, non-monarchical government.

524. Gustainis, J. Justin. *American Rhetoric and the Vietnam War*. New York: Praeger Publishers, 1993. 192 pages

Analyzes images of the war in presidential rhetoric, protest rhetoric, and in films, songs, comic strips, and other media.

525. Haiman, Franklyn S. *"Speech Acts" and the First Amendment*. Carbondale, IL: Southern Illinois University Press, 1993. 128 pages

Explores connections between the current trend toward legislation of "politically correct" speech and the first amendment ideal of free speech. Concludes that enforced silence, however well-intentioned, is unacceptable and inhibits the growth and development of a free democratic society.

526. Hamlett, Ralph A. "The Rhetoric of Synnationalism: A Model of Foreign Policy Discourse." *DAI* 53 (March 1993): 3044A.

Proposes a model for the analysis of United States foreign policy discourse to explain how popular opinion is constructed in that arena.

527. Heisey, D. Ray. "The Rhetoric of Anatoly Sobchak: Rule of Law Versus *Nomenklatura*?" *SCJ* 59 (Fall 1993): 60–72.

Applies an interaction approach to analyze how the language of democratic reform is used as a code for encouraging nationalism.

528. Hinck, Edward A. *Enacting the Presidency: Political Argument, Presidential Debates, and Presidential Character*. New York: Praeger, 1993. 272 pages

Rhetorical analysis of presidential and vice-presidential debates from 1960 to 1988.

529. Holloway, Rachel L. *In the Matter of J. Robert Oppenheimer: Politics, Rhetoric, and Self-Defense*. New York: Praeger Press, 1993. 144 pages

Analyzes the rhetoric of accusation and defense in the Atomic Energy Commision's 1953 effort to remove the American physicist from government service.

530. Howard, Charles Clayton. "A Lonely Place of Honor: A Rhetorical Analysis of the Movement to Amend the Constitution to Prevent Flag Burning." *DAI* 54 (July 1993): 27A.

Examines contrasting rhetorics used by both those desiring an amendment to the Constitution to protect the flag and by those who oppose such an amendment.

531. Kaufer, David S., and Kathleen M. Carley. "Condensation Symbols: Their Variety and Rhetorical Function in Political Discourse." *P&R* 26 (1993): 201–26.

Explores the content and usage of various condensation symbols such as buzzwords, pregnant place-holders, emblems, standard symbols, allusions, and stereotypes.

532. Lilley, Lins. "Entering the Presidential Race: A Comparison of Entrance Speeches of Minor Candidates and Major-Party Nominees." *DAI* 53 (May 1993): 3732A.

Analyzes speeches of ten minor candidates to describe the distinct communication patterns underlying the speeches in relation to the acceptance speeches of major-party candidates.

533. Lundberg, Lynne Katherine. "Can Feminist Theology Change Judeo-Christian Tradition? An Analysis of the Rhetorical Construction of Women's Place in the Church." *DAI* 54 (August 1993): 371A.

Combines biblical hermeneutics with argumentation theory to evaluate persuasiveness of interpretation; finds that reformist feminist theology is most persuasive.

534. Lyotard, Jean-François. *Political Writings*. Translated by Kevin Paul and Bill Readings. Minneapolis, MN: University of Minnesota Press, 1993. 353 pages

Provides a collection of essays published in French between 1956 and 1989 that trace the development of the "postmodern" in Lyotard's thought; looks at specific political and historical issues such as capital, Algeria, and World War II.

535. MacKinnon, Catharine A. *Only Words*. Cambridge, MA: Harvard University Press, 1993. 112 pages

Contends that pornography, racial and sexual harassment, and hate speech are acts of intimidation, subordination, terrorism, and discrimination, and should be legally treated as such.

536. McCormick, Lawrence Ray. "James Henry Thornwell and the Theological Justification of Slavery: A Study in the Development of a Proslavery Ideology." *DAI* 53 (January 1993): 2161A.

Examines the effectiveness of Thornwell's rhetorical strategies and arguments in his defense of slavery.

537. McLeod, Susan H., and Fred S. Schwarzbach. "WPA on Campus—What about the TAs? Making the Wyoming Resolution a Reality for Graduate Students." *WPA* 17 (Fall/Winter 1993): 84–86.

Tells how a comprehensive training program for TAs has fared according to the "Statement of Principles and Standards."

538. Medhurst, Martin J. *Dwight D. Eisenhower: Strategic Communicator*. Great American Orators, no. 19. New York: Greenwood Press, 1993. 256 pages

Analyzes Eisenhower's use of oratory in the Cold War, arguing that he knew exactly what he was doing, used half-truths strategically, was intentionally indirect, and chose his audiences and circumstances deliberately and tactically.

539. Medhurst, Martin J., ed. *Landmark Essays on American Public Address*. Landmark Essays. Davis, CA: Hermagoras Press, 1993. 235 pages

The essayists show their concern with the role of rhetoric in public speeches from 1925 until 1989.
Essayists: Baird, A.; Baskerville, Barnet; Block, Edwin; Bryant, Donald C.; Hochmuth, Marie; Leff, Michael; Lucas, Stephen E.; Mohrmann, G. P.; Parrish, Wayland; Reid, Loren D.; Thomssen, Lester; Wrage, Ernest J.; Wichlins, Herbert H.; Zarefsky, David.

540. Millen, Jonathan Howard. "A Social Constructionist Critique and Case Study of Mediation: No Complaints, No Choice, No Problem." *DAI* 53 (December 1992): 1726A.

Examines community mediation through case study and narrative analysis. Finds two significant problems in the overly simple concept of communication and the difficulty in defining success.

541. Milovanovíc-Barham, Cêlica. "Three Levels of Style in Augustine of Hippo and Gregory of Nazianzus." *Rhetorica* 11 (Winter 1993): 1–26.

Explains that Augustine's three levels of style in Christian oratory, with their emotional impacts on the audience, agreed with contemporary Latin and Greek practice.

542. O'Rourke, Daniel J., III. "In His Image: A Rhetorical Analysis of the Mythic Androcentrism of the Roman Catholic Church." *DAI* 53 (March 1993): 3045A.

Describes, interprets, and analyzes the androcentric rhetoric of the modern papacy of the Roman Catholic Church to determine its impact on women in the faith.

543. Patrick, Mary Webber. "*Ethos* in Epistles: Rhetorical Analyses of Ignatius' Epistles." *DAI* 53 (January 1993): 2357A.

Analyzes and evaluates Ignatius' use of rhetoric in constructing his moral self-portrait.

544. Patten, Neil Alexander. "Ashes in Their Mouths: A Rhetorical Profile of the 'Grassroots' Disarmament Movement in Bloomington, Indiana, 1980–1984." *DAI* 53 (May 1993): 3732A.

Examines how local-level participation defines national political movements through an analysis of local collective action and leadership patterns.

545. Rauch, Jonathan. *Kindly Inquisitors: The New Attacks on Free Thought*. Chicago: University of Chicago Press, 1993. 176 pages

Identifies three major threats to the system for producing knowledge: fundamentalists, intellectual egalitarians, and humanitarians. Traces attacks on free thought from Plato to Salman Rushdie.

546. Ross, Lena B., ed. *To Speak or Be Silent: The Paradox of Disobedience in the Lives of Women*. Wilmette, IL: Chiron Publications, 1993. 304 pages

The contributors critique the positioning of Middle Eastern, Native American, Western European, and African-American women in literature and mythology. They draw on research and experiences from anthropology, psychology, and literature to introduce new scholarship by, for, and about women.
Essayists: Abu-Lughod, Lila; Anderson, Teresa; Bennett, Jane Foress; Baruch,

Elaine Hoffman; Chen, Fan Pen; Cooke, Miriam; de Jager, Marjolijn; Gold, Nili Rachel Scharf; Gomez, Jewelle; Grossman, Judith; Hubback, Judith; Ouyang, Wen-chin; Perera, Sylvia Brinton; Rebolledo, Tey Diana; Ross, Lena B.; Roy, Manisha; Savitz, Carol; Smith, Patricia Clark; Watson, Jeanie; White-Lewis, Jane.

547. Scult, Allen. "The Limits of Narrative: Truth Aspiring Discourse in the Bible." *Rhetorica* 10 (Autumn 1992): 345–66.

Traces the hermeneutical performance of the core story of the Pentateuch; argues that truth-aspiring discourse must move beyond narrative invention.

548. Senecah, Susan Louise. "The Environmental Discourse of David Brower: Using Advocacy Advertising to Save the Grand Canyon." *DAI* 53 (January 1993): 2163A.

Examines the rhetorical, historical, cultural and ideological reasons why mass media pieces worked as the critical elements of a 1960s Sierra Club lobbying campaign.

549. Shell, Mark. "Babel in America; Or, The Politics of Language Diversity in the United States." *CritI* 20 (Autumn, 1993): 103–27.

Discusses problems inherent in the "unofficially anglophone America's understanding of itself." Argues for a reconception of the American national community.

550. Shoemaker, Kenneth Wayne. "Speaker and Audience Participants in Micah: Aspects of Prophetic Discourse." *DAI* 54 (October 1993): 1412A.

Applies rhetorical analysis and discourse analysis to Micah to explore the complex relations between the divine speaker and the prophetic speaker.

551. Sloop, John Martin. "Institutional and Cultural Discipline: The Changing Portrait of the Prisoner—1950 to1990." *DAI* 53 (January 1993): 2164A.

Explores the relationship between popular, mass-mediated messages and ideological

dimensions of the discipline; analyzes popular discourse about prisoners between 1950 and 1990.

552. Smith, Ralph R., and Russel R. Windes. "Symbolic Convergence and Abolitionism: A Terministic Reinterpretation." *SCJ* 59 (Fall 1993): 45–59.

Traces the origins of radical abolitionism to evangelical religion. Offers new directions for research in rhetorical movement studies.

553. Smith, Tony. *Dialectical Social Theory and Its Critics: From Hegel to Analytical Marxism*. SUNY Series in Radical Social and Political Theory, edited by Roger S. Gottlieb. Albany, NY: State University of New York Press, 1992. 192 pages

Uses dialectical reading to examine arguments against the Hegelian legacy in Marxism advanced by Lucio Colletti, Jon Elster and John Roemer, and Jean Baudrillard.

554. Smith-Howell, Deborah Sue. "Using the Past in the Present: The Rhetorical Construction of the Presidency." *DAI* 54 (October 1993): 1150A.

Finds that allusions to past United States presidents were prominent in contemporary public discourse; examines 24 textbooks, 518 *Time* articles, and presidential speeches.

555. Solan, Lawrence M. *The Language of Judges*. Chicago: University of Chicago Press, 1993. 232 pages

Argues that judges sometimes inaccurately portray how we use language, creating inconsistencies in their decisions and threatening the fairness of the judicial system.

556. Stanley, Gary Lee. "Controlling Myths of the New Religious Right: A Narrative Analysis of Pat Robertson's 1988 Presidential Campaign." *DAI* 53 (January 1993): 2165A.

Analyzes Robertson's 1988 presidential campaign from a dramatistic/narrative perspective. Places his campaign in the context of the rhetoric of the New Religious Right.

557. Stoll, Mark Richard. "Protestantism, Capitalism, and Nature in the United States." *DAI* 54 (October 1993): 1520A.

Examines environmental rhetoric through the twentieth-century; argues that in America both capitalism and environmentalism—both exploitation and preservation of nature—descend directly from Protestant doctrines and values.

558. Stromberg, Peter G. *Language and Self-Transformation: A Study of the Christian Conversion Narrative.* New York: Cambridge University Press, 1993. 164 pages

Studies how people work through emotional conflict by means of set patterns of language. Mentions psychotherapy as well as conversion narratives.

559. Stuckey, Mary E. "Remembering the Future: Rhetorical Echoes of World War II and Vietnam in George Bush's Public Speech on the Gulf War." *ComS* 43 (Winter 1992): 246–56.

Analyzes how, through his use of specific language choices, Bush's rhetoric supported the orientational metaphor of the World War II paradigm while rejecting the Vietnam paradigm.

560. Stygall, Gail. *Scenes from the Civil Courtroom: Rhetoric, Expertise, and Commonsense Narratives.* Cincinnati, OH: Conference on College Composition and Communication, March 1992. ERIC ED 349 569. 14 pages

Discusses the breakdown of professional and disciplinary rhetoric and the need to recover commonsense narrative in addition to academic reasoning and the rhetoric of expertise.

561. Sullivan, Patricia A. "Signification and African-American Rhetoric: A Case Study of Jesse Jackson's 'Common Ground and Common Sense' Speech." *ComQ* 41 (Winter 1993): 1–15.

Examines the political discourse of black rhetors who rely on African American patterns of signification.

562. Tarbox, James Jeffrey. "The Constitutive Function of Woodrow Wilson's Rhetoric, 1914–1917." *DAI* 53 (November 1992): 1324A.

Analyzes 28 of Wilson's speeches for success in creating collectivity in public; discusses four rhetorical techniques.

563. Thornborrow, Joanna. "Metaphors of Security: A Comparison of Representation in Defence Discourse in Post-Cold-War France and Britain." *D&S* 4 (1993): 99–119.

Compares metaphors used in press reports of two summit meetings regarding issues of security and defense and examines metaphoric representation of those issues within Europe.

564. Tiersman, Peter M. "Linguistic Issues in the Law." *Language* 69 (March 1993): 113–37.

Classifies and discusses current developments in the study of language and the law.

565. Wall, Beverly C. "Supreme Court Rhetoric: Explorations in the Culture of Argument and the Language of the Law." *DAI* 53 (April 1993): 3507A.

Analyzes opinion genre and the culture of argument as realized or symbolized in Supreme Court texts.

566. Whalen, David M. "The Consolation of Rhetoric: John Henry Newman and the Realism of Personalist Thought." *DAI* 54 (July 1993): 191A.

Examines the fundamental rhetorical nature of Newman's reasoning.

567. White, Cindy L., and Catherine A. Dobris. "A Chorus of Discordant Voices: Radical Feminist Confrontations with Patriarchal Religion." *SCJ* 58 (Spring 1993): 239–46.

Presents a genre analysis of three selected works. Uses a "motivational classification" method to identify anti-religious rhetoric.

568. Williams, L. Glen. "Thomas Paine and the Birth of American Patriotism." *DAI* 54 (October 1993): 1150A.

Examines Thomas Paine's rhetoric and its role in the American Revolution; argues that Paine "cast Americans as unique people with a moral mission."

569. Zulik, Margaret D. "The Active Force of Hearing: The Ancient Hebrew Language of Persuasion." *Rhetorica* 10 (Autumn 1992): 367–80.

Investigates how the Hebrew Bible "persuades" through the act of the hearer.

570. Zurakowski, Michele Marie. "Public Issue, Private Choice: The Rhetorical Construction of Woman's Place in News Coverage of the Ban the Bill Rally, February 28, 1990." *DAI* 53 (April 1993): 3411A.

Takes a case study approach to explain how abortion rights news coverage helps articulate women's place in popular culture.

2.4 COMPUTER AND LITERACY STUDIES

571. Allen, Michael. *Robin Hood in His Sherwood Forest: Audience, Gender and a Freshman Bulletin Board*. San Diego, CA: Conference on College Composition and Communication, March/April 1993. ERIC ED 358 463. 28 pages

Describes one teacher's use of a computer bulletin board in a composition class and the issues of audience and gender that were encountered and solved.

572. Amdahl, Mark. *"Aspects 1.0." C&C* 10 (November 1993): 89–92.

Describes the synchronous conference software program *Aspects* for the Macintosh computer.

573. Anderson, Peter Bøgh, Berit Holmqvist, and Jens F. Jensen, eds. *The Computer as Medium*. New York: Cambridge University Press, 1993. 400 pages

The contributors to this collection use three approaches to examine the impact of computers on communication. The first group, using a semiotic approach, analyses signs generated by computers; the second group discusses the rhetoric of computers as interactive media, using comparisons to literature, art, and academic discourse; and the third group examines the social implications of personal computers and computer networks.
Essayists: Anderson, Peter Bøgh; Bang, Jørgen; Brandt, Per Aage; Christensen, Jens; Hasle, Per; Holmqvist, Berit; Hougaard, Jens; Jensen, Jens F.; Jensen, Klaus Bruhn; Jørgensen, Keld Gall; Laursen, Bjørn; Liestøl, Gunnar; Markussen, Randi; Piotrowski, David; Qvortrup, Lars; Sørenssenn, Bjørn; Sorensen, Elsebeth Korsgaard.

574. Ang, Soon, and Cynthia M. Beath. "Hierarchical Elements in Software Contracts." *JOC* 3 (1993): 329–61.

The authors use legal and organizational theories to describe contractual elements governing external software development. They maintain that hierarchical elements will vary with transaction characteristics.

575. Bakoss, J. Yannis, and Erik Brynjolfsson. "From Vendors to Partners: Information Technology and Incomplete Contracts in Buyer-Supplier Relationships." *JOC* 3 (1993): 301–28.

The authors use theory of incomplete contacts to show that incentive considerations motivate buyers to limit the number of suppliers. They discuss the impact of information technology on customer-supplier relationships.

576. Bangert-Drowns, Robert L. "The Word Processor as an Instructional Tool: A Meta-Analysis of Word Processing in Writing Instruction." *RER* 63 (Spring 1993): 69–93.

Suggests that word processing users improved their writing but not their attitudes. Offers advice for a better use of technology. Bases his findings on 32 studies.

577. Barron, Terry. "Impacts of Information Technology on Organizational Size and Shape: Control and Flexibility." *JOC* 3 (1993): 363–87.

Constructs and analyzes optimization models of organizational design problems for hierarchical organizations. Points out that the model embodies information technology effects of control and "flexibility."

578. Barton, Regina. *Teaching across the Curriculum with the Macintosh and the Writing Center in the One Computer Classroom.* New York: New York City Teacher Centers Consortium, 1993. 123 pages

Describes Apple Macintosh computers and various software packages that can be used to teach composition.

579. Batistella, Edwin. "The Infohighway." *NebrHum* 3 (Winter 1993): 7–8.

Assesses moral, ethical, as well as practical implications of the information superhighway.

580. Batson, Trent. "ENFI Research." *C&C* 10 (August 1993): 93–101.

Studies Electronic Networks for Interaction (ENFI) to determine what changes occurred in student writings. Points out that further study is needed for more conclusive results.

581. Belanger, Kelly Renee. "Contextualizing Collaboration: Portraits of Writing Groups in Computer-Supported Classes." *DAI* 53 (February 1993): 2718A.

Studies three computer-supported classrooms where students produced shared documents.

582. Bernhardt, Stephen A. "The Shape of Text to Come: The Texture of Print on Screens." *CCC* 44 (May 1993): 151–75.

Presents nine categories which distinguish the features of an on-screen text from those of a hard-copy text; argues that electronic texts are more reader-text interactive.

583. Bolter, Jay David. "Alone and Together in the Electronic Bazaar." *C&C* 10 (April 1993): 5–17.

Presents the 1992 Computers & Writing Conference keynote address. Promotes hypertext as a "better environment for collaboration" which allows for a diversity of voices, contexts, and conclusions.

584. Bothel, Richard Thomas. "Copyright?? or Copywrong??" *CCJ* 64 (August/September 1993): 28–32.

Claims that if educators do not exercise accountability for correct use of media in classrooms, they may face new restrictive regulations.

585. Boudin, Kathy. "Participatory Literacy Education behind Bars: AIDS Opens the Door." *HER* 63 (Summer 1993): 207–32.

Recounts her efforts to build critical literacy teaching practices into skills-based curriculum at a women's prison. Uses subject of AIDS to link women's experiences to the acquisition of literacy skills.

586. Boyle, Frank T. "IBM, Talking Heads, and Our Classrooms." *CE* 55 (October 1993): 618–26.

Describes an IBM presentation on computers in the classroom; argues against "encroachment of information technologies in higher education."

587. Braddlee. "Virtual Communities: Computer-Mediated Communication and Communities of Association." *DAI* 54 (October 1993): 1134A.

Examines discursive practices and the communicative content of a community of writers separated by geographical space but connected via a computer network.

588. Brooks, Randy M. "Principles for Effective Hypermedia Design." *TC* 40 (August 1993): 422–28.

Describes four goals of an effective design: minimal document clutter, an appropriate sponsor image, easily accessible storage information, and minimal resource requirements.

589. Brown, Lady Falls. "The Daedalus Integrated Writing Environment." *C&C* 10 (November 1993): 77–88.

Explains changes that occur in a networked classroom, specifically the active learning environment it fosters.

590. Bruce, Bertram C., and Andee Rubin. *Electronic Quills: A Situated Evaluation of Using Computers for Writing in Classrooms.* Hillsdale, NJ: Lawrence Erlbaum Associates, 1993. 248 pages

Discusses the words and experiences of teachers and students who used QUILL— a software package developed by the authors to aid in writing instruction. Examines the role of technology in the practice and development of literacy.

591. Bruce, Bertram C., Joy Kreeft Peyton, and Trent Batson, eds. *Networked-Based Classrooms: Promises and Realities.* New York: Cambridge University Press, 1993. 312 pages

Fourteen essays outline the history of network-based classrooms and discuss ways they can transform writing instruction. Topics include authority within the classroom, collaborative writing, distance learning, and writing across the curriculum. *Essayists:* Bartholomae, David; Batson, Trent; Bruce, Bertram C.; Cochran, Cynthia; Fowles, Mary; Gillespie, Terlyn; Hadjuk, Thomas; Hartman, Karen; Kemp, Fred; Kremers, Marshall; Miller, J. Douglas; Neuwirth, Christine M.; Palmquist, Michael; Peyton, Joy Kreeft; Reynolds,

Thomas; Sirc, Geoffrey; Spitzer, Michael; Thompson, Diane.

592. Bruning, Stephen David. "An Examination of the Social, Psychological, and Communication Variables that Influence User Perceptions of Computer-Mediated Communication Technologies." *DAI* 54 (October 1993): 1148A.

Surveys a group with email access. Finds that control, position, motives in interpersonal communication, demographics, and amount of computer use were the most important variables predicting use.

593. Buckley, Liz, and Bill McCarron. "Teaching Writing on Computers: Mistakes and Recoveries." *ET* 25 (Winter 1993): 46–49.

Documents problems and successes of using a networked computer system in a developmental writing class and in a graduate-level writing class.

594. Bueno, Kathleen A., and Wayne A. Nelson. "Collaborative Second Language Learning with a Contextualized Computer Environment." *JEdM&H* 2 (1993): 177–208.

The authors investigate how contextualized computer environments affect peer interaction during second language learning; they focus on different kinds of cooperative interactions occurring in this environment.

595. Burke, Robin. "Intelligent Retrieval of Video Stories in Social Simulation." *JEdM&H* 2 (1993): 381–92.

Describes a multimedia retrieval system for educational stories; discusses its integration into an architecture for teaching complex social skills.

596. Busiel, Christopher. "*Verbum Interactive* and Multimedia in Eduation." *C&C* 10 (November 1993): 63–76.

Considers the "first-ever interactive multimedia 'magazine'" as a revolutionary convergence of print magazines features of sound, animation, and interactive segments.

597. Butler, Wayne Michael. "The Social Construction of Knowledge in an Electronic Discourse Community." *DAI* 53 (June 1993): 4236A.

Describes and analyzes how members of an academic electronic discourse community employing synchronous and asynchronous software socially construct knowledge of literary texts.

598. Carbone, Nick, Margaret Daisley, Ed Federenko, Dix McComas, Charles Moran, Dori Ostermiller, and Sherri Vanden Akker. "Writing Ourselves On-Line." *C&C* 10 (August 1993): 29–48.

Chronicles the online/offline voices of six instructors in networked classrooms. Notes that teachers as well as students have online voices.

599. Carlson, Patricia A., and George Gonzalez. "The Knowledge Board: Using Hypertext as an "Intelligent" Workspace for Writing Issue-Based Prose." *JEdM&H* 2 (1993): 417–43.

Describes conceptual design and prototype implementation of the Knowledge Board which integrates text and cognitive-support tools for professionals who compose complex prose.

600. Carter, Duncan. "Critical Thinking for Writers: Transferable Skills or Discipline-Specific Strategies?" *CompSt* 21 (Spring 1993): 86–93.

Questions whether thinking during the writing process is generic or domain specific.

601. Cavalier, Robert, and Thomas C. Reeves. "International Perspectives on the Impact of Computing in Education." *EdTech* 33 (September 1993): 7–10.

Introduces articles in a special issue on computer-based education in Australia, Brazil, Chile, China, Europe, Korea, and Malaysia.

602. Chapman, William. "Color Coding and the Interactivity of Multimedia." *JEdM&H* 2 (1993): 3–23.

Discusses color coding in multimedia presentations. Focuses on physical and psychological characteristics of color perception; makes recommendations for color selection.

603. Chidambaram, Laku, and Robert P. Bostrom. "Evolution of Group Performance over Time: A Repeated Measures Study of GDSS Effects." *JOC* 3 (1993): 443–69.

The authors use adaptive structuration theory to examine the impact of computer support on group performance over time. They find that performance improved only when groups faithfully appropriated the technology.

604. Chiou, Guey-Fa. "Some Potential Areas of Research and Development in the Space of Computer Based Learning." *EdTech* 33 (August, 1993): 19–23.

Supports computer-based learning through experience and the application of theories.

605. Collier, Judith Sandefur. "An Examination of the Effect of Learning Modality on Academic Gains of Nontraditional Students in Computer-Based Instructional Systems." *DAI* 53 (May 1993): 3846A.

Demonstrates that students who use computer-based instruction in reading and math show achievement regardless of which learning style was used.

606. Condon, William. "Selecting Computer Software for Writing Instruction: Some Considerations." *C&C* 10 (November 1993): 53–56.

Argues that software selection today is as difficult as 10 years ago. Suggests assessing pedagogical uses of software, its versatility, and its transparency to the user.

607. Connolly, Frank W., and Chuck Schneebeck. "The Community of Electronic Learners." *EDUCOM* 28 (May/June 1993): 36–37.

Discusses the formation of communities of electronic learners through computer networks. Compares face-to-face communication, speed of evolution of a community, and rights and responsibilities of individuals.

608. Cooke, Martin. *Modelling Auditory Processing and Organization.* New York: Cambridge University Press, 1993. 150 pages

Argues that giving computers the capacity to filter out unwanted signals, as humans do in understanding speech, would help develop speech recognition systems and hearing aids.

609. Crain, Jeanie C. "Storyspace: Hypertext Writing Environment." *CHum* 27 (April 1993): 137–41.

Describes the use of Storyspace to teach students to collaborate effectively during the writing process.

610. Crews, Kenneth D. *Copyright, Fair Use, and the Challenge for Universities: Promoting the Progress of Higher Education.* Chicago: University of Chicago Press, 1993. 256 pages

Explains copyright law and congressional guidelines affecting the use of photocopies, videotapes, software, and reserve rooms.

611. Curtis, Marcia, and Charles Moran. "Userhome, Sweet Userhome: A Review of Novell's *Netware.*" *C&C* 10 (November 1993): 63–76.

Presents a case study of how one campus incorporated a networked classroom into their pedagogical goals.

612. Cusack, Michael W. "Efforts to Simplify Human-Computer Communications." *IEEE* 36 (March 1993): 14–18.

Maintains that with increasing reliance on computer-generated information, computers that think, communicate, observe, calculate, and design must be available for nontechnical users.

613. Davis, Ben. "Looking and Learning through Computers." *EDUCOM* 28 (January/February 1993): 20–25.

Describes several projects underway at MIT to develop multimedia organizers, hypermedia linking tools, and collaborative tools for group design, decision making, and idea formulation.

614. DeSanctis, Gerardine, Scott P. Poole, Gary W. Dickson, and Brad M. Jackson. "Interpretive Analysis of Teach Use of Group Technologies." *JOC* 3 (1993): 1–29.

The authors propose using adaptive structuration theory to examine the impacts of new computing technologies. They examine three teams' adoption of a group decision support system.

615. DeWitt, Scott Lloyd. "Hypertextualizing Composition Instruction: A Research Study." *DAI* 53 (January 1993): 2279A.

Relates ideas of hypertext to current theories of reading and writing.

616. Dorwick, Keith. "*Seen:* Tutorials for Critical Writing." *C&C* 10 (November 1993): 101–8.

Recommends *Seen* as a student-centered, collaborative program.

617. Douglas, J. Yellowlees. "What Hypertexts Can Do That Print Narratives Cannot." *Reader* 28 (Fall 1992): 1–22.

Explores the potential of interactive reading and the freedom of choice it gives readers. Calls for a rethinking of reading theory in light of hypertext's nonlinearity.

618. Douglas, Suzanne G. "Digital Soup: The New ABCs of Distance Learning." *EDUCOM* 28 (July/August 1993): 22–25, 28–30.

Describes new information technologies that expand learning opportunities in higher education, both on and off campus. Discusses the possibilities for partnerships with telephone companies and provides a projection for the future.

619. Downing, Tim J. "The Application of a Spiral Curriculum Model of Technical Training." *EdTech* 33 (July 1993): 18–28.

Reveals factors that hinder the use of a spiral curriculum and provides examples of its success.

620. Dubinskas, Frank A. "Virtual Organizations: Computer Conferencing Organizational Design." *JOC* 3 (1993): 389–416.

Studies organizational structuring processes accompanying the introduction of computer conferencing into organizations. Proposes terms such as "virtual group" and "virtual organization" to describe groups created through computer conferencing.

621. Eiler, Mary Ann. "Perspectives on Software." *C&C* 10 (November 1993): 59–62.

Maintains that software should be functional, transparent, appropriate, and secondary to the students and teacher.

622. Eklundh, Kerstin. *The Use of 'Idea Processors' for Studying Structural Aspects of Text Production.* Espoo, Finland: NORDTEXT Symposium, May 1993. ERIC ED 359 768. 18 pages

Discusses the use of "idea processors" that allow students to compose a text within an outline and to experiment with different organizations for ideas during the process.

623. Ellerby, Janet Mason. "A Theatre of Responses: Using a Computer Bulletin Board to Enhance Interpretation." *Reader* 28 (Fall 1992): 80–92.

Argues for computer networking in literature classes; suggests student anonymity to promote discussion of differing ideas.

624. Evans, John F. "The CA Literature Class: A Perspective." *Reader* 28 (Fall 1992): 69–79.

Endorses the use of computers to study literature. Argues that it moves the focus from teacher's instruction to "student/ reader" reactions with text, other students, and teachers.

625. Farrow, Margaret. "Knowledge-Engineering Using HyperCard: A Learning Strategy for Tertiary Education." *JCBI* 20 (Winter 1993): 9–14.

Argues that designing HyperCard stacks can be a valuable learning strategy that provides qualitatively different learning experiences from traditional, tutorial presentations.

626. Faulkner, Susan Lossen. "Computers and Freshman Composition Instruction: A Study of Faculty Preparation and Classroom Performance." *DAI* 53 (February 1993): 2720A.

Investigates time divided between writing and instruction in a composition class with computer-assisted instruction.

627. Fawcett, Heather. "The *New Oxford English Dictionary* Project." *TC* 40 (August 1993): 379–82.

Describes why designeers selected a hybrid type of structured general markup language (SGML) for the new computerized *OED*. Points out its benefits.

628. Fey, Marion H. *Building Community through Computer Conferencing and Feminist Collaboration.* Indianapolis, IN: Computers and Writing Conference, May 1992. ERIC ED 351 683. 16 pages

Looks at a composition course taught entirely through computer-mediated instruction and influenced by a pedagogy of feminist collaboration. Argues that computers facilitate collaboration among writers by facilitating giving and receiving.

629. Fischer, Rick, and Elinor Kelley Gruism. "Grammar Checkers: Programs That May Not Enhance Learning." *JourEd* 47 (Winter 1993): 20–27.

Results show that students' performance was not enhanced by increased feedback, instructors' satisfaction was not increased, and students were not satisfied with computer responses.

630. Foa, Lin J. "Technology and Change: Composing a Four-Part Harmony." *EDUCOM* 28 (March/April 1993): 27–30.

Discusses the creation of policies in higher education to integrate new technology, tying the campus and community together by the use of e-mail.

631. Foltz, Peter William. "Readers' Comprehension and Strategies in Linear Text and Hypertext." *DAI* 54 (September 1993): 1700B.

Argues that although hypertexts give readers more flexibility in choosing paths to information, they choose strategies to maintain a coherent macrostructure.

632. Ford, Robert Gilbert. "Narration and the Network: Postmodernism and Freshman Composition." *DAI* 53 (January 1993): 2280A.

Argues that privileging of science and technology at the expense of narrative is not justified in distance education programs using modems. Maintains that narration is still a powerful force for legitimation of teachers and students.

633. Fortune, Ron. "*Toolbook*: A Hypermedia Authoring Program." *C&C* 10 (November 1993): 117–26.

Concludes that the power of *Toolbook* lies in its ability to develop hypertext and hypermedia applications that can be readily shared.

634. Fox, Tom. "Standards and Access." *JBW* 12 (Spring 1993): 37–45.

Argues that literacy standards in higher education should be "relentlessly plural" in representing "our solidarity with those who seek to reduce the violence of inequity."

635. Freebody, Peter, and Anthony R. Welch, eds. *Knowledge, Culture and Power; International Perspectives on Literacy as Policy and Practice*. The Pittsburgh Series in Composition, Literacy and Culture, edited by David Bartholomae and Jean Ferguson Carr. Pittsburgh, PA: University of Pittsburgh Press, 1993. 256 pages

Eleven essays investigate how issues of class and power are at work in literacy campaigns and government programs worldwide, as reflected in a variety of countries, including Nicaragua, India, the United States, Singapore, Australia, and Kurdistan.
Essayists: Ahai, Naihuwo; Collins, James; Faraclas, Nicholas; Freebody, Peter; Hassanpour, Amir; Kumar, Krishna; Kwan-Terry, Anna; Kwan-Terry, John; Lankshear, Colin; Limage, Leslie J.; O'Connor, Peter; Walton, Christine; Welch, Anthony R.

636. Gaines, Brian R. "An Agenda for Digital Journals: The Socio-Technical Infrastructure of Knowledge Dissemination." *JOC* 3 (1993): 135–93.

Discusses social and technical aspects of digital journals; projects how new forms of knowledge dissemination may evolve; analyzes the social role of scholarly communication.

637. Gaines, Brian R., and Nicholas Malcolm. "Supporting Collaboration in Digital Journal Production." *JOC* 3 (1993): 195–213.

The authors report on the development of a group-writing tool designed for collaborators with varying access to communication networks. They discuss a design which stresses current word-processing interfaces and work practices.

638. Gandell, Terry S. "The Effect of Opportunities Provided by Telecommunications on the Reading and Writing of Adult Augmentative Communicators Who Are Severely Disabled." *DAI* 54 (July 1993): 89A.

Investigates the effect of the increased opportunity to communicate via telecommunications on the reading and writing of adult augmentative communicators who are severely disabled.

639. Garrett, John R. "Digital Libraries: The Grand Challenge." *EDUCOM* 28 (July/August 1993): 17–21.

Describes the challenges to building a national digital library system including the selection of information, building networks, access, leadership, billing, and the training of the information poor.

640. Gerrard, Lisa. "Computers and Composition: Rethinking Our Values." *C&C* 10 (April 1993): 23–34.

Explores the academic tendency to value theory over teaching; questions its place among "computers and compositionists."

641. Giles, Thomas D. "Ideas in Practice: The Search Key as a Grassroots Grammar Checker." *JDEd* 16 (Spring 1993): 28–31.

Explains how to use the search feature in a word-processing program as an effective grammar teaching tool.

642. Glau, Gregory. "Citation, Version 2.0." *CHum* 27 (June 1993): 225–28.

Evaluates software that enables students to construct MLA and APA bibliographies in correct format.

643. Godfrey, Shauna. "A Community of Writers." *UEJ* 21 (1993): 22–25.

Describes online computer conferences to promote student discussion.

644. Goldstein, David K. "Computer-Based Data and Organizational Learning: The Importance of Managers' Stories." *JOC* 3 (1993): 417–42.

Explores how computer-based data is used by marketing managers. Discusses how managers share their insights within and outside the organization.

645. Goodman, Kenneth. "Intellectual Property and Control." *AM* 68 (September Supplement 1993): S88–91.

Argues against ownership of intellectual property and suggests that sharing infor-

mation "produces overwhelmingly good consequences."

646. Graves, Roger. *Virtual Realities for the Twenty-First Century*. San Diego, CA: Conference on College Composition and Communication, March/April 1993. ERIC ED 358 461. 11 pages

Discusses cuts to a composition program at a Canadian university. Argues that shrinking budgets and new information economy literacies may decimate large composition programs. Suggests bringing together representatives from existing groups to form something akin to the National Council for Teachers of English.

647. Gray, Susan H. *Hypertext and the Technology of Conversation: Orderly Situational Choice*. New Directions in Information Management, no. 31. Westport, CT: Greenwood Press, 1993. 280 pages

Presents a study of computer-human interaction.

648. Greenlaw, James C. "Reading between Worlds: Computer-Mediated Intercultural Responses to Asian Literature." *Reader* 28 (Fall 1992): 37–51.

Argues for educational and emotional benefits of establishing electronic mail key pals for Asian high school students in Canada and Japan.

649. Grice, Roger A., and Lenore S. Ridgway. "Usability and Hypermedia: Toward a Set of Usability Criteria and Measures." *TC* 40 (August 1993): 429–37.

Describes a special challenge of testing the usability of hypermedia but also notes commonalities with traditional materials.

650. Gruber, Sibylle. "Book Review: *Electronic Quills: A Situated Evaluation of Using Computers for Writing Classrooms*." *C&C* 10 (April 1993): 107–12.

Discusses Bertram Bruce and Andee Rubin's book on the implementation of QUILL in the Alaskan school system.

Points out that the theoretical framework—situated evaluation—needs to be explored in more detail.

651. Haley-James, Shirley. "Entries from a New E-Mail User's Notebook." *C&C* 10 (November 1993): 5–10.

Overcoming her fear of electronic unknowns, the author chronicles her growing competence in using e-mail in establishing international contacts in Baltic countries.

652. Haney, Steve, Molly Hepler, Doug Short, Kim Richardson, Hugh Burns, Dimitri Korhanis, Cynthia Selfe, Gail Hawisher, and Paul LeBlanc. "Forum: A Conversation about Software, Technology, and Composition Studies." *C&C* 10 (November 1993): 151–68.

Nine experts on academic software discuss the place of self-produced software, the future of the book publishing industry, the necessity for teacher technology training, and funding for technology resources.

653. Hannafin, Robert D., and Wilhelmina C. Savenye. "Technology in the Classroom: The Teacher's New Role and Resistance to It." *EdTech* 33 (June 1993): 26–31.

Examines resistance to technology and enhanced results when technology is used in the classroom.

654. Hansen, Craig J. "Flow, Form, Content, and Technology: A Model for Understanding Communication in a Business Setting (Volumes I and II)." *DAI* 53 (January 1993): 2355A.

Examines corporate social contexts through the eyes of a variety of disciplines; examines the impact of new computer-based communications technologies.

655. Hawisher, Gail E., and Charles Moran. "Electronic Mail and the Writing Instructor." *CE* 55 (October 1993): 627–43.

The authors assess rhetorical and pedagogical implications of the use of e-mail in writing classes. They also include an extensive list of available resources and listservs for English studies.

656. Hayes, John R. "Taking Criticism Seriously." *RTE* 27 (October 1993): 305–15.

Argues for the importance of empirical research methods in literacy studies.

657. Heaps, Allan. "Writers and Habitat: Securing a Viable Networked Computer-Assisted Environment for Communities of Writers." *UEJ* 21 (1993): 47–52.

Reviews various layouts for designing a computer writing room.

658. Heeren, Elske, and Betty Collis. "Design Considerations for Telecommunications-Supported Cooperative Learning Environments: Concept Mapping as a 'Telecooperation Support Tool.'" *JEdM&H* 2 (1993): 107–27.

The authors discuss design issues of electronic environments supporting distant cooperative problem solving and the idea of a telecommunications-supported environment. They introduce a telecooperation support tool termed "shared concept mapping tool."

659. Hepler, Molly. "Things to Consider When Evaluating Software." *C&C* 10 (November 1993): 57–58.

Suggests that English professionals should define the curriculum and then select the software that fits the curriculum. Recommends that they also need to select adaptable software and plan for continuing support and training.

660. Hinckley, Clair Marcia. "Writing in Context: A Study of Adult Women Planning and Writing with Word Processing." *DAI* 53 (June 1993): 6582B.

Studies oral and written planning. Finds that older writers planned more both conceptually and rhetorically.

661. Hirsch, Paul M. "Globalization of Mass Media Ownership: Implications and Effects." *ComR* 19 (December 1992): 677–81.

Argues that the globalization of ownership of mass media content, production, and technology has major implications for how we define audience and theories about media control.

662. Hodges, James E. "Electronic Aids in Writing." *TETYC* 20 (May 1993): 132–36.

Provides a brief survey of grammar-checkers and writing software.

663. Holden, Michael, and William Mitchell. "The Future of Computer-Mediated Communication in Higher Education." *EDUCOM* 28 (March/April 1993): 31–37.

Describes the results of a Delphi study conducted to gather information regarding the future of computer-mediated communication (CMC) in higher education. Finds that the greatest obstacle is faculty attitudes.

664. Horn, Dennis. "Network Collaboration with UNIX." *TCQ* 2 (Fall 1993): 413–29.

Studies the expanding role of computer networks in technical communication. Explores ways in which Internet and UNIX allow collaboration from classrooms to international contexts.

665. Horney, Mark. "A Measure of Hypertext Linearity." *JEdM&H* 3 (1993): 67–82.

Analyzes hypertext documents and hypertext authoring to determine navigation patterns. Highlights discrepancies in ideas about the nonlinearity of hypertext.

666. Howard, Tharon W. "Electronic Distribution of Hypermedia on Wide-Area Networking Systems: An Update." *TC* 40 (August 1993): 438–48.

Describes software which allows for an inexpensive access to hypermedia products by corporate and educational clients.

667. Howard, Tharon W. "The Rhetoric of Electronic Communities." *DAI* 53 (March 1993): 3889A.

Examines electronic discourse communities' theories about power and authoriza-

tion. Discusses how computer-mediated communication affects theoretical concepts of community.

668. Hubbard, Lori. "Developing a Collaborative Performance Support System for Practicing Teachers." *EdTech* 33 (November 1993): 39–45.

Suggests a computer support system that streamlines such things as professional development and communication between teachers, students, and administration.

669. Hull, Glynda. "Hearing Other Voices: A Critical Assessment of Popular Views on Literacy and Work." *HER* 63 (Spring 1993): 20–49.

Challenges simplistic views concerning literacy, its relation to the workplace and the declining economy. Cites ethnographies on workplace literacy and argues for rethinking the complex relationship of workplace and literacy.

670. Illich, Ivan. *In the Vineyard of the Text: A Commentary to Hugh's Didascalicon.* Chicago: University of Chicago Press, 1993. 176 pages

Studies Hugh of St. Victor's *Didascalicon* as a historic moment between the leap from monastic texts (designed for oral, collective recitation) to scholastic works (texts organized for silent, contemplative, individual study). Argues that the era of bookish texts is passing with the advent of computers.

671. Jacques, Richard, Blair Nonnecke, Jenny Preece, and Diane McKerlie. "Current Designs in HyperCard: What Can We Learn?" *JEdM&H* 2 (1993): 219–37.

Presents results of an evaluation of hypersystems. Examines how stack design affects purpose, content, structure, navigation and control, and presentation of information.

672. Janangelo, Joseph. "Book Review: *Re-Imagining Computers and Composition:*

Teaching and Research in the Virtual Age." C&C 10 (November 1993): 89–94.

Concludes that the text encourages readers "to think critically about computers" and that it offers "specific plans for educational reform and teacher activism."

673. Johnson-Eilola, Johndan. "Control and the Cyborg: Writing and Being Written in Hypertext." *JAC* 13 (Fall 1993): 381–400.

Examines a networked computer-assisted composition classroom in postmodern terms.

674. Joyner, Randy L., Vivian Arnold, and B. June Schmidt. "Technology and Keyboarding Accuracy." *BEdF* 47 (April 1993): 16–19.

Argues that teachers need to be more aware of sources of common keyboarding errors made by secondary and postsecondary students.

675. Jurafsky, Daniel Saul. "An On-Line Computational Model of Human Sentence Interpretation: A Theory of the Representation and Use of Linguistic Knowledge." *DAI* 53 (April 1993): 5295B.

Describes a model of human sentence interpretation, including construction-based interpretative grammar (CIG), and SAL, an online interpreter.

676. Karovsky, Penelope. *Real Time Literacy.* San Francisco: American Educational Research Association, April 1992. ERIC ED 348 652. 17 pages

Argues that the educational use of computers is changing how people think. Maintains that it is directing culture toward a more functional and self-conscious form of literacy.

677. Kelley, Robert T. "Virtual Realism: Virtual Reality, Magical Realism, and Late Twentieth-Century Technologies of Representation." *DAI* 53 (March 1993): 3209A.

Compares computer-generated artificial reality and the magical realism of Morrison, Silko, and Rushdie to show how

they force users or readers to envision alternative realities.

678. Kemp, Fred. "Who Programmed This? Examining the Instructional Attitudes of Writing-Support Software." *C&C* 10 (November 1993): 9–24.

Analyzes equipment, software, pedagogy, and teacher as four elements of writing instruction using computers. Notes that software is "the most ideological and most unforgiving" element.

679. Key, Chris Dewayne. "Life Out of Context: Life in Text." *DAI* 53 (March 1993): 4933B.

Explores how autoethnographic writings, stories, journals, letters, e-mail, essays, dialogues, and poems establish the self in the act of writing and self-creation.

680. Killingsworth, M. Jimmie. "Product and Process, Literacy and Orality: An Essay on Composition and Culture." *CCC* 44 (February 1993): 26–39.

Discusses the ideological and social history of conflicts between product/process and literacy/orality in composition studies.

681. Knoblauch, C. H., and Lil Brannon. *Critical Teaching and the Idea of Literacy.* Portsmouth, NH: Boynton/Cook, 1993. 227 pages

Examines the rhetoric of ongoing literacy debates and their curricular implications by critiquing definitions of "literacy" from across political spectrums.

682. Lang, Susan M. *Creating a Community of Learners Using Hypertext.* Indianapolis, IN: Computers and Writing Conference, May 1992. ERIC ED 350 600. 13 pages

Discusses the use of hypertext to facilitate writing in literature courses by encouraging revision, the integration of ideas and texts, and collaboration among student writers.

683. Lang, Susan Michelle. "Three Traditions of Texts: Theoretical Implications of Using

Computers in the Field of English Studies." *DAI* 53 (February 1993): 2778A.

Explores the history and theoretical implications of using computers in both instruction and scholarship in English Studies.

684. Lansman, Marcy, John B. Smith, and Irene Weber. "Using the *Writing Environment* to Study Writer's Strategies." *C&C* 10 (April 1993): 71–92.

Describes the four composing modes of *Writing Environment* which also provides researchers with data on the composing strategies of the user. Discusses a study using the program.

685. Lapsley, Joyce H., and Pamela L. McLeod. "Teaching Desktop Publishing in a Windows Environment." *BEdF* 47 (April 1993): 43–44.

Explains the basic commands of the Windows environment and how the convenience of windows lends itself well to desktop publishing instruction.

686. LeBlanc, Paul J. *Writing Teachers Writing Software: Creating Our Place in the Electronic Age.* Advances in Computers and Composition Studies, edited by Gail E. Hawisher and Cynthia L. Selfe. Urbana, IL and Houghton, MI: NCTE and Computers and Composition Press, 1993. 188 pages

The book focuses on faculty development of software for composition studies. It describes the authors of the tools, their methods, and the reception of their software, as well as the implications their work has for future developers.

687. Lee, Yungbin B., and James D. Lehman. "Instructional Cuing in Hypermedia: A Study with Active and Passive Learners." *JEdM&H* 2 (1993): 25–37.

Examines the assumption that students actively seek out available embedded information. Results indicate that students are not equally willing to explore hypermedia environments to obtain information.

688. Lehner, Franz. "Quality Control in Software Documentation Based on Measurement of Text Comprehension and Text Comprehensibility." *IPM* 29 (1993): 551–68.

Introduces Readability Measuring System (RMS) as a tool for evaluating software documentation. Reviews existing approaches and principles of evaluation. Points out that RMS uses Hypercard and Macintosh computers.

689. Liebman, Sheldon. "Multimedia Versus Desktop Video." *Videography* 18 (August 1993): 90–94.

Attempts to define the word *multimedia* and explains its importance for video professionals.

690. Long, Thomas L., and Christine Pedersen. *Critical Thinking about Literature through Computer Networking.* Orlando, FL: Annual Computer Conference of the League for Innovation in the Community College, October 1992. ERIC ED 358 875. 26 pages

Discusses a computer-oriented, classroom-based research project focusing on 49 first-year college students enrolled in an interactive composition course utilizing computers.

691. Lu, Alvin. "Jack in the Text: From Multi-Media to Hypertext." *ETC* 50 (Winter 1993/94): 496–500.

Reviews hypertext books. Looks at both print adaptations and multimedia and hypertext versions of the same book.

692. Macedo, Donaldo P. "Literacy for Stupidification: The Pedagogy of Big Lies." *HER* 63 (Summer 1993): 183–206.

Critiques specialization, instrumentalist literacy and mechanical learning of reading skills. Examines the failure to use critical literacy to link bodies of knowledge and to read the word and the world.

693. MacKinnon, Alistair, and Clesson S. Bush. "Technology for Education: What Is the Federal Role?" *EdTech* 33 (April 1993): 33–34.

Urges to push for stronger federal agenda of technology in education to promote literacy.

694. Marlow, Eugene. "Electronic Communications Media: Massaging the Messages." *TC* 40 (August 1993): 453–56.

Offers guidelines for multimedia production and audience analysis.

695. McLellan, Hilary. "Hypertextual Tales: Story Models for Hypertext Design." *JEdM&H* 2 (1993): 239–60.

Argues that the design of instructional hypermedia programs should include stories. Discusses types of story components and provides a taxonomy of story structures.

696. Merickel, Alan P. "Some Thoughts about Computers and Composition: How Did I Get Here and Where Am I Headed?" *TETYC* 20 (May 1993): 128–31.

Presents a personal account of his experiments with networking and computer conferencing.

697. Migliareses, Piero, and Emilio Paolucci. "Cooperation Support through the Use of Group Decision Systems." *JOC* 3 (1993): 215–43.

Uses organizational theory to analyze the role of group decision support systems; discusses a prototype designed to support production-planning problems by improving communication.

698. Mims, James. "Focusing the Big Picture." *UEJ* 21 (1993): 2–8.

Offers an approach to computerized peer response groups.

699. Monroe, Rick. *Writing and Thinking with Computers: A Practical and Progressive Approach*. Urbana, IL: National Council of the Teachers of English, 1993. 121 pages

Stresses the need for teachers to design language-arts curricula using computers. Offers suggestions for using specific software features to teach "without abandoning reading, writing, thinking, listening,

and speaking." Argues for linked classroom networks to promote student collaboration. Includes sample lessons.

700. Moran, Charles. "The Winds, and the Costs, of Change." *C&C* 10 (April 1993): 35–44.

Argues that like medicine and banking, education is discovering that computer investments are not profitable. Asserts that the next 10 years will move faculty and students fully into the information age.

701. Morrell, Kenneth, Gary Marchionini, and Delia Neuman. "Sailing Perseus: Instructional Strategies for Hypermedia in the Classics." *JEdM&H* 2 (1993): 337–53.

Describes assignments instructors used to integrate the HyperCard-based system *Perseus* into their courses; evaluates *Perseus* as a teaching tool.

702. Mountain, Lee. "Home-to-Home Network Interaction between Teacher-Education Students and Children." *EdTech* 33 (February 1993): 41–43.

Suggests computer network connections between these two groups of students in the form of penpalling to establish communication and learning.

703. Mulvihill, Peggy. "*Storyspace*: A Deep and Welcome Emptiness." *C&C* 10 (November 1993): 127–34.

Presents a case study of a user's first encounter with Macintosh computers, *Storyspace*, and hypertext.

704. Myers, Linda, ed. *Approaches to Computer Writing Classrooms: Learning from Practical Experience*. Literacy, Culture, and Learning: Theory and Practice, edited by Alan C. Purves. Albany, NY: State University of New York Press, 1993. 225 pages

Presents 13 essays on the design of computer writing facilities and classrooms for writing courses, on adapting teaching styles for computer-assisted environments, and on programs at 12 colleges and universities.

Essayists: Balester, Valerie M.; Batson, Trent; D'Agostino, Karen Nilson; Gerrard, Lisa; Green, Robert C.; Handa, Carolyn; Hawisher, Gail E.; Holdstein, Deboarah; Johnson-Eilola, Johndan; Kemp, Fred; Myers, Linda; Pemberton, Michael A.; Selfe, Cynthia L.; Selfe, Richard J.; Sitko, Barbara; Thomas, Gordon.

705. NCTE Instructional Technology Committee. "NCTE Guidelines for Review and Evaluation of English Language Arts." *C&C* 10 (November 1993): 37–44.

Presents the full text of the 1981 guidelines that can be used "by educators at all levels to evaluate educational software."

706. Nicholl, Sheldon Scott. "Language Acquisition by Computer: Learning Categories, Agreement and Morphology under Psychological Constraints." *DAI* 53 (January 1993): 3604B.

Describes CAM (Categories, Agreement, and Morphology), a computer model of several aspects of language acquisition. Focuses on English and Cheyenne.

707. Nowaczyk, Ronald H., and E. Christopher James. "Applying Minimal Manual Principles for Documentation of Graphical User Interfaces." *JTWC* 23 (1993): 379–88.

Contends that the documentation of graphical user interfaces should include few, if any screens. Points out that icon and button information appear beneficial.

708. Nydahl, Joel. *An Experiment in Computer Ethics: Clustering Composition with Computer Applications.* Indianapolis, IN: Computers and Writing Conference, May 1992. ERIC ED 350 676. 16 pages

Explores "clustering" and computer literacy in a first-year composition course structured around four subthemes: technology/society, gender, education, and ethics and computers in business.

709. Palmquist, Michael E. "Network-Supported Interaction in Two Writing Classrooms." *C&C* 10 (November 1993): 25–57.

Compares student interaction in two classrooms: one group wrote research papers for a general audience; the other group wrote for professionals.

710. Palumbo, David B., and Doris Prater. "The Role of Hypermedia in Synthesis Writing." *C&C* 10 (April 1993): 59–70.

Palumbo and Prater maintain that hypermedia can facilitate the construction of meaning for learners and assist in the development of higher order thinking skills if the users follow the suggestions made by the authors.

711. Pennington, Martha C. "Computer-Assisted Writing on a Principled Basis: The Case against Computer-Assisted Text Analysis for Nonproficient Writers." *Lang&E* 7 (1993): 43–59.

Analyzes computer-assisted writing programs to determine their effectiveness in learning.

712. Pennington, Martha C. "Modeling the Student Writer's Acquisition of Word Processing Skills: The Interaction of Computer, Writing, and Language Media." *C&C* 10 (November 1993): 59–79.

Presents a general theoretical framework and a research program on word processing in relation to language learning and the acquisition of composing skills.

713. Penrod, James I. "Reflections on IT Planning: A Decade of Transition." *EDUCOM* 28 (March/April 1993): 22–26.

Discusses changes in information technology in higher education from personal to work group, from system islands to integrated systems, and from internal to inter-enterprise systems.

714. Picciane, Anthony G. "The Five Points: The Design of a Multimedia Program on Social History." *JEdM&H* 2 (1993): 129–47.

Describes content, pedagogy, organization and technical design of a multimedia program; evaluates approaches used to design a videodisc-based interactive program.

715. Piro, Vincent F. "Using Multicultural Texts in the Composition Class." *CompC* 6 (March 1993): 4–6.

Examines how students can respond to texts in multicultural anthologies. Argues for approaches that open classes to new perspectives. Includes a bibliography of multicultural readers.

716. Poole, Marshall Scott, Michael Holmes, Richard Watson, and Gerardine DeSanctis. "Group Decision Support Systems and Group Communication: A Comparison of Decision Making in Computer-Supported and Non-supported Groups." *ComR* 20 (April 1993): 176–213.

Investigates the impacts that computerized group decision support systems (GDSS) have on group decision-making processes.

717. Posey, Evelyn J. "Word Processing in the Basic Writing Classroom: The Promise of Classroom Research." *TETYC* 20 (February 1993): 23–30.

Studies 13 students and indicates that the greatest advantage of word processing is that students write more.

718. Posey, Evelyn J. *"Writer's Helper for Windows*: A Comprehensive Prewriting and Revising Program." *C&C* 10 (November 1993): 93–100.

Points out that *Writer's Helper for Windows* "introduces computers as a tool to support a writing community, encouraging students to generate ideas, draft, and revise as part of a comprehensive, recursive process."

719. Puccio, P. M. "The Computer-Networked Writing Lab: One Instructor's View. ERIC Digest." ERIC Clearinghouse, Indiana University, Bloomington, IN, 1993. ERIC ED 353 604. 4 pages

Lists several advantages of computer-networked writing labs which may be absent from conventional classrooms.

720. Pullen, Mary Chesteen. "A Comparison of Writing Performance Using Conventional

and Computer-Based Writing Techniques." *DAI* 54 (October 1993): 1328A.

Compares writing samples composed by third-grade girls using either microcomputers or pencil-and-paper. Finds that computer-generated samples differed significantly in T-unit length and total number of words but not in readability or content quality.

721. Raven, Mary Elizabeth. "Analyzing and Adapting to a Multiple Audience: A Study of Two Writers in the Computer Industry." *DAI* 54 (July 1993): 28A.

Presents an ethnographic study of two technical writers of computer documentation and analyzes multiple and sometimes conflicting adaptations made.

722. Regan, Alison. "'Type Normal Like the Rest of Us': Writing, Power, and Homophobia in the Networked Classroom." *C&C* 10 (November 1993): 11–23.

Argues for all students to contribute in networked and traditional classrooms; notes that lesbians and gays feel alienated and less likely to be empowered to write.

723. Rein, Gail L., Clyde W. Holsapple, and Andrew B. Whinston. "Computer Support of Organization Design and Learning." *JOC* 3 (1993): 87–120.

The authors examine the significance of developing multi-user, computer-based environments supporting organization design activities. They introduce a working perspective of an organization design and discuss prototype technology supporting this perspective.

724. Repman, Judi, Herman G. Weller, and William Lan. "The Impact of Social Context on Learning on Hypermedia-Based Instruction." *JEdM&H* 2 (1993): 283–98.

The authors discuss the impact of variations in social context during collaborative hypermedia-based instruction. Their results indicate a variability in approaches to and articulation of ideas.

725. Reynolds, Thomas J. "Hemingway and Basic Writers: A Computer-Based Reader-Response Study." *Reader* 28 (Fall 1992): 52–68.

Studies marginalized students' interpretations of Hemingway's "The End of Something," through computer network responses and collaboration.

726. Robbins, Bruce, ed. *The Phantom Public Sphere*. Cultural Politics, vol. 5, edited by the Social Text Collective. Minneapolis, MN: University of Minnesota Press, 1993. 310 pages

The essays question the notion of public sphere in the context of new communications technology.
Essayists: Andersen, Robin; Appadurai, Arjun; Aronowitz, Stanley; Berlant, Lauren; Carpignano, Paolo; DiFaxio, William; Fraser, Nancy; Jameson, Fredric; Keenan, Thomas; Polan, Dana; Robbins, Bruce; Ross, Andrew; Warner, Michael; Yúdice, George; Zerillo, Linda.

727. Rodrigues, Dawn. "Pedagogy in the Networked Writing Class: The Importance of Local Knowledge." *Dialogue* 1 (Fall 1993): 44–64.

Argues that students primarily interacting with each other online has become the dominant approach in networked writing classrooms and inadvertently suppresses other pedagogies; describes an alternative network pedagogy.

728. Romano, Susan. "The Egalitarian Narrative: Whose Story? Which Yardstick?" *C&C* 10 (August 1993): 5–28.

Questions whether networked classrooms can be called egalitarian. Looks at her networked, decentered, collaborative, student-centered classroom and points out that it does not produce quantitative evidence of positive change from her Mexican-American students' online writings.

729. Russell, Charles G. "Linguistic Virtual Reality." *ETC* 50 (Fall 1993): 155–56.

Defines virtual reality as a world accessible by technology and subject to manipulation by those who can access it.

730. Russell, Ethel. "Networking and the Developmental Classroom." *CollM* 11 (May 1993): 149–41.

Argues that a networked writing classroom establishes a sense of audience and purpose and thus facilitates writers' development.

731. Savolainen, Reija. "The Sense-Making Theory: Reviewing the Interests of a User-Centered Approach to Information Seeking and Use." *IPM* 29 (1993): 13–28.

Argues that a paradigm shift from a technology-centered to a user-centered theory includes an analysis of audience and influences designs for information processing systems.

732. Schiller, Scott S. "Multimedia Equipment for Distance Education." *M&M* 30 (November/December 1993): 36–37.

Defines distance learning programs and technologies for educators as well as students. Includes names and addresses of online and telecommunications providers.

733. Schleifer, Neal H. "The Effects of Using Computers in Writing Instruction on Writing Apprehension and Attitude toward Using Computers." *DAI* 53 (May 1993): 3880A.

Finds that gender was the only significant factor among student subjects.

734. Schramm, Robert J., and Grace E. Rich. "CAI Versus Textbook for Grammar and Punctuation Skills." *BEdF* 47 (April 1993): 48–52.

Presents research that indicates that computer-assisted instruction is an effective method for supplementing grammar and punctuation instruction in business communication classes.

735. Schwartz, Helen J. "Planning for New Majority Students." *EDUCOM* 28 (March/April 1993): 38–42.

Looks at a pilot project at Indiana University—Purdue University at Indianapolis, called the Interactive Learning Community, which lends computers with modems to students who are over 25 with job and/or family responsibilities.

736. Search, Patricia. "HyperGlyphs: Using Design and Language to Define Hypermedia Navigation." *JEdM&H* 2 (1993): 369–80.

Discusses criteria for hypermedia interfaces; illustrates how graphic design and language help users become active participants in the navigation process.

737. Search, Patricia. "Hyperglyphs: Using Design and Language to Define Hypermedia Navigation." *TC* 40 (August 1993): 414–21.

Describes an experiment designed to identify the best structural and user-navigation methods of hypermedia.

738. Shapiro, Elayne June. "Productivity, Satisfaction, Leadership and Interaction: A Comparison of Two Communication Networks in a Software Development Team Context, A Communication Perspective on Chief Programmer and Egoless Programming Teams." *DAI* 54 (October 1993): 1150A.

Looks at 18 teams of four programmers each divided into two groups, one with centralized communication network, the other decentralized; finds no significant performance differences.

739. Slatin, John M. "*Hypercard* and the Extension of Writing." *C&C* 10 (November 1993): 109–16.

Explains virtues and limitations of the program. Discusses the increased writing activities it brings with it.

740. Smith, William E. "Computers Versus Paper in Delivering News Story Rewrite Advice." *JourEd* 48 (Spring 1993): 52–59.

Shows that computer users were more successful in writing leads, that they felt they learned more, and that men were more successful than women. Does not find any differences in the retention of learning.

741. Soloway, Elliot, Mark Guzdial, and Kenneth E. Hay. "Reading and Writing in the Twenty-First Century." *EDUCOM* 28 (January/February, 1993): 26–29.

The authors describe students' multimedia composition with *MediaText*—"a multimedia document processor that makes it relatively easy to incorporate video clips, music clips, sound clips, animations, and still images."

742. Spetalnick, Terrie. "Privacy in the Electronic Community." *EDUCOM* 28 (May/June 1993): 38–40.

Discusses privacy issues in the electronic community; highlights digital information versus print products.

743. Stager, Susan. "Individual Rights Versus Institutional Responsibilities." *EDUCOM* 28 (May/June 1993): 41–44.

Discusses the rights of individuals versus institutional responsibilities as addressed in *The Bill of Rights and Responsibilities for Electronic Learners*.

744. Stefater, Sharon Gardner. "A Study of the Revision Strategies Employed by High School Students Using Word Processing in a Process-Oriented Writing Class." *DAI* 53 (May 1993): 3885A.

Concludes that teachers must develop specific teaching strategies if students are to use word processors correctly.

745. St. Pierre, Keith Alan. "The Effect of Computer-Assisted and Traditional Instruction on Ninth-Grade English Composition and Academic Self-Concept." *DAI* 53 (February 1993): 2671A.

Argues that the effects of computer-assisted instruction on writing achievement, general academic self-concept in English, composition, and word processing are insignificant.

746. Street, Brian V., ed. *Cross-Cultural Approaches to Literacy*. New York: Cambridge University Press, 1993. 321 pages

The 12 essays give accounts of literacy practices in different cultures. They examine teenagers' expressive writing, their spontaneous collaborative writing, and the uses of literacy in everyday lives of Hmong refugees in Philadelphia.
Essayists: Baynham, Mike; Besnier, Niko; Bledsoe, Caroline H.; Bloch, Maurice; Camitta, Miriam; Kulick, Don; Lewis, I. M.; Probst, Peter; Reder, Stephen; Robey, Kenneth M.; Rockhill, Kathleen; Shuman, Amy; Stroud, Christopher; Weinstein-Shr, Gail; Wikelund, Karen Reed.

747. Streibel, Michael J. "Queries about Computer Education and Situated Critical Pedagogy." *EdTech* 33 (March 1993): 22–26.

Examines theories and practices of current computer-assisted composition pedagogies.

748. Sullivan, Peggy. "Computer-Aided Publishing: Focusing on Documents." *C&C* 10 (November 1993): 135–50.

Classifies types of software programs used to produce written documents and defines terms used for computer-created documents. Includes an appendix of design and publishing resources.

749. Sundermeier, Michael, and Bob Whipple. *Beginning the Computer Community: Establishing a Computer Writing Classroom*. Indianapolis, IN: Computers and Writing Conference, May 1992. ERIC ED 350 690. 24 pages

The authors describe their efforts to establish a writing community by establishing a computer-writing lab for composition students and faculty.

750. Susser, Bernard. "Networks and Project Work: Alternative Pedagogies for Writing with Computers." *C&C* 10 (August 1993): 63–89.

Originally presented at the Eighth Conference on Computers & Writing, the essay argues that nonnetworked classes can apply "the advantages of networked classrooms using alternative pedagogies."

751. Takayoshi, Pamela. "Women and E-mail: Issues of Gender and Technology." *ELQ* 15 (May 1993): 7–10.

Suggests that electronic mail is not as gender-neutral as it might seem.

752. Taylor, James R., and Elizabeth J. Van Every. *The Vulnerable Fortress: Bureaucratic Organization and Management in the Information Age*. Toronto: University of Toronto Press, 1993. 283 pages

Argues that traditional organizational management structures cannot deal with emerging information-economy structures; discusses implications for departmental organization.

753. Taylor, Paul. "Evaluating Software: What Thoreau Said to the Designer." *C&C* 10 (November 1993): 45–52.

Points out that good educational software adheres to a theoretical focus, user action, consistency, connectivity, flexibility, and simplicity.

754. Tomlin, Susan Santoro. "The Stigma of Illiteracy." *DAI* 53 (February 1993): 2994A.

Argues, from evidence obtained by interviews, that managing the stigma of illiteracy requires a network of family and kin using specific techniques to hide information.

755. Tsail, Daniel E. "Instantiation and Recognition Encodings: Descriptive and Constructive Computer-Aided Design Mechanisms." *DAI* 54 (September 1993): 710A.

Explores how computer-aided design affects design composition.

756. Tuman, Myron. "Campus Word Processing: Seven Design Principles for a New Academic Writing Environment." *C&C* 10 (August 1993): 49–62.

Provides insight into creating "campus word processing" to create a true community of learners. Presents seven design principles and a four-step model.

757. Valacich, Joseph S., David Paranka, Joey F. George, and J. F. Nunamaker, Jr. "Communication Concurrency and the New Media: A New Dimension to Media Richness." *ComR* 20 (April 1993): 249–76.

The authors argue that groups using computer mediation outperform groups using verbal communication because it can support an unlimited number of parallel and distinct communication episodes.

758. Vyborney, Wende Michelle. "Computer Reasons and Human Power: Epideictic Strategies in Popularized Scientific Discourse on the Nature and Potential of Computer Technology." *DAI* 53 (December 1992): 1728A.

Examines *ethos*, metaphor, and textual organization and finds an Aristotelian epistemology in pro-computer works in contrast with a Socratic anti-computer position.

759. Walther, Joseph B. "Construction and Validation of a Quantitative Measure of Impression Development." *SCJ* 59 (Fall 1993): 27–33.

Tests interpersonal impression development in computer-mediated communication and traditional interactions. Finds a correlation with cognitive complexity.

760. Webster, Sally, and Frank W. Connolly. "Responsible Citizenship in the Electronic Community." *EDUCOM* 28 (May/June 1993): 32–35.

Discusses education values incorporated into *The Bill of Rights and Responsibilities for Electronic Learners*, especially access and control over personal information, and respect for the rights of others.

761. West, Thomas, W., and Stephen L. Daigle. "Higher Education in the Information Age: Project Delta." *EDUCOM* 28 (July/August 1993): 31–34.

Describes California State University's Project DELTA (Direct Electronic Learning Teaching Alternative). Presents the context of the project, planning steps, and lessons learned during planning.

762. Wresch, William. "The Imminence of Grading Essays by Computer—25 Years Later." *C&C* 10 (April 1993): 45–58.

Argues that three computer-graded student essay projects reveal the "traits of student writing and the traits of writing evaluators."

763. Zimmerman, Beverly. "Teaching in a College Computer Classroom: Paradox and Promise." *UEJ* 21 (1993): 42–46.

Outlines problems and successes of beginning computer-assisted writing classes and preparing teachers and students for using the computer facility.

See also 1407

2.5 ADVERTISING, PUBLIC RELATIONS, AND BUSINESS

---

764. Aldred, Gerald J., and Erik A. Thelen. "Are Textbooks Contributions to Scholarship?" *CCC* 44 (December 1993): 466–77.

Argues for the potential of textbooks to serve as sites of scholarly contributions to the field of composition.

765. Baker, Margaret Ann. "Form and Substance." *JTWC* 23 (1993): 159–70.

Discusses how a reader can be enticed to read a direct mail sales letter.

766. Beard, John D., and David L. Williams. "A Professional Profile of Business Communication Educators and Their Research Preferences." *JBC* 30 (July 1993): 269–95.

The authors present the results of an ABC survey about training, background, research interests, and methodology. They find consensus on research topics but differences over methodology.

767. Bourne, David Alan, Lois Josephs Fowler, and David H. Fowler. "Seeking Compliance: Individualizing Form Letters by Computer." *JTWC* 23 (1993): 353–70.

The authors argue that individualized form letters of medical advice improve compliance more than impersonal form letters. They point out applications to technical writers.

768. Brennan, Ian. "Moderators of the Complex Allegoric Advertising Execution-Brand Attitude Relationship." *DAI* 54 (August 1993): 598A.

Indicates that the persuasiveness of an allegoric add is moderated by a need for cognition but not by advertising message involvement.

769. Dulek, Ronald. "Models of Development: Business Schools and Business Communication." *JBC* 30 (July 1993): 315–31.

Maintains that business colleges develop horizontally or vertically. Argues that the adopted model affects how teachers teach and what sort of research is required to get tenure.

770. Goodwyn, Andrew. "News from Nowhere: Reading the Media." *EJ* 82 (September 1993): 60–65.

Argues that students need to learn critical reading at an early age in order to understand and appreciate texts at a later stage.

771. Haineault, Doris-Louise, and Jean-Yves Roy. *Unconscious for Sale: Advertising, Psychoanalysis, and the Public.* Translated by Barbara Kerslake, and Kimball Lockart. Theory and History of Literature, no. 86. Minneapolis, MN: University of Minnesota Press, 1993. 214 pages

Models a psychoanalytic interpretation of the rhetoric of advertising and its implications for subjectivity in postmodern society.

772. Harris, Norma J. "Negotiating Employment: A Microethnography of the Job Interview." *DAI* 54 (September 1993): 915A.

Studies a job interview and provides relational information on how participants use the process to discover intentions and reach decisions.

773. Hearit, Keith Michael. "Organizations, *Apologia*, and Crises of Social Legitimacy." *DAI* 53 (November 1992): 1323A.

Analyzes 11 cases of corporate *apologia* for naming strategies, values, and rhetorical tasks. Concludes that *apologia* "reaffirms faith" in society hierarchy.

774. Helmer, James. "Storytelling in the Creation and Maintenance of Organizational Tension and Stratification." *SCJ* 59 (Fall 1993): 34–44.

Argues that discourse is both the medium and the product of the power relations that characterize organizational behavior.

775. Huettman, Elizabeth. "Using Triangulation Effectively in Qualitative Research." *BABC* 56 (September 1993): 42.

Discusses the effectiveness of a qualitative study. Points out that Geoffrey A. Cross's study raises questions about collaboration and group dynamics.

776. Inguanti, Joseph John. "Postmodern Photography in America: Advertising and Politics." *DAI* 54 (July 1993): 10A.

Uses feminist, Marxist, psychoanalytic, and literary theory in identifying and defining postmodern photography through the study of human form.

777. Lowery, Tina Marie. "The Relation between Syntactic Complexity and Advertising Persuasiveness." *DAI* 53 (April 1993): 3402A.

Three experiments demonstrate the negative effects of language complexity on readers' motivation as well as their ability to process information.

778. Malaviya, Prashant. "Advertising Context Effects on Consumer Memory and Judgment: A Dual-Process Model of Elaboration." *DAI* 54 (July 1993): 249A.

Suggests that contexts differ to the extent to which they consume the limited resources available for target processing.

779. Monroe, Craig, Mark G. Borzi, and Vincent S. DiSalvo. "Managerial Strategies for Dealing with Difficult Subordinates." *SCJ* 58 (Spring 1993): 247–54.

Identifies four strategies in descending order of frequency: forcing, collaboration, minimal coping, and structural strategies.

780. Rockafello, Deborah Susan. "Practices and Opinions of Business Leaders Regarding Literacy in the Workplace." *DAI* 54 (September 1993): 741A.

Surveys 300 New Jersey business leaders to examine the extent of workplace literacy training and opinions of business leaders regarding the importance of literacy on the job.

781. Rymer, Jone. "Using Qualitative Research to Generate Theory." *BABC* 56 (September 1993): 42–44.

Discusses the effects of a qualitative study. Argues that Yates and Orliowski's study "represents a broadening of the management perspective on writing."

782. Shelby, Annette Nevin. "Organizational, Business, Management, and Corporate Communication: An Analysis of Boundaries and Relationships." *JBC* 30 (July 1993): 241–67.

Sets out a theory-based analysis of the four subject areas taught in business schools.

783. Sherblom, John C., Claire F. Sullivan, and Elizabeth C. Sherblom. "The What, the Whom, and the Hows of Survey Research." *BABC* 56 (December 1993): 58–64.

Presents five points to consider when constructing effective research surveys.

784. Spilka, Rachel. "The Value of a Flexible, Cautionary Approach to Data Gathering in Qualitative Research." *BABC* 56 (September 1993): 40–41.

Discusses the effectiveness of a qualitative study. Points out the problems of finding an appropriate data gathering technique.

785. Spinks, Nelda, and Barron Wells. "Are Preferences of Small Companies Likely to Agree with Those of Large Corporations concerning Résumés and Application Letters?" *BABC* 56 (September 1993): 28–29.

Presents the results of a study that shows that small and large companies have the same preferences in job application materials.

786. Springer, Craig Michael. "Society's Soundtrack: Musical Persuasion in Television Advertising." *DAI* 53 (December 1992): 1727A.

Develops a specialized methodology to extend rhetorical criticism to the music of television advertising. Examines Willie Nelson's song in the Environmental Defense Fund as an example.

787. Theus, Kathryn T. "Organizations and the Media Structures of Miscommunication." *MCQ* 7 (August 1993): 67–94.

Concludes that "discrepancies in communication may result not only from reporting routines but also from the organization's own ideologies governing communication."

788. Winsor, Dorothy A. "Using Qualitative Research to Generate Questions and Contextualize Writing." *BABC* 56 (September 1993): 39–40.

Discusses the effectiveness of Killingsworth and Steffens' qualitative study.

2.6 LITERATURE, FILM, AND THEATER

789. Ashurst, Edwin G., III. "A Dialogic Consideration of Folk Motifs in Popular English Drama, 1760–1860." *DAI* 54 (July 1993): 373A.

Identifies and examines rhetorical functions of folk motifs.

790. Ayres-Ricker, Brenda. "Dickens' Dissenting Women: Subversion of Domestic Ideology." *DAI* 53 (March 1993): 3219A.

Analyzes Dickens' treatment of women who operated outside Victorian patriarchal regulations; observes Dickens' questioning, however subtle, of the conventional ideology of womanhood.

791. Barton, Sabrina Bass. "Rearranging the Furniture: The Apparatus of Subjectivity in the 1950s Cinema." *DAI* 53 (February 1993): 2578A.

Emphasizes the constitution of femininity and masculinity through props, gestures, language, and space; advances a feminist rereading of 1950s movies.

792. Bender, Madge Helene. "The Rhetoric of Birth Control: 'The Love Rights of Women' in the Early Twentieth-Century Novels of Henry James and Theodore Dreiser." *DAI* 54 (October 1993): 1360A.

Analyzes the rhetorical approach of nineteenth-century physicians and social commentators. Argues that women were authorized to control sexuality, resulting in social power, autonomy, and position.

793. Berko, Lili. "Surveying the Surveilled: Video Space and Social Change." *DAI* 53 (January 1993): 2137A.

Considers the role of video in a postmodern context by applying a dialogic framework that relies on writings by Bakhtin and Foucault.

794. Bernstein, Susan Naomi. "Writing as Process and Metaphor in Selected Works of Louisa May Alcott, Margaret Fuller, Herman Melville, and Harriet Jacobs." *DAI* 54 (November 1993): 1800A.

Suggests that rhetorical purposes of mid-nineteenth-century American prose and contemporary French feminism are similar in presenting arguments for social change through unconventional stylistics.

795. Bibby, Michael. "'Where Is Vietnam?' Antiwar Poetry and the Canon." *CE* 55 (February 1993): 158–78.

Argues that the academic canon's exclusion of most Vietnam antiwar poetry is an attempt to "revise the war and the conflicts in ideology it provoked."

796. Bizup, Joseph M., and Eugene R. Kintgen. "The Cognitive Paradigm in Literary Studies." *CE* 55 (December 1993): 841–57.

Introduces attempts by Tsur, Cureton, Babuts, and Turner to apply insights from cognitive science to literary study, thereby reintroducing "the subject as an explanatory category."

797. Bowser, Maria Christina. "The Role of Suasion in *Les Liasons Dangereuses.*" *DAI* 53 (April 1993): 3545A.

Shows how the characters from *Les Liasons Dangereuses* use rhetoric in their letters as forms of suasion, including persuasion, negotiation, and manipulation.

798. Buck, R. A. "Politeness, Institutions, and Discourse Structure: A Sociolinguistic Approach to the Novels of E. M. Forster." *DAI* 54 (December 1993): 1728A.

Illuminates how readers use their knowledge of the communicative principles of conversation to make sense of the linguistic choices made by Forster's characters.

799. Charney, Leopold Joseph. "Just Beginnings: Film Studies, Close Analysis, and the Viewer's Experience." *DAI* 53 (May 1993): 3711A.

Analyzes film openings to argue for the "hermeticism" of film analysis.

800. Devenyi, Jutka. "Metonymic Variations in Drama: Fragmenting Body and Soul." *DAI* 53 (February 1993): 2606A.

Draws on Burke's, Kristeva's, and Barker's theories and observations to argue for a relationship between fragmented representations of subject and metonymic drama structure.

801. Dimendberg, Edward. "Film Noir and Urban Space." *DAI* 53 (January 1993): 2137A.

Considers film noir in relation to changes in American space after 1945; uses diverse methodologies and critical theories, including literary criticism.

802. Donlon, Jocelyn Hazelwood. "The Personal Narrative in Black and White Southern Fiction." *DAI* 54 (November 1993): 1802–3A.

Combines studies of orality and literacy with theories of folklore and narrative to determine how southern novels orchestrate 'spoken' personal narratives.

803. Doreski, C. K. *Elizabeth Bishop: The Restraints of Language*. New York: Oxford University Press, 1993. 180 pages

Analyzes how Bishop's rhetorical strategies shaped the aesthetic and thematic concerns of her poems and short stories.

804. Duffala, Joyce. "The Rittenberg/Kreitzer Theater-Based 'Active Communicating' Process and Interpersonal Communication in the Corporation: A Participatory Study." *DAI* 54 (July 1993): 2A.

Examines contemporary definitions of and perceived lack of preparation in interpersonal communication as described by corporate professionals.

805. Edwards, Steven Earl. "Three Original Plays." *DAI* 53 (February 1993): 2606A.

Explains his methodology for writing scripts with actable dialogue and playable characters.

806. Ellerby, Janet. "A Psychology of Terror." *Reader* 29 (Spring 1993): 8–13.

Explores the lack of cathartic closure in Joan Didion's *Salvador*. Cites psychological evidence of the influence of Sigmund Freud and Julia Kristeva.

807. Falk, Alice. "'It Is to the Greeks That We Turn': Greek and Women Writers." *DAI* 53 (March 1993): 3221A.

Explores how Browning, Eliot, Harrison, and Woolf used the centrality of Greek studies to overcome feminine marginality.

808. Fludernik, Monika. *The Fictions of Language and the Languages of Fictions*. New York, NY: Routledge, 1993. 552 pages

Presents a "detailed analysis of free indirect discourse as it relates to narrative theory and the crucial problematic of how speech and thought are represented in fiction."

809. Freguson, Delta. "Woman Identification as a Radical Dynamic in Women's Performance." *DAI* 53 (January 1993): 2166A.

Discusses how woman-identification has informed ritual, performance art, theater, and political action.

810. Guillory, John. *Cultural Capital: The Problem of Literary Canon Formation*. Chicago: University of Chicago Press, 1993. 408 pages

Argues that canon formation is the creation and distribution of literary culture as well as an access to literary production and consumption. Points out that educational institutions have a larger role in the distribution of cultural capital because they regulate access to literacy.

811. Hahn, Gregory. "Anti-Copyright: Eighteenth- and Twentieth-Century Arguments against Copyright." *DAI* 54 (October 1993): 1350A.

Provides a conceptual history of institutional relationships of law and literature, from common law opposition to modern and postmodern literary practice.

812. Hillenbrand, Mark Michael. "The Great Inspirers: A Mentoring Theory of Playwright Development." *DAI* 54 (November 1993): 1599A.

Examines the development of young playwrights in mentoring situations.

813. Hollis, Susan Tower, Linda Pershing, and M. Jane Young, eds. *Feminist Theory and the Study of Folklore*. Champaign: University of Illinois Press, 1993. 416 pages

The contributors cover girls' games, political cartoons, quilting, Pentecostal preachers, daily housework, Egyptian goddesses, tall tales, and birth.
Essayists: Davis-Floyd, Robbie E.; Fox, Jennifer; Goodwin, Marjorie Harness; Green, Rayna; Hollis, Susan Tower; Hughes, Linda A.; Ice, Joyce; Kodish, Debora; Lawless, Elaine J.; Mark, Vera; Miller, Elaine K.; Mitchell, Carol; Levin, Judith; Pershing, Linda; Phillips, Marilynn J.; Saltzman, Rachelle H.; Sawin, Patricia E.; Seriff, Suzanne; Shuman, Amy; Turner, Kay; Yocom, Margaret R.; Young, M. Jane.

814. Iser, Wolfgang. *The Fictive and the Imaginary: Charting Literary Anthropology*. Baltimore, MD: The Johns Hopkins University Press, June 1993. 416 pages

Looks at literature as a form of make-believe. Develops a method of literary anthropology to explore literary culture. Represents an underpinning and continuation of reader-response theory.

815. Kensur, Oscara. *Dilemmas of Enlightenment: Studies in the Rhetoric and Logic of Ideology*. Berkeley, CA: University of California Press, 1993. 268 pages

Describes how Dryden, Voltaire, and other writers of the Enlightenment co-opted the arguments of their opponents to resolve contradictory intellectual and political commitments.

816. Kim, Sung Chul. "Towards a Postmodern Theatre." *DAI* 53 (January 1993): 2166A.

Deconstructs the writings of Antonin Artaud on theater from a postmodern perspective.

817. Kipnis, Laura. *Ecstasy Unlimited: On Sex, Capital, Gender, and Aesthetics*. Minneapolis, MN: University of Minnesota Press, 1993. 308 pages

Presents essays on "popular culture, politics, aesthetics, feminism, and postmodernism" from the viewpoint of a working artist.

818. Krueger, Christine L. *The Reader's Repentance: Women Preachers, Women Writers, and Nineteenth-Century Social Discourse*. Chicago: University of Chicago Press, 1993. 350 pages

Discusses a female evangelical tradition that shaped nineteenth-century social and literary discourse.

819. Levine, George, ed. *Realism and Representation: Essays on the Problem of Realism in Relation to Science, Literature, and Culture*. Science and Literature, edited by George Levine. Madison, WI: University of Wisconsin Press, 1993. 330 pages

The essays examine whether there is a knowable reality, how it may be known, and what the implications for a variety of disciplines are.
Essayists: Beer, Gillian; Churchland, Paul; Ermarth, Elizabeth; Hayles, N. Katherine; Jordanova, Ludmilla; Levine, George; Livingston, Paisley; Miller, J. Hillis; Miller, Richard; Ritvo, Harriet; Robbins, Bruce; Rorty, Richard; Schaffer, Simon; Scholes, Robert; Sigman, Jill; van Fraassen, Bas C.

820. Love, Harold. *Scribal Publication in Seventeenth-Century England*. New York: Oxford University Press, 1993. 392 pages

Discusses why some writers and composers preferred to publish their works in handwritten form long after the advent of the printing press.

821. Ludlow, Jeannie. "Writing Monahsetah: Native American Poets (and) Writing the Body." *DAI* 54 (September 1993): 981A.

Locates, develops, and explores intersections among feminist literary criticism, Native American women's poetry, and poststructuralist theory.

822. McCredie, Wendy Jane. "Ethics and Poetics: Toward Ethical Interpretive Praxis." *DAI* 54 (October 1993): 1357A.

Concludes that literary works remind us of linguistic condition and our moral obligation to interpret and reinterpret actions. Maintains that negative dialectics provides a theoretical base to understand Lacan's psychoanlytical models of linguistic structures.

823. McDowell, Michael J. "Finding Tongues in Trees: Dialogical and Ecological Landscapes in Henry David Thoreau, Robinson Jeffers, and Leslie Marmon Silko." *DAI* 54 (July 1993): 179A.

Argues that these writers offer ecologically structured views of the landscape by incorporating into their works a dialogic interplay of voices and values.

824. McHenry, Elizabeth Ann. "Setting Terms of Inclusion: Storytelling as a Narrative Technique and Theme in the Fiction of Zora Neale Hurston, Eudora Welty, Leslie Marmon Silko and Maxine Hong Kingston." *DAI* 54 (November 1993): 1805A.

Tests the value of claims by social scientists and humanists that the stories of literary writers often function to record ethnography in the twentieth century.

825. McKerrow, Raymie E. "Visions of Society in Discourse and Art: The Failed Rhetoric of Social Realism." *ComQ* 41 (Summer 1993): 355–66.

Examines the failure of discourse and art during the 1920s and 30s social realism period; focuses on a rhetorical analysis of the discourse of social reform.

826. Meaney, Geraldine. *(Un)like Subjects: Women, Theory, and Fiction.* New York: Routledge, 1993. 288 pages

Examines the relationship between women and writing; focuses on theorists Hélène Cixous, Luce Irigaray, Julia Kristeva, and practitioners Doris Lessing, Angela Carter, and Muriel Spark.

827. Middleton, Joyce Irene. "Orality, Literacy, and Memory in Toni Morrison's *Song of Solomon.*" *CE* 55 (January 1993): 64–75.

Argues that Morrison's "intermingling" of forms (oral storytelling and modern novel) "privileges" oral memory and complicates the relationship between, and readers' assumptions about, these forms.

828. Nichols, Glen Freeman. "Textual Adaptations for Amateur Performance in Quebec: 1875–1908." *DAI* 54 (November 1993): 1600A.

Examines the adaptation of foreign works to confirm acceptable conventions of local culture.

829. Noland, Daniel W. "Textual Analysis, Agency and Joan Didion's *Salvador.*" *Reader* 29 (Spring 1993): 21–26.

Studies semantics and syntax to explore the condition of El Salvador.

830. Okur, Nilgun Anadolu. "Afrocentricity as a Generative Idea in the Study of African American Drama." *JBS* 24 (September 1993): 88–108.

Argues that Asante's notion of Afrocentricity is a more useful paradigm than Aristotle's *Poetics* when analyzing the rhetorical content of African American drama.

831. Page, Judy Lynn. "The Relative Autonomy of Reading Practices by Critical, Cultural, and Social Formations: An Ethnographic and Textual Analysis of Reentry Women Students' Interpretations of 'Educating Rita.'" *DAI* 53 (January 1993): 2137A.

Traces "relative autonomy" of discursive practices across a critical, cultural, and social formation by diverse "interpretive communities." Uses ethnography and textual analysis.

832. Papp, James R. "Parody, Cognition, Rhetorical and Social History." *DAI* 54 (October 1993): 1347A.

Proposes a three-dimensional model to reveal multiple operations of parody.

833. Pati, Mitali Raychaudhuri. "Beyond Tudor Paradigms: Politics and Language in Renaissance History." *DAI* 53 (May 1993): 3735A.

Analyzes Renaissance rhetorical strategies to explore political reality via the language act.

834. Perkins, Sally J. "The Performance of Gender: A Rhetorical Analysis of Contemporary Feminist Theatre." *DAI* 53 (February 1993): 2603A.

Argues that the rhetorical critic can illuminate the persuasive strategies in feminist theater; maintains that theater itself provides texts for a study of the contemporary feminist movement.

835. Peters, William H. *A Study of Diverse Teaching Approaches to Literature*. Louisville, KY: National Council of Teachers of English, November 1992. ERIC ED 355 544. 32 pages

Examines the effects of aesthetic, efferent, and aesthetic/efferent teaching approaches on 38 English secondary teachers' responses to literature.

836. Pickering, Barbara Ann. "The Rhetoric of Visual Images: An Analysis of Pro-Choice/Pro-Life Films." *DAI* 54 (October 1993): 1149A.

Examines seven films in the abortion debate using Burke's theory of dramatism.

837. Rushdy, Ashraf H. A. "Families of Orphans: Relation and Disrelation in Octavia Butler's *Kindred*." *CE* 55 (February 1993): 135–57.

Argues that Butler's text is simultaneously a novel of memory and historical novel, and that her achievement is "to make memory transformative."

838. Scholz, Anne-Marie W. "Domesticating Female Mastery: Reading Jane Austen in America, 1826–1926." *DAI* 54 (October 1993): 1432A.

Creates renewed rapport between history and literature by tracing the significance of how theories of fiction have included, rather than excluded, women authors.

839. Schweninger, Lee. "Toward an Ecofeminism." *Reader* 29 (Spring 1993): 27–31.

Discusses the message of empowerment resulting from an ecofeminist reading of Joan Didion's *Salvador*.

840. Sloniowski, Jeannette Marie. "The Cinema of Cruelty: Affective Rhetoric in the Cinema." *DAI* 54 (November 1993): 1575A.

Examines aesthetics of masochism and the grotesque as reflected in theories of Artaud and the Cinema of Cruelty.

841. Smith, Beverly Bronson. "The Ecology of Nativism in the American Theater, 1917–1929: A Semiotic Study." *DAI* 53 (February 1993): 2608A.

Uses semiotics to examine forms of nativism exhibited in 47 professionally produced plays.

842. Smith, Richard C. "Margins of the Modern: Aesthetics and Subjectivity in California Art and Poetry Movements, 1925–1975." *DAI* 54 (July 1993): 294A.

Examines the reception of European avant-garde aesthetic theories in mid-twentieth-century California.

843. Stoneley, Peter Nicholas. "Mark Twain and the Feminine Aesthetic." *DAI* 53 (January 1993): 2374A.

Conceptualizes how Twain manipulated popular ideology of femininity and designated epochs and modes of experience according to gender.

844. Thompson, Craig Bunyard. "Speaking of Identities: The Presentation of American Indian Experience." *DAI* 54 (September 1993): 935A.

Examines how beliefs in cultural identity intersect with notions of individualism, gender, and class in texts by and about Native Americans.

845. Trotter White, Ruth E. "Autoethnography and the Sense of Self in the Novels of Toni Morrison." *DAI* 54 (August 1993): 569A.

Shows that Morrison has ordered components which must be embraced by an oppressed people in order to achieve an evolved sense of self.

846. Vallin, Marlene Boyd. *Mark Twain: Protagonist for the Popular Culture*. Westport, CT: Greenwood Press, 1992. 308 pages

Treats Mark Twain as a public speaker, analyzing his rhetoric, lectures, and occasional speeches and discussing his impact on listeners.

847. Veeser, Harold, ed. *The New Historicism Reader*. New York, NY: Routledge, 1993. 288 pages

Attempts to "offer everything required to know, teach, and practice New Historicism." The contributors discuss Renaissance and Reagan studies, American realism, English romanticism, gender studies, and feminism.

848. von Gunden, Thomas James. "Snaring the Spectator: Narration, Sexual Difference, Film Noir." *DAI* 54 (November 1993): 1575A.

Analyzes how Hollywood's representations of sexual differences contribute to gendered narrative thematics, subject address, and spectator response.

849. Walsh, Jane M. "Myth and Imagination in the American Story: The Coronado Expedition, 1540–1542." *DAI* 54 (August 1993): 576A.

Demonstrates the manner in which myth and literature function as organizing structures for historical events.

850. Waxman, Barbara. "The Catholic Church in a World of Masculine Violence: A Postmodern Feminist Response." *Reader* 29 (Spring 1993): 32–37.

Examines the role of the Catholic Church in connection with the relationship of women and the masculine military.

851. White, Craig H. "Sphere of Influence, Star of Empire: American Renaissance Cosmos." *DAI* 53 (March 1993): 3228A.

Presents a rhetorical history of the antebellum culture's "separate spheres," reinterpreted through women-authored texts, the history of science, and manifest destiny.

852. Williams, Roland L. "Sweet Music: A Sounding of American Narratives." *DAI* 54 (December 1993): 2208A.

Establishes a relationship between slave narratives and white autobiography of the eighteenth century.

853. Witayasakpan, Jiraporn. "Nationalism and the Transformation of Aesthetic Concepts: Theater in Thailand during the Phibun Period." *DAI* 53 (January 1993): 2167A.

Examines the use of laws, guidelines, and government directions to change aesthetics, ethics, manners, and behavior of Thai people.

854. Zaczek, Barbara Maria. "The Letter: A Female Territory under Male Auspices?" *DAI* 53 (April 1993): 3521A.

Relates epistolary writing to Foucault's notion of discipline. Discusses how female correspondents use the transgressive potential of a letter to defy and challenge the law of decorum.

855. Zamora, Bobbie Jean. "The Connecting Moment: Virginia Woolf, the Reader, and the Act of Reading." *DAI* 53 (March 1993): 3211A.

Demonstrates that Woolf saw reader and writer as jointly altering ways texts may be read.

2.7 READING

856. Baker, Isabel, and Patricia Mulcahy-Ernt. *Expressive Writing Events to Improve Reading*

Comprehension and Abstract Thinking of Nonproficient College Learners. San Antonio, TX: Annual Meeting of the National Reading Conference, December 1992. ERIC ED 353 585. 19 pages

Reports on an experimental study of 90 students at a suburban community college which found that the opportunities to respond in expressive writing enhanced reading comprehension.

857. Calinescu, Matei. *Rereading.* New Haven, CT: Yale University Press, February 1993. 336 pages

Describes dynamics of rereading and explores the sometimes complementary, sometimes conflicting relationships between reading and rereading.

858. Casteles, Anne, and Max Coltheart. "Varieties of Developmental Dyslexia." *Cognition* 47 (May 1993): 149–80.

The authors use data from a large-scale study of reading patterns; they discover distinct varieties of developmental dyslexia.

859. Chovan, William L., and Kristina Roberts. "Deaf Students' Self-Appraisals, Achievement Outcomes, and Teachers' Inferences about Social-Emotional Adjustment in Academic Settings." *PMS* 77 (December 1993, Part I): 1021–22.

Finds a positive but small correlation between reading achievement and self-concept for 35 deaf students age nine to 19.

860. Coltheart, Max, Brent Curtis, Paul Atkins, and Michael Haller. "Models of Reading Aloud: Dual-Route and Parallel-Distributed-Processing Approaches." *PsyR* 100 (October 1993): 589–608.

The authors defend the position that skilled reading uses lexical and nonlexical routes from print to speech. They argue that the dual-route model explains six basic facts about reading.

861. Daneman, Meredyth, and Murray Stainton. "The Generation Effect in Reading and Proofreading: Is It Easier or Harder to Detect Errors in One's Own Writing." *R&W* 5 (September 1993): 297–313.

Questions the effect of text familiarity on proofreading. Uses text generation and proofreading task.

862. Darden, Ellen C. "Adult New Readers: The Impact on Family." *DAI* 54 (September 1993): 1107A.

Explores changes that occurred in marital, child, and family relationships when an adult becomes literate.

863. Davidson, J. "Bakhtin as a Theory of Reading." Center for the Study of Reading, Urbana, IL, 1993. ERIC ED 359 502. 24 pages

Shows how Bakhtin's "Discourse in the Novel" and "The Problem with Speech Genres" demonstrate his theories of language, representation, and interpretation. Compares Bakhtin's theories with reader-response criticism; concludes with ways for reformulating reading theory.

864. Dickstein, Morris. "Damaged Literacy: The Decay of Reading." *Profession* 93 (1993): 34–40.

Argues that the widening gap between common readers and academic critics is marked by the reader's passive acceptance and the critic's active interrogation of the text.

865. Dreher, Mariam Jean, and Rachel F. Brown. "Planning Prompts and Indexed Terms in Textbook Search Tasks." *JEdPsy* 85 (December 1993): 662–69.

The authors investigate text search as a type of strategic reading. They point out that planning prompts and presence of indexed terms increased search performance. They suggest further research for context and evaluation.

866. Forbes, Cherly Ann. "Toward a Model of Reading Writing as Oral Discourse." *DAI* 53 (January 1993): 2347A.

Presents a model of reading that points to a written discourse that is interactive as oral discourse.

867. Franan, Jacqueline. *Mapping: Organizing News Stories for Improved Readability. Does It Work?* Montreal, Quebec, Canada: Association for Education in Journalism and Mass Communication, August 1992. ERIC ED 349 545. 33 pages

Investigates college students' reactions to a news story written in traditional "inverted pyramid" format and the same story rearranged into "mapped" format.

868. Frazier, Diedra W. "Transfer of College Developmental Reading Students' Textmarking Strategies." *JRB* 25 (March 1993): 17–41.

Discusses a case study of four students who were taught textbook-annotating and who were asked to mark their biology books. Finds that they did not transfer the technique to other content courses.

869. Friedland, Ellen Susan. "The Effect of Context Instruction on the Vocabulary Acquisition of College Students." *DAI* 53 (May 1993): 3857A.

Examines the effects of two types of context instruction on the ability of developmental college readers to determine word meaning from context.

870. Gaffney, J. S. "Reading Recovery: Widening the Scope of Prevention for the Lowest Achieving Readers." Urbana, IL, Center for the Study of Reading, 1993. ERIC ED 360 624. 20 pages

Describes how reading recovery increases the possibility of literacy success, especially in the context of the regular/special education initiative. Presents implications for reorganizing school and teacher education programs.

871. Ginsberg, Michael. "The Things They Carry: Multiple Contexts in the Responses of Adolescents to Literature." *DAI* 54 (October 1993): 1301A.

Examines relationships between reading and psychological constructs of possible selves. Uses transcripts from a reading group.

872. Goetz, Ernest T., Mark Sadoski, Zhaleh Fatemi, and Rebecca Bush. *Readers' Responses to Brief News Articles.* Louisville, KY: National Council of Teachers of English, November 1992. ERIC ED 355 486. 16 pages

Extends an investigation of readers' imaginative processes (spontaneous imagery and emotional response) to newspaper articles.

873. Hall, Richard H., and Rose Blair. "Knowledge Maps and Spatial-Verbal Processing: A Temporal Analysis." *PMS* 77 (October 1993): 611–21.

The authors discuss recall testing using spatial text displays (knowledge maps) and traditional texts. They detect a high correlation of main idea/detail in map group on recall.

874. Hartman, Douglas K. "Intertextuality and Reading: The Text, the Reader, the Author, and the Context." *L&E* 4 (1992): 295–311.

Examines the influence that postmodern theories of intertextuality and intertextually informed research have had on notions of text, reader, author, and context.

875. Husebye-Hartman, Elizabeth Anne. "Causal Elaborative Inferences in Text Comprehension: Implications for Psychology and Reading." *DAI* 53 (May 1993): 3849A.

Demonstrates that causal structure determines whether readers make specific forward inferences.

876. Johnson, Dianne Kaye. "The Relationship of Reading, Attitudes and Learning Strategies to Writing in College Freshmen." *DAI* 53 (May 1993): 3815A.

Examines factors that contribute to reading ability, reading attitudes, learning strategies, and writing ability of first-year composition students. Includes demographic data.

877. Kline, Rebecca Rylander. "The Social Practice of Literacy in a Program of Study Abroad." *DAI* 54 (November 1993): 1785A.

Depicts reading behaviors of eight under-graduate participants in a junior-year-abroad program in France.

878. Lehr, Fran, and Jean Osborn, eds. *Reading, Language, and Literacy Instruction for the Twenty-First Century.* Hillsdale, NJ: Lawrence Erlbaum, 1993. 312 pages

Demonstrates how research on important issues relative to textbook design can advance our knowledge about what makes textbooks effective learning tools. This can inform policy makers, publishers, and those involved in textbook selection. *Essayists:*Adams, M. J.; Anderson, R. C.; Copeland, K.; Gaskins, J. W.; Greaney, V.; Grundin, H. U.; Harris, V. J.; Hiebert, E. H.; Kerr, B. M.; Mason, J. M.; Meyer, L. A.; Nagy, W. L.; O'Flahavan, J.; Osborn, J.; Pearson, P. D.; Pinnell, G. S.; Ridley, J. T.; Scott, J. A.; Squire, J. R.; Stahl, S. A.; Stallman, K. A.; Stephens, D.; Trabasso, T. R.; Wardrop, J. L.; Williams, J. P.; Winsor, P.

879. Lemke, J. L. "Intertextuality and Educational Research." *L&E* 4 (1992): 257–67.

Describes patterns of intertextuality and offers examples that illuminate the semantic bases of these patterns.

880. Long, Debra L., and Jonathan M. Golding. "Superordinate Goal Inferences: Are They Automatically Generated during Comprehension?" *DPr* 16 (January/June 1993): 55–73.

The authors maintain that superordinate goals (major causal relations) in a text are more likely to be generated in comprehension tasks than subordinate goals.

881. Lorch, Robert F., Jr. "Integration of Topic and Subordinate Information during Reading." *JEPL* 19 (September 1993): 1071–81.

Interprets the results of four experiments as demonstrating that readers integrate subordinate information with relevant topics as well as with immediate local context.

882. Lorch, Robert F., Jr., Elizabeth Pugzles Lorch, and Madeline A. Klusewitz. "College Students' Conditional Knowledge about Reading." *JEdPsy* 85 (June 1993): 239–52.

A study on strategic reading identified 10 categories representing a typology of reading situations. The authors point out that further research should investigate additional reading situations and individual differences.

883. Lowe, Kaye. "Reading: A Perspective on Life." *DAI* 54 (October 1993): 1199A.

Suggests that through a holistic perspective including participants' stories, experiences and understandings, we can better understand contexts in which reading failure and success occur; Argues that curriculum and pedagogy should encompass beliefs and understandings of learners.

884. Mahony, Diana Louise. "The Role of Sensitivity to Word Structure in the Development of Reading Skill." *DAI* 54 (August 1993): 1123B.

Finds that deficiencies in syntactic category knowledge are associated with reading failure. Points out that they persist into adulthood.

885. Meyer, Bonnie J. F., Michael Marsiske, and Sherry L. Willis. "Text Processing Variables Predict the Readability of Everyday Documents Read by Older Adults." *RRQ* 28 (July–September 1993): 235–49.

The authors present a model for predicting how well older adults (52–93) can read nonnarrative and nonexpository texts.

886. Mills, Carol Bergfeld, Virginia A. Diehl, Deborah P. Birkmire, and Lien-chong Mou. "Procedural Text: Predictions of Importance Ratings and Recall by Models of Reading Comprehension." *DPr* 16 (July/September 1993): 279–315.

Tests referential and causal models and emphasizes relations between outcomes. Points out that neither model accurately predicted recall of procedural discourse.

887. Moravcsik, Julia E., and Walter Kintsch. "Writing Quality, Reading Skills, and Domain Knowledge as Factors in Text Comprehension." *CJEP* (June 1993): 360–74.

Investigates three passages to determine the relationship of writing quality, reading skills, domain knowledge, and comprehension.

888. Napoli, Anthony R., and George J. Hiltner III. "An Evaluation of Developmental Reading Instruction." *JDEd* 17 (Fall 1993): 14–28.

The authors suggest research paradigms which represent a viable evaluation alternative when randomized grouping is not practical.

889. Newton, Evangeline Vlanton. "University Students as Readers of Literature within a Response-Centered Composition Classroom." *DAI* 53 (February 1993): 2667A.

Observes how two first-year college students interacted with literary texts in a reader-centered classroom where the pedagogy reflected current sociopsycholinguistic theories of reading.

890. Pritchard, Ruie Jane. "Developing Writing Prompts for Reading Response and Analysis." *EJ* 82 (March 1993): 24–32.

Proposes that writing before, during, and after reading improves response skills and protects readers from interpreting texts solely based on emotions or abstract elements.

891. Quinn, Kathleen Benson. "The Effect of Dialogue Journals and Cooperative Learning Groups on Underprepared College Students' Reading Comprehension and Course Attitudes." *DAI* 54 (August 1993): 472A.

Compares dialogue journals and study groups as student-centered approaches to reading with traditional teacher-directed approaches.

892. Rankin, Joan L. "Information-Processing Differences of College-Age Readers Differ-

ing in Reading Comprehension and Speed." *JRB* 25 (September): 261–78.

Finds that good comprehenders excel poor ones when tested for information-processing performance. Contends that differences in working memory may be a cause.

893. Schraw, Gregory, Suzanne E. Wade, and Carol Anne M. Kardash. "Interactive Effects of Text-Based and Task-Based Importance on Learning from Text." *JEdPsy* 85 (December 1993): 652–61.

Three experiments show higher recall with high task-based importance, although both impose strong constraints on prose learning. They found that reading from a perspective increases recall.

894. Short, Kathy G. "Researching Intertextuality within Collaborative Classroom Learning Environments." *L&E* 4 (1992): 313–33.

Presents a study of generative characteristics in literature circles. Calls for an intertextual research of classroom learning environments.

895. Shuman, R. Baird. "The Past as Present: Reader Response and Literary Study." *EJ* 82 (September 1993): 30–32.

Argues that education has to be seen in global terms. Points out that students need to be introduced to multiculturalism.

896. Stavros, Annette M. "Structuring Literacy Instruction: A Study of the Effects of IBM's Writing to Read Program on Teacher Attitudes and Behaviors." *DAI* 54 (August 1993): 504A.

Studies the effects of a highly structured literacy program on teacher attitudes toward literacy instruction.

897. Stephens, Diane, J. Gaffney, J. Weinzierl, J. Shelton, and C. Clark. "Toward Understanding Teacher Change." Center for the Study of Reading, Urbana, IL, 1993. ERIC ED 361 667. 24 pages

Analyzes classroom practices and beliefs of four teachers trained on the methods of Reading Recovery over a two year period. Concludes that the practices are influenced by social contexts. Recommends that educators redefine pre-service and in-service training.

898. Suh, Soyoung, and Tom Trabasso. "Inferences during Reading: Converging Evidence from Discourse Analysis, Talk-Aloud Protocols, and Recognition Priming." *JMemL* 43 (June 1993): 279–300.

The authors investigate the circumstances under which good inferences occur while reading narratives.

899. Swaan, Rolf A., and Herre van Oostendorp. "Do Readers Construct Spatial Representations in Naturalistic Story Comprehension?" *DPr* 16 (January/June 1993): 125–43.

The authors argue that readers do not normally construct detailed spatial representations implicit in a text unless they receive instructions to do so.

900. Symons, Sonya, and Michael Pressley. "Prior Knowledge Affects Text Search Success and Extraction of Information." *RRQ* 28 (July-September 1993): 250–61.

The authors argue that search efficiency of undergraduates in a full-year introductory psychology course varied based on their prior knowledge of textbooks.

901. Trabasso, Tom, and Soyoung Suh. "Understanding Text: Achieving Explanatory Coherence through On-Line Inferences and Mental Operations in Working Memory." *DPr* 16 (January/June 1993): 3–34.

The study finds that a discourse-analytic approach using think-aloud protocols can identify readers' inferences and predict where in a text readers make global inferences.

902. van den Broek, Paul, and Robert F. Lorch, Jr. "Superordinate Goal Inferences: Are They Automatically Generated during Comprehension?" *DPr* 16 (January/June 1993): 75–98.

The authors point out that readers can represent causal relations not only between events that occur close together but also between those that occur further apart.

903. Vine, Harold A., Jr., and Mark A. Faust. "Situating Readers-Part Five: What Disempowers Meaning-Making?" *EJ* 82 (March 1993): 33–36.

The authors discuss abstracting a theme statement as a disempowering practice for students. They conclude that readers need to explore thematic concerns and questions to understand a particular situation.

904. Vine, Harold A., Jr., and Mark A. Faust. "Situating Readers-Part Six: What Empowers Meaning-Making?" *EJ* 82 (April 1993): 75–78.

The authors maintain that empowered readers try to understand a situation, focus on their concerns, and be aware of the self and the other.

905. Wade, Suzanne, Gregory Schraw, William M. Buxton, and Michael T. Hayes. "Seduction of the Strategic Reader: Effects of Interest on Strategies and Recall." *RRQ* 28 (April–June 1993): 92–114.

The authors found that college students acted strategically except when they encountered seductive details (interesting but not important information) to which they gave a great deal of time.

906. Walczyk, Jeffrey J. "Are General Resource Notions Still Viable in Reading Research?" *JEdPsy* 85 (March 1993): 127–35.

Uses two experiments to assess subcomponent processes (i.e., word recognition, semantics) against reading rate. Proposes that readers who control rate compensate for inefficiencies and make high-level inferences.

907. Weber, Rose-Marie. "Even in the Midst of Work: Reading among Turn-of-the-Century Farmers' Wives." *RRQ* 28 (October-December 1993): 292–302.

Examines the role of reading in the lives of farm women by analyzing the content of extension bulletins sent to the women.

908. Wenger, Michael J., and Jan H. Spyridakis. "Reduced Text Structure at Two Text Levels: Impacts on the Performance of Technical Readers" *JTWC* 23 (1993): 333–52.

Studies textual coherence at the word and paragraph level. Discusses the implications for information design.

909. West, Richard, Keith E. Stanovich, and Harold R. Mitchell. "Reading in the Real World and Its Correlates." *RRQ* 28 (January–March 1993): 34–50.

Readers and nonreaders in airports showed that individuals high in print exposure displayed more extensive vocabularies and cultural knowledge than did individuals with low exposure.

910. Willows, Dale M., Richard S. Kruk, and Evelyne Corcos, eds. *Visual Processes in Reading and Reading Disabilities*. Hillsdale, NJ: Lawrence Erlbaum, 1993. 476 pages

The articles bring together a broad range of evidence that concerns the role of visual information in reading and reading disabilities.
Essayists: Aaron, P. G.; Beale, I. L.; Breitmeyer, B. G.; Corballis, M. C.; Corcos, E.; Evans, H. M.; Feldman, L. B; Forsberg, H.; Garzia, R. P.; Guillemard, J. C.; Humphreys, G. W.; Kennedy, A.; Kruk, R. S.; Lehmkuhle, S.; Massaro, D. W.; Olson, R. K.; Pollatsek, A.; Rayner, K.; Riddoch, M. J.; Sanocki, T.; Seymour, P. H. K.; Stanovich, K. E.; Stein, J. F.; Terepocki, M.; Venezky, R. L.; Watson, C.; Wilkins, A.; Williams, M. C.; Willows, D. M.

911. Winsor, P., W. E. Nagy, J. Osborn, and J. O'Flahaven. "Structural Analysis: Toward an Evaluation of Instruction." Urbana, IL, Center for the Study of Reading, 1993. ERIC ED 360 625. 30 pages

The authors evaluate structural analysis instruction and practice drills in teachers' manuals and student workbooks. They identify systematic deficiencies and recommend emphasizing the strategic use of word parts within contexts.

912. Wolfe, Donald Eugene. "A Connectionist Model of Letter and Word Recognition." *DAI* 54 (August 1993): 949B.

Describes a new computational model of human reading processes. Bases his argument on the assumption that letter recognition is not necessarily hierarchically related to word recognition.

2.8 LINGUISTICS, GRAMMATICAL THEORY, AND SEMANTICS

913. Adamson, H. D. "Social and Processing Constraints on Relative Clauses." *AS* 67 (Summer 1992): 123–33.

Examines the "frequency of relative clauses in the speech of two social classes" and discusses zero relatives in children's speech.

914. Bailey, Guy, and Margie Dyer. "An Approach to Sampling Dialectology." *AS* 67 (Spring 1992): 3–20.

The authors offer a random-sample telephone survey as a practical, efficient, and reliable research method for linguistic studies.

915. Barber, Charles. *The English Language: A Historical Introduction*. New York: Cambridge University Press, 1993. 299 pages

Provides an account of the development of the English language in its sounds, vocabulary, and grammar. Emphasizes the diversity of sources and its present character as a world language.

916. Berthoff, Ann E. "The Semiotics of Narrative [response to Egan, *L&E* 5 (1993)]." *L&E* 5 (1993): 175–79.

Criticizes Egan's argument as "radically flawed" and as a diversion from the argument of *Romantic Understanding*. Examines Egan's concepts of narrative, binary opposition, and abstraction.

917. Botha, Rudolf. *Twentieth-Century Connections of Language*. Cambridge, MA: Blackwell Publishers, 1993. 364 pages

Analyzes twentieth-century language; focuses on theorists such as Bloomfield, Chomsky, Dummett, Fodor, Katz, Labov, Popper, Quine, Sapir, Saussure, Skinner, and Wittgenstein. Discusses the influences of language on metaphysics.

918. Bourdieu, Pierre. *Language and Symbolic Power*. Translated by Gino Raymond and Matthew Adamson. Cambridge, MA: Harvard University Press, 1993. 302 pages

Maintains that when individuals use language in particular ways, they deploy their accumulated linguistic resources and implicitly adapt their words to the demands of the social field or market that is their audience.

919. Brent, Doug. "What a Composition Teacher Needs to Know about General Semantics." *CompC* 5 (January 1993): 4–6.

Describes the influence of General Semantics on composition instruction; argues that it conflicts with contemporary rhetorical theory. Offers critical thinking exercises.

920. Bromberger, Sylvain. *On What We Know We Don't Know: Explanation, Theory, Linguistics, and How Questions Shape Them*. Center for the Study of Language and Information. Chicago: University of Chicago Press and Center for the Study of Language and Information, 1993. 232 pages

Presents nine essays on the role that questions play in shaping how we investigate the world. The contributors discuss the limitations of our ability to conceive, formulate, connect, and assess questions and answers.

921. Brown, Becky. "The Social Consequences of Writing Louisiana French." *LSoc* 22 (March 1993): 67–101.

Finds that social change is bringing about the creation of code (written Louisiana French), which in turn is bringing about language maintenance.

922. Caldas, Stepen J., and Suzanne Caron-Caldas. "Rearing Bilingual Children in a Monolingual Culture: A Louisiana Experience." *AS* 67 (Fall 1992): 290–96.

The authors chronicle their experiences in raising their children bilingually in a monolingual culture.

923. Cannon, Garland. "Malay(sian) Borrowings in English." *AS* 67 (Summer 1992): 134–62.

Presents results of research on borrowings in English. Includes two appendices offering primary and secondary Malay borrowings.

924. Chen, Rong. *Ambiguity Can Be Pragmatic, and a Good Thing, Too*. Urbana, IL: Conference on Pragmatics and Language Learning, April 1992. ERIC ED 351 699. 16 pages

Argues that ambiguity in speech can be deliberate as well as unintended. Points out that ambiguities invoke words or phrases with both literal and idiomatic meaning. Maintains that a listener may acknowledge either meaning depending on her own communicative goal.

925. Clark, Herbert H. *Arenas of Language Use*. Center for the Study of Language and Information. Chicago: University of Chicago Press and Center for the Study of Language and Information, 1993. 430 pages

Argues that a common ground must exist for people to understand one another. Shows how people infer this common ground from past conversations, immediate surroundings, and shared cultural backgrounds.

926. Corson, David J. "Discursive Bias and Ideology in the Administration of Minority Group Interests." *LSoc* 22 (June 1993): 165-91.

Finds that injustices and distorted communication easily arose in administrative meetings when the interests of a culturally different group were not represented.

927. Coulmas, Florian. *Language and Economy*. Cambridge, MA: Blackwell Publishers, 1993. 392 pages

Uses socio-linguistic settings to explore the relationship between economic forces and linguistic development. Discusses how the economy impacts language and examines how language influences economic equality.

928. Crismore, Avon, Raija Markkanen, and Margaret S. Steffensen. "Metadiscourse in Persuasive Writing." *WC* 10 (January 1993): 39-71.

The authors study the effects of culture and gender on the use of textual and interpersonal discourse markers in 40 essays by Finnish and American university students.

929. Cuestos, Fernando. "Writing Processes in a Shallow Orthography." *R&W* 5 (March 1993): 17-28.

Discusses two experiments performed to determine if spelling models for languages with a deep orthography are similar to those with a shallow orthography.

930. Davis, Lawrence, and Charles L. Houck. "Can She Be Prestigious and Nice at the Same Time? Perceptions of Female Speech in Hoosierdom." *AS* 67 (Summer 1992): 115-22.

The authors analyze the responses of male and female participants from east-central Indiana and rank Northern and Southern dialects according to socioeconomic status and personality traits.

931. Davis, Lawrence, and Charles L. Houck. "Is There a Midland Dialect Area?—Again." *AS* 67 (Spring 1992): 61-70.

The authors dispute Midland as a separate dialect area and find it instead to be a "large linear transition area" located between Northern and Southern dialect areas.

932. Ding, Ersu. "Meaning and Power: A Study in the Marxist Theory of Language." *DAI* 53 (April 1993): 3507A.

Argues that Marxist theory presupposes an omnipotent subject but emphasizes inequality in and behind speech acts due to an uneven distribution of productive means and products of labor.

933. Drake, H. L. *Teaching Critical Thinking by Way of General Semantics*. Rohnert Park, CA: Conference on Critical Thinking & Educational Reform, August 1992. ERIC ED 350 630. 13 pages

Compares Alfred Korzybski's and Richard Paul's theories of critical thinking. Advocates using general semantics as a tool for teaching critical thinking through observing, evaluating, and arriving at informed, fair judgments.

934. Erneling, Christina E. *Understanding Language Acquisition: The Framework of Learning*. Albany, NY: State University of New York Press, 1993. 256 pages

Draws on the work of Austrian philosopher Ludwig Wittgenstein to develop an alternative to the theories of language acquisition by the linguist Jerry Fodor.

935. Fairclough, Norman. "Intertextuality in Critical Discourse Analysis." *L&E* 4 (1992): 269-93.

Explores the concept of "intertextuality" and demonstrates its usefulness for discourse analysis.

936. Farr, Marcia. "Essayist Literacy and Other Verbal Performances." *WC* 10 (January 1993): 4-38.

Compares academic discourse to performance styles of two Mexican immigrants speaking at community meetings. Suggests viewing nonmainstream discourses as correctives and perspectives on academic literacy.

937. Ferreira, Fernanda. "Creation of Prosody during Sentence Production." *PsyR* 100 (April 1993): 233–53.

Argues for a model of prosody that addresses the relationship of pauses in sentence production and syntax.

938. Fishelov, David. "Poetic and Nonpoetic Simile: Structure, Semantics, and Rhetoric." *PoT* 14 (1993): 1–23.

Models formal, structural, and semantic rules for producing and receiving nonpoetic similes; concludes that poetic similes are defined by a cluster of deviations from these rules.

939. Fludernik, Monika. "Narratology in Context." *PoT* 14 (1993): 729–61.

Reviews six recent books by applying pragmatics to literary texts; concludes that pragmatics supplements conventional narratology by explaining how texts are framed generically, diachronically, and empirically.

940. Foorman, B. R., and J. Lieber. "The Eternal Context: Affective and Cognitive Egocentricity [response to Egan, *L&E* 5 (1993)]." *L&E* 5 (1993): 165–74.

Contrasts Egan's affective scripts with Piaget's cognitive egocentricity. Argues that children's narratives, proper at one developmental stage, will seem stunted at later developmental stages.

941. Ford, Cecilia E. *Grammar in Interaction: Adverbial Clauses in American English Conversation.* New York: Cambridge University Press, 1993. 165 pages

Analyzes the use of temporal, conditional, and causal clauses in American conversation. Distinguishes between different functions in initial and final positions.

942. Gardner, Howard. "From Conflict to Clarification: A Comment on Egan's 'Narrative and Learning: A Voyage of Implication' [response to Egan, *L&E* 5 (1993)]." *L&E* 5 (1993): 181–85.

Though wary of endorsing any one mode of learning, Gardner salutes Egan's argument and recommends her theory of development.

943. "1992 George Orwell Award Nominees." *QRD* 19 (January 1993): 7–10.

Provides author, title, and publication information for the 19 nominees, briefly summarizing each book to give reasons behind the nomination.

944. Gilbert, Pam. "Narrative as Gendered Social Practice: In Search of Different Story Lines for Language Research." *L&E* 5 (1993): 211–18.

Argues that educational research should examine "power of storying" to regulate and order cultural life as well as to create different cultural life. Uses gender and literacy as examples.

945. "The Gobblies at the Gate." *QRD* 19 (April 1993): 14.

Argues that language is threatened more by "mouthers of gobbledygook" then by "Attila the DJ." Urges Clinton's administration to control language, not be controlled by it.

946. Graham, Theresa, and Michelle Perry. "Indexing Transitional Knowledge." *DP* 29 (July 1993): 779–88.

The authors analyze verbal specificity of children's speech and describe a new method for indexing the point at which a child acquires new knowledge.

947. Gray, Robert R. "Monitoring and Grammatical Morpheme Accuracy in the English Compositions of Japanese University Students." *DAI* 53 (March 1993): 3193A.

Finds that form-focused writing instruction can help error-prone learners to improve grammatical production accuracy in ESL composition.

948. Gregg, Robert J. "The Survey of Vancouver English." *AS* 67 (Fall 1992): 250–67.

Presents the results of SVEN (Survey of Vancouver English), a major urban dialect survey which began in 1978, and which is regarded as an "extensive database."

949. Greville, G., Norman M. Fraser, and Scott McGlashan, eds. *Heads in Grammatical Theory*. New York: Cambridge University Press, 1993. 340 pages

The contributors discuss how various grammatical theories define a "head," the principal elements in a noun phrase. *Essayists:* Borsley, Robert D.; Cann, Ronnie; Comrie, Bernard; Corbett, Greville G.; Fraser, Norman M.; Hawkins, John A.; Hudson, Richard A.; McGlashan, Scott; Nichols, Johanna; Payne, John; Radford, Andrew; Vincent, Nigel; Zwicky, Arnold M.

950. Gundaker, Grey. "'Without Parse of Script': The Interaction of Conventional Literacy and Vernacular Practice in African American Expressive Culture." *DAI* 54 (July 1993): 226A.

Explores the interaction of scripts, graphic signs, practices, and approaches to African American narrative texts.

951. Gundel, Jeanette K., Nancy Hedberg, and Ron Zacharski. "Cognitive Status and the Form of Referring Expressions in Discourse." *Language* 69 (June 1993): 274–307.

Explains forms of reference by speakers' assumptions about addressee's knowledge and attention, using "cognitive statuses."

952. Hall, John Robert. "Linguistic Markers of Association as Persuasive Devices in Mediated Appeals." *DAI* 53 (May 1993): 3731A.

Argues that the success of mediated appeals can be partially explained by the interaction between linguistic and extra-linguistic variables.

953. Halliday, M. A. K. "Towards a Language-Based Theory of Learning." *L&E* 5 (1993): 93–116.

States that "language development is learning how to mean"; calls for learning theories based on the principle that learning language and learning through language are simultaneous.

954. Harland, Richard. *Beyond Superstructuralism*. New York, NY: Routledge, 1993. 224 pages

Maintains that the "next advance beyond post-structuralism depends on replacing word based theories with syntagm-based theories." Argues that the "effect of combining words grammatically can transform the very nature of meaning."

955. Harris, R. Allen. "Generative Semantics: Secret Handshakes, Anarchy Notes, and the Implosion of *Ethos*." *RR* 12 (Fall 1993): 125–59.

Looks at the *ethos* of a group of linguists (general semanticists) over the course of its brief history.

956. Hayakawa, Alan R. "Remembering Don Hayakawa." *ETC* 50 (Fall 1993): 131–35.

Presents a memoir by Hayakawa's son who is working on the sixth edition of *Language in Thought and Action*.

957. He, Agnes Weiyun. "Language Use in Peer Review Texts." *LSoc* 22 (September 1993): 403–20.

Delineates linguistic features of 13 texts written by students attempting to help one another revise midterm papers. Suggests that peer review constitutes a genre.

958. Hicks, Deborah. "Narrative Discourse and Classroom Learning: An Essay Response to Egan's 'Narrative and Learning: A Voyage of Implications' [*L&E* 5 (1993)]." *L&E* 5 (1993): 127–48.

Agrees with Egan's thesis that narrative has an important role in classroom learning. However, she proposes a view of narrative as a family of discourses, not a single genre, and suggests that they are a part of the social constructs from which they arise.

959. Hill, Jane H., and Judith T. Irvine, eds. *Responsibility and Evidence in Oral Discourse*. New York: Cambridge University Press, 1993. 316 pages

Twelve essays explore ways in which speakers in a range of cultures attribute responsibility for acts and states of affairs. The essayists consider different kinds of discourse, including ritual divination, giving of evidence in trials, fieldwork conversations, and junior-high-school students' narratives of fights.
Essayists: Bauman, Richard; Bendix, Edward H.; Besner, Niko; Chafe, Wallace; Du Bois, John W.; Duranti, Allesandro; Hill, Jane H.; Irvine, Judith T.; Kuipers, Joel C.; Maranhão, Tullio; Philips, Susan U.; Shuman, Amy; Zepeda, Ofelia.

960. Hinton, Geoffrey E., David C. Plaut, and Tim Shallice. "Simulating Brain Damage." *ScAm* 269 (October 1993): 76–82.

Discusses possible treatments for acquired dyslexia and language processing problems caused by head injuries through experiments using computer-simulated neurons.

961. Holloway, Joseph E., and Winifred K. Vass. *The African Heritage of American English*. Bloomington, IN: Indiana University Press, 1993. 240 pages

Discusses topics such as Bantu words in the Gullah dialect, Africanisms of Bantu origin in Black English, and Africanisms in contemporary American English.

962. Holt, Daniel, ed. *Cooperative Learning: A Response to Linguistic and Cultural Diversity*. Language in Education: Theory and Practice: ERIC Clearinghouse on Languages and Linguistics, 1993. 196 pages

The collection provides teacher trainers with a theoretical framework and practical strategies for creating successful group activities and for fostering discussions among students from diverse language backgrounds in elementary and secondary education.
Essayists: Alvarez, Mary; Chips, Barbara; Cooper, Carole; Cromwell, Carole; Gilligan, Angie; Gonzales-Greeson, Sue; Heredia-Arriga, Sue; Holt, Daniel; Kagan, Soencer; Madric, Corine; McGroarty, Mary; Spencer, Sue; Wallace, Diane.

963. Hopper, Paul, and Elizabeth Closs Traugott. *Grammaticalization*. New York: Cambridge University Press, 1993. 277 pages

The authors introduce a process by which ordinary nouns and verbs change over time to serve as grammatical elements such as auxiliaries, case markers, or sentence connectives. They use data from different languages.

964. Horning, Alice S. *The Psycholinguistics of Readable Writing: A Multidisciplinary Exploration*. Norwood, NJ: Ablex, 1993. 216 pages

Reviews research in linguistics, psychology, reading, and writing, and applies it to readable writing. Concludes that psycholinguistic redundancy and cohesion are crucial to readability.

965. Ilyashov, Anatoli Michael. "What Does Conservative Mean?" *QRD* 20 (October 1993): 9.

Analyzes the difference between "conservatives" in Russia and the United States. Argues that the media causes confusion by using the same term for "two different things."

966. Johansen, Jorgen Dines. *Dialogic Semiosis: An Essay on Signs and Meaning*. Advances in Semiotics, edited by Thomas A. Sebeok. Bloomington, IN: Indiana University Press, 1993. 357 pages

Discusses Hiemslev's linguistics and Peirce's semiotics with an emphasis on the relation between utterer and interpretant in a dialogic process. Explains Peirce's ideas of "common ground" and "universe of discourse."

967. Jubien, Michael. *Ontology, Modality, and the Fallacy of Reference*. New York: Cambridge University Press, 1993. 144 pages

Argues that proper names express special properties belonging to the things they name.

968. Justus, Carol F. "Review Article: Implications of the Evolution of Writing." *Diachronica* 10 (Spring 1993): 97–110.

Reviews Denise Schmandt-Besserat's *Before Writing, Vol. 1: From Counting to Cuneiform*.

969. Kasher, Asa, ed. *The Chomskyan Turn*. Cambridge, MA: Blackwell Publishers, 1993. 416 pages

Includes two new papers by Noam Chomsky, "Linguistics and Adjacent Fields" and "Linguistics and Cognitive Sciences." Contains articles on linguistics as semantics, pragmatics, phonology, and psychological issues brought about by Chomsky's studies.
Essayists: Bromberger, Sylvain; Chomsky, Noam; Fromkin, Victoria A.; Halle, Morris; Hornstein, Norbert; Kasher, Asa; Lappin, Shalom; Leiber, Justin; Matthews, Robert J.; May, Robert; Newmeyer, Frederick; Pylyshyn, Zenon W.; Reinhart, Tanya; Rizzi, Luigi; Rothstein, Susan, D.; Wexler, Ken.

970. Kretzschmar, William A., Jr. "Isoglosses and Predictive Modeling." *AS* 67 (Fall 1992): 227–49.

Discusses "appropriate roles for qualitative isoglosses" and qualitative methods for an analysis of linguistic features.

971. Kuiper, Koenraad. "The Oral Tradition in Auction Speech." *AS* 67 (Fall 1992): 279–89.

Examines contemporary auction speech to infer the "linguistic character of auctions in the English tradition."

972. Kuno, Susumu, and Ken-ichi Takami. *Grammar and Discourse Principles: Functional Syntax and GB Theory*. Chicago, IL: University of Chicago Press, 1993. 221 pages

Critiques recent research in government-binding theory.

973. Labov, William. *Principles of Linguistic Change*. Cambridge, MA: Blackwell Publishers, 1993. 720 pages

Examines linguistic change to identify the principles of change and to analyze the development of linguistic structures. Focuses on how changes come about and how change itself becomes essential to the linguistic system.

974. Lakoff, George. "Metaphor and War." *QRD* 19 (July 1993): 9–12.

Argues that metaphors can be "pernicious," then identifies five predominant metaphors and analyzes how they functioned in the Gulf War.

975. Leap, William L. *American Indian English*. Salt Lake City, UT: University of Utah Press, 1993. 323 pages

Examines linguistic and sociolinguistic aspects of varieties of English spoken by Navajo, Hopi, Ute, and other Native American groups. Documents the influence of ancestral languages on Indian English.

976. Lucy, John A., ed. *Reflexive Language: Reported Speech and Metapragmatics*. New York: Cambridge University Press, 1993. 424 pages

The essayists examine the ability of natural language to represent its own structure through explicit statements about use. They discuss theories of reflexiveness, analyze case studies, and discuss implications for research.
Essayists: Banfield, Ann; Briggs, Charles; Caton, Steve C.; Crapanzano, Vincent; Hanks, William F.; Hickmann, Maya;

Janowitz, Naomi; Lee, Benjamin; Lucy, John A.; Mertz, Elizabeth; Moore, Robert E.; Parmentier, Richard J.; Silverstein, Michael; Urban, Greg.

977. Malkiel, Yakov. *Etymology*. New York: Cambridge University Press, 1993. 244 pages

Examines goals, assumptions, and approaches of etymological research over the past two centuries, comparing it to an etymological study in ancient and medieval times.

978. Mao, LuMing R. "I Conclude Not: Toward a Pragmatic Account of Metadiscourse." *RR* 11 (Spring 1993): 265–89.

Shows how metadiscourse is linked to a specific rhetorical context; looks comparatively at metadiscourse in the Western and Chinese rhetorical contexts.

979. Maranda, Michael J. "Wales: A Case Study in Linguistic Nationalism." *DAI* 54 (August 1993): 693A.

Suggests that linguistic nationalism in Wales is related to preserving group identity.

980. Marcus, Gary. "Negative Evidence in Language Acquisition." *Cognition* 46 (January 1993): 53–85.

Argues that children's unlearning of grammatical errors can be explained by nature of their "internal learning mechanisms."

981. Matthews, P. H. *Grammatical Theory in the United States: From Bloomfield to Chomsky*. Cambridge Studies in Linguistics. New York: Cambridge University Press, 1993. 296 pages

Provides a history of American linguistic theory; concentrates on the ideas of Bloomfield and Chomsky.

982. McKee, John DeWitt. "I Am Crippled." *QRD* 19 (July 1993): 12–13.

Uses his own experiences with cerebral palsy to argue against politically correct terms; believes that political correctness "weakens—indeed pollutes" language.

983. McKoon, Gail, Gregory Ward, Roger Ratcliff, and Richard Sproat. "Morphosyntactic and Pragmatic Factors Affecting the Accessibility of Discourse Entities." *JMemL* 43 (February 1993): 56–75.

The results of six experiments show that a successful pronominal reference is a function of both the pragmatic and syntactic context of the prior discourse.

984. McQuillan, Gene. "You Are Here(?): Cartography, Unreliability, Erasure, Vigilance." *CEAF* 23–24 (Summer/Winter 1993–1994): 4–8.

Examines how cartographic mapping relates to linguistic mapping, focusing on a student project to "map" the distribution of power on a college campus.

985. Mey, Jacob. *An Introduction to Pragmatics*. Cambridge, MA: Blackwell Publishers, 1993. 336 pages

Provides an introduction to pragmatics by reviewing Austin, Grice, Searle, and Sacks. Explores the complexities and uses of language.

986. Miller, Linda J. "An Analysis of Language in a Series of 1987 Congressional Hearings on AIDS." *DAI* 54 (July 1993): 320A.

Focuses on "signal language" used to describe or discuss people with AIDS, and the moral, ideological, religious, and emotional metamessages underlying such language.

987. Moore, Robert C. *Logic and Representation*. Center for the Study of Language and Information, CSLI Lecture Notes, Number 39. Chicago: University of Chicago Press and Center for the Study of Language and Information, 1993. 430 pages

Applies formal logic to modeling and reasoning about knowledge and belief, including reasoning about one's own beliefs and the semantics of sentences about knowledge and belief.

988. Murray, Thomas E. "Social Structure and Phonological Variation on a Midwestern College Campus." *AS* 67 (Summer 1992): 163–174.

Shows how midwestern college students "use phonological variation as a means of associating or disassociating themselves with" certain social groups.

989. Myhill, John. *Typological Discourse Analysis*. Oxford, England: Blackwell Publishers, 1993. 240 pages

Develops a method for describing and comparing the functions of grammatical constructions in different languages.

990. Navidi, Mandana. "The Role of the Mass Media in the Iran-Contra Affair: An In-Depth Study of the Media's Language Specifically with Regards to Crisis-Reporting in the United States, Iran, and Germany (Volumes I and II)." *DAI* 53 (April 1993): 3513A.

Examines relationships between linguistic differences and ideological differences in persuasive, manipulative and impersonal journalism.

991. Nylvek, Judith A. "Is Canadian English in Saskatchewan Becoming More American?" *AS* 67 (Fall 1992): 268–78.

Examines data collected in Saskatchewan that shows that American English has influenced the pronunciation of young Canadian speakers of English.

992. Padden, Carol A. "Lessons to Be Learned from a Young Deaf Orthographer." *L&E* 5 (1993): 71–86.

Suggests that misspellings in freewritings of deaf writers, ages four to 10, are based on a different analysis of the English orthographic system.

993. Palacas, Arthur L. "Attribution Semantics: Linguistic Worlds and Point of View." *DPr* 16 (July/September 1993): 239–77.

Points out that a semantic theory requires representations of text that take account of indirect speech, deictic orientation, and the expressive, as well as informational aspects of language.

994. Pappas, Christine C. "Questioning Our Ideologies about Narrative and Learning: Response to Egan [*L&E* 5 (1993)]." *L&E* 5 (1993): 157–64.

Suggests that learning theories based on an ideology about the primacy of narrative will not help children appreciate how thought is reflected in various disciplines nor how those disciplines are realized by certain semiotic systems of linguistic genres.

995. Parker, Frank, and Kim Sydow Campbell. "Linguistics and Writing: A Reassessment." *CCC* 44 (October 1993): 295–314.

Argues that the theoretical orientation of linguistics can "inform" the practical orientation of writing research and pedagogy. Offers four examples.

996. Parks, Douglas R., and Raymond J. DeMallie. "Plains Indians' Native Literatures." *Boundary* 19 (Fall 1992): 105–47.

Offers document histories and linguistic notes on the translation, editing, and publication of Pawnee and Lakota native language texts.

997. Perdue, Clive, ed. *Adult Language Acquisition: Cross-Linguistic Perspectives, Volume 1: Field Methods*. New York: Cambridge University Press, 1993. 253 pages

The 24 contributors to this volume worked together in a European Science Foundation-sponsored project to study linguistic problems faced by adult immigrants to France, Germany, Great Britain, The Netherlands, and Sweden. The volume outlines field methods used to gather and analyze data for longitudinal case studies. *Essayists:* Allwood, Jens; Becker, Angelika; Bhardwaj, Mangat; Bremer, Katharina; Broeder, Peter; Carroll, Mary; Dietrich, Rainer; Edwards, Jane; Extra, Guus; Feldweg, Helmut; Kelly, Ann; Klein, Wolfgang; Levelt, Pim; Noyau, Colette; Perdue, Clive; Porquier, Rémi; Roerts, Celia; Simonot, Margaret; Slobin, Dan; Strömqvist, Sven; van Hout, Roeland; Vasseur, Marie-Thérèsa; Véronique, Daniel; Voionmaa, Kaarlo.

998. Perdue, Clive, ed. *Adult Language Acquisition: Cross-Linguistic Perspectives, Volume 2: The Results.* New York: Cambridge University Press, 1993. 253 pages

This volume outlines the results from a European Science Foundation-sponsored study of linguistic problems faced by adult immigrants to France, Germany, Great Britain, The Netherlands, and Sweden. *Essayists:* Allwood, Jens; Becker, Angelika; Bhardwaj, Mangat; Bremer, Katharina; Broeder, Peter; Carroll, Mary; Dietrich, Rainer; Edwards, Jane; Extra, Guus; Feldweg, Helmut; Kelly, Ann; Klein, Wolfgang; Levelt, Pim; Noyau, Colette; Perdue, Clive; Porquier, Rémi; Roerts, Celia; Simonot, Margaret; Slobin, Dan; Strömqvist, Sven; van Hout, Roeland; Vasseur, Marie-Thérèsa; Véronique, Daniel; Voionmaa, Kaarlo.

999. Scholes, Robert, ed. *Literacy and Language Analysis.* Hillsdale, NJ: Lawrence Erlbaum, 1993. 232 pages

The essayists investigate interconnections between language and literacy in terms of structures of language as well as the linguistic contexts of literacy. They maintain that claims regarding descriptions of the linguistic competence of native speakers contain phonemic, morphemic, and sentential constructs that are applicable only to literate language users. *Essayists:* Bugarski, R.; Ehri, L. C.; Karanth, P.; Meyer, P. G.; Miller, J.; Nigam, R.; Olson, D. R.; Patel, P. G.; Prakash, P.; Rekah, D.; Scholes, R. J.; Suchitra, M. G.

1000. "So Much for Free Speech." *QRD* 20 (October 1993): 4–5.

Reports on the destruction of "almost all" copies of a campus newspaper and the aftermath. Finds the free speech defense "doublethink."

1001. Starks, Donna J. "Aspects of Woods Cree Syntax." *DAI* 54 (September 1993): 992A.

Analyzes the syntax of the Algonquian language spoken at South Indian Lake, Manitoba.

1002. Stirling, Lesley. *Switch-Reference and Discourse Representation.* New York: Cambridge University Press, 1993. 354 pages

Analyzes how the sharing of a grammatical subject is indicated across clause boundaries. Refers to a wide range of world languages.

1003. Thomas, Linda. *Beginning Syntax.* Cambridge, MA: Blackwell Publishers, 1993. 192 pages

Provides a basic introduction to syntax for undergraduates.

1004. Thonus, Terese. "Anderson, Maicon, and Thyago: 'English' Names in Brazil." *AS* 67 (Summer 1992): 175–89.

Discusses and explains the influence of "English on male naming practices in Brazil" during a twenty-year period.

1005. Tirone, Nicholas Dominick. "The Question of an Extra-Linguistic Reality: Between Derrida and Bergson." *DAI* 54 (July 1993): 205A.

Examines Derrida's notion of *différance* and hermeneutically employs it in a reading of Bergson's crucial dualisms to reveal that the "between" is not represented by linguistic oppositions.

1006. Turner, Mark. "Language Is a Virus" *PoT* 13 (1992): 725–36.

Shows that we interpret metaphors that present "bare equations" as instances of basic everyday metaphors. Argues that we use various conceptual instruments to interpret them.

1007. Twardon, Andrew Andrezej. "Discourse Connectives and Personality Style: Differences in Use and in Cognitive Representation." *DAI* 54 (October 1993): 1345A.

Studies differences in the use of connectives by subjects who self-rated their performance according to four personality styles.

1008. Van Ness, Silke. "The Pressure of English on the Pennsylvania German Spoken in Two West Virginia Communities." *AS* 67 (Spring 1992): 70–82.

Analyzes variations in the past participle prefix and the loss of the prefix in two speech communities.

1009. Vavra, Ed. "Welcome to the Shoe Store?" *EJ* 82 (September 1993): 81–84.

Maintains that teachers need to know grammar in order to provide appropriate reading materials and exercises. Uses a psycholinguistic model to teach syntax.

1010. Verburg, T. Larry. "The Politics of Technical Language." *TC* 40 (August 1993): 448–52.

Applies Orwell's analysis of political language to technical language; argues that the latter allows for easy manipulation and obscuring.

1011. Verkuyl, Henk J. *A Theory of Aspectuality: The Interaction between Temporal and Atemporal Structure*. New York: Cambridge University Press, 1993. 426 pages

Analyses how sentences indicate various kinds of time reference. Looks at both verbs and noun phrases.

1012. Wardhaugh, Ronald. *Investigating Language: Central Problems in Linguistics*. Cambridge, MA: Blackwell Publishers, 1993. 272 pages

Focuses on issues of linguistics while exploring possible answers for questions facing linguists. Includes a glossary of terms.

1013. Warner, Anthony R. *English Auxiliaries: Structure and History*. New York: Cambridge University Press, 1993. 304 pages

Examines auxiliary verbs, showing how lexical properties are central to their

grammar. Traces their historical development.

1014. Wells, Gordon. "Reevaluating the IRF Sequence: A Proposal for the Articulation of Theories of Activity and Discourse for the Analysis of Teaching and Learning in the Classroom." *L&E* 5 (1993): 1–37.

Develops an integrated framework for describing and analyzing classroom discourse by using Leontiev's activity theory in connection with Halliday and Hasan's discourse theory.

1015. Wilkinson, Louise Cherry, Elaine R. Stillman, Leslie Alexander Mitzberg, and Margaret Aurilo. "Narrative Analysis: Filtering Individual Differences in Competence [response to Egan, *L&E* 5 (1993)]." *L&E* 5 (1993): 195–210.

Argues that a chosen method for analyzing narratives can filter the cognitive complexity of narrative production; maintains that an underlying structure analysis shows more about an "oral" narrator's strengths and weaknesses than do story grammar and cohesion analysis.

1016. Williams, James D. "Rule-Governed Approaches to Language and Composition." *WC* 10 (October 1993): 542–68.

Problematizes Chomskian rule-governed grammars and social-constructive rhetorics based on them. Suggests that connectivist theories of language better explain how writers use discourse to express local knowledge.

1017. Winford, Donald. "Another Look at the Copula in Black English and Caribbean Creoles." *AS* 67 (Spring 1992): 21–60.

Gives quantitative and structural evidence of connection between Black English vernacular and Caribbean English Creole.

1018. Wong, Wing-Kwong Caesar. "A Computational Theory of Affective Connotation: Application to Text Understanding and Revision." *DAI* 54 (October 1993): 2076B.

Argues that Charles Osgood's connotative dimensions should extend to evaluation, activeness, power, and well-being; introduces several affective relationships; develops connotation lexicon, thesaurus, and patterns of use in a cognitive model of reading and revising processes.

1019. Woods, John. "Dialectical Blindspots." *P&R* 26 (1993): 251–65.

Concludes that *ad hominem* pronouncements are highly complex structures which cannot be dismissed as simply dialectical fallacies.

1020. Zalewski, Jan Pawel. "Redefining the Global Grammar: Towards the Development of a Communicatively-Oriented Pedagogical Grammar of English as a Second Language." *DAI* 53 (June 1993): 4306A.

Reexamines Burt's 1975 proposal for global grammar to help develop a pedagogically useful description of English morpho-syntax.

1021. Zeitlin, Amanda Dargan. "American Talkers: The Art of the Sideshow Carnival Pitchman and Other Itinerant Showmen and Vendors." *DAI* 53 (March 1993): 3326A.

Categorizes the rhetoric of the "pitch," discovering similar structures used in auctions, carnivals, and street sales.

1022. Zuber, Sharon, and Ann M. Reed. "The Politics of Grammar Handbooks: Generic *He* and Singular *They*." *CE* 55 (September 1993): 515–30.

Finds that most grammar handbooks are reluctant to endorse singular "they" as correct usage with indefinite antecedents. Notes the tension between colloquial usage and written standards.

2.9 PSYCHOLOGY

1023. Barnard, Suzanne. "Reconsidering Psycholinguistics' Project: Language as

Praxis in Lacan and Kristeva." *DAI* 53 (June 1993): 6529B.

Uses Lacan (subject as dialogic) and Kristeva (relationship of affect and language) to define language as human, social, temporal, and material.

1024. Blasko, Dawn, and Cynthia M. Connine. "Effects of Familiarity and Aptness on Metaphor Processing." *JEPL* 19 (March 1993): 295–308.

Results of five experiments indicate that subjects showed evidence of "figurative activation" when metaphors are high-familiar or low-familiar.

1025. Bowser, June. "Are We Paying Enough Attention to Creativity?" *Leaflet* 92 (Fall 1993): 21–27.

Applies research findings on creativity to academia; stresses small, personal settings, group work, positive outlooks, and trust in intuition.

1026. Breedin, Sarah Dubois. "The Relationship of Semantic and Syntactic Aspects of Verb Representation." *DAI* 53 (January 1993): 3812B.

Looks at the language processing system by studying verb representation; includes semantic complexity and conceptual constituents.

1027. Burman, Erica, and Ian Parker, eds. *Discourse Analytic Research: Repertoires and Readings of Texts in Action.* New York: Routledge, 1993. 192 pages

Presents essays on discourse research in psychology.
Essayists: Burman, Erica; Gill, Rosalind; Marks, Deborah; Marshall, Harriette; Macnaghten, Philip; Moir, James; Parker, Ian; Raabe, Bianca; Stenner, Paul; Widdicombe, Sue.

1028. Carrell, Patricia L., and Laura B. Monroe. "Learning Styles and Composition." *MLJ* 77 (1993): 148–62.

Investigates the relationships of learning styles to writing performance for basic writers, traditional first-year composition students, and ESL composition students.

1029. Chrysler, Susan Theresa. "The Effects of Gender Stereotypes on Pronoun Comprehension." *DAI* 54 (December 1993): 3369B.

Argues that readers change mental assumptions about the gender of pronoun antecedents as their stereotype-based inferences are updated by new information.

1030. Coleochi, Cheryl Ann. "An Evaluation of the Bilingual Vocational Education Program." *DAI* 53 (January 1993): 3766B.

Evaluates an ESL program for refugee youth run by Catholic Charities of Richmond, VA.

1031. Curren, Mary T., and Katrin R. Harich. "Performance Attributions: Effects of Mood and Involvement." *JEdPsy* 85 (December 1993): 605–9.

The authors point out that mood bias varied in 80 undergraduates depending on perceived importance of outcome and performance outcome. Variables were locus, causal stability, and controllability.

1032. Edwards, Derek, and Jonathan Potter. "Language and Causation: A Discursive Action Model of Description and Attribution." *PsyR* 100 (January 1993): 23–41.

Proposes a model for investigating everyday causation as a remedy for problems in a linguistic category model and a conversational model.

1033. Finet, Dayna. "Effects of Boundary Spanning Communication on the Sociopolitical Delegitimation of an Organization." *MCQ* 7 (August 1993): 36–66.

Explores the relationship between communication by an organization's members with external affiliates and the organization's sociopolitical perceptions of correctness.

1034. Finke, Laurie. "Knowledge as Bait: Feminism, Voice, and the Pedagogical Unconscious." *CE* 55 (January 1993): 7–27.

Discusses and illustrates how "psychoanalysis might reveal the unconscious of feminist pedagogy" and how a "feminist pedagogy might repoliticize psychoanalysis."

1035. Friedman, Bonnie. *Writing Past Dark: Envy, Fear, Distraction, and Other Dilemmas*. New York: Harper Collins, 1993. 128 pages

Explores writers' fears and distractions which contribute to writer's block.

1036. Frith, Uta. "Autism." *ScAm* 268 (June 1993): 108–14.

Examines language acquisition and use among autistic children.

1037. Furlong, Peter R. "Personal Factors Influencing Informal Reasoning of Economic Issues." *JEdPsy* 85 (March 1993): 171–81.

Points out that dialogical reasoning occurred only with prompting. Suggests to use reflective inquiry that allows for multiple perspectives.

1038. Graesser, Arthur C., and Cathy L. McMahen. "Anomalous Information Triggers Questions when Adults Solve Quantitative Problems and Comprehend Stories." *JEdPsy* 85 (March 1993): 136–51.

The authors point out that deletion triggers more questions than contradictions or irrelevancies. They suggest that social barriers prevent questioning in classrooms.

1039. Gutterriez, Felipe Rochon. "Rhetoric, Ideology, and the Imagination." *DAI* 53 (April 1993): 3408A.

Explores an approach to the imagination through the dialogue between being/subjectivity and the variously-constituted structures of meaning.

1040. Hegarty, Mary. "Constructing Mental Models of Machines from Text and Diagrams." *JMemL* 43 (December 1993): 717–42.

Describes the roles of text and diagrams in the construction of mental models of machines. Discusses the processes of integrating them into reading strategies.

1041. Hoagland, John. "Critical Thinking: A Socratic Model." *Arg* 7 (1993): 291–311.

Advances a concept of critical thinking based on the Socratic model and describes it enacted in the process of argument analysis.

1042. Howard-Rose, Dawn, and Philip H. Winne. "Measuring Component and Sets of Cognitive Processes in Self-Regulated Learning." *JEdPsy* 85 (December 1993): 591–604.

The authors study cognitive engagement on two levels (acquisition, transformation) in a model of self-regulated learning. The analysis revealed that measures of SRL are not coherent.

1043. Infante, Dominic A., Carol M. Anderson, Matthew M. Martin, Anita D. Herington, and Jungkee Kim. "Subordinates' Satisfaction and Perceptions of Superior's Compliance-Gaining Tactics, Argumentativeness, Verbal Aggressiveness and Style." *MCQ* 6 (February 1993): 302–26.

Concludes that perceived communication traits of superiors have an effect on the subordinates' satisfaction with superiors.

1044. Jackson, Dorothy, and Margaret Jelinek. "Differential Use of Constraining Questions by Gender and Matrix." *PMS* 77 (December 1993): 887–93.

Points out that in visual/perception problem-solving tasks, women favored perceptual questioning strategies while men favored hypothesis-seeking strategies. Shows that cognitive style and tempo are influential factors.

1045. Johnson-Laird, Philip N., and Eldar Shafir. "The Interaction between Reasoning and Decision Making: An Introduction." *Cognition* 49 (October/November 1993): 1–9.

The article introduces a special issue devoted to reasoning and decision making.

Explores three reasons for the interactions between these two traditions.

1046. Kellogg, Ronald T. "Observations on the Psychology of Thinking and Writing." *CompSt* 21 (Spring 1993): 3–41.

Considers from a psychological perspective the linkage between how writers compose and how well they compose.

1047. Kincheloe, Joe L., and Shirley R. Steinberg. "A Tentative Description of Post-Formal Thinking: The Critical Confrontation with Cognitive Theory." *HER* 63 (Fall 1993): 296–320.

The authors challenge Piagetian and postmodernist thought processes and develop a post-Piagetian cognitive theory which draws from and moves beyond feminist, critical, and postmodernist thought. They establish a framework for a "post-formal" way of thinking which provides practitioners with a new outlook on curriculum development and teaching practices.

1048. Langer, Philip, and David Chiszar. "Assessment of Critical Thinking Courses." *PMS* 77 (December 1993): 970.

The study measures evaluative thinking in four undergraduate critical thinking courses. The results indicate varied instruction or narrow definition of critical thinking.

1049. Larkey, Linda Kathryn. "Perceptions of Discrimination during Downsizing." *MCQ* 7 (November 1993): 158–80.

Concludes that "perceptions of ethnic discrimination moderately correlates with perceptions of selection fairness and information access during the layoff process."

1050. Lehrer, Richard, and Joan Littlefield. "Relationships among Cognitive Components in Logo Learning and Transfer." *JEdPsy* 85 (June 1993): 317–30.

The authors argue that four cognitive components (working memory, representation, metacognition, performance) are necessary to acquire Logo (computer language) and to transfer knowledge. Discusses two methods of instruction which are equally effective.

1051. Levi, Don S. "The Limits of Critical Thinking." *IL* 14 (Spring/Fall 1992): 131–45.

Critiques the view that "deep disagreements" exist where no argument can actually address what is at issue. Uses abortion as an example.

1052. Lilling, Andrea Matte. "The Relationship between Referential Activity and Insight: A Psychoanalytic Psychotherapy Process Study." *DAI* 53 (January 1993): 3780B.

Finds language and emotion linked. Argues that verbalizing and gaining insight into significant emotional experiences helps subjects "recognize, contain and regulate emotions . . . and behaviors."

1053. Link, Austin Peter. "Where Id Was, There Ego Shall Be: The Politics of Metaphor in Freud's Theories of the Structure of the Mind." *DAI* 54 (October 1993): 2179B.

Applies feminism, Nietzsche's theories, and a recent philosophical understanding of metaphor to examine political implications of Freud's metaphors.

1054. Meyer, John C., and Beverly Davenport Sypher. "Personal Constructs as Indicators of Cultural Values." *SCJ* 58 (Spring 1993): 227–38.

Concludes that acknowledging constructs as a set of principles around which culture is created and maintained may help understand message choices and reduce organizational conflicts.

1055. Meyer, Sheree L. "Refusing to Play the Confidence Game: The Illusion of Mastery in the Reading/Writing of Texts." *CE* 55 (January 1993): 46–63.

Suggests that modes of interpretation and response derived from feminist and psychoanalytic theories can provide alternatives to "mastery," here associated with formal argumentation.

1056. Miller, Joseph Michael. "The Social Representation of Self and the Role of Narrative in the Sociolinguistic Construction of Autobiographical Discourse." *DAI* 53 (January 1993): 3837B.

Focuses on narrative as a social cognitive frame; finds that autobiography is a social construction of self.

1057. Miller-Johnson, Marilyn. "A Study on the Impact of Journal Writing and Parenting Information on Self-Esteem, Emotional Adjustment, Parental Attitudes and Knowledge of Child Development with Adolescent Mothers." *DAI* 54 (September 1993): 1676A.

Examines the effects of structured journal writing and the dissemination of parenting information.

1058. Mphahlele, Es'kia. "Educating the Imagination." *CE* 55 (February 1993): 179–86.

Argues for the need to "rescue the imagination" by "recapturing" the power of oral expression using the written word and providing a fuller "context for protest."

1059. Mwamwenda, Tuntufye S. "Formal Operations and Academic Achievement." *JPsy* 127 (1993): 99–103.

Maintains that students who had attained Piaget's formal operations stage performed better in a psychology course than those who had not.

1060. Mwamwenda, Tuntufye S. "Sex Differences in Formal Operations." *JPsy* 127 (1993): 419–25.

The author's study of African students found that gender is not a statistically significant factor in performance of formal operations.

1061. Nielsen, Kirsten. "Cognitive Constraints and Situational Factors Affecting Speech and Writing." *DAI* 54 (August 1993): 1131B.

Evaluates the effects of cognitive and stylistic factors on syntax; explores the relationship between syntax and content.

1062. Novak, Cynthia Cornell. "College-Bound Writers: An Attributional Study of the Effects of Writing-Specific Self-Concept, Success and Failure, and Normative Versus Mastery Feedback on the Motivated Behavior of Help Seeking." *DAI* 53 (June 1993): 4258A.

Investigates the impact of writing-specific self-concepts, success and failure, and mastery versus normative feedback on the psychological processes associated with writing.

1063. Ochser, Robert S. *Physical Eloquence and the Biology of Writing.* Albany, NY: State University of New York Press, 1993. 223 pages

Stresses neurological foundations of written English. Discusses inate abilities not enhanced by formal learning. Describes a writing curriculum stressing the subconscious processes rather than planned, rehearsed, and formally practiced activities.

1064. Pavitt, Charles. "Describing Know-How about Group Discussion Procedure: Must the Representation Be Recursive?" *ComS* 43 (Fall 1992): 150–70.

Examines subtasks which calls for different "styles" of thinking required for successful participation in a small decision-making group while maintaining coherent discussion among group members.

1065. Polk, Thad Anderson. "Verbal Reasoning." *DAI* 53 (February 1993): 4355B.

Validates verbal reasoning and proposes that most people reason without reasoning-specific (syllogistic) processes. Argues that they apply linguistic processes to encode and reencode in deductive reasoning.

1066. Ricco, Robert B. "Revising the Logic of Operations as a Relevance Logic: From Hypothesis Testing to Explanation." *HD* 36 (May/June 1993): 125–46.

Discusses the concept of the interdependent and semiotic relationship between reality and knowledge as found in Piaget's last two books.

1067. Roberts, Richard Miller. "The Production of Figurative Language: Function and Context." *DAI* 53 (February 1993): 4402B.

Examines communicative goals accomplished by the use of hyperbole, idioms, indirect requests, irony, meiosis, metaphor, rhetorical questions, and simile.

1068. Robins, Shani, and Richard E. Mayer. "Schema Training in Analogical Reasoning." *JEdPsy* 85 (September 1993): 529–38.

The authors point out that schema induction was enhanced when analogical problem solving was taught. They conclude that "active responding does not necessarily constitute active learning."

1069. Sadoski, Mark, Ernest T. Goetz, and Joyce B. Fritz. "Impact of Concreteness on Comprehensibility, Interest, and Memory for Text: Implications for Dual Coding Theory and Text Design." *JEdPsy* 85 (June 1993): 291–304.

The authors argue that interesting (concrete) information is recalled better than uninteresting (abstract) information. They evaluate "dual coding theory versus schema theory" and suggest "guidelines for text design."

1070. Semb, George B., John A. Ellis, and John Araujo. "Long-Term Memory for Knowledge Learned in School." *JEdPsy* 85 (June 1993): 305–16.

The authors propose that students remember what they learn in college courses. They find that tutors retain more knowledge than tutees, suggesting positive effects of overlearning.

1071. Shafir, Eldar, Itamar Simonson, and Amos Tversky. "Reason-Based Choice." *Cognition* 49 (October/November 1993): 11–36.

The authors consider the role of reason and arguments in the decision making process

1072. Sidanius, Jim. "The Interface between Racism and Sexism." *JPsy* 127 (1993): 311–22.

A 1986 study of university students reveals a strong correlation between racism and sexism in men.

1073. Smith, Kris Marie. "Gender Differences and the Impact of College on White Students' Racial Attitudes." *DAI* 53 (May 1993): 3819A.

Finds that gender influences how white students perceive affirmative action in relation to students of color.

1074. Spence, Ellen Louise. "Psychophysiology and Memory: The Encoding and Retrieval of Affective Text." *DAI* 53 (April 1993): 5955B.

Concludes that both encoding and retrieval of narratives vary significantly with affective versus emotionally neutral content.

1075. Stanovich, Keith E., and Anne E. Cunningham. "Where Does Knowledge Come From? Specific Associations between Print Exposure and Information Acquisition." *JEdPsy* 85 (June 1993): 211–29.

The authors point out that print exposure contributes to knowledge acquisition across individuals. Their results challenge the view that knowledge acquisition is determined "only by cognitive components" encoding and storing information.

1076. Swoboda, Debra Antoinette. "The Moral Language of Political Activists." *DAI* 54 (July 1993): 550B.

Studies 50 activists; finds that political ideology is less important to their language than the moral framework for describing beliefs and attributes necessary to worthwhile living.

1077. Twist, Donald Anthony. "A Dramatistic Analysis of Morton Kelsey's Argument for the Compatibility of Analytic Psychology and Christianity." *DAI* 53 (March 1993): 3047A.

Examines Kelsey's arguments for compatibility of analytic psychology and Christi-

anity from the critical perspective of Burke's dramatism.

1078. Waddill, Paula Jane. "The Mental Representation of Narrative: All Stories Are Not Created Equal." *DAI* 53 (May 1993): 6019B.

Argues that causal connections and thematic relationships differ sharply in processing and remembering folk tales versus anecdotal narratives on everyday events.

1079. Wade, Elizabeth. "Communicating about Narrative (In)Accuracy." *DAI* 54 (August 1993): 1131B.

Argues that hedges and narrative purpose (such as persuasion), as well as local and global cues to factual accuracy, affect interpretation.

1080. Whittlesea, Bruce W. A. "Illusions of Familiarity." *JEPL* 19 (November 1993): 1235–53.

Examines the concept of familiarity in terms of a fluency heuristic; suggests that familiarity relies on perceptual fluency and the fluency of conceptual processing.

1081. Wiley, Mark. "How to Read a Book: Reflections on the Ethics of Book Reviewing." *JAC* 13 (Fall 1993): 477–92.

Argues that book reviews are important in defining a community and essential to a discipline's identity.

1082. Wilson, Stephanie Gray. "Syntactic Processing as an Automatic Process: Evidence from Artificial and Natural Languages." *DAI* 54 (July 1993): 533B.

Uses a psycholinguistic viewpoint to argue that syntactic processing may not be a function of the structure of the language processor but an automatic process developed through experiences.

2.10 EDUCATION

1083. Abadiano, Helen Regalado. "Cohesion Strategies and Genre in Expository Prose: A

Comparison between the Writings of Sixth-Grade Children of Ethnolinguistic Cultural Groups and Their Literacy Materials." *DAI* 54 (November 1993): 1706A.

Results suggest that the quality and kinds of "models" of writing introduced to children may be crucial to developing their writing skills.

1084. Angelo, Thomas A. "A 'Teacher's Dozen': Fourteen General, Research-Based Principles for Improving Higher Learning in Our Classrooms." *AAHE* 45 (April 1993): 3–7.

Describes learning theories and evaluates the relative success of their application to specific teaching strategies.

1085. Burke, Jim. "The Standards Movement Explained and Considered." *CalE* 29 (Winter 1993): 20–21, 30.

Presents a brief history of the education reform movement since *A Nation at Risk*; outlines the involvement of the NCTE and affiliates, specific projects, and potential concerns.

1086. Carlisle, Kenneth E. "The Politics of Educational Reform." *EdTech* 33 (May 1993): 43–47.

Argues that current and future competition for foreign resources necessitates better education.

1087. Clotfelter, Charles T., and Michael Rothschild, eds. *Studies of Supply and Demand in Higher Education*. National Bureau of Economic Research. Chicago: University of Chicago Press, 1993. 288 pages

The contributors provide an economic analysis of the nature of competition in higher education and higher education's use of resources. They also discuss who chooses to purchase what kind of education and why.
Essayists: Brewer, Dominic J.; Cameron, Stephen V.; Clotfelter, Charles T.; Constantinides, George M.; Cook, Philip J.; Ehrenberg, Ronald G.; Feldstein, Martin; Frank, Robert H.; Getz, Malcolm; Green,

Jerry R.; Hannshek, Eric A.; Hauser, Robert M.; Heckman, James J.; Kuh, Charlotte V.; Ladd, Helen F.; Manski, Charles F.; McPherson, Mechael S.; Merton, Robert C.; Quigley, John M.; Rees, Daniel I.; Rothshield, Michael; Rubinfeld, Daniel L.; White, Lawrence J.

1088. Cole, Ardra L., and J. Gary Knowles. "Teacher Development Partnership Research: A Focus on Methods and Issues." *AERJ* 30 (Fall 1993): 473–95.

Reflects on alternative ways to study teaching and teacher development. Focuses on teacher-researcher partnership in collaborative research.

1089. Craig, Robert. "Vico as Educator: Values, Self-Development, and Synthesis." *JT* 28 (Spring/Summer 1993): 7–11.

Discusses Vico's view of education as a "moral activity" based on a reasoned and passionate utilization of language.

1090. D'Amico-Samuels, Deborah. "Perspectives on Assessment from the New York City Adult Literacy Initiative: A Critical Issues Paper." Literacy Assistance Center, New York, NY, November 1991. ERIC ED 357 658. 50 pages

Reviews the current assessment process; explores a few changes in direction and in practice.

1091. Edwards, Ronald G. "Cultural Diversity and Education Reform: A New Philosophy of Education." *MultiR* 2 (September 1993): 44–46.

Contains an annotated bibliography of texts that argue for the importance of cooperation, administrative decentralization, the need for critical thinking, values that promote action, and teacher empowerment.

1092. Ewald, Helen Rothschild. "A Comment on the November 1992 Issue of *College English*." *CE* 55 (April 1993): 440–41.

Comments that articles by Caughie, Stotsky, Deletiner, and Bloom discuss difficulties of nonhierarchical classrooms and suggests discussions about pedagogical ethics.

1093. Fisher, Edith Maureen. "Behavioral Diversity: The 'Win-Win' Model." *MultiR* 2 (June 1993): 40–42.

Argues that the "win-win" model of behavior diversity teaches individuals to discover insights about themselves and others.

1094. Henson, Mark, and R. R. Schmeck. "Learning Styles of Community College Versus University Students." *PMS* 76 (February 1993): 118.

The authors point out that the scores on the Inventory of Learning Processes of 178 undergraduates suggest that community college students "mistook *acting* like good students for being good university students."

1095. Hill, Herbert, and James E. Johnes, Jr., eds. *Race in America: The Struggle for Equality.* Madison, WI: University of Wisconsin Press, 1993. 465 pages

The collection consists of essays from a 1989 Wisconsin conference in honor of *Brown Versus Board of Education*; they cover civil rights history, educational reform, and implications for race and education.
Essayists: Bell, Derrick; Brittain, John C.; Carter, Robert L.; Chambers, Julius L.; Clark, Kenneth B.; Farley, Reynolds; Hill, Herbert; Jones, James E., Jr.; Jones, Nathaniel R.; Liebman, James S.; Lyman, Stanford M.; Morris, Aldon; Morris, Milton D.; Orfield, Gary; Takaki, Ronald; Williams, Eddie N.; Williams, Patricia J.

1096. Kahaney, Phyllis, Linda A. M. Perry, and Joseph Janangelo, eds. *Theoretical and Critical Perspectives on Teacher Change.* Norwood, NJ: Ablex, 1993. 210 pages

The contributors explore changes in educational settings. They discuss education in connection with gender stereotypes, social rules, liberation theory, and computer-supported writing environments.

Essayists: Brannon, Lil; Britton, James; Diamond, C. T. P.; Gilligan, Carol; Graves, Gary; Hawisher, Gail E.; Kramarae, Cheris; Lee, Diane M.; Martin, Laura M. W.; Newman, Denis; Pradl, Gordon M.; Selfe, Cynthia L.; Sinnott, Jan D.; Steiner, Joan N.; Tappan, Mark B.; Vaughan, Margaret E.

1097. King, James R. *Professing and Postmodernity: Social Construction of Teaching Selves.* San Antonio, TX: Annual Meeting of the National Reading Conference, December 1992. ERIC ED 353 580. 14 pages

Reports on a study that examined the interaction of teacher and student in a methods preparation course.

1098. Kuh, George D. "In Their Own Words: What Students Learn Outside the Classroom." *AERJ* 30 (Summer 1993): 277–304.

Finds that students do not consider their background as important for out-of-classroom learning.

1099. Marsh, Herbert W., and Lawrence Roche. "The Use of Students' Evaluations and an Individually Structured Intervention to Enhance University Teaching Effectiveness." *AERJ* 30 (Spring 1993): 217–51.

Study suggests that student evaluations coupled with consultation is effective in improving teaching success.

1100. Myers, Miles, and James Moffett. *Curriculum for the 21st Century: Free to Dream Revisited.* [Audiocassette]. Urbana, IL: NCTE, 1993.

The speakers discuss ways to help *all* learners in our educational system; they cover the use of standards in education, equitable education for all, multicultural diversity and pluralism, and "community learning systems."

1101. Ogbu, John. *Understanding Cultural Diversity and Learning.* [Audiocassette]. Urbana, IL: NCTE, 1993.

Addresses the Conference on English Education Luncheon at the 1992 NCTE Convention; argues that we should focus on the benefits of what multicultural diversity introduces to the classroom rather than on how schools "handle" diversity.

1102. Peers, Michele G. "A Teacher/Researcher's Experience with Performance-Based Assessment as a Diagnostic Tool." *JR* 37 (April 1993): 544–48.

Describes an informal integrated reading/writing assignment that identifies a student's control of reading, writing, and content. Includes a general scoring rubric.

1103. Schecter, Sandra R., and Shawn Parkhurst. "Ideological Divergences in a Teacher Research Group." National Center for the Study of Writing and Literacy, 1992. ERIC ED 354 524. 32 pages

Describes a two-year study of a well-supported, university-affiliated teacher research group. Argues that the concept of ideology used to emphasize beliefs about society, politics, and cognition are intimately bound up in teacher researchers' perspectives.

1104. Sommers, Nancy. "I Stand Here Writing." *CE* 55 (April 1993): 420–28.

Sommers reflects on her life and teaching and how "sources" influence both.

1105. Spanos, William V. *The End of Education: Toward Posthumanism.* Pedagogy and Cultural Practice, edited by Henry Giroux and Roger Simon. Minneapolis, MN: University of Minnesota Press, 1993. 277 pages

Deconstructs traditional, humanist models of pedagogy and proposes a new "postmodern" model based on the discourses of Heidegger, Derrida, and others.

1106. Srocki, Bernadine Mary. "The Impact of a Folklore Project on Communication Skills, Cultural Awareness and Teacher Attitudes." *DAI* 53 (January 1993): 2282A.

Presents an ethnographic study examining the positive effects of a folklore project on teacher concerns, development of students' oral and written literacy skills, and cultural awareness.

1107. Steiner, Joan Naomi. "A Comparative Study of the Educational Stances of Madeline Hunter and James Britton." Urbana, IL, National Council of Teachers of English, 1993. NCTE Concept Paper Series No. 6. ERIC ED 359 546. 87 pages

Finds that Hunter depicts teachers as knowledge dispensers while Britton sees teachers as helping students to learn actively. Considers implications for learning, curriculum development, and student-teacher roles. Discusses the use of each approach in practical terms.

1108. Takemura, Kazuhisa. "Protocol Analysis of Multistage Decision Strategies." *PMS* 77 (October 1993): 459–69.

Discusses a study in which 25 students used combinations of different decision-making strategies over time depending on the cognitive demand of the task.

1109. Trend, David. "The Center Will Not Hold: Contests of Meaning in Culture and Education." *DAI* 54 (September 1993): 742A.

Addresses the way knowledge is regulated and meaning is shaped in various social constructions.

1110. Vandenburg, Peter John. "The Politics of Knowledge Dissemination: Academic Journals in Composition Studies." *DAI* 54 (October 1993): 1358A.

Analyzes the role of scholarly journals' editorial practices in the professionalization of composition studies and the marginalization of nonpublishing composition teachers. Includes suggestions for editorial reform.

1111. Zilversmith, Arthur. *Changing Schools: Progressive Education Theory and Practice, 1930–1960.* Chicago: University of Chicago Press, 1993. 248 pages

Examines the impact of Dewey's ideas at the national and local level. Aims to improve the understanding of the role of progressives' ideas in determining school practices. Discusses the relationship between educational ideas and educational practices.

2.11 JOURNALISM, PUBLISHING, TELEVISION, AND RADIO

1112. Aden, Roger C., and Christina L. Reynolds. "Lost and Found in America: The Function of Place Metaphor in *Sports Illustrated*." *SCJ* 59 (Fall 1993): 1–14.

Analyzes the rhetorical dimensions of the leisure ethic presented by *Sports Illustrated*. Sees it as a way to cope with a culture dominated by a machine metaphor.

1113. Austin, Alexandra Eloise. "Audience Processing of Mass Media Messages Concerning AIDS." *DAI* 53 (January 1993): 2159A.

Investigates how different audiences for Safe Sex/AIDS information campaigns perceive mass media messages concerning AIDS.

1114. Caelleigh, Addeane S. "Role of the Journal Editor in Sustaining Integrity in Research." *AM* 68 (September Supplement 1993): S23–29.

Examines the changing roles of editors of science literature as enforcers of high ethical standards among authors and institutions.

1115. Clark, Ginger. "Linking Genre Analysis with Interpretive Processes: A Foundation for Exploring the Motives and Gratifications of Female Television Viewers." *DAI* 53 (March 1993): 3029A.

Employs genre analysis, issues of interpretive processes, and the concept of oral culture to explore motives and gratifications of female television viewers.

1116. Cummings, Kate. "The Double Scene of Televised AIDS Campaigns." *Pre/Text* 13 (Fall/Winter 1992): 67–77.

Examines the rhetoric of current AIDS public service announcements; argues that ads are homophobic.

1117. Cumings, Rick Allen. "An Analysis of Television Network News Coverage of the TWA 847 Crisis." *DAI* 53 (June 1993): 4128A.

Studies the conflicting rhetoric of three major networks' news coverage of the TWA hijacking.

1118. Eberts, Michael Albert. "Comparing Groups of California Community College Newspapers: A Search for Editorial Independence." *DAI* 53 (January 1993): 2526A.

Posits that college newspapers owe their rights to freedom of speech rather than freedom of the press. Surveys current practices in California.

1119. Edwards, Janis L. "Pictorial Images as Narratives: Rhetorical Activation in Campaign 88 Political Cartoons." *DAI* 54 (September 1993): 722A.

Examines drawings for features of narrative and uses of rhetorical strategies "providing commentaries on the absence of the ideal."

1120. Emke, Ivan. "Speaking of AIDS in Canada: The Texts and Contexts of Official, Counter-Cultural, and Mass Media Discourses Surrounding AIDS." *DAI* 53 (February 1993): 3009A.

Analyzes the social construction of AIDS as set into the discourse of government, media, and counter-culture.

1121. Erickson, Keith V., Cathy A. Fleuriet, and Lawrence A. Hosman. "Prolific Publishing: Professional and Administrative Concerns." *SCJ* 58 (Summer 1993): 328–38.

Argues that studies on "prolific publishing" are methodologically weak and may communicate the message that scholarship is a "numbers game."

1122. Evertz, Kathy Jo. "Selling the Lady: Commercialization and the 1986 Statue of Liberty Centennial." *DAI* 53 (January 1993): 2134A.

Addresses questions surrounding the denunciation of the commercialization of Liberty during the 1986 Centennial celebrations. Reveals contemporary American attitudes about a national icon during the past century and the Reagan years.

1123. "A Free and Independent Press." *QRD* 19 (April 1993): 7.

Comments on how the press responds when the "military invade in secret."

1124. Haws, Dick. *Touring the Newsroom: An Inside Look at Newspapers*. Ames, IA: Iowa State University Press, 1993. 96 pages

Presents traditions, behaviors, and attitudes encountered in newsrooms. Discusses "bad" and "good" newspapers, editors, corrections, codes of ethics, evaluations, hackwriters, public relations people, objectionable language, polls, readership, sexism, coverage of sexual assault, salaries, and surreptitious taping.

1125. Heiens, Richard A. "The Influence of Newspaper, Radio, and Television Publicity on Sales of the State of Colorado's Lottery Product, Lotto." *DAI* 54 (October 1993): 1463A.

Examines variables influencing lottery sales in the state of Colorado.

1126. Heller, Karen S. "Silence Equals Death: Discourses on AIDS and Identity in the Gay Press, 1981–1986." *DAI* 54 (August 1993): 574A.

Examines press coverage of AIDS in two gay newspapers in San Francisco and New York City between 1981–86.

1127. Hesske, Steve. "Imagewordimage: Postmodernism, Television, and Writing (Teaching)." *DAI* 54 (September 1993): 909A.

Examines the relationships among writing, teaching, writing theory, and commercial television.

1128. Hutton, Frankie. *The Early Black Press in America, 1827 to 1860*. Westport, CT: Greenwood Press, 1993. 208 pages

Discusses editors and the editorial content of 17 magazines and newspapers of the African American middle class.

1129. Jolliffe, Lee. *Persuasive Elements of 100 Successful Magazine Query Letters*. Montreal, Quebec, Canada: Association for Education in Journalism and Mass Communication, August 1992. ERIC ED 351 676. 32 pages

Compares successful and unsuccessful persuasive letters. Argues that the use of concrete words, vividness, cohesion, human interest, vocabulary diversity, and an opening narrative made for successful letters.

1130. Kennedy, George. "News about the News: Changes and Challenges." *ETC* 50 (Summer 1993): 3–16.

Looks at criteria journals use to decide what is newsworthy; suggests that those criteria need to change as journalists face the future.

1131. Leon, Mark Robert. "The Dialectic of Truth and News: Implications of Truth in News Narrative." *DAI* 54 (October 1993): 1395A.

Examines news reporting from a truth theoretic perspective and proposes a resonance theory to analyze news narrative more effectively.

1132. Morley, David. *Television, Audiences, and Cultural Studies*. New York: Routledge, 1993. 336 pages

Provides an introductory overview of the "development of audience research from a cultural perspective." Focuses on the "role of the media in articulating public and private spheres of experience and in the social organization of space, time and community."

1133. Morris, Barbra. "From Hooked on TV to Hooked on Books." *UEJ* 21 (1993): 28–31.

Describes an approach that uses television to help teach basic notions about narrative constructions of reality.

1134. National Council of Teachers of English. "Guidelines for Dealing with Censorship of Nonprint Materials." Urbana, IL, National Council of Teachers of English, 1993. 12 pages

Offers suggestions for administrators and teachers in using nonprint media and in resisting attempts to censor such materials.

1135. Nero, Charles Isidore. " 'To Develop Our Manhood': Free Black Leadership and the Rhetoric of the New Orleans *Tribune*." *DAI* 53 (March 1993): 3045A.

Focuses on *Tribune* editorials in 1864 and 1865 and their rhetorical technique to redefine racial situation, relationships, and people.

1136. Pfau, Michael, and Jong Guen Kang. "The Relationship between Media Use Patterns and the Nature of Media and Message Factors in the Process of Influence." *SCJ* 58 (Spring 1993): 182–91.

Results reflect media choice, targeting designs of commercials, and political and public service messages across print, radio, and television media.

1137. Phillips, Donna Burns, Ruth Greenberg, and Sharon Gibson. "*College Composition and Communication*: Chronicling a Discipline's Genesis." *CCC* 44 (December 1993): 443–65.

Reviews the development of the physical format, the conversants, and the subject matter of *CCC* from 1950 to 1993.

1138. Raymond, James C. "I-Dropping and Androgyny: The Authorial *I* in Scholarly Writing." *CCC* 44 (December 1993): 478–83.

Discusses three criteria for using authorial "I" in scholarly writing, namely topical relevance, authoritative voice, and the energy of novelty and dissent.

1139. Schooler, Caroline. "Enhancing Cognitive and Behavioral Responses to Televised Health Messages: The Role of Positive Appeals." *DAI* 53 (March 1993): 3030A.

Discusses the effects of televised health promotional messages. Bases her study on cognitive and behavioral hypotheses.

1140. Shea, Preston Tuckerman. "The Rhetoric of Authority in the *New England Courant*. (Volumes I and II)." *DAI* 53 (January 1993): 2519A.

Examines themes, rhetoric, imagery, and gender in the weekly *New England Courant* (1721–1726) published by James and Benjamin Franklin. Analyzes questions of authority in civil and church politics.

1141. Shoos, Diana, Diana George, and Joseph Comprone. "Twin Peaks and the Look of Television: Visual Literacy in the Writing Class." *JAC* 13 (Fall 1993): 459–75.

The authors analyze *Twin Peaks* to demonstrate how television constructs meaning, how that meaning is coded, and how those codes might be deconstructed.

1142. Simpson, Paul. *Language, Ideology, and Point of View*. Interface. New York, NY: Routledge, 1993. 208 pages

Focuses on the way in which speakers and writers linguistically encode their beliefs, interests, and value systems in a wide range of media.

1143. "Top Censored Stories of 1992." *QRD* 19 (April 1993): 7.

Reports awards given by Project Censored and provides addresses for the complete list.

1144. Wood, Jeremy. "Advocacy: Commitment, Polarization and the Edge of Slime." *DAI* 53 (May 1993): 4073A.

Analyzes media discourse to find that advocates structure discourse according to their commitment to an issue; points out that advocacy is morally precarious, presenting commitment-favoring interpretations as truth.

1145. Zelizer, Barbie. "Has Communication Explained Journalism?" *JC* 43 (Autumn 1993): 80–88.

Uses four metaphors—journalism as performance, as narrative, as ritual, and as interpretive community—to argue for a more interdisciplinary approach to journalism.

1146. Ziegler, Dhyana. "Breaking through the Barriers: Using Video as a Tool for Intercultural Communication." *JBS* 24 (December 1993): 159–77.

Documents a video letter exchange project as an effective tool for fostering intercultural communication and understanding between Africans and African Americans.

See also 740

2.12 PHILOSOPHY

1147. Agassi, Joseph. "The Heuristic Bent." *P&R* 26 (Winter 1993): 9–17.

Argues that there is more than one dimension of rationality. Points out that the degree of efficiency of any problem-solving may differ in different dimensions.

1148. Beaney, Michael. "The Bond of Sense: An Essay in the History of Analytic Philosophy." *DAI* 53 (April 1993): 3551A.

Examines certain themes on the rise and development of analytic philosophy. Focuses on the relationship between Aristotelian and Fregean logic, and the emergence and evolution of interest in questions of meaning.

1149. Campbell, Jay G. "A Critical Survey of Some Recent Philosophical Theories of Metaphor." *DAI* 53 (January 1993): 2378A.

Argues that Robert Fogelin's version of the elliptical-simile theory is the most promising of recent theories of metaphor.

1150. Dasenbrock, Reed Way. "A Response to 'Language Philosophy, Writing, and Reading: A Conversation with Donald Davidson.'" *JAC* 13 (Fall 1993): 523–38.

Explores how Davidson's philosophy of language can be applied to composition pedagogy.

1151. Delany, C. F. *Science, Knowledge, and Mind: A Study of the Philosophy of C. S. Peirce.* Notre Dame, IN: University of Notre Dame Press, 1993. 188 pages

Discusses the American philosopher's critique of Cartesianism and other aspects of his philosophy of science and mind. Argues that Peirce's views can serve as a corrective in contemporary debates over such issues as the social and historical nature of science.

1152. Dunne, Joseph. *Back to the Rough Ground: Phronesis and Techne in Modern Philosophy and in Aristotle.* Notre Dame, IN: University of Notre Dame Press, 1993. 624 pages

Considers how Aristotle's distinction between the philosophical concepts of *phronesis* and *techne* is dealt with in his own works and in those of nineteenth- and twentieth-century philosophers such as John Henry Newman, R. G. Collingwood, Hannah Arendt, Hans Georg Gadamer, and Jürgen Habermas.

1153. Gaskins, Richard H. *Burdens of Proof in Modern Discourse.* New Haven, CT: Yale University Press, 1993. 368 pages

Analyzes legal, philosophical, scientific, social, and other examples of "arguments from ignorance," a form of reasoning in which conclusions depend on a lack of compelling information. Shows that one position wins by default if the opponents cannot prove it wrong.

1154. Hausman, Carl B. *Charles S. Peirce's Evolutionary Philosophy.* New York: Cambridge University Press, 1993. 247 pages

Discusses Peirce's version of pragmatism, his theory of signs, his phenomenology, and his theory of continuity.

1155. Hiltz, Stephen Charles. "Concerning Thought, Truth, and Realism: Essays on the Vicissitudes of Representation." *DAI* 54 (October 1993): 1394A.

Examines connections between thought and language and the reality of thought and description; isolates issue of realism with respect to truth from realism-nominalism and realism-idealism controversies; argues that realism rests on conflation of truth conditions and representation in sentences.

1156. Johnson, Christopher. *System and Writing in the Philosophy of Jacques Derrida.* New York: Cambridge University Press, 1993. 252 pages

Analyzes Derrida's theory of writing; argues that Derrida was influenced by contemporary natural science and systems theory.

1157. Johnston, Araminta Stone. "The Moral of the Story/The Story of the Moral: The Primacy and Narrative in the Lives of Persons." *DAI* 53 (March 1993): 3258A.

Examines the Western philosophical view of stories in narratives as inferior to logical philosophy, concluding that the long-held view is both incorrect and pernicious.

1158. Lloyd, Genevieve. *The Man of Reason: "Male" and "Female" in Western Philosophy.* 2d ed. Minneapolis, MN: University of Minnesota Press, 1993. 146 pages

Explores metaphors of "maleness" in philosophical thought, with particular attention to the association of masculinity with reason or rational thought and to the relativism of recent philosophical thought.

1159. Lyotard, Jean-François. *The Postmodern Explained: Correspondence 1982–1985.* Translated by Don Barry, Bernadette Maher, Julian Pefanis, Virginia Spate, and Morgan Thomas. Minneapolis, MN: University of Minnesota Press, 1993. 141 pages

Uses his letters addressed to young philosophers to explain his thought.

1160. Roberts, Lawrence D. *How Reference Works: Explanatory Models for Indexicals, Descriptions, and Opacity.* Albany, NY: State University of New York Press, 1993. 192 pages

Combines cognitive science and the philosophies of language and mind in a study of how referring expressions work in natural language.

1161. Staller, Mark Lewis. "Rhetoric and Philosophy in the Platonic Dialogues: Plato's Presentation of Rhetoric, Philosophy, and Sophistic in Five Selected Dialogues." *DAI* 54 (December 1993): 2182A.

Examines five dialogues to discover Plato's persuasive intentions and strategies.

1162. Weinsheimer, Joel C. *Eighteenth-Century Hermeneutics: Philosophy of Interpretation in England from Locke to Burke.* New Haven, CT: Yale University Press, February 1993. 272 pages

Deals with hermeneutical issues in British scriptural, legal, historical, political, and literary interpretation. Concludes that hermeneutics in eighteenth-century England became the site of a contest between reason and history.

1163. Wells, Susan. "The Malaprop in Spite of Herself: A Desperate Reading of Donald Davidson [response to Kent, *JAC* 13 (Winter 1993)]." *JAC* 13 (Fall 1993): 517–22.

Maintains that Davidson's language philosophy is not sustained by rationality and cannot support interventions into understanding language, though he has provided necessary philosophic tools for further discussion.

2.13 SCIENCE AND MEDICINE

1164. Alexandrov, Daniel, and Anton Struchkov. "Bakhtin's Legacy and the History of Science and Culture: An Interview with Anatolii Akhutin and Vladimir Bibler." *Configurations* 1 (Fall 1993): 335–86.

The authors respond to Bakhtin's genre and dialogue theories. They provide an explanation of the "multi-stage-ness" of concentric dialogic communities in science.

1165. Ames, Sue Ann Wooster. "Multiple Spoken and Written Channels of Communication: An Ethnography of a Medical Unit in a General Hospital." *DAI* 54 (August 1993): 369A.

Presents an ethnographic study of language in an acute care unit. Examines nursing care notes, nursing intershift notes, and physician notes on charts.

1166. Ashmore, Malcolm. "The Theatre of the Blind: Starring a Promethean Prankster, a Phoney Phenomenon, a Prism, a Pocket, and a Piece of Wood." *SocStSc* 23 (February 1993): 67–106.

Discusses Robert Wood's 1904 manifestation which established the nonexistence of Rene Blondot's "N-rays" through a "rhetoric of undiscovery," forcing readers to "see the nothing that was there."

1167. Barnard, David. "Commentary on Simone de Beauvoir's *A Very Easy Death*." *AM* 68 (October 1993): 772–73.

Suggests that studying texts which focus on the emotional and intellectual sides of dying can help medical students understand the needs of dying patients.

1168. Bazerman, Charles. "Forums of Validation and Forms of Knowledge: The Magical Rhetoric of Otto von Guericke's Sulfur Globe." *Configurations* 1 (Spring 1993): 201–28.

Discusses von Guericke's account of his famous demonstration and the "rhetorical world his account was part of."

1169. Blakeslee, Ann Madeline. "Inventing Scientific Discourse: Dimensions of Rhetorical Knowledge in Physics." *DAI* 53 (February 1993): 2787A.

Presents a socio-rhetorical analysis of three physicists. Focuses on a whole rhetorical process by which they sought to position their work.

1170. Blakeslee, Ann M. "Reader and Authors: Fictionalized Constructs of Dynamic Collaborations?" *TCQ* 2 (Winter 1993): 23–35.

Presents a case study of collaboration among physicists, biologists, and chemists, which suggests a socially constructed, dynamic audience.

1171. Blau, Shawn F. "Cognitive Darwinism: Rational Emotive Therapy." *ETC* 50 (Winter 1993): 403–41.

Based on Ellis's ideas, Blau points out that there should be a way for a person to learn from his or her thoughts. Argues that by constructing a meaningful mental scene, a person can assess whether or not to go into a caution mode.

1172. Brugess, Curt, and Jennifer Skodis. "Lexical Representation and Morpho-Syntactic Parallelism in the Left Hemisphere." *B&L* 44 (February 1993): 129–38.

The authors suggest that the traditional notion of left-hemispheric specialization for syntactic processing can be extended to the retrieval of lower-level morphological representations.

1173. Campanario, J. M. "Consolation for the Scientist: Sometimes It Is Hard to Publish Papers That Are Later Highly Cited." *SocStSc* 23 (May 1993): 342–62.

Analyzes 316 commentaries by authors of highly-cited scientific papers and shows that peer reviewers resist endorsing innovative papers. Argues for better evaluative criteria.

1174. Cichon, Elaine J., and Jon T. Masterson. "Physician-Patient Communication: Mutual Role Expectations." *ComQ* 41 (Fall 1993): 477–89.

The researchers examine physician-patient communication as it relates to expectations they hold for themselves and for each other.

1175. Cohn, Victor. "A Madison Avenue Spin on Medical Terms." *AM* 67 (February 1992): 102–3.

Argues against the popular use of "health-care" jargon and its "commercialization and dehumanization" of the physician-patient relationship.

1176. Crawford, T. Hugh. "An Interview with Bruno Latour." *Configurations* 1 (Spring 1993): 247–69.

Latour and Crawford discuss Serres, Foucault, Lyotard, Feyerabend, Bloor, post-modernism, the debate between realists and constructivists, actor-network theory, and semiotics.

1177. Cullen, David J., and Anne Macaulay. "Consistency between Peer Reviewers for a Clinical Specialty Journal." *AM* 67 (December 1992): 856–59.

Analyzes reviewing practices of nonmembers and members of a journal's editorial board.

1178. Dittrich, Lisa R. "Commentary on May Sarton's *Recovering*." *AM* 67 (February 1992): 96–97.

Analyzes the journal entry of a mastectomy patient and finds lessons for medical students.

1179. Donley, Carol. "Commentary on Joseph Chaikin's Speech for Accepting the Fifth Annual Edwin Booth Award." *AM* 67 (December 1992): 832–33.

Examines the importance of speech and body language to a stroke victim.

1180. Donnelly, Carol M., and Mark A. McDaniel. "Use of Analogy in Learning Scientific Concepts." *JEPL* 19 (July 1993): 975–89.

Results of four experiments indicate that subjects better comprehend new information when concepts are expressed analogically.

1181. Forsythe, D. E. "Engineering Knowledge: The Construction of Knowledge in Artificial Intelligence." *SocStSc* 23 (August 1993): 445–77.

Argues that engineers who design artificial intelligence ignore crucial complexities of knowledge acquisition. Points out that these deletions are reflected in the resultant technology.

1182. Friedman, Paul J. "Background and Advice to Faculty Serving on Ad Hoc Committees of Inquiry Concerning Questions of Research Integrity." *AM* 68 (September Supplement 1993): S100.

Provides several guidelines to help clarify faculty roles in assessing research integrity.

1183. Futrell, Wiley Michael. "Jeremy Rifkin Challenges Recombinant DNA Research: A Rhetoric of Heresy." *DAI* 53 (March 1993): 3043A.

Analyzes a broad range of Rifkin's rhetorical artifacts and those of scientists engaged in recombinant DNA research against criteria developed to identify and understand heresy.

1184. Graves, Heather Ann Brodie. "The Rhetoric of Physics: An Ethnography of the Research and Writing Processes in a Physics Laboratory." *DAI* 53 (April 1993): 3885A.

Argues that physicists use rhetoric in all stages of the knowledge creation process.

1185. Halliday, M. A. K., and J. R. Martin. *Writing Science: Literacy and Discursive Power*. The Pittsburgh Series in Composition, Literacy and Culture, edited by David Bartholomae and Jean Ferguson Carr. Pittsburgh, PA: University of Pittsburgh Press, 1993. 283 pages

The authors focus on the use of language and literacy issues in scientific research and in science classrooms. They discuss "systemic functional linguistics" and its application to the discursive technology of science; professional literacy within scientific disciplines; and the ways scientific knowledge is construed and reproduced in schooling.

1186. Halperin, Edward C., Janice Scott, and Stephen L. George. "Multiple Authorship in Two English-Language Journals in Radiation Oncology." *AM* 67 (December 1992): 850–56.

Examines reasons for the apparent increase in multiple authors of scholarly scientific articles.

1187. Harris, Lauren Julius. "Broca on Cerebral Control for Speech in Right-Handers and Left-Handers: A Note on Translation and Some Further Comments." *B&L* 45 (July 1993): 108–20.

Reanalyzes Broca's views on the relationship of handedness to speech representation. Bases his argument on a new translation of Broca's later articles.

1188. Hatfield, David L. "The Rhetoric of Science: A Case Study of the Cold Fusion Controversy." *DAI* 53 (February 1993): 2787A.

Discusses to what extent a rhetorical analysis of cold fusion discourse may increase an understanding of the controversy.

1189. Hawkins, Anne Hunsaker. "Commentary on Linda Pastan's 'Ethics.'" *AM* 67 (March 1992): 172–73.

Examines the use of ethics learned through the humanities to widen medical students' awareness.

1190. Hensel, William A., and Teresa L. Rasco. "Storytelling as a Method for Teaching Values and Attitudes." *AM* 67 (August 1992): 500–504.

Encourages teachers to share personal stories with their medical students to help them learn from mistakes and to form their own values.

1191. Herndl, Carl, and Vicki Taylor. *What Does Resistance Look Like in Nonacademic Discourse?* San Diego, CA: Conference on College Composition and Communication, March/April 1993. ERIC ED 357 350. 17 pages

A case study of an environmental biologist at a military test facility reveals that ideological issues of quantification versus qualification appeared regularly.

1192. Hoyningen-Huene, Paul. *Reconstructing Scientific Revolutions: Thomas S. Kuhn's Philosophy of Science.* Translated by Alexander T. Levine. Chicago, IL: University of Chicago Press, 1993. 310 pages

Traces Kuhn's work over four decades from the period before his 1962 work, *The Structure of Scientific Revolutions*, to the present.

1193. Hunt, D. Daniel, Carol F. MacLaren, Craig S. Scott, Joseph Chu, and Lisa I. Leiden. "Characteristics of Dean's Letters in 1981 and 1992." *AM* 68 (December 1993): 905–11.

The authors present the results of national surveys which examine the characteristics of writers of medical school dean's letters. Suggests adherence to AAMC guidelines.

1194. Hurst, Peter Jonathan. "The Research University as an Organizational Context for Collaboration: Cross-Departmental Research Collaboration in Environmental Studies." *DAI* 53 (May 1993): 3814A.

Surveys 212 University of Michigan faculty; explores cross-disciplinary collaboration; finds that dissatisfaction is related to research orientation and tenure status.

1195. Kalamaras, George. "Confronting the Canon of Science: Gender and the Role of Informal Writing in Constructing Disciplinary Knowledge." *CompSt* 21 (Spring 1993): 78–85.

Maintains that the discourse of science, particularly biology, can be powerful but exclusive.

1196. Kesselring, Linda J. "Putting Trauma Care in Writing: Parallels between Doctors'

and Nurses' Responsibilities and Textbook Presentations." *JTWC* 23 (1993): 129–35.

Demonstrates that the distant and impersonal nature of medical writing that is criticized by technical writing scholars may be required by trauma surgeons who publish their work.

1197. Laird, Frank N. "Participatory Analysis, Democracy, and Technological Decision Making." *STHV* 18 (Summer 1993): 341–61.

Argues that scientific and technological policy should be subject to democratic, pluralistic norms and that it should be established through participatory analysis satisfying democratic criteria and emphasizing participant knowledge.

1198. Latour, Bruno. "Pasteur on Lactic Acid Yeast: A Partial Semiotic Analysis." *Configurations* 1 (Winter 1993): 129–45.

Shows how literary techniques can be applied productively to human and nonhuman elements in scientific writing.

1199. Latour, Bruno. *We Have Never Been Modern*. Translated by Catherine Porter. Cambridge, MA: Harvard University Press, 1993. 168 pages

Proposes that modernity is a matter of faith in scientific methods, relying on the distinctions between nature and society, human and thing. Argues that this distinction is challenged by debates over the ozone, global warming, and deforestation which makes it increasingly difficult to keep nature and culture separate.

1200. Lindqvist, Svante. "The Spectacle of Science: An Experiment in 1744 Concerning the Aurora Borealis." *Configurations* 1 (Winter 1993): 57–94.

Argues that the content of a scientific article as well as the form of publication are important for historians.

1201. Lubrano, Linda L. "The Hidden Structure of Soviet Science." *STHV* 18 (Spring 1993): 147–75.

Records collaborative research of 107 physicists, chemists, and biologists of the former Soviet Union which reveals open professional communication and an unexpected pluralism of scientific elites.

1202. Makoul, Gregory Thomas. "Perpetuating Passivity: A Study of Physician-Patient Communication and Decision-Making." *DAI* 53 (May 1993): 3732A.

Describes how physicians and patients discuss health problems; examines the utility of reciprocal determinism to communication studies.

1203. Margolis, Howard. *Paradigms and Barriers: How Habits of Mind Govern Scientific Belief*. Chicago: University of Chicago Press, 1993. 288 pages

Interprets Kuhn's paradigm shifts. Argues that breaking down particular habits of mind is key to understanding processes through which one model is supplanted by another.

1204. Martin, Brian. "The Critique of Science Becomes Academic." *STHV* 18 (Spring 1993): 247–59.

Ascertains that approaches centered in radical critique will revitalize science studies, moving scholars away from "the study of science as it is serving society as it is."

1205. McCrae, Murdo William, ed. *The Literature of Science: Perspectives on Popular Science*. Athens, GA: University of Georgia Press, 1993. 321 pages

Presents 16 essays on the language, rhetoric, history, and hermeneutics of popular scientific writing.
Essayists: Anderson, Charles M.; Angyal, Andrew J.; Clarke, Bruce; Eger, Martin; Fahnestock, Jeanne; Kelley, Robert T.; Masur, Louis P.; McRae, Murdo William; Pegg, Barry; Pitts, Mary Ellen; Porush, David S.; Russell, Doug; Stone, David A.; Wassertein, Alan G.

1206. Mehlenbacher, Brad. "Rhetorical Moves in Scientific Proposal Writing: A Case Study from Biochemical Engineering." *DAI* 54 (October 1993): 1337A.

Argues that although rhetoricians and sociologists treat scientific and technical writers as nonreflective and arhetorical, proposal writing requires numerous rhetorical devices.

1207. Miller, Christine M. "Framing Arguments in a Technical Controversy: Assumptions about Science and Technology in the Decision to Launch the Space Shuttle *Challenger*." *JTWC* 23 (1993): 99–114.

Explores three dominant conceptions of science and technology which appear to account for why engineers failed to persuade managers not to launch the *Challenger*.

1208. Mulkay, M. "Rhetorics of Hope and Fear in the Great Embryo Debate." *SocStSc* 23 (November 1993): 721–42.

Points out that the 1990 British parliamentary debate on human embryo research suggests a need for preserving scientific rhetoric, showing how opposing rhetorics may affect future scientific research appraisals.

1209. Pakes, Gary E. "Writing Clinical Investigator's Brochures on Drugs for a Pharmaceutical Company." *JTWC* 23 (1993): 181–89.

Maps a streamlined, succinct, and easily readable format for the clinical investigator's brochure by closely paralleling research and development history of the drug.

1210. Peters, Thomas Nathan. "A Rhetorical Project for Understanding Scientific Change." *DAI* 53 (January 1993): 2162A.

Uses scientific argument to test theories of scientific change encountered in the literature of the history, philosophy, sociology, and rhetoric of science.

1211. Pfeifer, Mark P., and Gwendolyn L. Snodgrass. "Medical School Libraries' Handling of Articles That Report Invalid Science." *AM* 67 (February 1992): 109–13.

Results show that few medical libraries identify scientifically invalid articles they have.

1212. Pycior, H. M. "Reaping the Benefits of Collaboration while Avoiding Its Pitfalls." *SocStSc* 23 (May 1993): 301–23.

Argues that Marie Curie's "rise to prominence" was less the consequence of collaborative research with her husband than independent papers on the physics and chemistry of radioactivity.

1213. Rouse, Joseph. "What Are Cultural Studies of Scientific Knowledge?" *Configurations* 1 (Winter 1993): 1–22.

Argues that cultural studies aims to construct "authoritative knowledge of the world" by exploring how the sciences establish meaning.

1214. Sauer, Beverly. "Demand Modeling, New Mode Problems, and the $64 Question: Technological Utopianism in America's Race to Develop High Speed Rail Technology." *IEEE* 36 (September 1993): 144–51.

Analyzes two reports. Argues that proposal writers who argue for untried and untested visionary designs face ethical and rhetorical dilemmas.

1215. Schryer, Catherine F. "Records as Genre." *WC* 10 (April 1993): 200–234.

Reviews theories of genre; analyzes how record-keeping promotes certain kinds of literacies and marginalizes others in a college of veterinary medicine.

1216. Selzer, Jack. *Understanding Scientific Prose*. Rhetoric of the Human Sciences. Madison, WI: University of Wisconsin Press, 1993. 388 pages

Fifteen essays illustrate methods of rhetorical criticism and scholarship on the rhetoric of science. They offer deconstructionist, feminist, sociolinguistic, reader-response, and other analyses of the rhetoric in one scientific article, "The Spandrels of San Marco and the Panglossian Paradigm: A Critique of the Adaptionist Programme" (1979) by Stephen Jay Gould and Richard Lewontin.

Essayists: Bazerman, Charles; Charney, Davida; Couture, Barbara; Fahnestock, Jeanne; Gould, Stephen Jay; Gragson, Gay; Halloran, S. Michael; Herndl, Carl; Journet, Debra; Lyne, John; Miller, Caroline; Myers, Greg; Rhoades, Georgia; Rosner, Mary; Selzer, Jack; Wells, Susan; Winsor, Dorothy.

1217. Sharf, Barbara F. "Reading the Vital Signs: Research in Health Care Communication." *ComM* 60 (March 1993): 35–41.

Examines health communication including physician-patient communication, health information dissemination, and social support.

1218. Shulkin, David J., James E. Goin, and Rennie Drummond. "Patterns of Authorship among Chairmen of Departments of Medicine." *AM* 68 (September 1993): 688–92.

Provides results from the study of senior physicians' publishing patterns over a 12-year period.

1219. Sismondo, S. "Some Social Constructions." *SocStSc* 23 (August 1993): 515–53.

Argues that contemporary social construction metaphors are not equally valuable or reliable when applied to science studies. Sees "neo-Kantian" or "idealist" constructions as least useful of all.

1220. Slaughter, Sheila. "Beyond Basic Science: Research University Presidents' Narratives of Science Policy." *STHV* 18 (Summer 1993): 278–302.

Maintains that narratives of research university presidents now celebrate marketable technology rather than the "fruits of research." Points out that scholarly entrepreneurial activity will be rewarded over other university research.

1221. Smith, Wilbur L. "The Need to Train Residents to Write Effectively." *AM* 67 (October 1992): 659.

Recommends placing more emphasis on writing skills in residency programs so that less "ambiguity, lack of clarity, and unnecessary verbiage" are found in medical records.

1222. Stair, Thomas O., and John M. Howell. "Using Imaginary Patients to Test Students' Clinical Documentation Skills." *AM* 67 (August 1992): 550.

Examines a standardized method for critiquing medical students' abilities to write patient histories.

1223. Stillman, Paula L. "Technical Issues: Logistics." *AM* 68 (June 1993): 464–68.

Discusses the role of "standardized" patients in helping teach medical students oral and written communication skills.

1224. Theriot, Nancy M. "Women's Voices in Nineteenth-Century Medical Discourse: A Step toward Deconstructing Science." *Signs* 19 (1993): 1–31.

Studies women's voices in medical discourse—as patients and physicians—as a means to seeing gender and science as mutually constituting.

1225. Thompson, Dorothea K. "Arguing for Experimental 'Facts' in Science: A Study of Research Article Results Sections in Biochemistry." *WC* 10 (January 1993): 106–28.

Identifies six rhetorical moves used in the results sections of biochemistry articles; demonstrates their persuasive nature.

1226. Tolbert, Jane Thornton. "A Case Study of a Seventeenth-Century Gatekeeper: The Role of Nicolas-Claude Fabri de Peiresc in the Dissemination of Science through the Correspondence Networks." *DAI* 53 (April 1993): 3410A.

Examines the role of rhetoric, personality, and social status in Peiresc's promotion of the dissemination of scientific discoveries.

1227. Welsh, Jim. "Commentary on Steven Spielberg's 'Jurassic Park.'" *AM* 68 (September 1993): 662–63.

Examines the public's image of science as mirrored in current films such as *Jurassic Park*.

1228. Wright, Susan. "The Social Warp of Science: Writing the History of Genetic Engineering Policy." *STHV* 18 (Winter 1993): 79–101.

Argues that methodologies sensitive to the operations of power, especially as expressed in discourse, can bridge the gulf between political theory and the social studies of science.

See also 138, 142, 164, 165

2.14 CROSS-DISCIPLINARY STUDIES

1229. Ackerman, John M. "The Promise of Writing to Learn." *WC* 10 (June 1993): 334–70.

Argues that both theoretical and empirical studies of cross-curricular writing have overstated its merits as a technology and as a "mode of learning."

1230. Aczel, Peter, David Israel, Stanley Peters, and Yasuhiro Katagiri, eds. *Situation Theory and Its Applications, Volume 3.* Center for the Study of Language and Information, CSLI Lecture Notes, Number 37. Chicago: University of Chicago Press, 1993. 430 pages

The editors include a collection of essays from the Third International Conference on situation theory and its applications. The contributors aim to create a theory of information and provide a common set of tools for an analysis of phenomena from cognitive science, AI, linguistics, logic, philosophy, and mathematics.

Essayists: Barwise, Jon; Coons, Robert C.; Cooper, Robin; Crimmins, Mark; Devlin, Keith; Gabday, D. M.; Georgeff, Michael; Ginzburg, Jonathan; Haglund, Bjorn; Hwang, Chung Hee; Lager, Torbjorn; Morley, David; Poesio, Maffino; Rao, Anand; Rosenberg, Duska; Schubert, Lenhart K.; Schulz, Stephen, M.; Westerstahl, Dag.

1231. Arnold, Louise, and T. Lee Willoughby. "Curricular Integration at the University of Missouri—Kansas City School of Medicine." *PMS* 76 (February 1993): 35–40.

Presents a longitudinal study of 547 BA/MD degree (six year) students which suggests that interdisciplinary learning increases critical thinking, clinical ability, and rapport with patients.

1232. Bishop, Wendy. *Genre as 'Field Coverage'—Division in Writing Instruction Erase Our Common Ground.* Louisville, KY: National Council of Teachers of English, November 1992. ERIC ED 352 661. 15 pages

Argues that writing courses should emphasize writing commonalities, process instruction, and genre experimentation rather than segregating different genres such as technical writing and creative writing.

1233. Cortazzi, Martin. *Narrative Analysis.* Bristol, PA: Falmer Press, 1993. 224 pages

Analyzes narratives from a variety of perspectives. Draws on models from sociology, psychology, literary analysis, and anthropology.

1234. Desplanques, Marie-Annick. "Women, Folklore and Communication: Informal Social Gatherings in a France-Newfoundland Context." *DAI* 53 (June 1993): 4428–29A.

Explores the dynamics of verbal interaction in a number of folklore genres.

1235. Edwards, Ronald G. "Multiculturalism and Its Link to Quality Education and Democracy." *MultiR* 2 (June 1993): 12–14.

Contends that the international or global perspective on multicultural education cuts across cultural boundaries.

1236. Ervin, Elizabeth. "Interdisciplinarity or 'An Elaborate Edifice Built on Sand'? Rethinking Rhetoric's Place." *RR* 12 (Fall 1993): 84–105.

Discusses complex relationships between the disciplines of history and rhetoric.

1237. Farris, Christine. *Disciplining the Disciplines: The Paradox of Writing across the Curriculum Claims.* San Diego, CA: Conference on College Composition and Communication, March/April 1993. ERIC ED 358 468. 13 pages

Argues that WAC may provide a means of overarching the traditional academic departmental writing specialization, but institutional constraints may play an important role in determining what WAC can and cannot do.

1238. Fitzgerald, Thomas K. *Metaphors of Identity: A Culture-Communication Dialogue.* Albany, NY: State University of New York Press, 1993. 264 pages

Combines anthropology, psychology, and other disciplines in a study of personal identity, communication, and culture.

1239. Goldsmith-Conley, Elizabeth Harriet. "Art as Argument: A Rhetorical Approach to Teaching Literature and Painting." *DAI* 53 (January 1993): 2280A.

Shows that a rhetorical approach emphasizing questions of audience, purpose, and technique helps to mediate conflicts about content and pedagogy in the literature and art curriculum and will promote critical thinking skills in students.

1240. Hanson, Michele. "The Library as Laboratory for Interdisciplinary Studies." *TETYC* 20 (October 1993): 222–28.

Discusses a composition assignment that incorporates library visits in teaching basic search strategies.

1241. Heath, Shirley Brice, and Milbrey W. McLaughlin, eds. *Identity and Inner-City Youth: Beyond Ethnicity and Gender.* New York: Teachers College Press, 1993. 256 pages

The contributors discuss neighborhood-based organizations that serve inner-city youngsters through rituals, processes, and structures that make room for building identities. They address issues of collaboration across organizations, the role of gangs in social control, and the historical roles of ethnicity and gender in youth organizations.
Essayists: Ball, Arnetha; Fine, Gary Alan; Hansol, Elisabeth; Heath, Shirley Brice; James, Thomas; Langman, Juliet; McLaughlin, Milbrey W.; Mechling, Jay; Vigil, James Diego.

1242. Huff, Linda. *The Voice of a Composition Person in the Midst of Disciplinary Diversity.* San Diego, CA: Conference on College Composition and Communication, March/April 1993. ERIC ED 356 471. 9 pages

Points out that English departments are becoming more theory centered. Argues that composition specialists must identify the ideological pedagogies they uphold in their classrooms and the language they use as a vehicle for their own voice.

1243. Hutchinson, Mary. *The Composition Teacher as Drudge: The Pitfalls and Perils of Linking across the Disciplines.* San Diego, CA: Conference on College Composition and Communication, March/April 1993. ERIC ED 359 553. 7 pages

Argues that writing across the curriculum, as it has evolved, serves only to perpetuate the stereotype that composition is tangential to the "content courses" and that composition teachers are inferior "copy editors."

1244. Johnsen, John. *Anthropology 101 and English 101: Ethnography as Data Source and Text.* San Diego, CA: Conference on College Composition and Communication,

March/April 1993. ERIC ED 358 457. 5 pages

Discusses how linking an anthropology and an English class through an ethnography project increases opportunities for collaborative writing as well as an appreciation of ethnography as literature.

1245. Jones, Robert, and Joseph J. Comprone. "Where Do We Go Next in Writing across the Curriculum?" *CCC* 44 (February 1993): 59–68.

Reviews recent literature, discusses critical problems, and offers solutions for instituting WAC programs.

1246. Journet, Debra. "Biological Explanation, Political Ideology, and 'Blurred Genres': A Bakhtinian Reading of the Science Essays of J. B. S. Haldane." *TCQ* 2 (Spring 1993): 185–204.

Examines biologist and Marxist J. B. S. Haldane's essays to show how science and politics are connected.

1247. Journet, Debra. "Interdisciplinary Discourse and 'Boundary Rhetoric': The Case of S. E. Jelliffe." *WC* 10 (October 1993): 510–41.

Examines rhetorical hurdles faced by an early twentieth-century physician attempting to reconcile conflicting genres, values, and methodologies in neurology and pschoanalysis.

1248. Keessen, Jan, and Majorie Ann White. *WAC—An Answer to Multicultural Diversity.* San Antonio, TX: Minority Student Today Conference, October, 1991. ERIC ED 348 693. 8 pages

Explores the need to establish interdisciplinary guidelines to foster more effective writing instruction.

1249. Keessen, Jan, and Majorie Ann White. *Writing across the Curriculum. 'Wanted: Guidelines for Teaching Writing in Nonwriting Courses.'* Cincinnati, OH: Conference on College Composition and Communication, March 1992. ERIC ED 348 693. 8 pages

Explores the need to establish interdisciplinary guidelines to foster more effective writing instruction.

1250. Reynolds, Nedra. "*Ethos* as Location: New Sites for Understanding Discursive Authority." *RR* 11 (Spring 1993): 325–38.

Explores *ethos* as location of social identity(ies) from which people write; argues for a critical awareness of *ethos* in the construction of composition texts, syllabi, and other public forums in which composition is discussed.

1251. Sands, Roberta G. "'Can You Overlap Here?': A Question for an Interdisciplinary Team." *DPr* 16 (October/December 1993): 545–64.

Proposes that organizational discourse can reflect conflicts between members of different disciplines skeptical about using conventions from other fields.

1252. Schrag, Sonja Simonson. "The Discourse of Music Scholarship." *DAI* 53 (February 1993): 2800A.

Argues that musicologists, performers, composers, and teachers represent themselves as scholars and generate new knowledge through writing, dialogue, and argumentation.

1253. Sensenbaugh, Roger. "Writing across the Curriculum: Toward the Year 2000." ERIC Clearinghouse on Reading and Communication Skills, 1993. ERIC ED 354 549. 3 pages

Concludes from summarizing more than 300 ERIC database items concerning WAC published between 1990 and 1992 that the WAC movement will continue to be important in the year 2000.

1254. Shotter, John. *Cultural Politics of Everyday Life: Social Constructionism, Rhetoric, and Knowing of the Third Kind.* Toronto: University of Toronto Press, 1993. 240 pages

Argues for an experiential rather than theoretical basis for epistemology.

1255. Stewart, Penny. "Cross-Curricular Grading: H. P. Grice's Principle in Every Teacher's Repertoire." Portales, NM, Eastern New Mexico University, 1993. ERIC ED 355 553. 7 pages

Proposes that to establish credibility in student evaluation, teachers should grade according to Grice's "cooperative principle" theory.

1256. Tchudi, Stephen, ed. *The Astonishing Curriculum: Integrating Science and Humanities through Language.* Urbana, IL: NCTE, 1993. 168 pages

Fifteen essays studying the interrelations of science and humanities illustrate successful "ways of celebrating and capitalizing on the interdisciplinary and linguistic openness of young children; of enriching learning through discovery and expression in the middle, junior high, and senior high years; and of synthesizing knowledge with understanding in college and university programs."
Essayists: Abt-Perkins, Dawn; Blanchette, Brad; Bridgman, Terrie; Carroll, Pamela Sissi; Carvelas, Betty; Cohn, Ann Watson; Cousin, Patricia Tefft; Fox, Roy F.; Gallard, Alejandro J.; Gallas, Karen; Goodney, David E.; Jacobs, Erica; Long, Carol S.; Maguire, Mary H.; Mathers, Kathy; Maylath, Bruce; Moore, Jane; Pagnucci, Gian; Parren, Lauren; Pastore, Judith Laurence; Peetoom, Adrian; Pope, Mike; Prentice, Linda; Shutler, Jean Rohner; Wolfe, Lila F.

1257. Thaiss, Chris. "When Is a Program?" *CompC* 6 (December 1993): 8–9.

Questions the traditional model of an academic program and explores less formal definitions of a WAC program.

1258. Walsh, S. M. *How to Develop a Program for Writing across the Curriculum with an Established Faculty in a Period of Retrenchment.* Richmond, VA: National Council of Teachers of English, March 1993. ERIC ED 358 449. 10 pages

Discusses the role played by educational consultants in the development of WAC programs. Points out that veteran faculty members may be unwilling to change their teaching styles.

1259. Weston, Ruth D. "Science by Poetry, Fiction by Geometry: Interdisciplinary Reading and Writing." *CEA* 55 (Winter 1993): 71–76.

Discusses teaching interdisciplinary critical thinking skills and helping students understand the connections among analytical skills used in various disciplines.

1260. Whitney, Anne. *Art Therapy: What Does It Have to Say to Writing Teachers?* San Diego, CA: Conference on College Composition and Communication, March/April 1993. ERIC ED 359 554. 8 pages

Discusses the connection between art therapy and the teaching of writing; argues that both are processes aimed at self-discovery.

3

Teacher Education, Administration, and Social Roles

3.1 TEACHER EDUCATION

1261. Anderson, Jim. "Journal Writing: The Promise and the Reality." *JR* 36 (December 1992/January 1993): 304–9.

Discusses problems associated with journal writing in teacher education programs such as overuse, ethics, goals and grading. Discusses considerations that should be made when rethinking the role of journals.

1262. Anson, Chris M., Joan Graham, David A. Jolliffe, Nancy S. Shapiro, and Carolyn H. Smith. *Scenarios for Teaching Writing: Contexts for Discussion and Reflective Practices*. Urbana, IL and University Park, PA: National Council of Teachers of English and The Alliance for Undergraduate Education, 1993. 195 pages

The authors present a collection of case studies and discussion materials which define particular moments in teaching writing. They encourage an examination of instructional practices.

1263. Beard, Pauline, and Susan Danielson. "Teacher to Teacher: A Dialogue on the 'Art' of Teaching English." Portland State University, 1993. ERIC ED 354 531. 26 pages

Presents a survey questionnaire concerning classroom practices of 50 randomly sampled high school, community college, and university English teachers in the Portland, Oregon area. Finds that most teachers emphasized that their writing classes had become more student-oriented and were becoming more text-based to develop reading and analytic skills.

1264. Bizzell, Patricia. *Academic Discourse and Critical Consciousness*. Pittsburgh, PA: University of Pittsburgh Press, 1993. 304 pages

Presents essays that document the author's experiences teaching writing for over 10 years. Focuses on how students from diverse backgrounds learn to use language.

1265. Blalock, Susan E. "The Tutor as Creative Teacher: Balancing Collaborative and Directive Teaching Styles." *JGTAD* 1 (Summer 1993): 61–65.

Describes a program that requires TAs to work as writing tutors in addition to receiving more general classroom pedagogy preparation. Points out that TAs transfer experience from a collaborative teaching model (tutoring) to a directive teaching model, improving the overall quality of instruction.

1266. Boardman, Kathleen Ann. "Teaching Experience: New Writing Instructors in a College Program." *DAI* 53 (January 1993): 2347A.

Traces how six new teaching assistants in a one-semester teacher preparation program came to view and enact their roles as teachers and writers.

1267. Bottoms, Laurie. "Notes to My Student Teachers: Last Class before Graduation." *V&R* 4 (Spring 1994): 53–60.

Stresses the importance of writing for both students and their teachers.

1268. Cochrane-Smith, Marilyn, and Susan L. Lytle, eds. *Inside/Outside: Teacher Research and Knowledge.* New York: Teachers College Press/Columbia University, 1993. 310 pages

Includes essays by literacy teacher-researchers and student teachers; provides an analytical introduction by the co-editors; and focuses on teachers as reflective practitioners. Discusses the implications of practice for theory.
Essayists: Baum-Brunner, Shelley; Belzer, Alisa; Black, Leslie; Bousel, Howard; Brody, Dara; Brown, Shirley; Buchanan, Judy; Byer, Leah Beth; Cimakasky, Linda; Cochrane-Smith, Marilyn; Colgan-Davis, Penny; Cornman, Elizabeth; Crouse, Madeleine Rawley; Coy, Deborah; Farmboy, Deidré R.; Fecho, Robert; Feldgus, Elieen Glickman; Freilech, Pamela; Greenspur, Karen; Harris, Mickey; Hartman, Barbara; Headman, Robin; Hilton, Dimitrios; Joe, Samona; Johnston, Patricia; Jumpp, Deborah; Kanevsky, Rhoda

Drucker; Klavens, Janet; Mahoney-Hanley, Maureen; Miller, Teresa Donato; Patton, Keith; Powers, Elizabeth; Ritchie, Marjorie Callahan; Roers, Pamela; Schefer, Debra Miller; Sims, Michele; Synder, Jeni; Starr, Penny A.; Strieb, Lynne Yermanock; Swenson, Jan; Wunner, Kathleen E.; Winklestein, Bruce.

1269. Craig, Judith S., and Robert C. Ostergren. "Establishing an Effective, Voluntary Teaching Assistant Training Program in a Large, Decentralized University Setting." *JGTAD* 1 (Summer 1993): 75—83.

Describes a university-wide program designed to bring together experienced and inexperienced TAs from many disciplines into small-group workshops. Points out that workshops need to address community-wide issues and concerns.

1270. Crepps, Sandra. "Journal, What Journal?" *V&R* 4 (Spring 1994): 3–11.

Describes the use of journals for integrating and reflecting on many aspects of teachers' daily lives.

1271. Davidson, J., and B.C. Bruce. "Inquiring about Inquiry." Center for the Study of Reading, Urbana, IL, 1993. ERIC ED 362 849. 17 pages

The authors identify challenges teachers face when restructuring teacher education in areas of technology and interdisciplinary approaches to inquiry. They propose that teachers-in-training connect ideas across broad subject domains and emphasize experiential and child-centered techniques.

1272. Faery, Rebecca Blevins. "Teachers and Writers: The Faculty Writing Workshop and Writing across the Curriculum." *WPA* 17 (Fall/Winter 1993): 31–42.

Proposes that a faculty writing workshop helps writing teachers improve their teaching because it keeps them mindful of the experience of writing.

1273. Gappa, Lavon. "The Teaching Associate Program: A Collaborative Approach." *JGTAD* 1 (Spring 1993): 25—32.

Describes a GTA training program that combines discipline-specific teacher preparation with a collaborative approach to interdisciplinary research and instruction preparation. Points out that university-wide collaborations were facilitated by department-selected liaisons and experienced TAs called Teaching Associates.

1274. Gibson, Sharon S. *Faculty and Student Communities: The Interactive Contexts of Teachers and Learners.* Louisville, KY: National Council of Teachers of English, November 1992. ERIC ED 355 551. 16 pages

Proposes that writing teachers should draw on their own use of collaborative techniques in attempting to develop similar support groups within the writing classrooms and in the larger university community.

1275. Hall, Dennis R. "*ComPost*: A Writing Program Newsletter and Its Rationale." *WPA* 17 (Fall/Winter 1993): 75–82.

Describes the newsletter developed by the University of Louisville as a vehicle to promote cohesiveness and stability in the writing program.

1276. Han, Eunhye. "Reflective Thinking in Journal Writing: A Case Study of Six Pre-service Teachers." *DAI* 54 (September 1993): 803A.

Examines how preservice teachers approach the task of their own journal writing in terms of reflective thinking.

1277. Hutchings, Pat. "Preparing Graduate Students to Teach." *AAHE* 45 (February 1993): 11–15.

Provides an interview with Leo Lambert, editor of a recently published guide for training TAs; includes specific mentoring strategies.

1278. Kagan, Dona M. "Contexts for the Use of Classroom Cases." *AERJ* 30 (Winter 1993): 703–23.

Reviews the history of case-based instruction in teacher education, showing three uses—as instructional materials, as raw data in research, and as catalysts for change.

1279. Kelly, Kathleen Ann, Laurie Nardone, and Scot Petersen. *To Have or Have Not: The Foucauldian Quandary of Control in Teacher-Training.* Cincinnati, OH: Conference on College Composition and Communication, March 1992. ERIC ED 348 674. 23 pages

Presents three separate discussions of how Foucault's theories provide a way of understanding the power dynamics present in teacher-training and how teaching styles develop.

1280. Keyes, Melissa Ann. "Measuring Changes in Educator Attitudes as a Result of Technical Assistance in Sex Equity." *DAI* 53 (May 1993): 3775A.

Investigates the use of technical assistance to promote sex equity among educators in K–12 public schools.

1281. Li, Xiao-Ming. "A Celebration of Tradition or of Self? An Ethnographic Study of Teachers' Comments on Student Writing in America and in China." *DAI* 53 (May 1993): 3829A.

Examines commonly shared criteria of "good writing" among American and Chinese teachers. Argues that the notion of "good writing" has to be placed in a historical and cultural context.

1282. Low, Patricia Jeanine. "Literate Learners: The Evolution of Teacher Research at the Bread Loaf School of English (Vermont)." *DAI* 54 (November 1993): 1709A.

Presents interviews with Bread Loaf Program participants.

1283. McCleary, Bill. "Training of TAs Takes Surprising Turn for the Better, Survey Finds." *CompC* 6 (April 1993): 1–3, 6.

Summarizes information on TA training programs in *Preparing Graduate Students to Teach*, edited by Leo Lambert and Stacey Lane Tice.

1284. Metz, Virginia Ellen. "Training Teachers to Teach Writing: Impact on Teacher Attitudes and Student Products." *DAI* 54 (November 1993): 1765A.

Examines teachers' apprehensions with their own writing and how this is transferred to students. Proposes a way to reduce this apprehension.

1285. Meyer-Reimer, K., and B. C. Bruce. "Building Teacher-Researcher Collaboration: Dilemmas and Strategies." Center for the Study of Reading, 1993. ERIC ED 357 331. 13 pages

Examines ethical dimensions of teacher-researcher collaboration. Explores problems related to topics such as including identifying roles of teachers and researchers as well as time, institutional, and political constraints. Lists conditions for successful collaboration.

1286. Newkirk, Thomas, ed. *Nuts and Bolts: A Practical Guide to Teaching College Composition*. Portsmouth, NH: Heinemann-Boynton/Cook, 1993. 216 pages

Eight essays address practical concerns of beginning teachers of composition, based on the "oral culture" (or "lore") from the writing program at the University of New Hampshire.
Essayists: Gallenger, Bruce; Chiserie-Strater, Elizabeth; Harrigan, Jane; Newkirk, Thomas; Qualley, Donna; Rule, Rebecca; Sullivan, Patricia A.; Wheeler, Sue.

1287. Nilson, Linda B. "Training TAs in Disciplinary Clusters: A Cost-Effective Alternative to Departmental Programs." *JGTAD* 1 (Spring 1993): 33—41.

Describes an interdisciplinary training program that brings together TAs from methodologically similar departments (such as humanities and social sciences) into teacher-orientation seminars. Discusses advantages and disadvantages of the program.

1288. Norton, Mary F. "Visions of the Future: Utopian and Apocalyptic Designs." *CEAF* 23–24 (Summer/Winter 1993–1994): 15–17.

Argues that the teacher's role in multidisciplinary courses includes the new discourse of culture and ethnography.

1289. Patterson, Leslie, Carol Minnick Santa, Kathy G. Short, and Karen Smith, eds. *Teachers Are Researchers: Reflection and Action*. Neward, DE: International Reading Association, 1993. 248 pages

Four essays outline the concept of teacher-research, followed by 20 essays of teacher-researchers reflecting upon the research process as seen in their classrooms. They offer examples of studies conducted at a variety of educational levels, detailing how they as teacher-researchers pursued their inquiries while still teaching.
Essayists: Atwell, Nancie; Boody, Robert M.; Brinkley, Ellen H.; Cline, Dawn M.; Clyde, Jean Anne; Condon, Mark W. F.; Crowell, Caryl G.; Daniel, Kathleen; Fiderer, Adele; Gibson, Christine M.; Hancock, Jan; Heichel, Laura G.; Hirtle, Jeannine S.; Hubbard, Ruth Shagoury; Isakson, Marne B.; Jongsma, Kathleen Stumpf; Lee, Sharon; McFarland, Katherine P.; McLean, Mari M.; Miller, Tristan M.; Nocerino, Mary Ann; Patterson, Leslie; Patton, Lee; Pierce, Kathryn Mitchell; Power, Brenda Miller; Reimer, Kathryn Meyer; Santa, Carol Minnick; Shannon, Patrick; Short, Kathy G.; Smith, Karen; Sommer, Mary Kenna; Stansell, John C.; Stephens, Diane; Whitin, Phyllis E.; Wood, Katie; Zuercher, Nancy T.

1290. Peters, William H. *Critical Conditions for Effective Writing Strategies for Language Diverse Learners.* Louisville, KY: National Council of Teachers of English, November 1992. ERIC ED 355 543. 8 pages

Stresses the role of teacher ethnosensitivity in the language-diverse classroom for maximizing students' writing potential.

1291. Pytlik, Betty P. *A Short History of Graduate Preparation of Writing Teachers.* Louisville, KY: National Council of Teachers of English, November 1992. ERIC ED 355 545. 14 pages

Reviews the history of writing teacher preparation in the United States.

1292. Romano, Tom. *The Teacher Celebrates Writing.* Louisville, KY: National Council of Teachers of English, November 1992. ERIC ED 355 516. 18 pages

Suggests complementing one's professional writing of academic articles by writing narratives for personal enjoyment and fulfillment.

1293. Schecter, Sandra R., and Shawn Parkhurst. "Ideological Divergences in a Teacher-Research Group." *AERJ* 30 (Winter 1993): 771–98.

Studies roles played by ideology in a teacher research group. Argues for the importance of accounting for ideological differences in a particular study.

1294. Strickland, Kathleen, and James Strickland. *Un-Covering the Curriculum: Whole Language in Secondary and Postsecondary Classrooms.* Portsmouth, NH: Heinemann-Boynton/Cook, 1993. 240 pages

Presents stories, strategies, and examples of student work from whole language classrooms.

1295. Sydow, Debbie. *Professional Development Issues for Community College Faculty.* San Diego, CA: Conference on College Com-

position and Communication, March/April 1993. ERIC ED 357 364. 12 pages

A survey study shows that most community college English faculty in Virginia are engaged in professional development activities. Also finds that more time is needed for professional development.

1296. Tremmel, Robert. "Zen and the Art of Reflective Practice in Teacher Education." *HER* 63 (Winter 1993): 434–58.

Discusses the benefits of incorporating Zen Buddhist practice of "mindfulness" into reflective teaching and teacher education programs.

1297. Trickey, Karen B. "Reflecting on Practice Together: A Case Study of Dialogue between Experienced and Beginning Art Teachers." *DAI* 54 (November 1993): 1645A.

Shows benefits of art teachers working collaboratively and at all levels of experience for the purpose of expanding growth as artists and teachers.

1298. Walvoord, Barbara E. "How to Get Disciplined-Based Faculty into WAC Workshops." *CompC* 5 (January 1993): 8–9.

Argues that WAC supporters should think of themselves "as being in the business of faculty development, rather than in the business of writing across the curriculum."

1299. Watson, Karilee, and Mary Ann Traxler. *Writing across the Curriculum: Creating a Professional Writing Sequence for a Teacher Education Program.* Louisville, KY: Association of Independent Liberal Arts Colleges for Teacher Education, June 1992. ERIC ED 351 294. 19 pages

Discusses a program that includes writing competency as part of teacher training. Points out that education students submit writing portfolios as a demonstration of their professional development.

1300. Welch, Nancy. "Resisting the Faith: Conversion, Resistance, and the Training of Teachers." *CE* 55 (April 1993): 387–401.

Describes her experience of teacher instruction. Argues that its "convergent" model was really one of conversion.

1301. Wenner, Barbara Britton. *Personal Histories of Four Composition Teachers: How Much Have We Changed?* San Diego, CA: Conference on College Composition and Communication, March/April 1993. ERIC ED 357 391. 12 pages

Finds that teachers seemed inspired rather than strangulated by their regard for theory; suggests that thoughtful proliferation and evolution of theory in the classroom was the trend.

1302. White, John O. "A Look at California's New Standards for Preparing and Assessing English Teachers." *CalE* 29 (Fall 1993): 10–11, 17, 19.

Summarizes 12 standards for English teacher preparation adopted by the California Commission on Teacher Credentialing and their effect on college teacher-training programs.

1303. Wilhoit, Stephen. "Learning (and Relearning) to Teach." *Inland* 16 (Fall/Winter 1993): 14–17.

Offers five guidelines for training new writing instructors.

1304. Wilson, Donald. *Retread: The (Re)Shaping of an Untrained Composition Teacher.* Pittsburgh, PA: Annual Meeting of the college English Association, March 1992. ERIC ED 353 582. 8 pages

Uses personal narrative to illustrate difficulties experienced by beginning teachers who are burdened with heavy workloads, inadequately trained, and faced with a mixture of different pedagogies.

1305. Zubizarreta, John. "Shared Scholarship in the Emerging Professoriate." *CEAF* 23–24 (Summer/Winter 1993–1994): 12–14.

Examines the role of research and scholarship in quality teaching.

3.2 ADMINISTRATION

1306. "ADE Policy Statement and Guidelines." *ADE* 105 (Spring 1993): 43–48.

Provides statements and policies on good practice (teaching, evaluation, scholarship), use of outside reviewers, class size and workload, and use of adjunct faculty.

1307. "ADE Statement on the Use of Part-Time and Full-Time Adjunct Faculty." *ADE* 104 (Spring 1993): 62.

Outlines problems caused by the growing number of adjunct faculty. Presents guidelines for limiting the number of appointments and for addressing concerns of adjuncts.

1308. Allen, Virginia. "A Comment on 'Teaching College English as a Woman' [response to Bloom, *CE* 54 (November 1992)]." *CE* 55 (September 1993): 552–56.

Calls for action against injustices to part-time composition instructors.

1309. Berger, Mary Jo. "Funding and Support for Basic Writing: Why Is There So Little?" *JBW* 12 (Spring 1993): 81–89.

Explains the budgeting process in higher education. Recommends strategies for teachers and administrators trying to increase funding for basic writing programs.

1310. Bishop, Wendy. "Writing Is/And Therapy? Raising Questions about Writing Classrooms and Writing Program Administration." *JAC* 13 (Fall 1993): 503–16.

Points out that writing instructors often become therapists. Calls for analogies between writing instruction and therapy to become a part of conference papers and journal articles.

1311. Bishop, Wendy, and Gay Lynn Crossley. "Doing the Hokey Pokey? Why Writing Program Administrators' Job Conditions Don't Seem to Be Improving." *CompSt* 21 (Spring 1993): 46–59.

Traces the difficult working conditions of WPA to the ill definition of duties, conflicts with senior faculty, and a feminization of the role.

1312. Brown, Ted. "Unkind Cuts: Rethinking the Rhetoric of Academic Job Rejection Letters." *CE* 55 (November 1993): 770–78.

Analyzes several sample letters; argues that applicants deserve to be treated with more consideration and dignity when being rejected.

1313. Capps, Randall. "Communicating Sudden Change in Task and Culture: The Inglis Montmagny Story." *IEEE* 36 (March 1993): 30–34.

Highlights 10 principles to administer the socio-technical concept which is the foundation of self-directed work teams. Presents a case study of Inglis Montmagny.

1314. "The Corbett Editorship of *CCC*, 1974–1979." *Focuses* 6 (Winter 1993): 97–100.

Notes the author's editorship. Argues against an overemphasis on a narrowly defined type of scholarship about promotion and tenure.

1315. Gappa, Judith M., and David W. Leslie. *The Invisible Faculty: Improving the Status of Part-Timers in Higher Education*. San Francisco: Jossey-Bass, 1993. 324 pages

Offers employment profiles of part-time faculty members and proposes institutional policies to improve their status and enhance their contributions to the academic community. Draws on interviews with 467 administrators and faculty members at 18 colleges and universities.

1316. Gebhardt, Richard. "Editor's Column." *CCC* 44 (December 1993): 439–42.

Outlines three issues related to scholarship and the "academic reward system."

1317. Gunner, Jeanne. "The Status of Basic Writing Teachers: Do We Need a 'Maryland Resolution'?" *JBW* 12 (Spring 1993): 57–63.

Analyzes composition studies and the impact of professional statements by the Wyoming Conference, CCCC, and the Council of Writing Program Administrators. Recommends a resolution which would reassert the value of teaching.

1318. Hillman, Linda. *Nontenure Track Positions in Writing Programs: A Narrative of One*. Boston, MA: Conference on College Composition and Communication, March 1991. ERIC ED 353 601. 14 pages

Reports on the politics involved in the employment renewability of 10 female nontenure-track writing faculty at DePaul University, Illinois.

1319. Howard, Rebecca Moore. "Power Revisited: Or, How We Became a Department." *WPA* 16 (Spring 1993): 37–49.

Describes Edward M. White's "institution-changing strategies" and tells how the writing program at Colgate became the Colgate Department of Interdisciplinary Writing.

1320. Hult, Christine. *The Organization and Administration of an Undergraduate Writing Emphasis*. San Diego, CA: Conference on College Composition and Communication, March/April 1993. ERIC ED 358 479. 14 pages

Discusses developing and administering college writing programs in addition to literature programs.

1321. Kolson, Kenneth, and Sandee Yuen. "On Reconciling Teaching and Research." *AAHE* 45 (February 1993): 7–10.

Describes university programs that encourage classroom research and projects involving collaboration between faculty and students.

1322. Lemon, Hallie S., Joan Livingston-Webber, Randy Smith, Kris Jacobus, and Therese

Purdy. *The Permanent Temps' Lament: Why Not Tenure Status?* San Diego, CA: Conference on College Composition and Communication, March/April 1993. ERIC ED 356 483. 51 pages

> Recounts the history and experiences of a group of permanent "temporary" writing instructors trying to gain tenurable status at Western Illinois University.

1323. Letourneau, Kathrine C. "Sex Type, Achievement Motivation and Locus-of-Control in Female Administrators and Female Teachers." *DAI* 54 (December 1993): 2014A.

> Results support the presence of dualistic sex traits and high locus of control in female administrators. Findings question the trait of competitiveness assigned to administrators.

1324. Lovitt, Carl R. "Three South Carolina Institutions Co-Host First Regional Writing across the Curriculum Conference." *CompC* 6 (May 1993): 10–12.

> Describes a writing across the curriculum conference held February 18–19, 1993, which focused on teaching and institutional issues.

1325. McCleary, Bill. "Higher Education Must End 'Two-Tier Faculty,' New Book Says." *CompC* 6 (December 1993): 1–3.

> Reports on *The Invisible Faculty: Improving the Status of Part-Timers in Higher Education* by Judith Grappa and David Leslie. Discounts myths about part-timers and recommends alternative career tracks.

1326. McCleary, Bill. "We Do Not Get Off to a Flying Start on Enforcing the Wyoming Resolution." *CompC* 6 (May 1993): 10–12.

> Describes efforts to form an "enforcement committee" for the Wyoming Resolution. Appends a 1991 CCCC proposal for implementing the resolution.

1327. McDonald, James C. *Louisiana and the Wyoming Resolution: A Survey of Writing Programs.* Cincinnati, OH: Conference on College Composition and Communication, March 1992. ERIC ED 357 390. 17 pages

> Reports on a study that surveyed 21 college writing programs in Louisiana about the working conditions for writing teachers.

1328. Montgomery, Nancy. *The Teacher's Role in the Writing Workshop.* Cincinnati, OH: Conference on College Composition and Communication, March 1992. ERIC ED 354 536. 9 pages

> Uses her observations of the writing workshop activities of three teachers to provide information on teacher and student roles in successful workshops.

1329. Phelps, Louise Wetherbee. "A Constrained Vision of the Writing Classroom." *Profession* 93 (1993): 46–54.

> Draws on her experiences as a writing program administrator to demonstrate the need for teachers to enact their personal ethics without imposing them on their students.

1330. Seitz, James E. "Eluding Righteous Discourse: A Discreet Politics for New Writing Curricula." *WPA* 16 (Spring 1993): 7–14.

> Invites writing program administrators to consider Roland Barthes' distinction between "politics" and "the political" in developing effective writing curricula.

1331. Stanley, Linda C. "Problems and Principles in Maintaining WAC Programs." *CompC* 6 (October 1993): 8–9.

> Suggests tying WAC to the Wingspread Conference's "Seven Principles for Good Practices in Undergraduate Education" to explain and defend WAC programs.

1332. Steeples, Christine. "A Computer-Mediated Learning Environment for Adult Learners: Supporting Collaboration and Self-Direction." *JEdM&H* 2 (1993): 443–54.

> Discusses issues of learner collaboration and learner independecne in relation to

concepts of public and private spaces within electronic learning environments.

3.3 SUPPORT SERVICES

1333. Aleo, Cynthia. "Does a Comma Splice Have Horns?" *WLN* 17 (May 1993): 9.

Compares tutoring to being a matador in the bullring. Argues that tutors must adapt techniques to individual clients instead of using only one strategy for all students.

1334. Amato, Katya. "Making Bricks without Straw: The Fate of One Writing Center." *WLN* 17 (June 1993): 4–7.

Questions whether centers should continue when state budget cuts reduce the facilities to a volunteer effort.

1335. Baker, Richard. "Tutors' Column: The Payoff." *WLN* 17 (March 1993): 9.

Points out that small triumphs are as important as great success stories.

1336. Barrios, Amy. "Tutors' Column: When Writing Is Not the Issue." *WLN* 17 (February 1993): 9–10.

Points out that students may reveal personal or academic needs in tutorials. Advises to refer emotionally-distressed students for counselling and to help others acquire the tools of academic discourse.

1337. Bartosenski, Mary. "Spellbound by a Clean Page." *WLN* 18 (November 1993): 8–9.

Points out that students dislike revising "perfect looking" texts produced by laser printers. Providing scrap paper and colored pens, tutors enable students to begin necessary revision.

1338. Birdsall, Mary Pat. "Using Response Journals for Problem-Solving in the Writing Center." *WLN* 17 (April 1993): 12–16.

Maintains that consultants can ensure continuity of instruction, discuss students' ex-

pectations, share concerns and techniques, maintain morale, express self-doubt, write to learn decrease isolation and develop a friendly atmosphere.

1339. Bishop, Wendy. "Writing from the Tips of Our Tongues: Writers, Tutors, and Talk." *WCJ* 14 (Fall 1993): 30–43.

Argues that talk about writing that occurs between students and writing center tutors should be understood as a central collaborative activity supporting acts of composing.

1340. Brainard, David. "Tutoring and Learning Disabilities." *WLN* 17 (May 1993): 15–16.

Argues that learning disabled students think in "learning disabled language." Points out that they must accept their thinking and then "transpose this language into standard language." Cites ways to assist these students.

1341. Brendel, Gail. "Tutors' Column." *WLN* 18 (October 1993): 11–12.

A "familiar-professional" relationship with clients enables Brendel to study their style without confusing it with their personal needs.

1342. Broadbent, Marianne, and Hans Lofgren. "Informative Delivery: Identifying Priorities, Performance, and Value." *IPM* 29 (1993): 683–701.

The authors adapt critical success factor (CSF) methodology, priority and performance evaluation (PAPE), and cost-benefit analysis to an information services evaluation context.

1343. Carter, Barbara B. "A Mini-Course Serves Many Purposes." *WLN* 17 (March 1993): 14–16.

Cites six steps for creating an effective summary and points out four reasons why students have difficulty with summarizing journal articles.

1344. Clark, Irene L. "Portfolio Evaluation, Collaboration, and Writing Centers." *CCC* 44 (December 1993): 515–24.

Discusses the "creative confusion" generated at the USC Writing Center when a portfolio grading system replaced the department-produced final exam in writing courses.

1345. Clark, Irene L. "Portfolio Grading and the Writing Center." *WCJ* 13 (Spring 1993): 48–62.

Discusses several "persistently problematic" writing center issues which were highlighted when USC's first-year writing program shifted to portfolio evaluation of students' writing.

1346. Coll, Joan H., and Richard Coll. "Tables and Graphs: A Classification Scheme for Display Presentation Variables and a Framework for Research in the Area." *IPM* 29 (1993): 745–50.

The researchers demonstrate that the effectiveness of tables and graphs depends on variables such as users, task, data, and work group. They point out that formats must be studied in this context.

1347. Collins, Norma Decker. "The Role of a Writing Center in a Teacher Education Program." *WLN* 18 (December 1993): 6–7.

Argues that the methods used in a junior high writing center bridged the gap between theory and practice found in the traditional writing class.

1348. Cosgrove, Cornelius. "Explaining and Justifying Writing Centers: An Example." *WLN* 17 (April 1993): 1–4.

Argues that students and faculty have to be educated about the function of writing centers. Shares a newsletter which was created to explain how tutors work.

1349. Crump, Eric. "Voices from the Net: Shaping Writing Center Computer Labs." *WLN* 17 (February 1993): 4–6.

Discusses kinds of equipment and configuration for a computer lab. Points out

that directors need to consider maintenance problems, noise, heat, and arrangement of machines. Argues for laptop computers and laser printers as less intrusive than other equipment.

1350. Crump, Eric. "Voices from the Net: Talk about Talk in the Writing Center." *WLN* 17 (March 1993): 10–11.

Points out that tutors suggested using ESL techniques and encouraged students to listen to news programs, to read aloud, and to tape themselves speaking in order to learn standard spoken English.

1351. Crump, Eric. "Voices from the Net: The Causes and Consequences of Writing Center Dependency." *WLN* 17 (June 1993): 12–14.

Cites examples of negative dependency such as aggressive ESL or physically-disabled students as well as unsure nontraditional students. Argues that dependency becomes positive when the nurturing atmosphere encourages growth and independence.

1352. Crump, Eric. "Voices from the Net: Sharing Records: Student Confidentiality and Faculty Relations." *WLN* 18 (October 1993): 8–9.

Looks at the ethics of sending reports about tutorials to faculty members. Points out that some directors consider such reports as violating students' privacy.

1353. Crump, Eric. "Voices from the Net: Sharing Records, Part II: Political Considerations." *WLN* 18 (November 1993): 6–7.

Discusses whether writing centers should be seen as an extension or as an alternative to the classroom.

1354. Crump, Eric. "Voices from the Net: Weird (?) Topics: A Pressure Point in the Negotiation of Student Authority." *WLN* 18 (December 1993): 8–9.

Discusses tutor responses to offensive topics. Points out that they can discuss audience, purpose, and appropriateness, or even terminate the tutorial.

1355. deBeer, Liz. *Tutoring Strategies for LD College Students' Common Writing Errors.* Lincroft, NJ: Quill, April 1993. ERIC ED 356 488. 12 pages

Discusses ways to identify and categorize LD writing problems. Suggests strategies that tutors and teachers can use with LD writers by identifying common error patterns.

1356. DeCiccio, Albert. "Moving the Boundary: Putting the Idea of a Writing Center to the Test." *WLN* 17 (January 1993): 1–4.

Argues that "writing center pedagogy is at the cutting edge of educational reform" and should shape, not merely support or serve, future writing instruction.

1357. Delaney, Laurie, Hellen Fuller, Jennifer Kay, and Gratia Murphy. "Bridges between Faculty and Tutors: An Honest Look at Teacher/Tutor Relationships." *WLN* 18 (November 1993): 1–3.

The authors present four awkward situations for tutors: tutoring friends, interpreting assignments, reporting plagiarism, and respecting teachers' policies. They offer six guidelines for dealing with potential dilemmas.

1358. Denton, Thomas. "Peer Tutors' Evaluations of the Tutor Training Course and the Tutoring Experience: A Questionnaire." *WLN* 18 (November 1993): 14–16.

Describes types of questions asked, presents the responses in terms of percentages, analyzes and interprets these responses, and draws conclusions.

1359. Devenish, Alan. "Decentering the Writing Center." *WLN* 18 (September 1993): 4–7.

Details five strategies to decenter the writing center: communicating regularly with faculty; placing tutors in classrooms; tutoring in dormitories; sponsoring creative writing activities; and working with the larger community.

1360. Droll, Belinda Wood. "Teacher Expectations: A Powerful Third Force in Tutoring Sessions." *WLN* 17 (May 1993): 1–5.

Identifies teachers' rhetorical emphases by asking questions at the beginning of tutorials, by soliciting copies of assignments, model answers, and course syllabi, and by discussing writing informally.

1361. Easley, Rex. "The Collaborative Writing Workshop and the Classroom Tutor." *WLN* 17 (June 1993): 11, 14.

Explains a setup in which tutors assist their students working together in small, collaborative units during class time and who then meet with their students during lab time. Argues that this arrangement provides social and educational support for the participants.

1362. Fishbain, Janet. "Listening: To Establish Rapport, to Comprehend Student's Perceptions, to Hear an Essay, to Check a Student's Perceptions." *WLN* 18 (September 1993): 10–12.

Points out that "listening requires hearing words, recognizing tone, sensing body language, noticing voice pitch and rate of speech." Details the process and cites examples of "listening" to students.

1363. Fleming, Susan. "The Text as Authority Figure." *WLN* 18 (October 1993): 15–16.

Maintains that because adults frequently denied young women their curiosity and silenced their expression, they experience difficulty challenging authority figures and asserting their own viewpoints.

1364. Flynn, Thomas, and Mary King, eds. *Dynamics of the Writing Conference: Social and Cognitive Interactions.* Urbana, IL: NCTE, 1993. 127 pages

Eleven essays examine how the "social and cognitive interaction between students and teachers in writing conferences can promote the engagement of . . . higher-order thinking skills." The contributors discuss how the theory of conferences can benefit students and how students and teachers interact. They emphasize the shifting control of writing to the students themselves.

Essayists: Cosgrove, Cornelius; Fletcher, David C.; Horn, Susanna; Hurlow, Marcia L.; Johnson, JoAnn B.; Oye, Paula M.; Schjitzer, Thomas C.; Slattery, Patrick J.; Taylor, David.

1365. Franklin, Phyllis. "Scholars, Librarians, and the Future of Primary Records: A Talk Presented at the American Library Association, 1992." *ADE* 106 (Winter 1993): 6–12.

Cautions that primary texts may not be valued in the electronic era. Argues that librarians and scholars must share responsibility for preserving them.

1366. George, Claire. "Response to 'Writing Center Ethics.'" *WLN* 17 (April 1993): 7–8.

Describes working with a student and a faculty member who were mutually antagonistic. Recognizes her responsibility to be objective though both were at fault.

1367. Harris, Muriel, and Tony Silva. "Tutoring ESL Students: Issues and Options." *CCC* 44 (December 1993): 525–37.

Offers answers to questions frequently asked about tutoring ESL students in writing centers.

1368. Healy, Dave. "A Defense of Dualism: The Writing Center and the Classroom." *WCJ* 14 (Fall 1993): 16–29.

Points out that writing centers give students opportunities to develop the critical distance they need to become active participants in their own learning.

1369. Hemmeter, Tom, and Carolyn Mee. "The Writing Center as Ethnographic Space." *WLN* 18 (November 1993): 4–5.

Explains the concepts of interpersonal, textual, intertextual, environmental, and writing community spaces and describes how they impact the interaction between consultant and client.

1370. Hobson, Eric. "Coming In Out of the Silence." *WLN* 17 (February 1993): 7–8.

Endorses WCENTER (an e-mail list) which "offers the writing center community a unique, fast-and-flexible, and wide-ranging research and information network." Cites specific benefits to participants.

1371. Hobson, Eric Hughes. "Where Theory and Practice Collide: Beyond Essentialist Descriptions of the Writing Center." *DAI* 53 (May 1993): 3828A.

Argues that essentialist thought underlies the definitions of and discussions about the theoretical and practical nature of writing centers.

1372. Kennedy, Barbara L. "Nonnative Speakers in First-Year Composition Classes with Native Speakers: How Can Writing Tutors Help?" *WCJ* 13 (Spring 1993): 27–38.

Suggests types of activities for moving beyond decoding, dealing with culture-bound texts, culturally different organization patterns, and culturally determined discourse styles.

1373. Kennedy, Karen Sue. "Tutors' Column: What's in a Name?" *WLN* 18 (September 1993): 13.

Prefers term "consultant" to "tutor" because consultant suggests a student/student relationship whereas tutor indicates a teacher/student situation. Argues that consultations create an "interaction of perspectives."

1374. Kiedaisch, Sue Dinitz. "Look Back and Say 'So What': The Limitations of the Generalist Tutor." *WCJ* 14 (Fall 1993): 63–74.

Points out that although tutors with limited knowledge of writing conventions across disciplines may experience difficulties, tutoring as a generalist can be effective for several reasons.

1375. Kinkead, Joyce A., and Jeanette G. Harris, eds. *Writing Centers in Context: Twelve Case Studies.* Urbana, IL: NCTE, 1993. 274 pages

Fourteen essays present the histories, methods, and organization of successful writing centers in a variety of academic, social, and political contexts; though varying widely, each center has successfully met the needs of and influenced its specific situation. A final bibliographic essay covers many topics related to writing centers.

Essayists: Clark, Irene L.; Greene, Brenda M.; Harris, Muriel; Kiefer, Kathleen; Lotto, Edward; Mohr, Ellen; Momenee, Luanne; Mullin, Joan A.; Neff, Julie; Okawa, Gail Y.; Rodriques, Dawn; Simon, Linda.

1376. Klosterman, Nancy. "Tutors' Column: The Writing Center: Friend or Foe." *WLN* 18 (November 1993): 11–12.

After accepting a writing center scholarship, Klosterman experiences severe anxiety. She describes the training program and tutoring experiences that enable her to overcome her fears.

1377. Kucsma, Alexander J. "The Silent Tutor: Using Patterns to Teach Writing." *WLN* 17 (March 1993): 4–6.

Looks at a program in which faculty members provide the center with samples of successful writing assignments which their students can study and learn from "by looking and observing and mimicking."

1378. Laskowski, Briget. "'Hands-Off' in the Writing Center." *WLN* 18 (November 1993): 12.

Maintains that whether teaching computer skills or assisting students with their writing, tutors do not appropriate machines or papers to help students build their self-confidence.

1379. Leibrock, Shannon M., and Lisa C. Bernbaum. "Awards for Writers Reward Writing Centers." *WLN* 17 (May 1993): 12–14.

The authors describe the process involved in establishing and executing the awards. They point out that one benefit of the award is the improved reputation of the center. Cites specific benefits to tutors and students involved.

1380. Marmorstein, Donna. "The Tutor as Hard Laborer." *WLN* 17 (March 1993): 8.

Points out that compared to physically demanding jobs performed by family members and friends, tutoring seems easy. Argues that being sympathetic and emotionally responsive to students writing about unfortunate experiences is equally difficult.

1381. Marron, Peggy. "Tutoring Deaf Students: Another View." *WLN* 17 (January 1993): 15–16.

Argues that deaf students have special needs and cannot be tutored in the same manner as hearing students. Points out that learning to sign helped facilitate the tutorials.

1382. Mongeon, J. E. "It's That Time of Year." *WLN* 18 (October 1993): 14.

Argues that when time is limited, tutors focus on the introduction and thesis, the main points, and the conclusion, and they examine a paragraph for grammar and punctuation errors.

1383. Moody, Pam. "Tutors' Column: A Slight Case of Plagiarism." *WLN* 17 (January 1993): 9–11.

Experiences anger and betrayal when a client hostile to literature plagiarizes a paper. Learns, however, that students can appreciate other subjects as she appreciates literature.

1384. Olsen, Kai A., Robert R. Korfhage, Kenneth M. Sachatz, Michael B. Spring, and James G. Williams. "Visualization of a Document Collection: the VIBE System." *IPM* 29 (1993): 69–81.

Describes a prototype system of visual cues to enhance verbal keywords in document retrieval systems.

1385. Pemberton, Michael. "Writing Center Ethics." *WLN* 17 (January 1993): 14–15.

States that "ethics . . . are central to writing center operations." Solicits contributions and participation and points out that future columns will present situations that require ethical responses.

1386. Pemberton, Michael. "Writing Center Ethics." *WLN* 17 (March 1993): 6–7.

Points out that writing center people frequently idealize working one-to-one. Argues that few claims are completely true and that honesty is tempered with altruism and pragmatism.

1387. Pemberton, Michael. "Writing Center Ethics." *WLN* 17 (April 1993): 6–7.

Points out that because administrators control funding, they may request confidential information about tutors or faculty. Argues that directors may confront a "delicate balance of ethical judgements."

1388. Pemberton, Michael. "Writing Center Ethics." *WLN* 17 (May 1993): 6–7.

Questions whether the director of a writing center should reveal the name of a poorly performing teaching assistant to the administrators or observe the principle of confidentiality.

1389. Pemberton, Michael. "Writing Center Ethics." *WLN* 17 (June 1993): 15–16.

Discusses a case in which tutors cite four reasons why an ineffective TA's name should not be revealed to administrators.

1390. Pemberton, Michael. "Writing Center Ethics: Telling Stories In and Out of School." *WLN* 18 (October 1993): 4.

Argues that "the issue of confidentiality . . . is perhaps the single most ethically troublesome issue for anyone who works in writing centers." Questions whether anecdotes about clients violate confidentiality.

1391. Pemberton, Michael. "Writing Center Ethics." *WLN* 18 (December 1993): 10, 12.

Provides a variety of answers to the question "When confronted by the repugnant, the dishonest, or the potentially dangerous essay in a writing conference, what should we do?"

1392. Powers, Judith. "Bending the 'Rules': Diversifying the Model Conference for the ESL Writer." *WLN* 17 (February 1993): 1–3, 8.

Points out that collaborative methods fail to meet the needs of ESL writers. Argues that consultants frequently "adopt a didactic role" because of the academic nature of the subject.

1393. Powers, Judith K. "Rethinking Writing Center Conferencing Strategies for the ESL Writer." *WCJ* 13 (Spring 1993): 39–47.

Argues that to help ESL writers acquire the academic writing skills they need, conferencing strategies must shift to a more didactic approach, with faculty as informants.

1394. Roswell, Barbara Sherr. "The Tutor's Audience Is Always a Fiction: The Construction of Authority in Writing Center Conferences." *DAI* 53 (May 1993): 3830A.

Investigates how undergraduate tutors and writers construct authority in their talk about text.

1395. Rubenstein, Ilene. *Rx for Tutor Training.* San Diego, CA: Conference on College Composition and Communication, March/April 1993. ERIC ED 359 510. 21 pages

Proposes a training program designed to move writing tutors toward becoming paraprofessionals.

1396. Scott, Erica. *When Peers Are Not Equal: The Writing Center as a Discourse Community.* Louisville, KY: National Council of Teachers of English, November 1992. ERIC ED 355 514. 11 pages

Argues that the term "peer" is inappropriate to describe the tutor/tutee relationship in writing centers because tutors and tutees are members of different discourse communities.

1397. Selenak, Irv Cockriel, Eric Crump, and Elaine Hocks. "Ideas in Practice: Preparing Composition Teachers in the Writing Center." *JDEd* 17 (Fall 1993): 28–34.

Explores the effects that working in a writing center has on teaching assistants' assumptions about classroom teaching.

1398. Severino, Carol. "Writers Writing." *WLN* 17 (February 1993): 11–14.

Looks at a case in which students work twice weekly on individualized reading/writing tasks designed by their specific teacher/mentor, a graduate teaching assistant. Points out that novice teachers keep reading/teaching journals.

1399. Sherwood, Steve. "How to Survive the Hard Times." *WLN* 17 (June 1993): 4–8.

Argues that in order to survive, writing centers should justify their cost effectiveness, practice self-promotion, avoid becoming marginalized, ally themselves with learning centers, and move their centers out of English departments.

1400. Sherwood, Steve. "Humor and the Serious Tutor." *WCJ* 13 (Spring 1993): 3–12.

Suggests that using nonderisive humor can encourage collaborative environments by facilitating interactive language, creativity, and flexibility. Maintains that gentle humor frees students to do their best work.

1401. Sherwood, Steve. "White Lies in the Writing Center: The Fragile Balance between Praise and Criticism." *WLN* 18 (December 1993): 1–4.

Describes types of lies students and tutors tell. Concludes that truthful alternatives are preferable to lies.

1402. Simpson, Jeanne. "Planning for Computers in the Writing Center: First Drafts." *WLN* 17 (March 1993): 13–14.

Cites four basic considerations in selecting computers, programs, and printers: use, noise, heat, and space. Suggests role-playing tutorials with proposed computers, programs, and physical arrangements.

1403. Simpson, Jeanne. "The Challenge of Innovation: Putting New Approaches into Practice." *WLN* 18 (September1993): 1–3.

Points out that because of budget cuts and accountability, writing center administrators must become proactive in justifying their existence and they also need to become informed advocates for what they do.

1404. Simpson, Steven. "Tutors' Column." *WLN* 17 (April 1993): 9.

States that "tutoring friends in the writing center's environment can be a rewarding experience for both parties, if it is handled in a professional manner."

1405. Spooner, Michael. "Circles and Centers: Some Thoughts on the Writing Center and Academic Book Publishing." *WLN* 17 (June 1993): 1–3, 10.

Argues that publishable work should be research based and theoretical and should address issues writing centers share with the wider field of composition studies. Cites six specific topics.

1406. Taylor-Escoffery, Bertha. "The Influences of the Writing Center on College Students' Perceptions of the Functions of Written Language." *DAI* 53 (May 1993): 3885A.

Finds that writing centers enhanced basic writers' writing in the "expressive" and "transactional" domain, and reduced writing apprehension.

1407. Thaiss, Chris. "Of Havens, Nodes, and No-Center Centers." *Focuses* 6 (Summer 1993): 16–26.

Proposes that the writing center has become dispersed throughout the campus in writing across the curriculum programs but that it is still a clearinghouse of ideas.

1408. Thornus, Therese. "Assisting ESL/EFL Students in the Writing Center." *WCJ* 13 (Spring 1993): 13–26.

Suggests using students' native language to get ideas down, contrasting the first language with American English, and discussing different expectations in writing for an American academic audience.

1409. Upton, James. "We Hold These Truths to Be Sometimes Not So Self-Evident." *WLN* 17 (April 1993): 5, 8.

Cites five "not so self-evident" principles, including making the kind of learning happening in writing centers standard practice, helping writers become independent, and encouraging professional development of staff.

1410. Waldo, Mark L. "On the Running Board of the Portfolio Bandwagon." *WPA* 16 (Spring 1993): 15–26.

Argues that writing centers should be the logical residence for WAC programs.

1411. Weaver, Patti. "Tutors' Column: Angel and the Devil's Advocate." *WLN* 17 (June 1993): 9–10.

Experiences a moral dilemma when she disagrees with a student's thesis. Realizes that she cannot change the thesis, but she asks questions that make it less objectionable.

1412. Welch, Nancy. "From Silence to Noise: The Writing Center as Critical Exile." *WCJ* 14 (Fall 1993): 3–15.

Argues that writing centers should be viewed as places where students can productively engage the many (often competing) internalized "voices" that converge in their texts.

1413. Williams, Sharon. "Sentence Errors in the Writing Conference: The Little Red Caboose." *WLN* 18 (October 1993): 13–14.

Cites nine common errors. Creates a six-page, user-friendly handout using student writing samples and emphasizing revision. Includes samples showing problems and solutions. Points out that her handout is available upon request.

1414. Woo, Helen. "Tutors' Column: Expectations of a Tutor." *WLN* 18 (December 1993): 12, 11.

Becomes a tutor because of her negative writing experience and her compassion for struggling students. Idealizes tutoring, but soon learns not to glorify the process.

1415. Woolbright, Meg. "A Response to 'Contesting "The Idea of a Writing Center": The Politics of Writing Center Research.'" *WLN* 17 (January 1993): 11–13.

Argues "for caution and . . . clearer articulation of the political differences between research and tutoring." Maintains that researchers should question the system but not the tutoring situation.

1416. Woolbright, Meg. *Social-Constructionist Theory and the Writing Center: A House of Mirrors*. San Diego, CA: Conference on College Composition and Communication, March/April 1993. ERIC ED 357 359. 10 pages

Claims that an approach that privileges resistance and allows student and tutor to talk about their differences would be preferable to aiming for consensus.

1417. Yahner, William. "Explaining and Justifying Writing Centers: One MORE Example." *WLN* 18 (October 1993): 5–7.

Claims that centers encourage student retention, contribute to the professional development of novice and experienced writing instructors, provide an apprenticeship program for education majors, and facilitate WAC.

1418. Young, Virginia H. "Politeness Phenomena in the University Writing Conference." *DAI* 53 (June 1993): 4236A.

Analyzes 19 videotaped writing conferences to discuss the relationship of student comfort to manifestations of politeness phenomena in the teacher's comments.

3.4   ROLE IN SOCIETY

1419. Anaporte, J., Lil Brannon, Mary Ann Cain, Elizabeth J. Deis, Lowell T. Frye,

George Kalamaras, and Kate H. Winter. "Balancing the Personal and Professional: A Question of Quality." *WC* 10 (July 1993): 413–65.

The authors address problems faced by composition professionals. They discuss job-sharing, spouses in the same field, women with families, and the marginalization of composition faculty.

1420. Caplan, Paula. *Lifting a Ton of Feathers: A Woman's Guide to Surviving in the Academic World*. Toronto: University of Toronto Press, 1993. 273 pages

Presents anecdotal and analytical material on the ways men dominate academia. Discusses what women need to do to counteract that and advance their academic careers. Includes practical information on vitae, job applications, and interviews.

1421. Cronin, Frank C. "Roots of the Censorship Controversy: The Political Origins of Our Discipline." *Leaflet* 92 (Fall 1993): 17–20.

Suggests that censorship attempts reflect a continuing belief that the purpose of literature is to indoctrinate; traces political and religious influences on English literature.

1422. Edelman, Marian Wright. "Reprint: Winson and Dovie Hudson's Dream." *HER* 63 (Winter 1993): 463–91.

Provides an introduction to and reprint of Edelman's 1975 article raising questions on the current status of school desegregation four decades after the *Brown* decision.

1423. Freire, Paulo. *Pedagogy of Hope: Reliving Pedagogy of the Oppressed*. New York: Continuum Press, 1993. 192 pages

Continues his early work, *Pedagogy of the Oppressed*. Chronicles and synthesizes Latin American and other Third World people's struggles for education and empowerment.

1424. González, Roseann Dueñas. "Language, Race, and the Politics of Educational Failure: A Case for Advocacy." National Council of Teachers of English, 1993. NCTE Concept Paper Series No. 10. ERIC ED 359 549. 37 pages

Discusses difficulties imposed on Native American, Latino, African American, and Asian American students when they are labeled as deficient simply because their learning patterns are different from the dominant culture's; argues that teachers should adopt an "advocacy" model that seeks to combat inequities by forming coalitions with parents and communities.

1425. Huberman, Michael. *The Lives of Teachers*. Translated by Jonathan Neufeld. New York: Teachers College Press, 1993. 320 pages

Looks at 160 teachers to study the dynamics of a life-time spent in the classroom. Discusses the uniqueness of teaching and its connection with other professions.

1426. Johnston, Bill J. "The Transformation of Work and Educational Reform Policy." *AERJ* 30 (Spring 1993): 39–65.

Argues that educational reform has been tied to conceptions of labor in a society that is transforming its notions of work.

1427. Lardner, Ted, and Alan W. France. "Two Comments on 'Conceptualizing Writing as Moral and Civic Thinking' (and) Sandra Stotsky Responds [*CE* 54 (November 1992)]." *CE* 55 (November 1993): 801–10.

Challenges the possibility of separating personal civic responsibility from responsibility to the academic community.

1428. National Council of Teachers of English and Conference on College Composition and Communication. "The National Language Policy: A Position Statement from the Conference on College Composition and Communication." National Council of Teachers of English, 1993. 1 page

Explains NCTE's and CCCC's National Language Policy: why it was developed, and why the "English-Only" movement has a number of drawbacks.

1429. NCTE Task Force on Guidelines for Dealing with Censorship of Nonprint Materials. "Guidelines for Dealing with Censorship of Nonprint Materials." *Leaflet* 92 (Spring 1993): 13–24.

Gives rationale and principles underlying recommended guidelines, as well as guidelines themselves; lists resources for dealing with censorship.

1430. O'Reilley, Mary Rose. *The Peaceable Classroom*. Portsmouth, NH: Heinemann-Boynton/Cook, 1993. 184 pages

Argues for a "pedagogy of nonviolence" in teaching writing and reading that will help students make moral choices.

1431. Roberts, David H. "Three Areas of Parental Concern: A Letter to the Superintendent." *ELQ* 15 (February 1993): 7–9.

Confronts issues of grammar instruction in schools by answering parental concerns in three categories: process pedagogy, content (grammar versus writing), and changes in society.

1432. Schaafsma, David. *Eating on the Street: Teaching Literacy in a Multicultural Society*. The Pittsburgh Series in Composition, Literacy and Culture, edited by David Bartholomae and Jean Ferguson Carr. Pittsburgh, PA: University of Pittsburgh Press, 1993. 448 pages

Discusses the struggle of teaching literacy in a racially divided society, the effects of different cultural values, and the importance of story and storytelling in education. Presents multi-layered stories of the Dewey Center Community Writing Project in Detroit to illustrate literacy across multiple perspectives.

1433. Smith, Jeff. "Allan Bloom, Mike Rose, and Paul Goodman: In Search of a Lost Pedagogical Synthesis." *CE* 55 (November 1993): 721–44.

Concludes that Goodman's apprenticeship model of university education is a useful alternative to polarized positions (characterized by Rose and Bloom) of current cultural literacy debates.

1434. Tarvers, Jo Koster. "And Then You Do It for Money . . . : Lessons from a Teacher Turned Writing Consultant." *CompC* 6 (September 1993): 4–6.

Offers practical advice about working as a writing consultant to businesses.

1435. Taylor, Denny. "Living in an Adversarial Society." National Council of Teachers of English, 1993. NCTE Concept Paper Series No. 11. 34 pages

Analyzes ways in which teachers create artificial dichotomies between "poor" and "privileged." Argues that social, economic, and political realities make it imperative that teachers care for students' well-being in all areas.

1436. Williams, James D. *Program Administration in the Face of Political Correctness*. Cincinnati, OH: Conference on College Compostion and Communication, March 1992. ERIC ED 352 674. 10 pages

Argues for the teaching of writing and rhetoric as inseparable from democracy which assumes that students define themselves without instructor imposition.

3.5   OTHER

1437. Olbert, Sharon. "Storytelling Promotes Self-Esteem." *TETYC* 20 (Feburary 1993): 49–52.

Presents the story of a first-year teacher who encourages students to tell about their lives.

4
Curriculum

1438. Abrahamson, Priscilla A. "Between a Rock and a Soft Spot: Reviewing College Preparatory Writing." *EJ* 82 (October 1993): 14–20.

Concludes that writing preparation is dependent on the situation. Argues that writing tasks must be geared toward students' needs.

1439. Amore, Adelaide P. "Reconstruction Strategies for Reevaluation in Teaching Traditional American Texts." *Leaflet* 92 (Fall 1993): 6–11.

Argues that teachers can maintain the power of a text by presenting it both within its own and within a contemporary context.

1440. Andres, Sophia. *Images Bridging Home and Academic Cultures*. San Diego, CA: Conference on College Composition and Communication, March/April 1993. ERIC ED 359 536. 15 pages

Argues that student writers, beginning with a single image from their home life, can develop widening concentric circles of awareness of how their writing can convey thoughts, feelings, and emotions.

1441. Applebee, Arthur N. "Beyond the Lesson: Reconstructing Curriculum as a Domain for Culturally Significant Conversations." Albany, NY, National Research Center on Literature Teaching and Learning, 1993. ERIC ED 357 336. 27 pages

Argues that an effective curriculum requires a constructivist pedagogy in which teachers' and learners' roles are transformed to support the construction of meaning.

1442. Balester, Valerie. *Cultural Divide: A Study of African-American College-Level Writers*. Portsmouth, NH: Heinemann-Boynton/Cook, 1993. 184 pages

Analyzes eight African American students' writing and speaking to reveal their negotiation of Black English vernacular and academic discourse.

1443. Bannister, Linda. *Three Women Revise: What Morrison, Oates, and Tan Can Teach Our Students about Revision*. San Diego, CA: Conference on College Composition and Communication, March/April 1993. ERIC ED 355 542. 18 pages

Presents revision strategies of creative writers Toni Morrison, Joyce Carol Oates, and Amy Tan as a source of writing instruction for student writers.

1444. Barber, John F. "Why *I* Write." *EngR* 43 (1993): 5–6.

Reflects on his uses of writing, his success, and his failures. Offers strategies for teaching writing based on his experiences and insights.

1445. Barnett, Claudia. *Collaborative Ghost Writing*. Indianapolis, IN: Computers and Writing Conference, May 1992. ERIC ED 348 671. 9 pages

Explores ghost writing as a process in first-year and upper-level composition classes. Discusses how it can help students focus on their reading processes.

1446. Bender, Daniel. "Diversity Revisited, or Composition's Alien History." *RR* 12 (Fall 1993): 108–24.

Argues that practicing imitation can contribute to students' understanding of diversity.

1447. Berlin, James A., and Michael Vivion, eds. *Cultural Studies in the English Classroom*. Portsmouth, NH: Heinemann-Boynton/Cook, 1993. 344 pages

The 20 essayists discuss specific classroom and program approaches to integrating students' cultural experiences into their learning of reading and writing. *Essayists:* Balsamo, A.; Berlin, James A.; Blitz, M.; Brodkey, L.; Carino, P.; Farris, C.; Fleischer, C.; Foreman, J.; Fortier, M.; France, A. W.; George, D.; Hurlbert, C. M.; Kennedy, A.; McCormick, K.; Miller, R. E.; Morton, D.; Penticoff, R.; Robison, L.; Schriner, D. K.; Shoos, D.; Shumway, D.; Smith, P.; Smith, E., II; Vivion, M.; Zavarzadeh, M.; Zebroski, J. T.

1448. Bishop, Wendy. "Genre as 'Field Coverage'—Divisions in Writing Instruction." *Dialogue* 1 (Fall 1993): 28–43.

Discusses limitations of subdividing writing courses into separate fields (technical, creative, and poetry); advises writing teachers to rethink the writing curriculum.

1449. Bizzaro, Patrick. *Responding to Student Poems: Applications of Critical Theory*. Urbana, IL: National Council of the Teachers of English, 1993. 236 pages

Points out the lack of a systematic study of poetry-writing instruction. Examines poetry writing instruction in relation to composition theory, new criticism, reader-response theory, deconstruction, and feminist theory.

1450. Bock, Mary Ann. "Education with the People: 'Race,' Pedagogy and Literacy." *DAI* 54 (December 1993): 2131A.

Identifies ways in which race and particularly "whiteness" bear on literacy in education.

1451. Bolin, Bill. *A Multicultural Approach to Writing Assignments*. Pittsburgh, PA: College English Association Conference, March 1992. ERIC ED 350 619. 10 pages

Argues that because of the increasing number of minority students in colleges, writing teachers must be sensitive to cultural differences among students and between themselves and students. Maintains that expressive writing tasks, which allow students to draw from their own experiences to make knowledge, should be encouraged.

1452. Bradford, Richard. *The State of Theory.* New York: Routledge, 1993. 186 pages

Presents an overview of how critical theory operates in practice. Discusses gender, race, the gothic, the value of "theory guides" for students, and the impact of theory on teaching practice.

1453. Brandt, Deborah, Erika Lindemann, and Jack Selzer, eds. *Profiles of Writing Programs in the Alliance for Undergraduate Education.* University Park, PA: The Alliance for Undergraduate Education, 1993. 74 pages

The contributors describe the curriculum, administrative structure, student support services, staff, staff development, and reforms in progress of writing programs in 17 public research universities. In addition, seven brief essays address curricular, staffing, and administrative issues across all the institutions represented by the profiles.

1454. Bratcher, Suzanne. "Understanding Proofreading (or Frank Smith Meets the Surface Error)." *V&R* 4 (Spring 1994): 61–68.

Offers a method for teaching proofreading as a reading rather than writing skill.

1455. Callaway, Susan. *Constructing Knowledge about Resistance in Peer Tutoring: Multidisciplinary Approaches to Multicultural Contexts.* San Diego, CA: Conference on College Composition and Communication, March/April 1993. ERIC ED 357 348. 11 pages

Examines how a multidisciplinary approach shaped the construction of knowledge about resistance in peer tutoring in a multicultural context.

1456. Capossela, Toni-Lee, ed. *The Critical Writing Workshop: Designing Writing Assignments to Foster Critical Thinking.* Portsmouth, NH: Boynton/Cook, 1993. 225 pages

The essayists suggest applying writing theories to the teaching of critical thinking. Includes an annotated bibliography.
Essayists: Berkin, M.; Capossela, Toni-Lee; Coon, A. C.; Jenseth, R.; Jones, L.; Lawrence, S. M.; Nydahl, J.; Olson, C. B.; Pytlik, B.; Rubin, L.; Sandberg, K.; Zeiger, W.

1457. Casazza, Martha E. "Using a Model of Direct Instruction to Teach Summary Writing in a College Reading Class." *JR* 37 (November 1993): 202–8.

Describes and gives examples of the EMQA model such as explanation, modeling, questioning, and application, to teach the rules of summary writing.

1458. Cintorino, Margaret A. "Getting Together, Getting Along, Getting to the Business of Teaching and Learning." *EJ* 82 (January 1993): 23–32.

Examines student talk in small groups. Demonstrates how interaction becomes more productive as students gain social skills and experience working in groups.

1459. Cole, Karen Brobst. "Efficacy and Generalization of Instruction in Sequential Expository Writing for Students with Learning Disabilities." *DAI* 53 (January 1993): 2326A.

Investigates the effectiveness of teaching expository paragraph writing to students with disabilities.

1460. Conely, James. *A Class Exercise in Proofreading: Getting Students to Read What They Write.* Pittsburgh, PA: College English Association Conference, March 1992. ERIC ED 350 613. 7 pages

Describes writing instruction based on small group work designed to provide peer feedback. Argues that this method will decrease errors which are caused by a failure to read what is written. Stresses proofreading for logic and communication errors rather than mechanical errors.

1461. Cope, Bill, and Mary Kalantzis, eds. *The Powers of Literacy: A Genre Approach to Teaching Writing.* The Pittsburgh Series in Composition, Literacy and Culture, edited by David Bartholomae and Jean Ferguson Carr.

Pittsburgh, PA: University of Pittsburgh Press, 1993. 275 pages

Nine essays from theorists and practitioners introduce the genre approach to literacy teaching, which is a new educational paradigm distinct from the traditional and process pedagogies, and which emphasizes content, structure, and sequence.

Essayists: Callaghan, Mike; Christie, Frances; Cope, Bill; Cranny-Francis, Anne; Kalantzis, Mary; Knapp, Peter; Kress, Gunther; Macken, Mary; Martin, J. R.; Rothery, Joan; Slade, Diana.

1462. Couch, Lezlie Laws. "Old Voices/New Conversations: Sharing Drafts with Students." *EJ* 82 (December 1993): 30–33.

Sees writing as a collaborative process by which meaning emerges; points out that sharing drafts helps to discuss the writing process.

1463. Curry, Judson B. "A Return to 'Converting the Natives,' or Antifoundationalist Faith in the Composition Class.'." *RR* 12 (Fall 1993): 160–67.

Views the pedagogy of an antifoundationalist class as a process of religious conversion.

1464. Daisey, Peggy. "Three Ways to Promote the Values and Uses of Literacy at Any Age." *JR* 36 (March 1993): 436–39.

Describes how reading aloud, journal writing and bibliotherapy provided opportunities for students to experience the values and uses of literacy in a content-area reading course.

1465. Daisley, Margaret. *A Letter to My Mother*. Louisville, KY: National Council of Teachers of English, November 1992. ERIC ED 355 549. 17 pages

Details a teaching assistant's impressions of her first year of teaching in a university writing program.

1466. Duckart, Tracy B. "Collaborative Learning: Some Thoughts from a Yet-to-Be Teacher." *CalE* 29 (March/April 1993): 19, 21.

Uses Bruffee's and Vygotsky's theories to suggest that a teacher's primary responsibility is to invite students into a community in which they become co- and self-educators.

1467. Duncan, Carter. "The WPA on Campus—The Transformation of Instruction in Writing: Implications of Class Size." *WPA* 16 (Spring 1993): 72–75.

Gives reasons why increasing composition class sizes presents special instructional difficulties. Originally written at the request of the Oregon State Composition Advisory Committee.

1468. Dursky, Janice. *Emphasizing Collaborative Experiences in Reading/Writing Courses*. Kansas City, MO: Midwest Regional Reading and Study Skills Conference, March 1993. ERIC ED 355 506. 8 pages

Suggests ways to include collaborative learning experiences in reading/writing courses to improve communication skills.

1469. Eck, Phyllis I. "The Process in Revision: One Writing Program's Challenges and Changes, 1960–1990." *DAI* 53 (June 1993): 4305A.

Studies the extent to which changes in teaching revision at Bowling Green State University (Ohio) reflected the thinking of researchers in the field.

1470. Edleson, Daniel C. "Socrates, Aesops, and the Computer: Questioning and Storytelling with Multimedia." *JEdM&H* 2 (1993): 393–403.

Describes a computer-based teaching system that combines asking good questions with telling stories.

1471. Elbow, Peter. "The War between Reading and Writing and How to End It." *RR* 12 (Fall 1993): 5–24.

Argues that the academy values reading more than writing; describes the benefits of granting equal status to writing.

1472. Ferganchick-Neufang, Julia. "Reconciling Writing Differences: Collaboration/Gender Characteristics." *TETYC* 20 (October 1993): 194–203.

Maintains that mixed-gender collaborative writing helps bridge differences.

1473. Fine, Melinda. "'You Can't Just Say That the Only Ones Who Can Speak Are Those Who Agree with Your Position': Political Discourse in the Classroom." *HER* 63 (Winter 1993): 412–33.

Describes the dynamics surrounding the discussion of controversial issues and effects of hierarchical power in suppressing students' opposing viewpoints in a middle-school classroom.

1474. Franck, Marion R. "The Teachers as Student: An Inside-Out Adventure." *V&R* 4 (Spring 1994): 13–24.

Recounts what she learned about teaching and writing as a "student" in a colleague's advanced writing course.

1475. Geyer, Michael. "Multiculturalism and the Politics of General Education." *CritI* 19 (Spring 1993): 499–533.

Defines multiculturalism as a politics through which the concept of general education must now be negotiated.

1476. Gill, Kent, and the NCTE Committee on Classroom Practices, eds. *Ideas for the Working Classroom.* Classroom Practices in Teaching English. Urbana, IL: NCTE, 1993. 178 pages

The editors present 31 essays intended to "celebrate successful teaching practices in English." They point out that the articles were chosen because they emphasized practical, active, and independent learning, cross-disciplinary approaches, collaboration, and respect for differences."

Essayists: Allen, Kathy; Angelico-Hart, Dael; Barron, Ronald; Brough, Barbara Jones; Brown, Susan Reese; Burke, Jim; Coffey, Kathy; Dukes, Thomas; Earthman, Elise Ann; Fabiano, Theodore F.; Gerke, Diann; Goodson, F. Todd; Herz, Sarah K.; Johannessen, Larry R.; Kammer, Joel; Luboff, Gerald F.; McColley, Beverly A.; Meinhardt, Carol; Meyers, G. Douglas; Mink, JoAnna Stephens; Mollineaux, William R.; Oldham, Perry; Reissman, Rose Cherie; Rosenthal, Rose; Schultz, Joanna; Schwartz, Edythe H.; Schwartz, Phyllis B.; Victor, Daniel D.; Watson, Gary A.; Wilkins, Beverly; Zarnowski, Myra.

1477. Gill, Kent, and the NCTE Committee on Classroom Practices, eds. *Process and Portfolios in Writing Instruction.* Classroom Practices in Teaching English, vol. 26. Urbana, IL: NCTE, 1993. 99 pages

The 16 essays written by teachers describe methods they have used successfully, covering different stages of the writing process. The last half of the book is devoted to using writing portfolios, rather than separate papers, to evaluate and respond to students' writing.

Essayists: Bertisch, Carole Ackerson; Brady, Laura; Calabrese, Marylyn; DeToye, Lela M.; Figgins, Margo A.; Gallegher, Donald R.; Ingalls, Bob; Keiper, Robert W.; McWilliams, Betty; Murphy, Elaine; Nistler, Robert J.; Privitte, Linda LaMantia; Randsell, D. R.; Sharp, Anne; Thaiss, Christopher; Verner, Dan; Wilkins, Beverly; Young, Gail M.

1478. Gillespie, Maggie. "Placement Testing in Community Colleges: A Response to Hughes and Nelson." *CCR* 20 (February 1993): 59–69

Examines a 1991 study which discusses students' placement into first-year composition classes; proposes an alternative method of analysis.

1479. Golmic, Bruce Andrew. "Facilitating Change: An Ethnographic Study to Identify Interventions Applied during the Implementation of a Cooperative Integrated Reading and Composition Program." *DAI* 53 (April 1993): 3441A.

Uses ethnographic research to show a successful integration of a reading and composition program.

1480. Graves, Roger. "Composition in Canadian Universities." *WC* 10 (January 1993): 72–105.

Surveys 62 English- and French-language universities throughout Canada. Finds that much writing is housed in various academic departments instead of in large-scale first-year composition programs.

1481. Green, Bill, ed. *The Insistence of the Letter: Literacy Studies and Curriculum Theorizing.* The Pittsburgh Series in Composition, Literacy and Culture, edited by David Bartholomae and Jean Ferguson Carr. Pittsburgh, PA: University of Pittsburgh Press, 1993. 248 pages

The contributors argue that traditional notions of literacy need to be reconsidered in order to bring about changes in curriculum and instruction that will serve the interests of a multicultural student body and a multinational labor market.
Essayists: Burgess, Tony; Christie, Frances; Donald, James; Green, Bill; Hamilton, David; Hoskin, Keith; Lankshear, Colin; Luke, Allan; Luke, Carmen; Reid, William A.; Willinsky, John.

1482. Group, Kenneth Leroy, Jr. "An Emerging Model for Multicultural Literacy: A Case Study of What Teachers Know about the Instruction of Mainstreamed Language Minority Children." *DAI* 54 (September 1993): 806A.

Presents a model to provide knowledge, guidelines, and insight for teachers to facilitate meaningful literacy learning in a multicultural environment.

1483. Hagerty, John R. "Acknowledging Diversity and Reconciling Differences: The Crucial Role of Cultural, Social, and Political Assumptions in the Teacher-Student Dialogue." *DAI* 54 (August 1993): 499A.

Demonstrates that a flexible, balanced approach enables teachers to engage students in open, effective, and meaningful dialogues.

1484. Hansen, David T. "From Role to Person: The Moral Layeredness of Classroom Teaching." *AERJ* 30 (Winter 1993): 651–74.

Calls attention to multiple and subtle ways in which teachers have a moral impact on students. Defines morals as customary roles and as personal virtue.

1485. Hansen, Jane. "What Keeps Writing Alive in Our Classrooms?" *R&WQ* 9 (April/June 1993): 197–205.

Examines evaluation, reading, and experimentation and the ways they keep writing alive.

1486. Haring-Smith, Tori. *Learning Together: An Introduction to Collaborative Learning.* New York: HarperCollins, 1993. 106 pages

Provides novices with background information on collaboration as a learning strategy specifically applied to composition.

1487. Herndon, Kathleen M., and Priti Kumar. *Reconsidering the Melting Pot: Fostering Multicultural Awareness through Introductory Composition and Literature Courses.* Cincinnati, OH: Conference on College Composition and Communication, March 1992. ERIC ED 349 561. 34 pages

Focuses on the importance of helping students develop an awareness of their cultural heritage and an appreciation of the cultural heritage of others.

1488. Hesse, Douglas. "Teachers as Students, Reflecting Resistance." *CCC* 44 (May 1993): 224–31.

Maintains that first-year composition students and graduate student teachers share similar modes of resistance to texts and ways of thinking that challenge their "common sense" world views.

1489. Hinten, Marvin. "Tantalizing with Titles." *TETYC* 20 (October 1993): 211–13.

Presents a study in which students learn to use allusions, puns, rhyme, alliteration, and paradox to create effective titles.

1490. Hobson, Peter. "Is It Time for Another Look at Plato? A Contemporary Assessment of His Educational Theory." *JT* 28 (Fall/Winter 1993): 77–86.

Suggests that "with some modification," a return to Plato's educational theory could offer a "useful alternative model to present educational and social trends."

1491. Holloway, Karla F. C. "Cultural Politics in the Academic Community: Masking the Color Line." *CE* 55 (October 1993): 610–17.

Argues that intellectual borders have arisen in reaction to increasing diversity in the academic community. Calls for interdisciplinary pedagogies.

1492. Holt, Mara. "Knowledge, Social Relations, and Authority in Collaborative Practices of the 1930s and the 1950s." *CCC* 44 (December 1993): 538–55.

Discusses conceptions of knowledge, social relations, and authority involved in the collaborative pedagogies of the 1930s and 1950s.

1493. Hurlbert, C. Mark, and Samuel Totten, eds. *Social Issues in the English Classroom*. Urbana, IL: National Council of the Teachers of English, 1993. 357 pages

Presents articles from 25 concerned teachers and professors explaining why and how they integrate inquiry into troubling social issues with the study of language and literature and make it the subject of discussion and writing-to-learn activities. *Essayists:* Bell, Debbie; Blitz, Michael; Davenport, Doris; Giroux, Henry A; Hart, Ellen Louise; Hurlbert, C. Mark; Johnson, Roger T.; Kutzer, M. Daphne; Lankewish, Vincent A.; Mack; Nancy; Mason, Jimmie; Milanés, Cecilia Rodriguez; Parmeter, Sarah Hope; Shapiro, Alan; Stotsky, Sandra; Stumbo, Carol; Tassoni, John; Tayko, Gail; Totten, Samuel; Weiler,

Kathleen; Wright, William; Zebroski, James Thomas; Zins, Daniel.

1494. Inkster, Bob. *The Organizational Voice*. San Diego, CA: Conference on College Composition and Communication, March/April 1993. ERIC ED 356 496. 5 pages

Discusses how to use the writing class memo and committee reports to develop students' voice and sense of audience in writing.

1495. Irby, Janet. "Empowering the Disempowered: Publishing Student Voices." *EJ* 82 (November 1993): 50–54.

Uses group writing assignments, student interviews, and student evaluations to provide students with an empowered voice.

1496. Jones, Elizabeth, and Stacy Tibbetts. *Writing Skills for College Students*. University Park, PA: National Center on Postsecondary Teaching, Learning, and Assessment, 1993. 27 pages

Reviews studies concerning writing skills at the college level.

1497. Kappe, Frank, Hermann Maurer, and Nick Sherbakov. "Hyper-G: A Universal Hypermedia System." *JEdM&H* 2 (1993): 39–66.

Discusses the application of hypermedia technology in university environments. Describes ideas and concepts behind the hypermedia project Hyper-G as related to university applications.

1498. Kelly, Anthony E. "Designing Instructional Hypertext for Use in Lecture Note Review: Knowledge Engineering and Preliminary Testing." *JEdM&H* 2 (1993): 149–76.

Discusses principles that create a hierarchical and textual hypertext program used to trace students' review behavior. Presents instructional implications of computer-collected data.

1499. King, Cayle, and Bonnie Hawk. "Developing a Code of Ethics in the Collaborative

Classroom." *TETYC* 20 (October 1993): 206–10.

Presents exercises in acknowledging influences and crediting sources.

1500. Kinross, Robin. "Conversation with Erik Spiekermann." *IDJ* 7 (1993): 29–40.

Presents excerpts from a conversation with Erik Spiekermann, a German graphic designer who specializes in information and typeface design. Includes a critical discussion of typography.

1501. Klopping, Inge M. "Don't Lose Control!" *BEdF* 47 (April 1993): 41–42.

Asserts that teachers at every level of education should be prepared to teach keyboarding skills to prepare students for the workplace.

1502. Kloss, Robert J. "Stay in Touch, Won't You? Using the One-Minute Paper." *CollT* 41 (Spring 1993): 60–63.

Uses short student responses to discuss problems with course atmosphere as well as subject matter.

1503. Kutz, Eleanor, Suzy Groden, and Vivian Zamel. *The Discovery of Competence: Teaching and Learning with Diverse Student Writers*. Portsmouth, NH: Heinemann-Boynton/Cook, 1993. 216 pages

Explores possibilities for collaborative inquiry in program design, writing assessment, and multicultural curricula.

1504. Landberg, Gail L. "The Identification and Validation of Sociopsycholinguistic Strategies for Integrating Reading and Writing at the Postsecondary Level." *DAI* 54 (October 1993): 1302A.

Examines the use of sociopsycholinguistic strategies to improve reading and writing instruction; argues that contrary to recent research findings, reading, writing, speaking, and listening are still taught in isolation.

1505. Lange, Ellen. "*The New Yorker* in the Classroom: A Catalyst for Making Real

World Connections." *CompC* 6 (October 1993): 6–7.

Advocates *The New Yorker* over traditional readers and describes how students can "go beyond the text and connect reading with the real world."

1506. Langston, Mark, and Arthur Graesser. "The Point and Query Interface: Exploring Knowledge by Asking Questions." *JEdM&H* 2 (1993): 355–67.

Discusses point and query interface and its effectiveness as navigational system and pedagogical tool; concludes that the interface is applicable to goal-driven knowledge acquisition.

1507. Lankshear, Colin, and Peter L. McLaren, eds. *Critical Literacy: Politics, Praxis, and the Postmodern*. SUNY Series of Teacher Empowerment and School Reform, edited by Henry A. Giroux and Peter L. McLaren. Albany, NY: State University of New York Press, 1993. 288 pages

The contributors redefine the project of literacy by bringing to light new possibilities for liberation struggles both in and outside of schools.
Essayists: Anderson, Gary L.; Apple, Michael W.; Bee, Barbara; Berlin, James; Brady, Jeanne F.; Carlson, Dennis; Denski, Stan; Gee, James Paul; Giroux, Henry; Harris, Kevin; Hernandez, Adriana; Irvine, Patricia; Jules, Didacus; Lankshear, Colin; McLaren, Peter; Rockhill, Kathleen; Searle, Chris; Sholle, David.

1508. LaPointe, Linda. *Connections through Inclusion (Multicultural Writing Community of the Two-Year College)*. Cincinnati, OH: Conference on College Composition and Communication, March 1992. ERIC ED 348 691. 8 pages

Explores the two-year college as a multicultural environment providing necessary connections for all its students via cooperative learning.

1509. Latchaw, Joan. *Where Is the 'Critical' in Critical Thinking?* Cincinnati, OH: Conference on College Composition and Communication, March 1992. ERIC ED 350 599. 18 pages

Argues that the definition of critical thinking has evolved from problem solving skills to higher-order reasoning strategies. Discusses barriers to writing programs based on critical inquiry.

1510. Ledyard, John O. "The Design of Coordination Mechanisms." *JOC* 3 (1993): 121–34.

Discusses the theory of coordination mechanism design, using it to solve problems in organizational computing, and testing new mechanisms before going into the field.

1511. Lee, Carol D. *Signifying as a Scaffold for Literary Interpretation: The Pedagogical Implications of an African American Discourse Genre.* NCTE Research Reports, no. 26. Urbana, IL: National Council of the Teachers of English, 1993. 200 pages

Maintains that if we understand signifying, an African American pattern of oral discourse defined as a "rhetorical stance, an attitude toward language, and a means of cultural self-expression" given great value within African American communities, we can use it to help build bridges for teaching literacy skills to African American students.

1512. LeVan, Sally L. "Writing Projects and Teacher Balance: With Colleagues, Students, and Self." *DAI* 53 (April 1993): 3501A.

Explores how Writing Project participants balance a traditional hierarchical background and experiment with new knowledge.

1513. Logan, Shirley W. *Lessons from Four 'Bronze Muses' or How the Rhetoric of Nineteenth-Century African-American Women Can Inform Writing Instruction in the Twenty-First Century.* San Diego, CA: Conference on College Composition and Communication, March/April 1993. ERIC ED 357 337. 12 pages

Argues that the rhetorical strategies of Maria Stewart, Sojourner Truth, Frances E. W. Harper, and Ida B. Wells can be helpful in teaching writing to college students.

1514. Mackey, Margaret. "The Many Faces of Resistant Reading." *EJ* 82 (September 1993): 69–74.

Concludes that instructors need to take students' backgrounds and their divergent views into consideration when reading and discussing a text.

1515. Madraso, Jan. "Proofreading: The Skill We've Neglected to Teach." *EJ* 82 (February 1993): 32–41.

Suggests that students can improve their writing if they read a composition orally, focus on stylistic problems, and look at error patterns. Argues that computers can make proofreading more efficient.

1516. Mansfield, Margaret A. "Real World Writing and the English Curriculum." *CCC* 44 (February 1993): 69–83.

Argues that introducing professional writing assignments into introductory composition courses can improve students' understanding of audience, authority, and the writing process.

1517. May, Adrienne C. "Bridging the Gap: Toward a Comprehensive Undergraduate Writing Program Model." *DAI* 53 (June 1993): 4189A.

Develops seven criteria for a comprehensive undergraduate writing program model.

1518. McClure, Michael. *Composition as Fiction: Revising the Writing Classroom.* San Diego, CA: Conference on College Composition and Communication, March/April 1993. ERIC ED 358 462. 13 pages

Questions assumptions underlying writing instruction in higher education. Argues that students may benefit from writing fiction in the composition class, and teachers may gain a different perspective on students' roles.

1519. McFarland, Ron. "An Apologia for Creative Writing." *CE* 55 (January 1993): 28–45.

Offers an apologia by developing an extended analogy between poetry and baseball to counter recent attacks on contemporary poetry and creative writing programs.

1520. McMahan, Elizabeth. "Helping Women Become Writers." *TETYC* 20 (Feburary 1993): 42–45.

Maintains that teachers can point out sexism in language, help women find their voices in the classroom, raise feminist consciousness, and foster women's aspirations.

1521. Mead, Dana Gulling. *Autobiography and the Exploratory Essay*. Atlanta, GA: National Council of Teachers of English, November 1990. ERIC ED 350 672. 11 pages

Discusses how autobiography and writing of the exploratory essay can be used in college composition to explore the writing process.

1522. Meagher, Donald Gordon. "Perspectives on Literacy in a Community College: Interviews with Students and Faculty in English and College-Prep Departments (English Departments)." *DAI* 54 (December 1993): 2034A.

Examines community college faculty and student attitudes towards literacy; finds that students look for correctness and clarity whereas instructors have broader social concerns.

1523. Morenberg, Max. *"Come Back to the Text Ag'in, Huck Honey!"* Louisville, KY: National Council of Teachers of English, November 1992. ERIC ED 355 557. 10 pages

Promotes sentence combining activities in the classroom as part of the process approach. States that sentence combining activities can be joined with literature by having students create sentences similar to ones in literary texts.

1524. Musgrove, Laurence E. *Classical "Topoi" and the Academic Commonplace*. San Diego, CA: Conference on College Composition and Communication, March/April 1993. ERIC ED 357 366. 12 pages

Suggests that students should be introduced to a wide range of *topoi*—the dialectical, the common, the predictable, the particular, and the propositional.

1525. Nabors, Sherry Lynne. "College English Methods Texts: Signs of a Paradigm Shift?" *DAI* 54 (September 1993): 835A.

Reveals that a paradigm shift from current-traditional to process paradigm is imminent in English methods texts.

1526. Nardo, Anna K. "The Politics of Curriculum Change: Tales from the LSU English Department." *ADE* 105 (Fall 1993): 10–14.

Relates process and progress of curriculum reform that lead to three options in the English major: creative writing, literature, and writing and culture.

1527. Olbert, Sharon, and Kathryn Ring. "Scoring Peers' Papers: Teaching Audience Awareness and Generating Enthusiasm." *TETYC* 20 (December 1993): 300–305.

Discusses the results of a case study in which students in two paired classes graded each others' argumentative research papers.

1528. Parmeter, Sarah Hope. *Current Practices and Concerns of Teachers Integrating Lesbian and Gay Materials into the Composition Curriculum: Or, What Are We Doing and How Are We Doing It?* Boston, MA: Conference on College Composition and Communication, March 1991. ERIC ED 350 621. 13 pages

Acknowledges the value of gay and lesbian-inclusive composition courses but warns against a "neutral" curriculum. Argues that teachers need a clear and well-articulated purpose and plan to avoid volatile, homophobic discussions which marginalize already vulnerable students.

1529. Penman, Robyn. "Unspeakable Acts and Other Deeds: A Critique of Plain Legal Language." *IDJ* 7 (1993): 121–31.

Explains serious challenges of the movement to the legal profession; identifies problems with this movement.

1530. Peritz, Janice Heney. "Making a Place for the Poetic in Academic Writing." *CCC* 44 (October 1993): 380–85.

Explains how students' addition of an epigraph to an academic writing project helped them to "read and write in (de)constructive ways" which were "poetic."

1531. Perry, Theresa, and James W. Fraser, eds. *Freedom's Plow: Teaching in the Multicultural Classroom.* New York, NY: Routledge, 1993. 352 pages

Argues that "multicultural education should be at the center" of all discussions about American education. Parts I and II present voices and experiences of teachers "from first grade to college level," who are engaged in "multicultural education efforts."

1532. Poston, Carol. *Theory into Practice: Personal Voice, Process, and Portfolio.* San Diego, CA: Conference on College Composition and Communication, March/April 1993. ERIC ED 358 476. 10 pages

Proposes to teach process orientation toward the production of the college research paper; argues that students learn not just a subject but also a way of synthesizing ideas.

1533. Randic, Jasna. *The Role of Native American Tradition in the College Composition Classroom.* Cincinnati, OH: Conference on College Composition and Communication, March 1992. ERIC ED 351 691. 14 pages

Argues that writing students would benefit from an exposure to vivid imagery, innovative presentation of meaning, and nonlinear rhetoric of Native American literature. Maintains that native American

storytelling should be incorporated into writing classes.

1534. Ray, Ruth E. *The Practice of Theory: Teacher Research in Composition.* Urbana, IL: NCTE, 1993. 191 pages

Notes that theory and practice have often been falsely and hierarchically opposed and argues that the relationship between theory and practice must be rebuilt. Also explores the teacher-research movement, argues that graduate studies must prepare students to combine research and teaching, and shows how a feminist perspective can help accomplish this.

1535. Richards, Jane. "Tell Me, What Is Foxfire?" *CompC* 6 (November 1993): 4–7.

Describes practices and support networks for Foxfire approaches to teaching which emphasize experiential learning, reflection, and collaboration.

1536. Roberts, Richard M., and Roger J. Kreuz. "Nonstandard Discourse and Its Coherence." *DPr* 16 (October/December 1993): 451–64.

The authors argue that coherence does not depend on conventional structural relations, although these do facilitate comprehension. They maintain that like Cummings' poetry, schizophrenic language can be viewed as coherent.

1537. Roskelly, Hephzibah. "The Risky Business of Group Work." *ATA* 4 (Spring 1993): 1–5.

Suggests that group work helps students "find their own voice" while negotiating institutional and academic constraints.

1538. Runyon, Nancy Ann. "Incorporating the Syllogism into the Teaching of Writing: The Case of Four Selected Rhetoric Textbooks." *DAI* 54 (November 1993): 1786A.

Argues that first-year composition texts should teach traditional Aristotelian logic.

1539. Saeta, Elsa. "The Patterns of Discourse: Beyond Theory toward Practice." *ET* 24 (Spring 1993): 30–34.

Reviews major arguments for and against teaching modes of discourse. Redefines discourse patterns as "heuristic paradigms."

1540. Sandberg, Kate E. "An Investigation of the Promotion of Dialectical Thinking in College Classrooms." *DAI* 53 (May 1993): 3819A.

Examines how instructors promote dialectical thinking by inducing controversy, creating safe environments, using small groups and dialogue, and making appropriate assignments.

1541. Sandman, John, and Michael Weiser. "The Writing Autobiography: How to Begin a Two-Year College Writing Course." *TETYC* 20 (Feburary 1993): 18–22.

Discusses a diagnostic essay which asks students to assess their own competencies and to describe previous writing experiences.

1542. Shimek, Suzanne. "Strategies for Wading through Writer's Sludge." *V&R* 4 (Spring 1994): 33–42.

Uses "writer's sludge" instead of "writer's block" to describe the process of forging ahead when writing becomes arduous, slow, confusing, and messy.

1543. Sitler, Helen Collins. "What College Writing Instructors Expect and Why You Should Join the Resistance." *EJ* 82 (October 1993): 21–25.

Lists analytical papers, statements supported with evidence, drafts, appropriate terminology, and different research techniques as some of the expectations of college teachers. Argues that it is more important to teach a liberating pedagogy that involves students in the writing process.

1544. Smith, Frank. *Whose Language? What Power? A Universal Conflict in a South African Setting*. New York: Teachers College Press, 1993. 177 pages

Provides an ethnographic study of the author's participation in an empowerment project with black South Africans. Argues

that "empowerment does not come from language—language reflects power."

1545. Soderlund, Michael D. "Classroom Memos: Creating Purposeful Dialogue." *EJ* 82 (November 1993): 55–57.

Points out that memos address an authentic audience. Considers them more powerful than journals.

1546. Sommers, Elizabeth. *Student-Centered, Not Teacher-Abandoned: Peer Response Groups That Work*. San Diego, CA: Conference on College Composition and Communication, March/April 1993. ERIC ED 357 382. 12 pages

Offers suggestions for dealing with problems in peer response.

1547. Sotirou, Peter. "Articulating a Hermeneutic Pedagogy: The Philosophy of Interpretation." *JAC* 13 (Fall 1993): 365–80.

Explains hermeneutic pedagogy and contrasts it with expressivist and social constructionist pedgagogies.

1548. Stevens, L. Robert, Gus Seligmann, Julian Long, and Georgia Caraway, eds. *The Core and the Canon: A National Debate*. Southern Methodist University Studies in Composition and Rhetoric. Dallas, TX: Southern Methodist University Press, 1993. 560 pages

The essayists provide a collection of papers on Classic Learning Core presented at curriculum conferences sponsored by the University of North Texas. They point out that CLC emphasizes underlying unities of knowledge, study of classic and classical books and documents, critical and creative thinking, and a thorough mastery of reading, writing, and speaking skills.

Essayists: Alexander, Melodie; Baker, Derek; Baxter, Jerry; Baxter, Nancy Kerber; Behrens, Maurice G.; Berry, Benjamin D., Jr.; Cain, Elizabeth P.; Carlson, Charles P., Jr.; Carbone, Michael; Chadwick-Joshua, Jocelyn; Churchill, John; Clements Worsham, Fabian; Coates, Roslyn; Como, James; Cordero, Ronald

A.; Craft, William; Daley, J.; Damico, Anthony; Doerr, Arthur H.; Eddy, John P.; Fedo, David A.; Field, Carol Hammond; Fitch, Nancy Elizabeth; Flanders, Todd; Flynn, Thomas F; Fulkerson, Tahita; Geiger, John; Greenlaw, M. Jean; Hagen, Carol; Hairman, Robert; Hall, Carol; Hardy, Clifford A.; Harris, Joseph B.; Henderson, Allen H.; Herrick, Christopher W.; Idol, John; Johnson, Roger, Jr.; Johnes, Richard; Kohl, John C.; Kohl, Theresa Welch; Krause, Joseph; Lawson, Hughie G.; Marshall, Ernest; Martin, Floyd W.; Martin, Jerry L.; Marx, Steven; McClish, Glen; Miller, James; Montgomery, Garth; Mueller, Gene; Nelson, John S.; O'Connor, Lucy A.; Palmer, Leslie; Payne, Michael; Pickens, Donald K.; Quinn, Dennis; Rapple, Brendan A.; Raschke, Carl; Reed, Ronald F.; Ross, Gary; Schrock, John Richard; Seidel, Linda; Seligmann, G. L.; Simpson, Pat H.; Smith, James LeRoy; Stiles, Victoria M.; Tanner, James T. F.; Tate, Michael; Thompson, Leslie M.; Troy, Mary; Tucker, William R.; Waldinger, Albert; Webster, David S.; Wollan, Laurin A., Jr.; Yaffe, Martin D.; Zorn, Jeff.

1549. Tatum, Stephen. "'The Thing Not Named': Or, The End of Creative Writing in the English Department." *ADE* 106 (Winter 1993): 30–34.

Calls for redefining the purpose of creative writing programs and proposes closer links with theory and literature. Lists six ways to foster the programs.

1550. Thomas, Sharon K., and Marilyn Wilson. "Idiosyncratic Interpretations: Negotiating Meaning in Expository Prose." *EJ* 82 (January 1993): 58–64.

Discusses difficulties that arise when students' existing knowledge conflicts with new information in texts. Suggests three strategies for helping students negotiate meaning.

1551. Thompson, Becky W., and Sangeeta Tyagi, eds. *Beyond a Dream Deferred; Multicultural Education and the Politics of Excel-*

lence. Minneapolis, MN: University of Minnesota Press, 1993. 267 pages

The essayists outline different models of multiculturalism, discuss the approaches to implementing multicultural education, and describe specific programs at the university level.

Essayists: Andersen, Margaret L.; Bell, Derrick; Ditsch, Estelle; Duster, Troy; Hall, Lisa Kahaleole Chang; Hamonds, Evelynn; Hu-Dehart, Evelyn; Jackson, Earl Jr.; López, Ian Haney; Marks, Carole C.; Mohanty, Chandra Talpade; Omolade, Barbara; Thompson, Becky; Tyagi, Sangeeta; West, Cornel.

1552. Thompson, Tom. *Personality Preference and Student Responses to Teacher Comments*. San Diego, CA: Conference on College Composition and Communication, March/April 1993. ERIC ED 357 392. 10 pages

A study at The Citadel finds no relation between preferred learning style and responses to teacher comments.

1553. Tinberg, Howard. "Border-Crossings: Shaping the Academic Conversation." *ATA* 4 (Fall 1993): 8–12.

Notes that important contributions of community college instructors have to offer efforts to generate research and theory from within classroom practice.

1554. Tingle, Nick. "The Lessons of LINKs." *CompSt* 21 (Fall 1993): 60–74.

Discusses LINKs courses, which require students to co-enroll in a content- or discipline-specific course to become members of a "learning community."

1555. Tobin, Lad. *Writing Relationships: What Really Happens in the Composition Class*. Portsmouth, NH: Heinemann-Boynton/Cook, 1993. 165 pages

Examines day-to-day realities of a process-oriented composition class, emphasizing how interpersonal relationships affect the quality of instruction and learning.

1556. Traxler, Matthew J., and Ann Gernsbacher Morton. "Improving Written Communication through Perspective-Taking." *L&CP* 8 (August 1993): 311–34.

Examines three writing experiments which test communicative effectiveness; argues that writers are more successful when they visualize the reader's needs.

1557. Tucker, Tommy Neil. "The Wednesday Read: A Bridge for Writers." *TETYC* 20 (May 1993): 115–20.

Emphasizes the positive value of reading aloud to students as guest readers from the community come with their own selections.

1558. Wensson, Jackie Marie Eason. "Changes in Teaching Practices Related to the Colorado Writing Project, 1987–1991." *DAI* 53 (April 1993): 3438A.

Investigates practices employed by writing teachers who have participated in the Colorado Writing Project. Recognizes advantages of suggested methods and their impediments to success.

1559. Whitney, Robert Lawrence. "Making Meaning: A Philosophical Study of Changing Presuppositions in the Teaching of Writing." *DAI* 53 (May 1993): 3839A.

Explores the implications of "writing to learn" for pedagogical purposes and knowledge making.

1560. Wiemelt, Jeffrey. *Text, Context, and Shared Understanding: Refocusing on "Accountability" in Student Writing*. San Diego, CA: Conference on College Composition and Communication, March/April 1993. ERIC ED 358 514. 12 pages

Presents a language-centered social interactionist approach to writing. Maintains that the writer-reader interaction needs to be text-centered.

1561. Wiley, Mark. "Building a Rose Garden: A Response to John Trimbur [*JAC* 13 (Winter 1993)]." *JAC* 13 (Fall 1993): 529–33.

Reinterprets Trimbur's criticism of Mike Rose's *Lives on the Boundary* as veiled praise.

1562. Wilson, Gerald B. "The Value Students Found in High School Writing Portfolios." *DAI* 54 (September 1993): 802A.

Data indicate that student ownership and empowerment result from portfolio assessment.

1563. Wolcott, Willa. "A Metacognitive Approach to Remediation." *Focuses* 5 (Summer 1992): 18–26.

Studies integration of instruction in the writing process. Discusses the development of editing strategies and the inclusion of readings in connection with students' metacognition of learning processes.

1564. Yoder, Sharon Logsdon. "Teaching Writing Revision Attitudes and Copy Changes." *JourEd* 47 (Winter 1993): 41–47.

Results show that students perceived that revisions increased their grades or knowledge, that surface features were revised more frequently than macro-level features, and that formula assignments restrict revisions.

4.2 HIGHER EDUCATION

4.2.1 DEVELOPMENTAL WRITING

1565. Adams, Peter Dow. "Basic Writing Reconsidered." *JBW* 12 (Spring 1993): 22–36.

Asks whether basic writers are more likely to succeed in first-year composition if they are mainstreamed into writing classes. Reports research evaluating their success rates at community colleges.

1566. Bartholomae, David. "The Tidy House: Basic Writing in the American Curriculum." *JBW* 12 (Spring 1993): 4–21.

Shows how basic writing courses often "enact a rhetoric of exclusion [at] the center of a curriculum designed to hide or erase cultural difference."

1567. Becker, Susan. *Life-Long Learning: A Reality for All?* San Diego, CA: Conference on College Composition and Communication, March/April 1993. ERIC ED 357 380. 12 pages

Suggests ways to teach a diverse student body in composition classes in the community college.

1568. DiPardo, Anne. *A Kind of Passport: A Basic Writing Adjunct Program and the Challenge of Student Diversity.* Urbana, IL: NCTE, 1993. 202 pages

Presents an ethnographic study of a basic writing course for underprepared students at fictitious Dover Park University, a predominantly white institution in a Western state that has committed itself to increasing campus diversity.

1569. DiPardo, Anne. "Nested Contexts: A Basic Writing Adjunct Program and the Challenge of 'Educational Equity.'" National Center for the Study of Writing and Literacy, 1992. ERIC ED 354 523. 55 pages

Presents an ethnographic study of an adjunct writing program at a public university that had been overwhelmingly Anglo-American. Offers student portraits of a Latina and a Black man and suggests ways to improve the program.

1570. Douglas, Michael. "A Successful Individualized Writing Lab Module." *JDEd* 16 (Spring 1993): 24–26.

Sets forth benefits of using computer-assisted instruction in developmental writing.

1571. Fraizer, Daniel T. "Choice by Default: The Political Economy of Developmental Writing Textbooks (Volumes I and II)." *DAI* 54 (November 1993): 1708A.

Survey results show that teachers, editors, and publishing representatives share a confidence in institutional authority and assume that commodified textbooks improve writing.

1572. Gay, Pamela. "Rereading Shaughnessy from a Postcolonial Perspective." *JBW* 12 (Fall 1993): 29–40.

Analyzes Shaughnessy's characterization of basic writing teachers who try to convert the "natives" to academic culture. Advocates decolonizing and dialogic pedagogy which incorporates "difference as a source of strength."

1573. Hindman, Jane E. "Reinventing the University: Finding the Place for Basic Writers." *JBW* 12 (Fall 1993): 55–76.

Advocates a pedagogy that places "the source of English professors' authority within the discipline." Analyzes evaluation of placement exams.

1574. Jones, William. "Basic Writing: Pushing against Racism." *JBW* 12 (Spring 1993): 72–80.

Exposes the racism of writing programs which assume a "hierarchy of intelligence among races." Presents Black religious folk expressions and the blues as anti-racist. Analyzes the success of historically Black colleges.

1575. Laurence, Patricia. "The Vanishing Site of Mina Shaughnessy's *Errors and Expectations.*" *JBW* 12 (Fall 1993): 18–28.

Shows how recent reevaluations of Shaughnessy's book disregard "historical and political forces that shape the rhetoric and methodology of particular practitioners, scholars, and researchers."

1576. Lawrence, William Walters. "A Descriptive Study of Asian American Basic Writers." *DAI* 54 (December 1993): 2132A.

Concludes that the native culture can influence students' writing and reading practices in English.

1577. Lester, Mark. "Why Johnny Can't Correct His Errors." *Inland* 16 (Fall/Winter 1993): 22–25.

Argues that students' errors often escape their notice because they respond to their language as members of an oral, rather than a literate, culture.

1578. MacDonald, Ross B. "Developmental Students' Processing of Teacher Feedback in Composition Instruction." National Center for Developmental Education, vol. 8, no. 5, 1993. ERIC ED 354 965. 8 pages

Reviews literature on feedback in English education and social psychology. Sets forth theoretical conclusions and practical suggestions for developmental English instructors to use when providing feedback to composition students.

1579. Martone, Denice. "Ways in Which At-Risk College Writers Collaborate to Reconceptualize Their Essays in Response to the Varying Prompts That Exist during a Writing Conference." *DAI* 53 (February 1993): 2721A.

Examines the effects of writing conference sessions on four at-risk first-year college students.

1580. McAlexander, Patricia. *Mina Shaughnessy in the 1990s: Some Changing Answers in Basic Writing.* San Diego, CA: Conference on College Composition and Communication, March/April 1993. ERIC ED 359 562. 12 pages

Points out that Shaughnessy's ideas about basic writers are changing and becoming more inclusive. Presents four often interrelated reasons for writing underachievement.

1581. McCurry, Niki. "The Computerized Inventory of Developmental Writing Traits." Alaska Writing Program, February 1992. ERIC ED 357 375. 6 pages

Discusses the advantages of CIDWT for teachers who want to implement a process-writing approach in their classrooms.

1582. Schwimmer, Jill. "Community College English Teachers Who Teach Writing to Underprepared Students: Curricula Focus and Instructional Strategies." *DAI* 54 (October 1993): 1209A.

Describes basic-writing teaching methodologies of instructors in California community colleges; examines why some teachers are likely to adopt or reject alternative curricula and teaching strategies.

1583. Scott, Jerrie Cobb. "Literacies and Deficits Revisited." *JBW* 12 (Spring 1993): 46–56.

Shows how narrow definitions of literacy and teachers' "uncritical dysconsciousness" sustain deficit pedagogy in developmental programs. Urges basic writing professionals to implement a "pedagogy of success."

1584. Sonomura, Marion Okawa. "Idiomaticity in Basic Writing: Formulas and Idioms in the Writing of Some Multilingual and Creole-Speaking Community College Students." *DAI* 54 (October 1993): 1344A.

Examines how demands of idiomaticity, in contrast to grammaticality alone, affect academic acceptability of writing.

1585. Sternglass, Marilyn S. "Writing Development as Seen through Longitudinal Research: A Case Study Exemplar." *WC* 10 (April 1993): 235–61.

Describes a longitudinal study of writers starting college at three levels of writing skills. Details one three-and-a-half year case study of a developmental writer.

1586. Thorne, Sheila. "Prewriting: A Basic Skill for Basic Writers." *TETYC* 20 (February 1993): 31–35.

Argues that prewriting is crucial for basic writer but that teachers and textbooks often simplify and mechanize the process. Describes methods of making prewriting central.

1587. Truxaw, Patsy. "Mike Rose in the Secondary English Class: Challenging Notions on Nonfiction Instruction." *CalE* 29 (Winter 1993): 10–11, 23, 26.

Explains Rose's arguments for exposing basic writers to higher-level thinking and writing tasks than the personal narrative;

illustrates Rose's theory with a description of an actual class.

1588. Urschel, Linda Kathleen. "A Descriptive Study of Basic Writing Instruction in the Christian College Coalition." *DAI* 54 (October 1993): 1272A.

Presents data on basic writing instruction in a coalition of 77 Christian liberal-arts colleges compared against a similar study of all colleges. Finds that coalition schools generally reported similar curricula but with smaller class sizes and significantly more basic writing courses taught by tenure-track faculty.

1589. Young, Alice Virginia. "Remedial Education in Mississippi's Community and Junior Colleges." *DAI* 54 (December 1993): 2035A.

Surveys remedial programs to find that 33 percent of the assessed students were recommended for remedial writing classes and that the majority was placed in such classes.

4.2.2 FIRST-YEAR COLLEGE COMPOSITION

1590. Adler-Kassner, Linda, and Shawn Gillen. *Racing towards Academic Literacy: BMWs, Tollways, and Bridges*. San Diego, CA: Conference on College Composition and Communication, March/April 1993. ERIC ED 357 378. 18 pages

The authors analyze literacy autobiographies by undergraduates and point out that becoming academically literate is a Faustian bargain in which students must surrender themselves to academic literacy and lose their own identity.

1591. Ahlschwede, Margrethe. "Writing with Students: Beginning to Know." *ATA* 4 (Fall 1993): 1–4.

Advocates that instructors and students complete the assignments and share their writing with students.

1592. Allen, Paul. "What Would a Writer Do?" *ADE* 106 (Winter 1993): 6–12.

Discusses what the methods of poets and fiction writers can teach composition students. Analyzes five characteristics that can carry over to first-year writers of essays.

1593. Alton, Cheryl, and Kathleen Pfeiffer. "Two Comments on 'Crossing Lines' [response to Deletiner, *CE* 54 (November 1992)]." *CE* 55 (October 1993): 666–73.

Cautions against composition instructors acting as "pseudo psychiatrists" or therapists.

1594. Baker, Nancy Westrich. "The Effect of Portfolio-Based Instruction on Composition Students' Final Examination Scores, Course Grades, and Attitudes toward Writing." *RTE* 27 (May 1993): 155–74.

Compares portfolio-based and standard process approaches to instruction in first-year college composition courses; challenges some common beliefs about portfolio use.

1595. Bass, Barbara Kaplan. "The Mathematics of Writing: Shaping Attitudes in Composition Classes." *TETYC* 20 (May 1993): 109–14.

Compares writing anxiety with math anxiety; includes practical suggestions for combating both.

1596. Bishop, Wendy, ed. *The Subject Is Writing: Essays by Teachers and Students on Writing*. Portsmouth, NH: Heinemann-Boynton/Cook, 1993. 278 pages

This reader for first-year composition presents 25 esays on topics in composition studies, divided into five sections: "Growing into Writing," "Changing the Writing Classroom," "Writing in Progress," "To the Writer—Explanations and Advice," and "Writers, School, and Writing."
Essayists: Anson, C. M.; Belanoff, P.; Bishop, Wendy; Brown, A.; Corder, J. W.; D'Arcy, P.; Daniell, B.; Davis, K.; Dickson, M.; Fulwiler, T.; Harris, J.; Harris, M.; Kienenberger, D.; Kremers, C.; Lutz, E.; Loban, S.; McAndrew, D. C.; Murray,

D. M.; Ronald, K.; Roskelley, H.; Strickland, J.; Usatch, B.; Wolf, T.; Wyche-Smith, S.; Zebroski, J.

1597. Boehnlein, James. *The Humanities Base Classroom: Responding, Interacting, and Composing*. San Diego, CA: Conference on College Composition and Communication, March/April 1993. ERIC ED 357 349. 6 pages

Presents the pedagogy employed in composition instruction in the Humanities Base program at the University of Dayton.

1598. Boyle, Kevin. *Boning Up for the Research Paper*. Cincinnati, OH: Conference on College Composition and Communication, March 1992. ERIC ED 358 470. 7 pages

Suggests assigning a mock research paper about three weeks before the final research paper is due in which students must argue and support a position different from what they expect to take in their final paper.

1599. Braswell, Patricia. "Cabbage Worms and Critical Thinking." *TETYC* 20 (Feburary 1993): 64–70.

Discusses teaching problem solving in the research course.

1600. Carbone, Nick. "Trying to Create a Community: A First Day Lesson Plan." *C&C* 10 (November 1993): 81–88.

Stresses community of writers by beginning with computer writing, responding, and peer interaction on the first day, saving administrative matters for later. Discusses the use of e-mail for educational purposes.

1601. Chen, Yueh-Miao. "The Writing Development of College Students and Effective Instruction." *DAI* 53 (April 1993): 3463A.

Researches the relationship between instruction and writing development; identifies factors affecting writing development of college writers.

1602. Conley, Delilah Ferne. "The Effects of Audience on the Writing of College Freshmen." *DAI* 53 (January 1993): 2279A.

Studies the effects of audience on motivation, voice, and performance of three classes of first-year composition writers.

1603. Cubbage, Elinor Phillips. "The Effects of Explicit Instruction in Argumentation on Community College Freshmen's Persuasive Writing." *DAI* 54 (November 1993): 1651A.

Results show that informal logic instruction produced greater gains and more positive student perceptions than formal logic instruction.

1604. Davison, Phebe. *Social Contexts: Crossing (Exploring, Assaulting, Metabolizing?) Cultural Boundaries in the Classroom*. San Diego, CA: Conference on College Composition and Communication, March/April 1993. ERIC ED 357 377. 13 pages

Discusses an experimental, team-taught course on censorship in which students were allowed to select their own topics and their own kind of discourse.

1605. Dively, Ronda Leathers. "Religious Discourse in the Academy: Creating a Space by Means of Poststructuralist Theories of Subjectivity." *CompSt* 21 (Fall 1993): 91–101.

Discusses responding to students who write from a religious perspective. Points out that they have to read authors who refuse to accept convenient stereotypes for categorizing religious experience.

1606. Estrin, Herman. *Teaching Minority Students to Write Effectively*. Bloomington, IL: 1993. ERIC ED 358 487. 3 pages

Offers a six-step program to teach beginning minority students in urban public colleges and technical schools how to write effectively.

1607. Frisk, Philip Justin. *Rap Music and the First-Year Writing Curriculum*. Cincinnati, OH: Conference on College Composition and Communication, March 1992. ERIC ED 349 552. 22 pages

Discusses how rap music as a curricular material can aid student-writers and teachers in developing response techniques to academic texts.

1608. Harris, Joseph. "The Course as Text/The Teacher as Critic." *CE* 55 (November 1993): 785–800.

Suggests that for a profession where scholarship is "in" teaching, we seem to talk more about how we view ourselves as intellectuals than about teaching.

1609. Hashimoto, I. " 'Sentence Variety': Where Theory and Practice Meet and Lose." *CompSt* 21 (Spring 1993): 66–77.

Considers advice given to students about improving their style through sentence variety. Concludes that the advice is possibly incoherent and useless.

1610. Hayn, Judith A. "A Study of the Effects of Using Prewriting Strategies in Teaching Composition." *DAI* 53 (February 1993): 2664A.

Compares the effect of teaching prewriting with the effect of teaching traditional methods in the writing ability of 63 first-year composition students.

1611. Heba, Gary M. "Inventing Culture: A Rhetoric of Social Codes." *DAI* 53 (March 1993): 3130A.

Provides a theory and method for teaching cultural critique in composition courses by giving heuristics for interpreting the cultural information received from various media sources.

1612. Hess, Marlene A. *Creating a Collaborative Context for Critical Thinking in Composition*. San Diego, CA: Conference on College Composition and Communication, March/April 1993. ERIC ED 357 389. 10 pages

Describes the efforts of the director of a composition program to create an active learning environment that stimulates the imagination and enhances critical thinking.

1613. Hutto, David. "Gas Attacks and Gas Stations: Writing Dialogues from Poems." *ExEx* 38 (Spring 1993): 13–15.

Describes a writing assignment in which students imagine a dialogue between characters in two separate poems; notes that it encourages students to enjoy writing.

1614. Landis-Groom, Eileen. *Using Letters between Classes and Campuses to Improve Writing Skills*. Louisville, KY: National Council of Teachers of English, November 1992. ERIC ED 357 339. 30 pages

Reports on a correspondence method of teaching writing in which students exchanged drafts and peer critiques between the Florida and Arizona campuses of Embry-Riddle University.

1615. Lindemann, Erika. "Freshman Composition: No Place for Literature." *CE* 55 (March 1993): 311–16.

Argues that including literature in composition courses interferes with students exploring academic discourse. Maintains that teachers talk too much while students write too little.

1616. Lindstrom, Braden. "To Be an Artist: A Written and Oral Project." *TETYC* 20 (October 1993): 188–89.

Discusses a collaborative writing project in which students research a famous visual artist and then present a first-person monologue.

1617. Marinara, Martha. *Stirring the Ashes of Public Discourse*. Louisville, KY: National Council of Teachers of English, November 1992. ERIC ED 357 338. 20 pages

Connects autobiography and social critique and encourages students to see their social roles and the events in their lives as determined by cultural context.

1618. Martin, Deanna C., and David R. Arendale. "Supplementary Instruction: Improving First-Year Student Success in High-Risk Courses." National Resource Center for the

Freshman Year Experience, 1992. ERIC ED 354 839. 61 pages

Describes Supplementary Instruction, a student assistance program designed to improve academic success. Points out that it is based on the idea that if students are not successful in their courses, then perhaps colleges should change their teaching methods.

1619. Masiello, Lea. "Write at the Start: A Guide to Using Writing in Freshman Seminars." National Resource Center for the Freshman Year Experience, 1993. ERIC ED 354 841. 73 pages

Explores ways in which first-year college students can benefit from writing; offers concrete, practical suggestions for implementing writing in seminar courses.

1620. Mattingly, Carol. "Social Warrants and Classroom Practices." *DAI* 53 (March 1993): 3209A.

Finds inconsistencies and overlaps among feminism, Marxism, and social constructionism as applied to classroom practices such as personal experience, contextualization, and collaboration.

1621. McMahon, Patricia Lynn. "A Narrative Study of Three Levels of Reflection in a College Composition Class: Teacher Journal, Student Portfolios, Teacher-Student Discourse." *DAI* 54 (December 1993): 2042A.

Examines student portfolios; looks for ways to make students' writing experiences more meaningful.

1622. Megna, Mary Cease. "Research Writing: The Dynamic Interaction between Reader, Writer, and Text." *DAI* 53 (February 1993): 2667A.

Uses a Likert Scale for assessment to identify attitudes of 100 first-year college students toward research writing.

1623. Mirtz, Ruth M. "Shaping, Sharpening, and Other Theories of Meaning-Making in First-Year College Writers." *CompSt* 21 (Fall 1993): 75–90.

Uses two case studies to examine students' accounts of meaning-making in writing.

1624. Navarre, Joan. *Literary Theory and Composition Practice*. Cincinnati, OH: Conference on College Composition and Communication, March 1992. ERIC ED 348 695. 14 pages

Uses Bakhtin's concept of heteroglossia to challenge the idea that students' writing assignments should reflect a single voice. Examines a paper by a first-year college student which reflects culturally encoded communication through a shift in voice.

1625. Norton, Jody. "Cadillac Jack's Dog and Pony Show: Introducing Language Theory to the Beginning Student of Literature." *W&D* 11 (Spring 1993): 105–31.

Applies poststructuralist theory to an introductory literature classroom to examine the role of language, metaphor, and ideology operating in traditional and popular literature.

1626. Perrin, Robert. "Picks and Pans: Writing Critiques of Best and Worst Sources during Research." *ExEx* 39 (Fall 1993): 30–32.

Describes a classroom exercise which asks students to evaluate sources for a research paper, thereby keeping students writing and letting them practice documentation during research.

1627. Richer, David Louis. "The Effects of Two Feedback Systems on First-Year College Students' Writing Proficiency." *DAI* 53 (February 1993): 2722A.

Investigates the effects of feedback from peers and teachers given to first-year college students during different stages in their writing.

1628. Rileigh, Kathryn. "Toward a Palatable Research Paper Experience." *IHE* 18 (Winter 1993): 123–32.

Describes a five-stage technique for managing research paper assignments in upper division college courses. Presents students' positive reactions.

1629. Shea, Christopher. "What's Happened to Writing Skills." *CHE* (3 February1993): A33–34.

Does not find a general consensus among writing instructors from various campuses about the rumored decline in skills of entering first-year students. Points out that many teachers agree that the argument is "shallow."

1630. Sims, Margaret C. "The Classroom Writing Community: Looking at the Tie That Binds." *V&R* 4 (Spring 1994): 25–32.

Shows how a diverse community college writing class created a community.

1631. Swanson-Owens, Deborah Ann. "Learning to 'Invent the University': A Case Study of Students Acquiring and Applying Discourse Structure Knowledge in Two Freshman Composition Classes." *DAI* 54 (November 1993): 1662A.

Provides analyses which indicate that different rhetorical forms constrain and compel students to think and write in different composing strategies, mental operations, and text logic.

1632. Tate, Gary. "A Place for Literature in Freshman Composition." *CE* 55 (March 1993): 317–21.

Suggests that literature is important to composition courses by providing a resource to help students think, talk, and write about lives outside the academy.

1633. Teichmann, Sandra Gail. *Bridging the Gap between Peer Response and the Classroom and Teacher Expectations: Three Stories*. Indiana, PA: Peer Tutoring in Writing Conference, October 1992. ERIC ED 351 689. 14 pages

Describes a course which promotes peer response. Points out that the teacher sets criteria for evaluating writing, uses class time for discussing student texts, and involves students in the writing assessment by using peer-grading for their portfolios.

1634. Teichmann, Sandra Gail. "Tale Two: Teacher Writing with a First-Year Writing Class." *ELQ* 15 (October 1993): 5–7.

Provides the second part of a linked essay started by Wendy Bishop. Looks at a teacher's first composition class and the experience of writing along with her students.

1635. Thompson, Shirley Mae Smith. "The Effects of Peer Collaboration on Community College Freshmen's Writing, Socialization, and Attitudes." *DAI* 53 (May 1993): 3791A.

Results suggest that peer collaboration may have had a positive effect on students' writing, their socialization, and their attitudes toward writing.

1636. Vandenberg, Peter. *Compromise and Conciliation: Frame Alignment Theory in the Argument Class*. San Diego, CA: Conference on College Composition and Communication, March/April 1993. ERIC ED 357 341. 12 pages

Explains that consciously aligning one's own "frame" with someone else's can give rise to discursive practices that engage, critique, and embrace diverse points of view.

1637. Vogel, Mark W. "Reviews of Recent Composition Textbooks." *Focuses* 6 (Winter 1993): 101–51.

Reviews 13 readers and six rhetorics for those who choose textbooks used mainly in first-year English courses.

1638. Walsh, S. M. *Writers' Fears and Creative Inclinations—How Do They Affect Composition Quality?* San Diego, CA: Conference on College Composition and Communication, March/April 1993. ERIC ED 357 387. 10 pages

Reports on an experimental study of 255 first-year composition students at two campuses of the California State University System.

1639. Young, Linda P. "College Freshman Writing across the Curriculum: A Case Study of Students' Motivations for Revising." *DAI* 53 (June 1993): 4239A.

Examines how first-year college students adapt to discipline demands as they write across the curriculum. Focuses on revisions students made to three essays.

4.2.3 ADVANCED COMPOSITION

1640. Adams, Katherine H., and John L. Adams, eds. *Teaching Advanced Composition: Why and How*. Portsmouth, NH: Boynton/Cook, 1991. 312 pages

Eighteen essays present historical, theoretical and practical perspectives on courses in advanced composition. The editors include an afterword on needed scholarship in the field and a bibliography.
Essayists: Adams, Katherine H.; Adams, John L.; Anderson, C.; Ashton-Jones, Evelyn; Bloom, L. Z.; Carr, Janet; Carter, M.; Coe, R. M.; Covino, W. A.; Donovan, T. R.; Fahnestock, J.; Frey, O.; Gage, J. T.; Haring-Smith, T.; Keene, M. L.; Olson, G. A.; Penfield, E.; Ross, Mary Ellen; Wallace, Ray; Young, R.

1641. Benson, Nichola, Sarah Gurney, Judith Harrison, and Rachel Rimmershaw. "The Place of Academic Writing in Whole Life Writing: A Case Study of Three University Students." *Lang&E* (1993): 1–20.

Studies the views of three university students toward writing in relation to previous experiences with writing.

1642. Bishop, Wendy. "Tale One: Writing with a Writing Workshop." *ELQ* 15 (October 1993): 2–5.

Presents the first half of a linked essay which is concluded by Sandra Gail Teichmann. Details the experience of being an active writing participant in her graduate-level, advanced writing class.

1643. Howell, Charles. *Proposal for an Advanced Writing Course—Perspectives on Professional Knowledge*. San Diego, CA: Conference on College Composition and Communication, March/April 1993. ERIC ED 359 517. 13 pages

Proposes a course using rhetorical and linguistic concepts as tools for the examination of professional knowledge and professional education.

1644. Martin, Wanda. "Self-Aware and Learning to Change." *ATA* 4 (Fall 1993): 5–8.

Portrays composition as creating occasions for students to speak from the complexity of their cultural diversities.

1645. Sargent, Julia Elizabeth. "From Shallow Writing to Writing with Power: The Quantum Leap." *DAI* 53 (April 1993): 3437A.

Examines the development of a writer's confidence, skill, and "power" after being exposed to the creative writing process.

1646. Trudelle, Thomas. "Restless Minds Take Stock: Self-Evaluation of Student Journals." *ATA* 4 (Fall 1992): 10–16.

Reports how journals may be integrated into a course by using student-generated goal setting, progress reporting, and evaluative criteria.

4.2.4 BUSINESS COMMUNICATION

1647. Arnold, Vanessa D., and Gerry D. Roach. "Reach Out and Write Someone." *BEdF* 47 (February 1993): 25–27.

Asserts that writing letters to editors or elected officials may help students develop organized, logical, and persuasive writing.

1648. Blyler, Nancy Roundy. "Teaching Persuasion as Consensus in Business Communication." *BABC* 56 (March 1993): 26–31.

Explains how three rhetorical techniques help writers to build consensus with readers and enable them to argue more persuasively.

1649. Blyler, Nancy Roundy. "Teaching Purpose in a Business Communication Course." *BABC* 56 (September 1993): 15–20.

Presents strategies for teaching students how to consider the complexity of purposes for the business messages they write.

1650. Brady, Laura A. "A Contextual Theory for Business Writing." *JBTC* 7 (October 1993): 452–71.

Critiques traditional or formalist notions of conventions in business writing; posits an alternative concept based on context and intertext.

1651. Brockman, Elizabeth Blackburn, and Kelly Belanger. "You-Attitude and Positive Emphasis: Testing Received Wisdom in Business Communication." *BABC* 56 (June 1993): 1–5.

The authors describe a study which compares responses to a letter with and one without you-attitude and positive emphasis.

1652. Brown, Alvin R. "Methodologies for Teaching Grammar, Punctuation, and Spelling: Required Essentials for Developing Good Writers." *Leaflet* 92 (Spring 1993): 35–41.

Suggests approaches, with specific examples, for teaching grammar, spelling, and punctuation to junior college and business school students.

1653. Browne, Carmen D. "Office Etiquette." *BEdF* 47 (February 1993): 41–43.

Asserts that business educators have a responsibility to teach students the link between etiquette and professional success; provides an outline etiquette curriculum.

1654. Cassady, Mona. "Technology as Part of Business Communication." *BABC* 56 (September 1993): 36–38.

Discusses methods for teaching computer technology in business communication.

1655. Cirincione, Joseph A. "Revision and Business Writing: Checking the Numbers." *BABC* 56 (March 1993): 16–21.

Presents sentence openers, verb choices, and independent clauses as three "style checkpoints" for revision of business prose.

1656. Comerford, Linda. "Taking the 'GR' Out of Grammar." *BABC* 56 (March 1993): 12–15.

Describes a short course for punctuation and grammar.

1657. Darter, Marvin E., and Katherine T. Hoff. "A Communication-Rich Systems Design Project." *BABC* 56 (December 1993): 32–37.

Describes a computer information systems course that uses oral and written components.

1658. Dillon, W. Tracy. "Copia Rerum: Confronting Interlanguage with International Students." *JBTC* 7 (April 1993): 246–55.

Explores double translation as a method for encouraging second language business communicators to increase English proficiency.

1659. Driskill, Linda. "Ethical Issues in Business Communication: The Case of the Busy Consultant." *BABC* 56 (September 1993): 31.

Discusses a business communication ethics case.

1660. Dukes, Thomas. "Should We Teach Software Use in Business Communication?" *BABC* 56 (September 1993): 34–35.

Discusses problems of teaching business communication with computers; explains why the use of computer labs is necessary.

1661. Dulye, Linda. "Toward Better Two-Way: Why Communications Process Improvement Represents the Right Response during Uncertain Times." *IEEE* 36 (March 1993): 24–29.

Demonstrates in a case study of a Fortune 100 company that effective two-way communication between all levels of employees can improve productivity and morale.

1662. Dyrud, Marilyn A. "Should We Teach Computer Software in Business Communication Courses?" *BABC* 56 (September 1993): 35–36.

Discusses problems of teaching business communication with computers; explains why computer software should not be taught.

1663. Farris, Ann Kay. "The Effect of Background Knowledge and Coherence on Reader Understanding of Written Business Communication." *DAI* 54 (September 1993): 785A.

Concludes that without appropriate background knowledge readers may not understand a business communication text even if it is well written.

1664. Fiarhurst, Gail T. "Echoes of Vision when the Rest of the Organization Talks Total Quality." *MCQ* 6 (May 1993): 331–71.

Describes a case study of an organization that recently began implementing Demming's Total Quality. Identifies five framing devices and their success or failure.

1665. Forman, Janis. "Business Communication and Composition: The Writing Connection and beyond." *JBC* 30 (July 1993): 333–52.

Points out that citations in business communication articles show only a modest use of composition studies. Considers historical studies, critical theory, multicultural/literacy studies as three areas of composition research relevant to business communication.

1666. Freed, Richard C. "This Is a Pedagogical Essay on Voice." *JBTC* 7 (October 1993): 472–81.

Presents a heuristic to help writers understand and effectively employ voice in professional documents.

1667. Gale, Frederic G. "Teaching Professional Writing Rhetorically: The Unified Case Method." *JBTC* 7 (April 1993): 256–66.

Describes the unified case method as an alternative to traditional uses in professional writing pedagogy.

1668. Gantz, Charles R. *Understanding Organizations: Interpreting Organizational Communication Cultures*. Studies in Communications Processes. Columbia, SC: University of South Carolina Press, 1993. 224 pages

Focuses on organizational culture and presents both a blueprint and defense for analyzing communication messages.

1669. Gatenby, Bev, and Margaret C. McLaren. "Teaching International Topics in the Business Communication Course: A Survey of ABC Members beyond the United States." *BABC* 56 (December 1993): 10–15.

Presents the results of an international survey of business communication instructors.

1670. Greenwood, Ruth Ellen. "The Case Study Approach." *BABC* 56 (December 1993): 46–48.

Discusses the benefits of using case studies with writing groups.

1671. Grotticelli, Michael. "Seeing the Spoken Word." *Videography* 18 (June 1993): 61–65.

Discusses closed captioning and its impact on video production and communications. Describes methods firms use to produce captions and attract new business.

1672. Hardy, Jane E. "Getting Started in Tough Times: How Professionals Can Help Students." *PC* 13 (February/March 1993): 26–28.

Describes the advantages of a mentoring program for business communication students and demonstrates ways in which professionals in the field can develop a student mentoring program.

1673. Harrington, Frances Marie. "The Memo as Genre: A Paradigm of Context and Community." *DAI* 54 (August 1993): 507A.

Defines the memo as a genre of business discourse. Applies a situational paradigm of relevant theories from rhetoric and organizational management.

1674. Hayes, Ellis Arnold. "A Descriptive Study of Perceived and Assessed Business Letter Writing Problems of Bankers in Branch Locations." *DAI* 54 (July 1993): 66A.

Investigates business letter writing problems within the banking profession.

1675. Jameson, Daphne A. "Using a Simulation to Teach Intercultural Communication in Business Communication Courses." *BABC* 56 (March 1993): 3–11.

Describes a classroom exercise in business communication; discusses the need for work in intercultural communication.

1676. Jillson, Jean. "Instructional Ergonomics." *BEdF* 47 (February 1993): 34–35.

Explores the relationship between students' well-being and classroom assignments, equipment, and over-all environment.

1677. Kramer, Melinda G. *Suddenly, I Was One of Them! Why Writing Consultants Must Learn the Lessons of the Organization.* San Diego, CA: Conference on College Composition and Communication, March/April 1993. ERIC ED 357 381. 5 pages

Gives an account of a writing instructor's experience of becoming a corporate editor for Chevy Chase Federal Savings Bank in Washington, D.C.

1678. Lomo-David, Ewuuk, and Jack Hulbert. "Instructor Classroom Behaviors and Student Academic Success." *BEdF* 47 (April 1993): 12–15.

Presents the results of a study in which business students were asked what teaching behaviors contributed to their classroom success.

1679. Mascolini, Marcia, and Roberta Supnick. "Preparing Students for the Behavioral Job Interview." *JBTC* 7 (October 1993): 482–88.

Outlines strategies for helping students develop behaviorally based answers in job interviews.

1680. Mendelson, Michael. "A Dialogical Model for Business Correspondence." *JBTC* 7 (July 1993): 283–311.

Draws upon Bakhtin and Erasmus to construct a theory of business correspondence as a distinct rhetorical genre.

1681. Mulcahy, Kevin F. "Research on Written Composition: Implications for Business Communication." *BABC* 56 (March 1993): 22–25.

Applies 10 basic principles of composition research to the teaching of business writing.

1682. Nelson, Sandra J., and Laura MacLeod. "The Analytical Report." *BEdF* 48 (October 1993): 36–38.

Outlines and discusses assignment objectives, topic selection, and teaching techniques when developing an analytical report assignment.

1683. Nixon, Judy C., and Judy F. West. "Selected Data about Business Communication Courses in AACSB Schools." *BABC* 56 (June 1993): 6–9.

Presents the results of a survey of business communication instructors about trends in their courses.

1684. O'Rourke, James S., IV. "Ethical Issues in Business Communication: Grading the Work of Nonnative Speakers of English." *BABC* 56 (December 1993): 56–57.

Presents a case study concerning the evaluation of work by nonnative speakers of English.

1685. O'Rourke, James S., IV. "Intercultural Business Communication: Building a Course from the Ground Up." *BABC* 56 (December 1993): 22–27.

Discusses components of a course in intercultural communication.

1686. Perotti, Valerie S., and Carl Remus Bridges. "A Comparison of the Business Correspondence of Hong Kong and Ohio Business Students." *BABC* 56 (December 1993): 16–21.

Presents the results of a study of differences in assignments evaluated according to United States business writing standards.

1687. Pomerenke, Paula J. "Surveying the Writing Assigned in Functional Areas." *BABC* 56 (December 1993): 28–31.

Presents the results of a survey to ascertain the amount and kinds of writing required in departments within a college of Business.

1688. Quible, Zane K. "How We Should be Teaching Business Communication according to Findings of Writing Research." *BABC* 56 (September 1993): 25–27.

Discusses implications of research on writing for effective business communication instruction, particularly for students with substandard skills.

1689. Reinsch, N. L., Jr. "Ethical Cases in Business Communication: The Case of the Recycled Paper." *BABC* 56 (September 1993): 30–31.

Discusses a business communication ethics case.

1690. Reinsch, N. L., Jr., and Phillip V. Lewis. "Author Citation Patterns for The Journal of Business Communication, 1978–1992." *JBC* 30 (October 1993): 435–62.

Reviews publication and citation patterns; notes various trends including increased co-authorship.

1691. Rentz, Kathryn. "Editorial: Negotiating the Field of Business Communication." *JBC* 30 (July 1993): 233–40.

Points out that business communication scholars have no department home. Maintains that the field's disciplinary status with its conflicting research paradigms provides additional problems.

1692. Roebuck, Deborah Britt. "Providing Management Assistance to Clients of a Small

Business Development Center while Helping to Prepare Students for Business." *BABC* 56 (March 1993): 32–33.

Describes a business communication assignment that pairs student groups with clients from the business world. Points out that students' projects for clients include proposals and formal reports.

1693. Rogers, Priscilla S. "Analytic Measures for Evaluating Managerial Writing. Working Paper 647." School of Business Administration, Michigan University, Ann Arbor, January 1993. ERIC ED 353 579. 35 pages

Introduces the Analysis of Argument Measure based on Toulmin's rhetorical theory and the Persuasive Adaptiveness Measure based on Delia, Kline, and Burleson's ranking system.

1694. Rogers, Priscilla S., Vincent J. Brown, Geoffrey A. Cross, Kitty O. Locker, and Jane M. Perkins. "How Researchers Gain Access to Organizations." *BABC* 56 (March 1993): 42–48.

Describes arrangements to conduct ethnographic research in a research and development laboratory, an insurance company, a state agency, a factory, and a software development company.

1695. Roth, Lorie. "Education Makes a Difference: Results of a Survey of Writing on the Job." *TCQ* 2 (Spring 1993): 177–84.

Argues that employees with advanced education spend more time writing and revising reports than employees without a higher education. Calls for further research.

1696. Scott, James Calvert. "Preparing Business Correspondence the British Way." *BABC* 56 (June 1993): 10–17.

Describes organization, style, mechanics, and format as four characteristics of British business correspondence.

1697. Shaffer, Raymond J., Kevin T. Stevens, and William P. Stevens. "Assessing the Readability of Government Accounting Standards:

The Cloze Procedure." *JTWC* 23 (1993): 259–67.

Assesses the readability of business writing in the authoritative statements of the Governmental Accounting Standards Board and finds them unreadable by their users.

1698. Sharp, Helen M. "Structure Student Success in Indirect Writing." *BABC* 56 (December 1993): 49–50.

Describes three steps instructors can use to teach indirect writing.

1699. Shaw, Gary. "The Shape of Our Field: Business Communication as a Hybrid Discipline." *JBC* 30 (July 1993): 297–313.

Argues that business communication lacks cogency as a field. Sees it as being constituted of rhetoric, communication, and management.

1700. Siegel, Gerald. *Predicting Performance in Practical Writing: Factors That Influence Success in the Introductory Business Communication Course.* Pittsburgh, PA: College English Association Conference, March 1992. ERIC ED 350 618. 9 pages

Discusses a study which suggests an ability to predict individual students' performance in an introductory business course. Looks at questionnaires and demographic information which were used to develop personal and academic profiles of students and which were used to predict success and failure in the course. Finds that questionnaires are better predictors than formal testing.

1701. Stull, William, and Dennis LaBonty. "Teaching Interpersonal Skills in Entrepreneurship." *BEdF* 47 (February 1993): 10–12.

Discusses how to teach future entrepreneurs interpersonal skills through experiential learning.

1702. Thompson, Michael P. "The Skills of Inquiry and Advocacy." *MCQ* 7 (August 1993): 95–106.

Identifies a need for the use of advocacy and inquiry skills in organizations and in management communication curricula.

1703. Tippens, Dora. "Interculturalizing the Technical or Business Communications Course." *JTWC* 23 (1993): 389–412.

Defines and exemplifies problems of ethnocentrism, language barriers, and cultural differences; presents assignments and activities which suggest solutions and new pedagogies.

1704. Van Decker, Lori. *When You Do It for Money, Is the Customer Always Right? San Diego, CA: Conference on College Composition and Communication*, March/April 1993. ERIC ED 357 358. 9 pages

Provides guidelines for teaching writing in the corporate environment.

1705. Vesper, Joan F., and Karl H. Vesper. "Writing a Business Plan: The Total Term Assignment." *BABC* 56 (June 1993): 29–32.

Describes an assignment in which students write business plans as term projects.

1706. Vincent, Annette, and Melanie Meche. "It's Time to Teach Business Etiquette." *BEdF* 48 (October 1993): 39–41.

Outlines how to teach work etiquette as well as telephone, dining, correspondence, introduction, and cultural etiquette.

1707. Watts, Françoise. "The Art of French Business Letter Writing: Our Modern Form of 'Préciosité.'" *FLA* 26 (Summer 1993): 180–87.

Suggests activities for advanced French students which link the idiosyncratic, courtly, and theatrical conventions of business French with the seventeenth century cultural history.

1708. Weiss, Timothy. "'The Gods Must Be Crazy': The Challenge of the Intercultural." *JBTC* 7 (April 1993): 196–217.

Provides a framework for a pedagogy of intercultural communication. Discusses avenues for future research.

1709. Weiss, Timothy. *What Have You Packed in Your Suitcase? Going International Now and in the Twenty-First Century.* San Diego, CA: Conference on College Composition and Communication, March/April 1993. ERIC ED 357 388. 12 pages

Advocates revising metaphors of business, models of communication, conceptual frameworks of interculturalism and internationalism, and models of professional identity.

1710. Wiese, Michael. "Sex, Laws, and Videotape Marketing." *Videography* 18 (November 1993): 50–53.

Describes the design, development, and marketing of training videos about sexual harassment.

1711. Wiese, Michael. "What I've Learned about Infomercials, Part I." *Videography* 18 (July 1993): 34–36.

Discusses the development and targeting of infomercials as an important marketing tool.

1712. Williams, Jerri Lynn. "The Rhetoric of Ethos in Business and Technical Writing Textbooks." *DAI* 54 (August 1993): 166A.

Offers numerous arguments to support a rhetorical foundation for business and technical writing textbooks.

1713. Williams, Sherry Morgan. "A Study of the Effects of Grammatik IV on Selected Writing Errors Made by Business Writing Students." *DAI* 54 (September 1993): 786A.

Determines the effects on selected writing errors of business writing students. Maintains that Grammatik IV reduced errors in style, punctuation, and spelling.

4.2.5 SCIENTIFIC AND TECHNICAL COMMUNICATION

1714. Alciere, Rose Mary. "Avoiding Governmentspeak." *TC* 40 (May 1993): 262–64.

Offers suggestions for avoiding such government document styles as pompous wording, poor organization, and excessive length.

1715. Allen, Jo. "The Role(s) of Assessment in Technical Communication: A Review of the Literature." *TCQ* 2 (Fall 1993): 365–88.

Outlines ways to assess technical communication programs, courses, teachers, and students.

1716. Allen, Nancy J. "Community, Collaboration, and the Rhetorical Triangle." *TCQ* 2 (Winter 1993): 63–74.

Finds that collaboration in technical writing is positive and allows writers to "present themselves as inside members of an immediate community."

1717. Bantz, Charles R. *Understanding Organizations: Interpreting Communication Cultures.* Columbia, SC: University of South Carolina Press, 1993. 224 pages

Presents a method of analyzing the symbolic world of organizations by examining their written and verbal communications. Includes a case study by Charles Pepper.

1718. Baren, Robert. "Teaching Writing in Required Undergraduate Engineering Courses: A Materials Course Example." *EnEd* 82 (Spring 1993): 59–61.

Points out that to develop engineering students' writing skills, Temple University's Engineering College has established a communications center and has incorporated writing assignments in required undergraduate courses.

1719. Barnum, Carol, and Saul Carliner. *Techniques for Technical Communicators.* New York: Macmillan, 1993. 368 pages

The authors present a collection of articles on preparing, writing, editing, and evaluating documents in print and other media.

1720. Barton, Ben F., and Marthalee S. Barton. "Modes of Power in Technical and Professional Visuals." *JBTC* 7 (January 1993): 138–62.

Employs a Foucauldian model based on the Panopticon to analyze power inscription in technical visuals.

1721. Barton, Laurence. "New Avenues in Teaching Written Communication: The Use of a Case Study in Crisis Management." *JTWC* 23 (1993): 171–80.

Discusses the value of using case studies as tool for teaching business and technical writing.

1722. Battalio, John. "The Formal Report Project as a Shared-Document Collaboration: A Plan for Co-Authorship." *TCQ* 2 (Spring 1993): 147–60.

Describes a four-step plan for a collaborative report project by upperclass college students. The survey of report groups shows positive attitudes toward formal reports and collaboration.

1723. Beeson, Susan Ayers. "The Effect of Writing after Reading on College Nursing Students' Factual Knowledge and Synthesis of Knowledge." *DAI* 54 (October 1993): 1211A.

Argues that notetaking after reading improves factual knowledge to a higher degree than essay writing or no writing. Points out that essay writing helps students synthesize better than notetaking.

1724. Birkmaier, Craig. "Tell a Computer." *Videography* 18 (September 1993): 69–74.

Discusses new audio-visual Macintosh computers and softwares—their importance, advantages, and capabilities, as well as their impact on communications.

1725. Blyler, Nancy Roundy. "Theory and Curriculum: Reexamining the Curriculum Separation of Business and Technical Communication." *JBTC* 7 (April 1993): 218–45.

Examines historical and political conditions that have encouraged the conventional distinction between business and technical communication.

1726. Bosley, Deborah S. "Cross-Cultural Collaboration: Whose Culture Is It, Anyway?" *TCQ* 2 (Winter 1993): 51–62.

Examines Western cultural biases in models of student collaboration and suggests ways of "internationalizing" collaborative groups.

1727. Brasseur, Lee R. "Contesting the Objectivist Paradigm: Gender Issues in the Technical and Professional Communication Curriculum." *IEEE* 36 (September 1993): 114–23.

Argues for the inclusion of a course in gender issues in a technical communication curriculum. Describes the course and includes a reading list.

1728. Burnett, Rebecca E., and Ann Hill Duin. "Collaboration in Technical Communication: A Research Continuum." *TCQ* 2 (Winter 1993): 5–21.

The authors provide a method of organizing research on collaborative technical communication.

1729. Cintorino, Margaret A. "Writing for the Public." *EJ* 82 (March 1993): 54–57.

Presents a program that allows students to write and design new documents. Argues that students' technical writing skills improve when they "write for the public."

1730. Conklin, James. "The Next Step: An Integrated Approach to Computer Documentation." *TC* 40 (February 1993): 89–96.

Argues for technical communicators to become members of computer software development teams.

1731. Connor, Jennifer J. "Medical Text and Historical Context: Research Issues and Methods in History and Technical Communication." *JTWC* 23 (1993): 211–32.

Identifies and offers solutions to problems in recent studies of historical and medical text. Recommends directions for research in technical communications and the history of medicine.

1732. Davidson, W. J. "SGML, Authoring Tools for Technical Communication." *TC* 40 (August 1993): 403–9.

Describes the function and usefulness of SGML (Structured General Markup Language) as an alternative to word processing and desktop publishing in formatting a document.

1733. Dragga, Sam. "Women and the Profession of Technical Writing: Social and Economic Influences and Implications." *JBTC* 7 (July 1993): 312–21.

Examines the predominance of women in technical writing and teaching positions.

1734. Dutra, Andrea M. "Cognitive Writing: Creating a Reference Manual." *TC* 40 (May 1993): 258–60.

Considers elements such as headings, tables of contents, and visuals from a cognitive psychological standpoint. Identifies qualities which assist the reader.

1735. Fennick, Ruth, Mary Peters, and Lois Guyon. "Solving Problems in Twenty-First Century Academic and Workplace Writing." *EJ* 82 (February 1993): 46–53.

The authors maintain that students need to acquire writing skills that emphasize the interactive nature of written discourse. They argue for writing projects which solve "real-world problems."

1736. Flammia, Madelyn. "Avoiding Desktop Disasters: Why Technical Communications Students Should Learn about Mechanical Paste Up Techniques." *JTWC* 23 (1993): 287–95.

Describes a technical writing course in which students gain better understanding of principles of design and layout by using mechanical paste up techniques.

1737. Forman, Janis. "Task Groups and Their Writing: Relationships between Group Characteristics and Group Reports." *TCQ* 2 (Winter 1993): 75–88.

Study results show a high correlation between high quality of group reports and groups who had worked together previously.

1738. Garland, Ken. "Lead, Kindly Light: A User's View of the Design and Production of Illustrated Walkers' Guides." *IDJ* 7 (1993): 47–66.

Examines illustrated walking guides (in Great Britain) as serious aids to an increasingly popular leisure activity.

1739. Gerson, Steven M. "Teaching Technical Writing in a Collaborative Computer Classroom." *JTWC* 23 (1993): 23–31.

Describes his experiences in computerized technical writing classrooms which prepare students for writing collaboratively in business and industry.

1740. Graves, Heather Ann Brodie. "The Rhetoric of Physics: An Ethnography of the Research and Writing Processes in a Physics Laboratory." *DAI* 53 (May 1993): 3885A.

Explores the extent to which rhetoric plays a role in research and writing processes of physicists.

1741. Greenly, Robert. "How to Write a Résumé." *TC* 40 (February 1993): 42–48.

Begins with an outline of conventional résumés, then describes some currently used unconventional ones such as "baseball cards," electronic vitaes, and multimedia résumés.

1742. Hager, Peter J., and Ronald J. Nelson. "Chaucer's *A Treatise on the Astrolabe:* A 600-Year-Old Model for Humanizing Technical Documents." *IEEE* 36 (June 1993): 87–94.

The authors conclude that Chaucer's treatise has much to teach us about effective technical communication.

1743. Harris, John Sterling. "Poetry and Technical Writing." *JTWC* 23 (1993): 313–31.

Argues that the study of poetry can improve technical writing, and technical writing can improve poetry.

1744. Horton, William. "The Almost Universal Language: Graphics for International Documents." *TC* 40 (November 1993): 682–93.

Argues for a consideration of cultural differences when selecting graphics for international users.

1745. Human, Patricia Waggoner. "The Effects of Process Journal Writing on Learning in Mathematics: A Study of Metacognitive Processes." *DAI* 53 (May 1993): 3796A.

Proposes that math students' metacognitive awareness increases over time as a result of process journal writing.

1746. Hunt, Peter. "The Teaching of Technical Communication in Europe: A Report from Britain." *TCQ* 2 (Summer 1993): 319–30.

Examines technical communication skills needed for European economic conditions. Concludes that composition, text-handling, elicitation, and specialized technical areas are necessary.

1747. Kaufer, David S., David Fleming, Mark Werner, and Ann Sinsheimer-Weeks. "Collaborative Argument across the Visual-Verbal Interface." *TCQ* 2 (Winter 1993): 37–49.

Outlines a framework to describe a visual-verbal interface. Applies it to collaboration in graphic design.

1748. Kohl, John R., Rebecca O. Barclay, Thomas E. Pinelli, Michael L. Keene, and John M. Kennedy. "The Impact of Language and Culture on Technical Communication in Japan." *TC* 40 (February 1993): 62–73.

Describes the complexities of Japanese language and culture; discusses a survey of Japanese engineers on the technical communication they produce.

1749. Krambert-Walker, Carol. "The Need to Provide Writing Support for Academic Engineers." *IEEE* 36 (September 1993): 130–36.

Argues that on-the-job academic engineers require writing support. Describes support options including faculty writing centers, workshops, and orientation sessions.

1750. Kynell, Teresa. "The Student as Translator in the Technical Writing Classroom: The Challenger Disaster as Heuristic." *TETYC* 20 (May 1993): 145–51.

Students survey documents and miscommunications which led to the tragedy, rewrite crucial memos, and study reasons why warnings were ignored.

1751. Li, Rengen. "Creating Interactive DBT Lessons without Video" *EdTech* 33 (May 1993): 20–26.

Suggests how and why computer basic training should not rely on video components for effectiveness.

1752. Lindeborg, Richard A. "The Irresistible Electronic Message of the 1990s: A Case Study." *IEEE* 36 (March 1993): 152–57.

Describes a system for electronic distribution of information in a large organization.

1753. Little, Sherry Burgurs. "The Technical Communication Internship: An Application of Experiential Learning Theory." *JBTC* 7 (October 1993): 423–51.

Examines internships from the perspective of David Kolb's experiential learning theory.

1754. Markel, Mike. "An Ethical Imperative for Technical Communications." *IEEE* 36 (June 1993): 81–86.

Argues that Kant's second formulation of the categorical imperative—that we should treat ourselves and others as ends as well as means—is the basis of an ethics of technical communication.

1755. Markel, Mike. "Induction, Social Constructionism, and the Form of the Science Paper." *JTWC* 23 (1993): 7–22.

Compares prescriptive Baconian induction and descriptive social constructionism in the organization of the science paper.

Concludes that the ethical intent of the writer is a critical organizational factor.

1756. Markel, Mike. "Techniques of Developing Forecasting Statements." *JBTC* 7 (July 1993): 360–66.

Outlines four forecasting techniques to assist writers in creating contexts for readers of technical communication documents.

1757. Martin, Wanda. "What We Talk About when We Talk About Technical Communication." *IEEE* 36 (September, 1993): 165–68.

Reviews three theories and interpretations of technical communications as they apply to both the business and instructional concepts.

1758. Monmonier, Mark. *Mapping It Out: Expository Cartography for the Humanities and Social Sciences.* Chicago Guides to Writing, Editing, and Publishing. Chicago: University of Chicago Press, 1993. 352 pages

Introduces fundamental principles of graphic logic and design from the basics of scale to complex mappings of movement or change. Helps writers and researchers decide when maps are most useful and what formats work best in wide ranges of areas from literary criticism to sociology.

1759. Moore, Patrick, and Chad Fitz. "Using Gestalt Theory to Teach Document Design and Graphics." *TCQ* 2 (Fall 1993): 389–410.

Applies six principles of Gestalt to textual design to explain success and problems readers have comprehending text and graphics.

1760. Moran, Michael G. "The Road Not Taken: Frank Aydelotte and the Thought Approach to Engineering Writing." *TCQ* 2 (Spring 1993): 161–75.

Examines Aydelotte's use of thought movement to teach engineering students writing about issues relevant to their careers.

1761. Mulvany, Nancy C. *Indexing Books.* Chicago Guides to Writing, Editing, and Publishing. Chicago: University of Chicago Press, 1993. 352 pages

Discusses how to decide what is and what is not indexable and how to establish a structure of entries. Deals with the concept of indexing and how it fits into the publishing process, how to decide when to prepare one's own index and when to hire a professional, how to work with publishers' indexing guidelines and how to choose appropriate software.

1762. Norton, Robert. "Commentary: Graphic Excellence for the Technical Communicator." *JTWC* 23 (1993): 1–6.

Discusses applications of Edward Tufte's five principles of graphical excellence that technical communicators should embrace.

1763. Ochse, Daniel R. "An Analysis of the Student Journal as a Tool for Identifying and Resolving Writing Problems of Adult and Higher Education Students." *DAI* 54 (October 1993): 1258A.

Analyzes a technical writing course in which students used journals in a college to identify and discuss their own writing problems. Finds that journals tended to improve students' writing skills and their attitudes toward writing.

1764. Ornatowski, Cezar M., and Katherine Staples. "Teaching Technical Communication in the 1990s: Challenges and Perspectives." *TCQ* 2 (Summer 1993): 245–48.

The authors survey the growth and change of technical communication in professional and academic settings.

1765. Perkins, J. M. "Social Perspectives on Technology Transfer." *IEEE* 36 (December 1993): 185–89.

Reviews recent books by Doheny-Farina as well as F. Williams and D. V. Gibson. Argues that technology transfer is a rhetorical process that opens new roles for technical communicators.

1766. Pinelli, Thomas E., Rebecca O. Barclay, et al. "The Technical Communication Practices of Russian and U.S. Aerospace Engineers and Scientists." *IEEE* 36 (June 1993): 95–104.

Describes two cross-cultural studies of Russian and United States communication practices. Emphasizes the value generated by such studies.

1767. Proceedings of the 40th Annual Conference of the Society for Technical Communication. Arlington, VA: 1993. 610 pages

Presents a collection of papers presented in Dallas TX May 1993. Subjects include writing and editing; education, training and professional development; research and technology; management; visual communication; and chapter development.

1768. Raign, Kathryn Rosser, and Brenda R. Sims. "Gender, Persuasion Techniques, and Collaboration." *TCQ* 2 (Winter 1993): 89–104.

Examines the relationship between the gender of collaborative writers and their preconceptions about collaboration, persuasion, and gender.

1769. Redish, Janice, and Judith Ramey. "Measuring the Value Added by Professional Technical Communicators." *IEEE* 36 (September 1993): 158–64.

Describes an ongoing project that attempts to measure the value of technical communicators' work.

1770. Richardson, Malcolm, and Sarah Liggett. "Power Relations, Technical Writing Theory, and Workplace Writing." *JBTC* 7 (January 1993): 112–37.

Analyzes medieval business correspondence and the nuclear power industry to point out the macro, top-down power relations implicit in the internal rhetoric of organizations.

1771. Russell, David R. "The Ethics of Teaching Ethics in Professional Communication: The Case of Engineering Publicity at MIT in the 1920s." *JBTC* 7 (January 1993): 84–111.

Argues that ethical critiques of professional communication coming from teachers trained in literary studies are less efficacious than critiques from those within the business and technical communication professions.

1772. Ryan, Charlton. "Using Environmental Impact Statements as an Introduction to Technical Writing." *TCQ* 2 (Spring 1993): 205–13.

Explores the benefits and problems of using professional technical documents within a college-level technical writing course. Focuses on steps taken to complete the assignment.

1773. Sauer, Beverly A. "Sense and Sensibility in Technical Documentation: How Feminists' Interpretation Strategies Can Save Lives in the Nation's Mines." *JBTC* 7 (January 1993): 63–83.

Analyzes postaccident investigative reports from a feminist perspective.

1774. Schreiber, E. J. "From Academic Writing to Job-Related Writing: Achieving a Smooth Transition." *IEEE* 36 (December 1993): 178–84.

Sees developments in writing pedagogy (e.g., WAC, collaborative writing, concern for social context) as helping student writers move from classroom to "real world" settings.

1775. Schriver, Karen A. "Quality in Document Design: Issues and Controversies." *TC* 40 (May 1993): 239–57.

Discusses "quality movement" and ways of interpreting quality in document design; includes an annotated bibliography.

1776. Schultz, Donald Clyde. "The Acquisition of Writing Skills: Key Elements in the Background of Four Professionals." *DAI* 53 (January 1993): 2229A.

> Investigates backgrounds of four individuals who use writing in their jobs to determine influences on and importance of their writing.

1777. Shelton, S. M. "Multimedia." *TC* 40 (November 1993): 694–704.

> Offers a brief background and the strengths and weaknesses of multimedia. Includes a glossary.

1778. Sims, Brenda R. "Linking Ethics and Language in the Technical Communication Classroom." *TCQ* 2 (Summer 1993): 285–99.

> Examines current research on the ethics of technical writing and how writers control readers' perceptions of information.

1779. Slack, Jennifer Daryl, David James Miller, and Jeffrey Doak. "The Technical Communicator as Author: Meaning, Power, Authority." *JBTC* 7 (January 1993): 12–36.

> Analyzes four views of the communication process which can be used to compare differing descriptions of the technical communicator.

1780. Spilka, Rachel. "Collaboration across Multiple Organizational Cultures." *TCQ* 2 (Spring 1993): 125–45.

> Argues that rhetoricians should expand current models of workplace collaboration. Lists four limitations of these views and seven strategies for overcoming them.

1781. Sullivan, Patricia A., and James E. Porter. "Remapping Curricular Geography: Professional Writing in/and English." *JBTC* 7 (October 1993): 389–422.

> Posits a curricular geography for professional writing in order to examine its status within the English Departments and industry.

1782. Tebeaux, Elizabeth. "From Orality to Textuality in English Accounting and Its

Books, 1553–1680: The Power of Visual Presentation." *JBTC* 7 (July 1993): 322–59.

> Historical examination of verbal and visual text in accounting documents.

1783. Thralls, Charlotte, and Nancy Roundy Blyler. "The Social Perspective and Pedagogy in Technical Communication." *TCQ* 2 (Summer 1993): 249–70.

> Explores ties between social theories in technical writing pedagogy. Identifies four paradigms: social constructionist, ideologic, social cognitive, and paralogic hermeneutic.

1784. Thrush, Emily A. "Bridging the Gaps: Technical Communication in an International and Multicultural Society." *TCQ* 2 (Summer 1993): 271–83.

> Argues for raised awareness of cultural differences in "experience, common knowledge, structure of society, rhetorical strategies, and processing graphics" in the classroom.

1785. Tsui, Chia-Jung. "Teaching Preparations of Oral Presentations." *JTWC* 23 (1993): 73–79.

> Reports on a method combining lectures, videos, discussion, self-assessments, simulation, and peer evaluation for teaching oral presentations to industry professionals.

1786. Warren, Thomas L. "Three Approaches to Reader Analysis." *TC* 40 (February 1993): 81–88.

> Uses demographic (layperson, expert), organizational (role in an organization), and psychological (determining reader's needs) approaches to reader analysis.

1787. Weiss, Edmond H. "Of Document Databases, SGML, and Rhetorical Neutrality." *IEEE* 36 (June 1993): 58–61.

> Maintains that reader-configurable environments such as SGML permit readers to shape the message, empowering readers and disempowering writers. Explores implications of this change for writers.

1788. Wiebe, Alvin F., David Johnson, Glen A. Harcey, and Marti Teter. "The Task-Training Guidelines: A Powerful Format for How-To Instructional Training Manuals." *TC* 40 (February 1993): 49–61.

Describes a training format and set of guidelines which may be used to organize and present any process or operation.

1789. Winn, William, and Lee Mountain. "ID and Situated Learning: Paradox or Partnership?" *EdTech* 33 (March 1993): 16–21.

Examines assumptions behind instructional design and situated learning to select the best instructional methods.

1790. Wise, Mary R. "Using Graphics in Software Documentation." *TC* 40 (November 1993): 677–81.

Provides advice on graphical elements such as icons, headers, white space, and running headers and footers.

1791. Wood, Sarah Bane. "Response to Madelyn Flammia's 'A Desktop Publishing Course: An Alternative to Internships for Rural Universities' [response to Flammia, *TCQ* 1 (Fall 1992)]." *TCQ* 2 (Spring 1993): 215–17.

Takes issue with Flammia's portrayal of Murray State's technical writing program and its members.

1792. Zimmerman, Beverly. "Metaphor, Frame, and Nonverbal Communication: An Ethnographic Study of a Technical Writing Classroom." *IEEE* 36 (September 1993): 137–43.

Studies an undergraduate class in which the teacher is engaged in a productive conflict with assumptions embedded in textbook and classroom design.

1793. Zimmerman, Donald E., and Marilee Long. "Exploring the Technical Communicator's Roles: Implications for Program Design." *TCQ* 2 (Summer 1993): 301–17.

Suggests guidelines for a college technical communication curriculum including core courses, production skills, internships, and product-specific courses.

4.2.6 WRITING IN LITERATURE COURSES

1794. Bresnahan, Roger J. "This Text, My Body: Identity Politics in Literature Courses." *CEAF* 23–24 (Summer/Winter 1993–1994): 9–11.

Discusses the confrontation between interpretive authority and canon expression.

1795. Carter, Steven. "On Being Silent: Tragedy in the Classroom." *CEAF* 23 (Winter 1993): 3–5.

Discusses how to deal with typical reactions to the genre of tragedy in the classroom by examining assumptions brought to the text.

1796. Cole, Margaret Ann. "A Cognitive Model of Journal Writing of College Students in an Introduction to Literature Course." *DAI* 54 (September 1993): 792A.

Studies how college students use journals in understanding stories to develop more effective instructional/learning strategies.

1797. Downing, David B., and James J. Sosnoski. *Professing Literature in 2015*. San Diego, CA: Conference on College Composition and Communication, March/April 1993. ERIC ED 357 340. 12 pages

The authors argue that in a futuristic scenario, electronic environments and media might be used to foster a sense of connectivity and intellectual community in a literature seminar.

1798. Doyle, Mary Ann. "Rethinking Reading and Writing in the Study of Literature." *DAI* 54 (August 1993): 373A.

Explores the teaching style of a professor in a research university English department.

1799. Eastwood, David R. "Handing Out a Process." *CEAF* 23–24 (Summer/Winter 1993–1994): 21–23.

Models a technique that uses cartoon handouts to share interpretive strategies with students.

1800. Johanyak, Michael. "The 'Doing' Act of Writing: A Pedagogical Linking of Composition with Literature." *CEAF* 23 (Winter 1993): 1–3.

Provides a lesson plan for getting students actively participating in discussing and freewriting.

1801. Landis-Groom, Eileen. "Using Informal and Formal Speeches to Enhance Students' Writing Skills." *CalE* 29 (March/April 1993): 8–9, 26.

Describes how using informal and formal oral presentations can improve writing skills, sense of audience, and engagement with literature among students at a technical university.

1802. Morgan, Dan. "Connecting Literature to Students' Lives." *CE* 55 (September 1993): 491–500.

Calls for a student-centered approach to introductory literature, including the use of participatory learning methods of composition courses.

1803. Nystrand, Martin, Adam Gamoran, and Mary Jo Heck. "Using Small Groups for Response to and Thinking about Literature." *EJ* 82 (January 1993): 14–22.

A small group work study finds that less prescriptive activities enhance student autonomy, ownership of work, and production of knowledge. Finds that more structured group work does not improve student participation.

1804. Perham, Andrea J. *Collaborative Journals: A Forum for Encouragement and Exploration*. Louisville, KY: National Council of Teachers of English, November 1992. ERIC ED 355 555. 9 pages

Suggests keeping a looseleaf notebook on reserve in the library to serve as a collaborative journal, imitating the practices of a Romantic poetry course.

1805. Purves, Alan C. "The Ideology of Canons and Cultural Concerns in the Literature Curriculum." National Research Center on Literature Teaching and Learning, Albany, NY, 1991. ERIC ED 349 563. 19 pages

Addresses educators involved in planning curricula in literature; advocates an adoption of a broader view of literature and its teaching which values a text's cultural background.

1806. Rider, Janine. "The Book or the Movie?" *ELQ* 15 (December 1993): 8–10.

Describes how the novel and film versions of *A Handmaid's Tale* spurred writing.

1807. Sanzenbacher, Richard. "Thinking with Different Metaphors: Leaving the House of Consciousness." *CEA* 55 (Winter 1993): 15–26.

Discusses how to develop more conscious interpretive strategies for students in an upper-division literature course.

1808. Sheridan, Daniel. "Writing in Response to Literature: The Paper of Many Parts." *EJ* 82 (October 1993): 58–63.

Requires an initial response to a poem chosen by the student, a prose paraphrase, a report on an issue related to the poem, a parody of the poem, an interview, and a final response.

1809. Walker, Nancy A. "The Student Writer as Reader." *ADE* 106 (Winter 1993): 35–37.

Discusses how creative writing courses promote ways of reading, raise questions about pedagogy, advance intellectual life on campus, and are uniquely empowering.

1810. Williams, Lee. "Reading Literature and Making Meaning." *ELQ* 15 (December 1993): 2–4.

Suggests that too many teachers still do not examine their own beliefs about the nature of reading.

1811. Williams, Mary Duyckinck. "A Writing-Reading Connection: An Investigation of the Relationship between Poetic Writing and Aesthetic Reading." *DAI* 53 (May 1993): 3831A.

Focuses on the relationship between poetic writing and aesthetic reading as demonstrated by college students' responses to short stories.

4.2.7 COMMUNICATION IN OTHER DISCIPLINES

1812. Beall, Herbert, and John Trimbur. "Writing in Chemistry: Keys to Student Underlife." *CollT* 41 (Spring 1993): 50–54.

Reports on the effects of writing assignments in a large general chemistry course to increase students' sense of class participation and control over their learning.

1813. Beason, Larry. "Feedback and Revision in Writing across the Curriculum Classes." *RTE* 27 (December 1993): 395–422.

Examines revision processes in four WAC classes. Discusses teacher/peer response patterns as well as the issue of global versus nonglobal revision.

1814. Burgoon, Michael, Frank Hunsaker, and Edwin Dawson. *Human Communication.* 3rd ed. Thousand Oaks, CA: Sage, 1993. 380 pages

Provides students with a vocabulary for human communication theory; includes source credibility, language as power, demographic barriers to listening, conflict styles, interpersonal verbal control, and persuasion.

1815. Corman, Steven R., and Robert L. Krizek. "Accounting Resources for Organizational Communication and Individual Differences in Their Use." *MCQ* 7 (August 1993): 5–35.

Examines the use of self-report data within an organization. Discusses its future implications.

1816. Day, Lawrence H. *From Mere Formulas to the Bigger Picture: Helping Students in Introductory Physics See Interconnectedness.* San Diego, CA: Conference on College Composition and Communication, March/April 1993. ERIC ED 357 356. 5 pages

Claims that it is important for students in an introductory physics course to write as they learn.

1817. Dunn, Patricia. *English 101 and Chemistry 101: Examining Texts through Different Lenses.* San Diego, CA: Conference on College Composition and Communication, March/April 1993. ERIC ED 357 354. 13 pages

Discusses an eight-week project that linked English and Chemistry courses. Maintains that students developed a more sophisticated awareness of rhetorical strategies and demonstrated the confidence to view themselves as participants in knowledge-making.

1818. Greene, Stuart. "The Role of the Task in the Development of Academic Thinking through Reading and Writing in a College History Course." *RTE* 27 (February 1993): 46–75.

Examines the effects of writing an informational report and a problem-based essay on how students think and structure meaning in writing.

1819. Hadaway, Nelda H. "Using Writing to Teach and Learn Geometry." *DAI* 54 (July 1993): 117A.

Describes how geometry students can use writing to facilitate their thinking; concludes that writing can be a useful tool for students in constructing a knowledge of geometry.

1820. Johnson, Allen B. "Enhancing General Education Science Courses: Written Logs on Popular Media." *CollT* 41 (Spring 1993): 55–58.

Provides examples of at-risk students using focused response logs in Earth Science courses to connect class material to popular sources.

1821. Limbert, Claudia A. *Writing across the Curriculum: A How-To Plan for a 'Writing-in-the-Social Sciences' Class That Works.* Pittsburgh, PA: College English Association

Conference, March 1992. ERIC ED 350 620. 17 pages

Describes a writing-intensive social science course based on students' concern for their own community. Adapts Eliot Wigginton's "Foxfire" method and uses oral histories and primary data to produce and publish local histories.

1822. McLeod, Susan, and Margot Soven, eds. *Writing across the Curriculum: A Guide to Developing Programs.* Newbury Park, CA: Sage, 1992. 216 pages

Twelve essays include practical suggestions and materials for implementing a WAC program.
Essayists: Farris, Christine; Graham, Joan; Harris, Muriel; Harding-Smith, Tori; Kuriloff, Peshe C.; Magnotto, Joyce Neff; McLeod, Susan; Peterson, Linda H.; Sandler, Karen Wiley; Smith, Raymond; Soven, Margot; Stout, Barbara; Thaiss, Christopher; Walvoord, Barbara E.

1823. Murdick, William, Richard Grinstead, Phil Schaltenbrand, Richard Miecznikowski, and Ray Dunlevy. "Journal Writing and Active Learning in College Art Classes." *ELQ* 15 (October 1993): 10–14.

Describes art classes in which journal writing improved active learning and made learning more visible to the teacher.

1824. National Council of Teachers of English. "Learning through Language: A Call for Action in All Disciplines." National Council of Teachers of English, 1993. 1 page

Provides a rationale for why students in language-intensive classes learn better; describes practices that use effective language-based learning; offers suggestions for assessing teaching and assignments in terms of effective use of language learning.

1825. O'Brien, Sheila Ruzycki. "Writing to Learn about Gender, Race, and Class." *ATA* 4 (Fall 1993): 1–4.

Describes the role of writing in elucidating issues of gender, race, and class in an American Studies class.

1826. Pernecky, Mark. "Reaction Papers Enrich Economics Discussions." *CollT* 41 (Summer 1993): 89–91.

Provides guidelines and examples of response assignments that aid discussion and learning.

1827. Rishel, Thomas. *The Well-Tempered Mathematics Assignment.* San Diego, CA: Conference on College Composition and Communication, March/April 1993. ERIC ED 359 561. 13 pages

Describes how mathematics teachers have students write autobiographies, reading logbooks, and letters to increase an understanding of mathematical concepts.

1828. Soven, Margaret. "The Advanced Writing across the Curriculum Workshop: The Perils of Reintroducing Rhetoric." ERIC Clearinghouse, Indiana University, Bloomington, IN, July 1993. ERIC ED 357 385. 15 pages

Reports on difficulties encountered in an advanced workshop on writing across the curriculum at La Salle University, Pennsylvania.

1829. Soven, Margot. *Ethics, the Classics, and the Rhetorical Tradition: Integrating the Curriculum.* Colorado Springs, CO: Conference on Ethics and Teaching, August 1992. ERIC ED 357 360. 10 pages

Presents a seminar at La Salle University which explored how to integrate the historical, political, and ethical insights common in humanities courses with those in other disciplines, and also explored moral and political issues by distinguishing dialectic from scientific tradition.

1830. Sublett, Michael D. "A Model Essay: One Way to Improve Students' Writing." *CollT* 41 (Winter 1993): 11–14.

Presents a geography professor who describes guidelines and uses of a model essay in large and small social science courses.

1831. Weinberg, Steve. "Overcoming Skepticism about 'Writing across the Curriculum.'" *CHE* (16 June 1993): B-2, B-4.

Discusses and analyzes students enthusiasm in writing intensive courses in different disciplines; argues that most will work hard in courses in their majors.

1832. Wheeler, Thomas H. "Instructional Objectives and the Writer-Editor Relationship." *JourEd* 48 (Autumn 1993): 4–7.

Offers a sequence of projects which assist students to discover how reader demographics, copy editing, deadlines, and communication skills affect the partnership between editor and writer.

1833. Zerger, Sandra Dee. "Literacy in College: The Use of Evidence in Reading and Writing of Undergraduates in Three Disciplines." *DAI* 54 (December 1993): 2045A.

Ascertains how students are initiated into the discourse of their professions; notes that professors' feedback on texts is a contributing factor to a successful initiation.

4.3   ADULT AND GRADUATE EDUCATION

1834. Byrd, Mark. "Adult Age Differences in the Ability to Write Prose Passages." *EdGer* (July/August 1993): 375.

Investigates the factor of age difference in the abilities of two different groups to write short essays of various difficulty levels.

1835. Cebula, Dorothy Marie. "Literacy Practices of Five Adults with Histories of Reading Difficulties." *DAI* 53 (May 1993): 2774A.

Examines the relationship between reading, writing, and attitudes about literacy

as perceived by five adults with histories of reading difficulties.

1836. Collins, Rita. "People, Programs, and Politics: Two Case Studies of Adult Literacy Classes." *DAI* 53 (May 1993): 3774A.

Describes instructional practices in two urban literacy programs serving low-level adult readers; identifies practices which were effective in meeting students' needs.

1837. Cunanan, Esmeralda Sagmit. "The Association between Advanced Degrees in Educational Administration and the Career Paths of the Male and Female Graduates from the University of Illinois at Urbana-Champaign from 1985–1990." *DAI* 54 (November 1993): 1606A.

Presents findings which correspond to the national picture of male-dominated leadership in education.

1838. Dobrin, Sidney I. "Writing across the Graduate Curriculum." *Dialogue* 1 (Fall 1993): 65–77.

Argues that WAC programs should include a graduate component because students and professors alike have inaccurate, unclear ideas about how to write.

1839. Flannery, Daniele D., ed. *Applying Cognitive Learning Theory to Adult Learning.* San Francisco: Jossey-Bass, 1993. 86 pages

Provides a guide to cognitive-learning theory for instructors and program planners in adult and continuing education. *Essayists:* Blank, William E.; Brandt, Barbara LeGrand; Buckmaster, Annette; Farmer, James A., Jr.; Ferro, Trenton R.; Flannery, Daniele D.; Huber, Kay L.; James, Waynne B.; Stouch, Catherine A.; Wislock, Robert F.

1840. Hewitt, Lynne E., Judith F. Duchan, and Erwin M. Segal. "Structure and Function of Verbal Conflicts among Adults with Mental Retardation." *DPr* 16 (October/December 1993): 525–43.

The authors propose that arguments between residents in a group home showed a constrained discourse pattern and were not dysfunctional. They argue that verbal conflicts allowed for useful social interactions.

1841. "Highlights of the MLAs 1990 Survey: Recent and Anticipated Growth in English Doctoral Programs." *ADE* 106 (Winter 1993): 45.

Summarizes findings in six categories: institutional and departmental characteristics, applicants, applicants enrolled, enrollment patterns, future plans, and doctoral degrees granted.

1842. Huber, Bettina J. "Recent and Anticipated Growth in English Doctoral Programs: Findings from the MLA's 1990 Survey." *ADE* 106 (Winter 1993): 46–63.

Reports on institutional and departmental characteristics, applicants, applicants enrolled, enrollment patterns, future plans, and doctoral degrees granted by English, Comparative Literature, Linguistics, and Foreign Languages departments.

1843. Kemper, Susan, James D. Jackson, Hintat Cheung, and Cheryl A. Anagnopoulos. "Enhancing Older Adults' Reading Comprehension." *DPr* 16 (October/December 1993): 405–28.

The researchers point out that people over sixty had more difficulty reading texts with propositionally dense sentences and complex sentence structures than did college students.

1844. Koncel, Mary A., and Debra Carney. *When Worlds Collide: Negotiating between Academic and Professional Discourse in a Graduate Social Work Program*. Cincinnati, OH: Conference on College Composition and Communication, March 1992. ERIC ED 349 573. 11 pages

Discusses the design of a writing program by graduate students to identify and analyze distinctive writing needs. Explores argumentation, curriculum issues, and faculty response to the writing program.

1845. Kroeker, Tirza, and Margaret Henrichs. *Reaching Adult Learners with Whole Language Strategies*. Katonah, NY: Richard C. Owen, 1993. 231 pages

Presents individual and group strategies for teachers of reading and writing impaired adult students. Includes student stories as examples of its theoretical base.

1846. Literacy Volunteers of Greater Hartford, CT. "Welcome to Our World: A Book of Writings by and for Students and Their Tutors." Connecticut State Department of Education, Bureau of Adult Education, Hartford, CT, 1991. ERIC ED 353 857. 160 pages

Presents adult students' writings and their tutors' comments on them.

1847. Newman, Betty Sue Holley. "Bringing Books to Life: A Study of Southern Women's Literacies." *DAI* 53 (May 1993): 3776A.

Examines literacy development and self-selected readings of six women from the southern United States.

1848. Popken, Randall. "Genre Transfer in Developing Adult Writers." *Focuses* 5 (Summer 1992): 3–17.

Studies some principles and implications about students learning to move from reading and writing in one rhetoricial genre to another.

1849. Warren, Stephen. *Grandmothers in the Classroom: How College English Teachers Can Help Those Nontraditional Students*. Pittsburgh, PA: College English Association, March 1992. ERIC ED 352 646. 11 pages

Examines college English teachers helping nontraditional students gain confidence in class from real-life experiences. Discusses uses of free writing and discussion to improve attitudes.

1850. Windish, Charles. "Motivation of Intensive English Program Participants: A Factor Analytic Exploration." *DAI* 54 (September 1993): 782A.

Argues that adult education research methodologies can be successfully applied to ESL research.

4.4 ENGLISH AS A SECOND LANGUAGE

1851. Aghbar, Ali-Asgar, and Mohammed Alam. *Teaching the Writing Process through Full Dyadic Writing*. Vancouver, British Columbia, Canada: Teachers of English to Speakers of Other Languages., March 1993. ERIC ED 352 808. 19 pages

The authors report on a study of 31 ESL writers that investigated the effectiveness of writing with a partner as a technique in teaching composition. They find improvement in the first essays.

1852. Albertini, John. "Critical Literacy, Whole Language, and the Teaching of Writing to Deaf Students: Who Should Dictate to Whom?" *TESOLQ* 27 (Spring 1993): 59–73.

Gathers data from 87 NS and 55 NNS autobiographies to look at different perceptions of literacy. Concludes that a "back to basics" philosophy fosters a limited view of literacy. Advocates social constructivism.

1853. Allison, Desmond. "Sentence Sequence and Coherence: In Search of Readers' Problems in Academic Discourse." *HPLLT* 12 (April 1989): 29–38.

Describes a university study which looks at the relationship between sentence sequence and coherence in academic writing in a second language.

1854. Anziano, Michael C., and Verna Terminello. "Navajo Head Start: Teacher Training and Adult Literacy in a Local Context." *JR* 36 (February 1993): 372–78.

Describes how writing in a second language can be taught when the writer's native language is based largely on an oral rather than written modality.

1855. Barnes, Mary, Suzanne L. Medina, Josh Plaskoff, and Michelle M. Robertson. *A Metacognitive Strategy for Teaching Essay Planning to ESL Students: A Computer-Based Instructional Design*. San Francisco: Teachers of English to Speakers of Other Languages, March 1990. ERIC ED 359 802. 48 pages

Discusses a computer program designed to help nonnative speakers acquire metacognitive skills to design a well-organized essay.

1856. Bosher, Susan. "Developing a Writing Curriculum for Academically Underprepared College ESL Students." University of Minnesota, 1992. ERIC ED 352 843. 24 pages

Presents an overview of three writing courses for underprepared ESL students designed to bring them up to minimum first-year composition standards.

1857. Brickman, Bette. "Publishing ESL Student Writing." *TETYC* 20 (February 1993): 47–48.

Looks at the positive impact of producing an anthology of proverbs from ESL students' native countries.

1858. Brock, Mark N. "A Comparative Study of Computerized Text Analysis and Peer Tutoring as Revision Aids for ESL Writers." *DAI* 54 (August 1993): 913A.

Finds that tutoring is more helpful than text analysis in helping writers to improve content, clarify purpose, and consider reader needs.

1859. Brock, Mark N. "Three Disk-Based Text Analyzers and the ESL Writer." *JSLW* 2 (January 1993): 19–40.

Discusses how computer grammar aids for writing texts can be problematic for L2 texts. Shows how they can be used with ESL students.

1860. Canagarajah, A. Suresh. "Up the Garden Path: Second Language Writing Approaches, Local Knowledge, and Pluralism [response to Raimes, *TESOLQ* 25 (Autumn 1991)]." *TESOLQ* 27 (Summer 1993): 301–6.

Criticizes Raimes's uncommitted pluralism and argues for writing pedagogies which empower ESOL students.

1861. Carlile, Barbara Jane. "A Study of Cultural Differences in Nonverbal Communication among Nonnative Speakers of English." *DAI* 54 (November 1993): 1604A.

Recommends that the meaning of different forms of nonverbal communication be addressed in ESL classrooms.

1862. Chen, Dar-Wu. "A Study of the Relationship of ESL Students' English Language Proficiency and Writing Expertise, and Its Implications to the Curriculum of Teaching ESL Writing." *DAI* 53 (May 1993): 3826A.

Finds that five student subjects' intermediate-level TOEFL scores did not have an evident connection to subjects' English writing methods, process, or performance.

1863. Conlan, Sean Gerard. "Paradigmatic Language Training and Its Effect on the Reading and Writing Performance of Low-Literate Adults." *DAI* 54 (October 1993): 1196A.

Concludes that paradigmatic language structures can be taught to low-literate adults; maintains that both writing and reading performance substantially increased after language training.

1864. Coombe, Christine A. "The Relationship between Self-Assessment Ratios of Functional Literacy Skills and Basic English Skills Test Results in Adult Refugee ESL Learners." *DAI* 53 (May 1993): 3774A.

Discusses self-perceptions of adult refugee students' observations regarding their own functional literacy abilities in English as a second language.

1865. Crandall, JoAnn, and Joy Kreeft Peyton, eds. *Approaches to Adult ESL Literacy Instruction.* Language in Education: Theory and Practice.: ERIC Clearinghouse on Languages and Linguistics, 1993. 98 pages

The contributors describe five approaches to literacy instruction of adults. They discuss competency-based, whole language, language experience, participatory (Freirean), and learner-generated texts.

1866. Currie, Pat. "Entering a Disciplinary Community: Conceptual Activities Required to Write for One Introductory University Course." *JSLW* 2 (May 1993): 101–17.

Analyzes assignments of the university course. Discusses the conceptual demands made on students; shows how NNS writers struggle to meet those demands.

1867. Devine, Joanne, Kevin Railey, and Philip Boshoff. "The Implications of Cognitive Models in L1 and L2 Composing." *JSLW* 2 (September 1993): 203–25.

Analyzes data from 10 L1 and 10 L2 adult writers; explores metacognition of personal, task, and strategy variables. Concludes that cognitive models differ in two groups.

1868. Flowerdew, John. "Content-Based Language Instruction in a Tertiary Setting." *ESP* 12 (1993): 121–38.

Reports on the development of a large-scale content-based curriculum, which includes a composition university in Oman.

1869. Gipe, Joan P., Charles A. Duffy, and Janet C. Richards. "Helping a Nonspeaking Adult Male with Cerebral Palsy Achieve Literacy." *JR* 36 (February 1993): 380–89.

Describes an instructional program that was developed to assist an adult in learning to read and write.

1870. Hemmert, Amy. "Grammar-Writing Journals: Where Fluency and Form Meet." *LTeacher* 17 (March 1993): 47, 49, 69.

Describes a journal writing procedure that focuses on grammar correction as well as fluency.

1871. Hirano, Kinue. "The Effect of Time Limits on Objective Measures of EFL Proficiency in Japanese University Students." *JACET* 24 (1993): 21–39.

> The results show that differing time limits on a writing task had no significant effect on ten measures related to T-unit analysis.

1872. Jackson, Alan, and Mari Kikuchi. "College Reading Skills: Developing 'Food for Thought.'" *JACET* 24 (1993): 61–80.

> Describes a project that developed a reading comprehension program for Japanese EFL students, including textbooks, a testing aparatus, and course evaluation procedures.

1873. Johns, Ann. "Too Much on Our Plates: A Response to Terry Santos' 'Ideology in Composition: L1 and ESL.'" *JSLW* 2 (January 1993): 83–88.

> Denounces Santos' suggestion to adopt L1 composition ideology for ESL students without careful consideration of L2 student needs.

1874. Johns, Ann M. "Written Argumentation for Real Audiences: Suggestions for Teacher Research and Classroom Practice." *TESOLQ* 27 (Spring 1993): 75–90.

> Reviews literature on audience and researches composing processes of two bilingual grant writers. Advocates genre analysis and teaching authentic audience awareness to L2 writers.

1875. Kelley, Eileen F. "The Nonnative English Speaking Student in the Community College Developmental English Classroom: An Ethnographic Study." *DAI* 54 (August 1993): 443A.

> Suggests using students' cultural background knowledge rather than mere English proficiency as a basis for meaningful interaction between student and instructor.

1876. Kemp, John B. "Towards Proficiency as a Writing Class Teacher." *LTeacher* 17 (December 1993): 29, 31, 33, 43.

> Presents a personal account of writing instruction in a Japanese university; rec-

ommends journals, reports, and a process approach.

1877. Khongpun, Somsook. "Composing Processes of Thai High School Students: A Protocol Analysis." *DAI* 54 (October 1993): 1337A.

> Explores the composing processes of five Thai EFL students.

1878. Kimura, Takashi, Hitomi Masuhara, Atsushi Fukada, and Masao Takeuchi. "Effectiveness of Reading Strategy Training in the Comprehension of Japanese College EFL Learners." *JACET* 24 (1993): 101–20.

> The results of this study on reading strategy training showed no significant difference between pre- and post-tests, nor between experimental and control groups.

1879. Krashen, Stephen D. "The Effect of Formal Grammar Teaching: Still Peripheral [response to Lightbown and Pienemann, *TESOL* 27 (Winter 1993)]." *TESOLQ* 27 (Winter 1993): 722–25.

> Reviews Lightbown and Pienemann's critique of Krashen's article and concludes that grammar teaching is "peripheral and fragile."

1880. Lalas, Jose, and Tom Wilson. "Focus on Multicultural Schools: New Technologies for ESL Students." *M&M* 30 (March/April 1993): 18–21.

> Describes how computer technologies can aid lanaguage acquisition; lists software programs, interactive laserdiscs, and CD-ROM applications for oral and written English.

1881. Lane, Janet, Ellen Lange, and Mary Lowry. "ESL Students at Risk: Identification and Intervention." *CATESOL* 4 (Fall 1993): 39–54.

> The authors argue for writing samples and standardized tests to pinpoint ESL students who are considered high at-risk students.

1882. Lee, Yu-Chang. "Revision Breakdowns in Academic Writing of Chinese Graduate-

Level ESL Students." *DAI 54 (September 1993): 844A.*

Investigates revision breakdowns in the academic writing of five Chinese graduate-level ESL students.

1883. Liao, Lily Hwei-Mei Chen. "The Effects of Field-Independence on Second Language Acquisition through Computer-Assisted Instruction." *DAI* 53 (May 1993): 3788A.

Studies college ESL students' acquisition of English structure and expression in a CAI setting.

1884. Lightbown, Patsy M., and Manfred Pienemann. "Comments on Stephen D. Krashen's 'Teaching Issues: Formal Grammar Instruction' [response to Krashen, *TESOLQ* 26 (Summer 1992)]." *TESOLQ* 27 (Winter 1993): 717–22.

Critiques Krashen's discounting of formal grammar instruction. Points to studies by Swain, White, and Pienemann and recommends that SLA researchers work with teachers.

1885. Lynch, Brian, and Peter Coughlan. "Making Use of Computer-Assisted Language Learning in Higher Education: A Report from UCLA." *CATESOL* 4 (Fall 1993): 55–72.

Presents an overview and analysis of computer-assisted instruction in a language learning project for ESL service courses which includes individualized instruction in grammar, vocabulary and prewriting.

1886. Lynch, Tony, and Ian McGrath. "Teaching Bibliographic Documentation Skills." *ESP* 12 (1993): 219–38.

Argues that postgraduate ESL students require stronger skills in presenting bibliographic information; enumerates sources of guidance.

1887. MacLennan, Carol Helen Gordon. "Nonliteral Language and the Learner of English." *DAI* 53 (June 1993): 4297A.

Analyzes seven studies to determine the types of difficulties learners of English

might have with nonliteral language in education and employment situations.

1888. McAndrew, Donald A., and C. Mark Hurlbert. "Teaching Intentional Errors in Standard English: A Way to 'Big Smart English.'" *ELQ* 15 (May 1993): 5–7.

The authors argue that writers should not follow language rules rigidly but follow a route that allows more democratic and equitable language and culture.

1889. McKay, Sandra Lee. *Agendas for Second Language Literacy.* New York: Cambridge University Press, 1993. 151 pages

Discusses how social, economic, and political policies shape the teaching of second-language literacy to minorities in Anglophone countries. Calls for more awareness of immigrants' literacy in the original language.

1890. McKay, Sandra Lee. "Examining L2 Composition Ideology: A Look at Literacy Education." *JSLW* 2 (January 1993): 65–81.

Argues that ESL composition theory needs to address literacy concerns such as literacy as a social practice, plurality of literacies, and power issues.

1891. Mok, Waiching Enid. "Contrastive Rhetoric and the Japanese Writer of EFL." *JALT* 15 (November 1993): 151–61.

Surveys research on contrastive rhetoric with an emphasis on English and Japanese rhetorics; suggests implications for writing pedagogy.

1892. Mora, Raimundo. "Pragmatic Aspects of the Language Used in Three Selected ESL Classes." *DAI* 53 (May 1993): 2829A.

Points out that teacher silence often was the key to getting students to participate while student silence was a symptom of discomfort.

1893. Moragne é Silva, Michele. *First and Second Language Composing Processes across Tasks.* Vancouver, British Columbia, Canada: Teachers of English to Speakers of Other

Languages Conference, March 1992. ERIC ED 350 847. 21 pages

Presents a case study of a writer's composing processes in a variety of tasks in her native and nonnative language. Concludes that the composing processes used in native and nonnative languages are largely similar.

1894. Morris, Gertrude Mae. "Novice ESL Writing in Six Public School Students." *DAI* 54 (October 1993): 1343A.

Studies elementary students' abilities to write formal and unstructured assignments.

1895. Myers, Sharon A. "In Search of the Genuine Article: A Cross-Linguistic Investigation of the Development of the English Article System in Written Compositions of Adult ESL Writers." *DAI* 53 (January 1993): 2352A.

Analyzes the use of definite and indefinite English articles by adult ESL students from nine L1 backgrounds.

1896. Nelson, Gayle L., and John M. Murphy. "Peer Response Groups: Do L2 Writers Use Peer Comments in Revising Their Drafts?" *TESOLQ* 27 (Spring 1993): 135–41.

Videotapes four intermediate ESL writers during their interactions in a peer group; collects rough and final drafts. Suggests that teachers should reinforce collaborative learning.

1897. Olivares, Rafael A. *Using the Newspaper to Teach ESL Learners*. Newark, DE: International Reading Association, 1993. 104 pages

Suggests the use of newspapers with ESL students to teach language skills as well as math, science, and social studies. Includes activities to help develop language in context.

1898. Pennington, Martha. "Exploring the Potential of Word Processing for Nonnative Writers." *CHum* 27 (June 1993): 149–63.

Recommends using word processors to reduce unnecessary barriers for ESL students and to enable them to write more confidently.

1899. Pennington, Martha C. "A Critical Examination of Word Processing Effects in Relation to L2 Writers." *JSLW* 2 (September 1993): 227–55.

Reviews research on word processing, including software and hardware considerations. Concludes that research indicates continuing to use computers in L2 writing.

1900. Pennington, Martha C., and Sufumi So. "Comparing Writing Process and Product across Two Languages: A Study of Six Singaporean University Student Writers." *JSLW* 2 (January 1993): 41–63.

Shows there is little relationship between process skill and product quality across languages. Argues that the writing process is similar in students' L1 and L2.

1901. Peyton, Joy Kreeft, and Jana Staton. *Dialogue Journals in the Multilingual Classroom: Building Language Fluency and Writing Skills through Writing Interaction*. Norwood, NJ: Ablex, 1993. 240 pages

Describes how to implement and maintain dialogue journal writing in ESL classrooms. Presents a model of researchers working in collaboration with teachers to provide a context for research results.

1902. Phinney, Marianne, and Sandra Khouri. "Computers, Revision, and ESL Writers: The Role of Experience." *JSLW* 2 (September 1993): 257–77.

Videotapes four writers using a computer to compose one paper. Indicates that experience with computers rather than writing affects the quality of the paper.

1903. Rabideau, Dan. *Integrating Reading and Writing into Adult ESL Instruction*. Washington, DC: March 1993. ERIC ED 358 749. 4 pages

Describes some major reading and writing practices currently used in adult ESL programs. Maintains that process writing provides practice, experimentation, and communication with language in the context of helping students express their own ideas.

1904. Rabino, Linda. "The Bilingual Education Program in New York City Public Schools: An Anthropological Study of Education, Language, and Ethnicity." *DAI* 54 (August 1993): 575A.

Proposes that the bilingual program and related controversies are part of an ethnic boundary maintenance mechanism.

1905. Raimes, Ann. "The Author Responds [to Canagarajah, *TESOL* 27 (Summer 1993)]." *TESOLQ* 27 (Summer 1993): 306–10.

Explains that Canagarajah's article reported rather than proposed writing approaches. Argues against limiting writing classrooms to political inquiry.

1906. Ransdell, D. R. "Creative Writing Is Greek to Me: The Continuing Education of a Language Teacher." *ELTJ* 47 (January 1993): 40–46.

After studying a foreign language as a beginner, the author maintains that creative writing activities should be integrated into every beginning language learning class.

1907. Reynolds, Patricia R. "Evaluating ESL and College Composition Texts for Teaching the Argumentative Rhetorical Form." *JR* 36 (March 1993): 474–80.

Describes criteria that can be used to select texts for ESL students and reports the analysis of 14 current texts using those criteria.

1908. Rosow, La Vergna. "I Teach Grammar . . . in Process." *CalE* 29 (March/April 1993): 6–7, 23.

Describes community college ESL class practices that empower learners to ana-

lyze theory, make decisions, and to use language in context.

1909. Santos, Terry. "Response to Ann Johns [JSLW 2 (January 1993)]." *JSLW* 2 (January 1993): 89–90.

Responds to Johns's comments and stresses the integration of L1 and L2 ideologies rather than L2 blindly following L1 theory.

1910. Schecter, Sandra R., and Linda A. Harklau. *Writing in Nonnative Language: What We Know, What We Need to Know.* Vancouver, British Columbia, Canada: Annual Meeting of the Teachers of English to Speakers of Other Languages, March 1992. ERIC ED 353 825. 45 pages

Reviews empirical research on second language writing, responds to questions on the state of the art, and identifies an agenda for future research.

1911. Schmitt, Norbert. "Comparing Native and Nonnative Teachers' Evaluations of Error Seriousness." *JALT* 15 (November 1993): 181–91.

Shows that Japanese teachers of English judged grammatical errors on student compositions more harshly although they reported that comprehensibility was their most important criterion.

1912. Severino, Carol. "The 'Doodles' in Context: Qualifying Claims about Contrastive Rhetoric." *WCJ* 14 (Fall 1993): 44–62.

Argues that rethinking Kaplin's early work in contrastive rhetoric in light of subsequent research can lead to a more sophisticated understanding of cultural and linguistic differences.

1913. Severino, Carol. "The Sociopolitical Implications of Response to Second Language and Second Dialect Writing." *JSLW* 2 (September 1993): 181–201.

Based on three case studies of responding L2 and SESD writers, she discusses "separatist, accommodationist, and assimilationist" stances. Presents L2 composition teaching as political.

1914. Shizuka, Tetsuhito. "Effects of Different Editing Methods on EFL Writing Quality at High School Level." *JACET* 24 (1993): 139–58.

Compares four editing methods (direct correction, indication of error location, peer feedback, and unaided self-editing) and finds no significant differences among the four methods.

1915. Silva, Tony. "Toward an Understanding of the Distinct Nature of L2 Writing: The ESL Research and Its Implications." *TES-OLQ* 27 (Winter 1993): 657–77.

Considers 72 studies of L1, L2, and NES composing processes and products to present differences in L2 writing. Argues for a specialized pedagogy for L2 writers.

1916. Steer, Jocelyn. *Teaching in the Multicultural Classroom.* HarperCollins Resources for Instructors. New York: HarperCollins, 1993. 63 pages

Introduces teachers to research and pedagogical strategies for teaching ESL students in a composition classroom with both native and nonnative speakers.

1917. Sweedler-Brown, Carol O. "ESL Essay Evaluation: The Influence of Sentence-Level and Rhetorical Features." *JSLW* 2 (January 1993): 3–17.

Recommends special training because ESL writing is judged on sentence-level errors over rhetorical concerns by NS composition instructors.

1918. Tarone, Elaine, Bruce Downing, Andrew Cohen, Susan Gillette, Robin Murie, and Beverly Dailey. "The Writing of Southeast Asian-American Students in Secondary School and University." *JSLW* 2 (May 1993): 149–72.

Studies mainstreamed secondary ESL students; compares them with NS, immigrant, and international writers in first-year com-

position classes as to writing success and problems.

1919. Taylor, Marva Maria. "Bridging the Gap: Integrating Academic Content in a College Intermediate-Level ESL Course." *DAI* 54 (November 1993): 1710A.

Presents case studies of five ESL undergraduates subject to a new teaching approach designed to raise self-esteem and a sense of belonging.

1920. Thomas, Jacinta Catherine. "The Affective Experience of ESL Writers." *DAI* 53 (January 1993): 2353A.

Examines emotions reported by and observed in ESL students when they compose in English.

1921. Tillyer, David A. "World Peace and Natural Writing through E-Mail." *CollM* 11 (May 1993): 67–69.

Argues that e-mail communication seems more real and meaningful to ESL writers than does standard academic writing.

1922. Tsang, Wai King, and Matilda Wong. "Investigating the Process Approach to Writing." *JALT* 15 (November 1993): 163–79.

The authors point out that a process approach helped Chinese students improve content and organization of their English essays, but sentence-level improvement was minimal.

1923. Wu, Yiqiang. "First and Second Language Writing Relationship: Chinese and English." *DAI* 53 (June 1993): 4303A.

Assesses Chinese college student's apprehensions while writing in English and Chinese.

1924. Yamashita, Junko. "Reading in a Foreign Language: Reading Ability or Language Ability?" *JACET* 24 (1993): 159–78.

Finds that English reading comprehension ability of Japanese learners was predicted best by simple sentence processing ability, showing that FL reading problems are linguistic.

1925. Yardley, Gabriel A. J. "The Country Club Composition Class: A Writing Project for University English Majors." *LTeacher* 17 (April 1993): 25, 27, 29.

Describes a writing project for a mini-research paper on one aspect of a foreign country.

1926. Yoshihara, Karen. "Keys to Effective Peer Response." *CATESOL* 4 (Fall 1993): 17–37.

Describes the use of peer response groups with nonnative English writers. Details procedures used with community college students such as specific peer response reports submitted to the instructor.

1927. Zhang, Xiaolin. "English Collocations and Their Effect on the Writing of Native and Nonnative College Freshmen." *DAI* 54 (September 1993): 910A.

Examines possible correlations between knowledge and use of English collocations on the quality of first-year college writing. Finds that native writers perform significantly better than nonnative writers.

1928. Zhu, Hong. "Cohesion and Coherence in Chinese ESL Writing." *DAI* 53 (January 1993): 2233A.

Examines cohesion and coherence, language transfer, and interference in Chinese ESL writings. Explores similarities and differences between Chinese and English.

4.5 RESEARCH AND STUDY SKILLS

1929. Accetta, Randy. "JRGs? What the Heck Are Those?" *CalE* 29 (Winter 1993): 13, 26.

Explains the use of journal response groups (JRGs) to stimulate discussion, improve revision skills, and establish a sense of community among community college students.

1930. Boon, Kevin A. "Vertical Analysis of Word Choice." *TETYC* 20 (February 1993): 53–56.

Presents a visual diagram designed to help increase vocabulary.

1931. Daniel, Neil. "Confronting the Cult of Correctness." *ATA* 4 (Spring 1992): 12–14.

Observes that students need to be shown how to master editing conventions.

1932. Holmes, V. M., and E. Ng. "Word-Specific Knowledge, Word-Recognition Strategies, and Spelling Ability." *JMemL* 32 (April 1993): 230–57.

Study investigates good and poor adult spellers and supports the contention that "poor spellers attempt to recognize words using only partial cues."

1933. Kornhauser, Arthur W. *How to Study: Suggestions for High School and College Students*. 3rd ed. Chicago: University of Chicago Press, 1993. 64 pages

Offers strategies and advice on understanding material preparing for exams and assignments and acquiring skills for reading, note-taking, listening, and improving the use of time in the classroom and the library.

1934. Lubarsky, Nancy Louise. "Developing Writing through the Use of Intergenerational Interviews and Narratives." *DAI* 53 (January 1993): 2498A.

Studies the use of narratives and oral history interviews to develop critical thinking, writing, and learning skills.

1935. McCleary, Bill. "Writing Courses Found to Enhance Many Academic Skills." *CompC* 6 (November 1993): 1–3.

Summarizes Alexander Astin's findings on the effects of the number of writing courses on students' beliefs and academic development.

1936. McKeown, Margaret G. "Creating Effective Definitions for Young Word Learners." *RRQ* 28 (January/February/March 1993): 16–31.

> Analyzes dictionary definitions for cognitive processing and provides four guidelines for improving definitions.

1937. Pelham, Fran O'Byrne. "The Research Journal: Integrating Reading, Writing, and Research." *CompC* 6 (April 1993): 4–5.

> Describes a journal approach to teaching research writing that emphasizes process and discovery.

1938. Powers, Judith. *Helping the Graduate Thesis Writer through Faculty and Writing Center Collaboration*. San Diego, CA: Conference on College Composition and Communication, March/April 1993. ERIC ED 358 466. 14 pages

> Chronicles the efforts at the University of Wyoming writing center to deal with a 100 percent increase in conferences held with graduate student writers.

1939. Scott, Grant F. "Three Framers, Biography, and the Research Paper." *CEA* 55 (Spring/Summer 1993): 69–78.

> Outlines a research paper assignment which moves beyond the "objective report" to allow writers to situate themselves within the topic.

1940. Sutton, Brian Ward. "Undergraduates Writing Research Papers: Twenty-Four Case Studies." *DAI* 53 (May 1993): 3831A.

> Determines what students do from the time they receive a research-paper assignment until they hand in the finished paper.

1941. Tuckman, Bruce. *The Coded Elaborative Outline as a Strategy to Help Students Learn from Text*. Atlanta, GA: American Educational Research Association, April 1993. ERIC ED 357 075. 15 pages

> Reports on a study of 182 undergraduates who were required to write coded elaborative outlines (CEO) on textbook chapters. Results show that these students scored significantly higher on tests.

1942. Wells, Dorothy. "An Account of the Complex Causes of Unintentional Plagiarism in College Writing." *WPA* 16 (Spring 1993): 59–71.

> Details the complexities students encounter in writing the research paper. Discusses difficulties that may result in "plagiarism of desperation."

1943. White, Edward M. "Too Many Campuses Want to Sweep Student Plagiarism under the Rug." *CHE* (24 February 1993): A44.

> Calls for more extensive instruction in first-year English classes to diminish chances of inadvertent plagiarism; recommends reinforcement in courses in other disciplines as well.

4.6 OTHER

1944. Bernhardt, Bill. *Becoming a Writer: The Evidence from Teacher Autobiographies*. San Diego, CA: Conference on College Composition and Communication, March/April 1993. ERIC ED 356 492. 6 pages

> Reports on a study of 120 graduate students (English and Education) investigating shared common experiences in learning how to write. Points out that personal expression helped most.

5
Testing, Measurement, and Evaluation

5.1 EVALUATION OF STUDENTS

1945. Agnew, Eleanor. *Departmental Grade Options: The Silent Saboteur*. San Diego, CA: Conference on College Composition and Communication, March/April 1993. ERIC ED 356 478. 13 pages

Argues that institutional pressure to keep grades down can cast teachers who give high grades as poor teachers while protecting truly poor teachers from this evaluation.

1946. Aitken, Joan E., and Michael R. Near. "College Student Question-Asking: The Relationship of Classroom Communication Apprehension and Motivation." *SCJ* 59 (Fall 1993): 73–81.

Results suggest that motivation level is a better indicator of question-asking than classroom apprehension level.

1947. Black, Laurel, Donald A. Daiker, Jeffrey Sommers, and Gail Stygall. *Handbook of Writ-

ing Portfolio Assessment: A Program for College Placement*. Oxford, OH: Miami University Press, 1992. 85 pages

Provides a guide to implementing a writing portfolio assessment program for placement of incoming college students.

1948. Boynton, Victoria. "Collaborative Power Sharing." *CompC* 6 (February 1993): 6–8.

Describes a procedure in which students evaluate one another's papers that encourages them to address problems of difference. Argues that it also requires teachers to share power with students.

1949. Cameron, Thomas. "A Responsible Evaluation Instrument and Its Impact on a Developmental Writing Program." *TETYC* 20 (December 1993): 313–23.

Presents a nine-point holistic scale based primarily on whether a student's writing is reader- or writer-centered; argues that the scale helps to sequence the curriculum.

1950. Christian, Barbara. "Freshman Composition Portfolios in a Small College." *TETYC* 20 (December 1993): 289–97.

Stresses the positive outcome of a portfolio experiment conducted by three teachers at a community college.

1951. Connors, Robert J., and Andrea A. Lunsford. "Teachers' Rhetorical Comments on Students' Papers." *CCC* 44 (May 1993): 200–223.

The authors conclude that teachers' written responses have moved away from an emphasis on mechanics but are still grade and judgment driven.

1952. Dickson, Marcia. *Initial Opposition— Won't Portfolio Assessment Take Away Teacher Autonomy?* San Diego, CA: Conference on College Composition and Communication, March/April 1993. ERIC ED 357 384. 5 pages

Offers strategies for making portfolio assessment stronger by avoiding resistance of faculty.

1953. Dwyer, Herbert J., and Howard J. Sullivan. "Student Preferences for Teacher and Computer Composition Marking." *JEdR* 86 (January/February 1993): 137–41.

The authors point out that students preferred teacher marking because it was more personalized and thorough.

1954. Elbow, Peter. "Ranking, Evaluating, and Liking: Sorting Out Three Forms of Judgment." *CE* 55 (February 1993): 187–206.

Defines and discusses three different acts of assessment. Argues for teachers revising their own classroom practices of assessment.

1955. Gorrell, Donna. *Portfolios for New (and Experienced) Teachers of Writing.* San Diego, CA: Conference on College Composition and Communication, March/April 1993. ERIC ED 357 352. 11 pages

Narrates a teacher's experience with portfolio assessment, pointing out its advantages in making the processes of writing evident.

1956. Greenberg, Karen L. "The Politics of Basic Writing." *JBW* 12 (Spring 1993): 64–71.

Emphasizes a connection between effective instruction and valid assessment of students, courses, and programs. Urges teachers and administrators—rather than outside agencies—to undertake such assessment.

1957. Hamp-Lyons, Liz, and William Condon. "Questioning Assumptions about Portfolio-Based Assessment" *CCC* 44 (May 1993): 176–90.

Concludes that portfolios improved department assessment procedures not because of "inherent value" as assessment devices but because of increased faculty communication and cooperation.

1958. Hanson, F. Allan. *Testing Testing: Social Consequences of the Examined Life.* Berkeley, CA: University of California Press, 1993. 378 pages

Discusses two kinds of tests, the "authentic" which assesses a qualitative state (between innocent and guilty), and the "qualifying" which assesses fitness to "X" (perform a task); argues that tests construct and control as well as measure us.

1959. Hoffman, Bettina Judith. "Predictors of Performance on the Essay Section of the English Composition Test in the College Board Achievement Tests." *DAI* 54 (December 1993): 2126A.

Investigates the relationship between essay, math, and verbal scores; concludes that the essay score can be predicted from other data.

1960. Holt, Dennis. "Holistic Scoring in Many Disciplines." *CollT* 41 (Spring 1993): 71–74.

Discusses the usefulness of holistic assessment according to rubrics for lab reports, reviews, and essays across the curriculum.

1961. Kearns, Edward. "On the Running Board of the Portfolio Bandwagon." *WPA* 16 (Spring 1993): 50–58.

Examines "shallow arguments and confused purposes" that initiated enthusiasm for portfolios. Expresses skepticism rather than outright opposition to its use.

1962. Keller, Dana, James Crouse, and Dale Trusheim. "Relationships among Gender Differences in Freshman Course Grades and Course Characteristics." *JEdPsy* 85 (December 1993): 702–9.

The authors find that college courses with a higher percentage of women were those "in which high school grades and SAT scores are less important for earning higher course grades."

1963. Kingan, Mary E., and Richard L. Alfred. "Entry Assessment in Community Colleges: Tracking or Facilitating?" *CCR* 21 (Winter 1993): 3–16.

Argues for student-oriented assessment programs that incorporate all aspects of an institution and use the results to benefit students, programs, and services.

1964. Kramp, Mary Kay, and W. Lee Humphreys. "Narrative, Self-Assessment, and the Reflective Learner." *CollT* 41 (Summer 1993): 83–88.

Describes the results of allowing students to tell their stories of learning experienced in their courses.

1965. Mahala, Daniel, and Michael Vivion. "The Role of AP and the Composition Program." *WPA* 17 (Fall/Winter 1993): 43–56.

Demonstrates the importance of WPA awareness of the content of AP courses and the tests of College Board and Educational Testing Service.

1966. Marsella, Joy. "The Effects of a College Writing Placement Exam on High School

and College Students and Teachers." *CompC* 6 (May 1993): 4–7.

Reports that the University of Hawaii's extensive writing placement examination brought about improvements in high school and university writing instruction.

1967. Mayo, Wendell. *Peer Tutoring and Writing Assessment.* Indianapolis, IN: Assessment Workshops of Indianapolis, November 1992. ERIC ED 351 687. 10 pages

Maintains that a true evaluation of writing must include an assessment of how students negotiate meaning. Emphasizes that writing teachers must consider the transaction between student writer and peer reader in grading.

1968. McCarron, William E. "Portfolio Assessment and the Teaching of Writing." *ET* 25 (Fall 1993): 47–48.

Concludes that using portfolio assessment in a graduate technical writing course led to increased revision and better final products.

1969. Metzger, Elizabeth, and Lizbeth Bryant. "Portfolio Assessment: Pedagogy, Power, and the Student." *TETYC* 20 (December 1993): 279–88.

Surveys history, methods, and issues of portfolio assessment; answers common questions; includes a bibliography.

1970. Nace, John Edward. "An Anatomy of Assessment: A Qualitative Study of Conceptual Influences upon Placement Essay Raters' Scoring Decisions at a Large Urban Community College." *DAI* 53 (May 1993): 3830A.

Examines the influences on CCP placement essay raters' scoring decisions and the resultant outcomes for student placement into college-level and pre-college-level introductory writing and reading courses.

1971. Ou, Hung-Chang. "A Study of the Relationship between English Listening Comprehension and Student Motivation." *DAI* 53 (January 1993): 2348A.

Analyzes the relationship between the dynamics of learners' motivation and their achievement in language learning.

1972. Page Voth, Leslie Victoria. "The Effects of Goal Setting, and Goal Setting Combined with a Facilitation Strategy, on the Writing Performance of Students with Learning Disabilities." *DAI* 53 (January 1993): 2329A.

Compares writing performance in three essays written by students with learning disabilities using goal setting.

1973. Peckham, Irvin. "Beyond Grades." *CompSt* 21 (Fall 1993): 16–31.

Explains student response to a policy of not giving grades on essays. Discusses other incentives for improved performance.

1974. Perkins, Don Carlos. "Practice against Theory in Writing Proficiency Exams." *DAI* 54 (1993): 2132A.

Examines testing procedures at the University of Wisconsin-Milwaukee; argues that proficiency testing is informed by current-traditional methods rather than current theory.

1975. Peter, Joanne K. A. "Certain Uncertainties: New Literacy and the Evaluation of Student Writing." National Council of Teachers of English, 1993. NCTE Concept Paper Series No. 5. ERIC ED 356 481. 57 pages

Examines the conflict between teachers' evaluation of student writing by perception versus the possibility of absolute standards. Supports new literacy models of reading and writing.

1976. Plowman, Lydia. "Tracing the Evolution of a Co-Authored Text." *L&C* 13 (July 1993): 149–61.

Studies group writing to determine the concept of socially distributed cognition in the process of writing without computers.

1977. Price, Patricia Marie. "An Examination of Response to Literature and Myers-Briggs Personality Preferences in High-Ability Secondary School Students." *DAI* 54 (November 1993): 1660A.

Describes the correlation of students' written responses to a story, gender, literary quality of story, and the Myers-Briggs Personality Preferences test.

1978. Quible, Zane K. "Grading Techniques that Help Eliminate Teacher Burnout." *BEdF* 48 (October 1993): 32–34.

Asserts that objectivity in grading can decrease burnout. Provides model error checklists to simplify grading.

1979. Rieber, Lloyd. "Paraprofessional Assessment of Students' Writing." *CollT* 41 (Winter 1993): 15–18.

A business professor describes the advantages of hiring experienced nonstudent copy editors to mark, evaluate, and comment on student papers.

1980. Roy, Emil L. "Computerized Scoring of Placement Exams: A Validation." *JBW* 12 (Fall 1993): 41–54.

Concludes that holistic exam-reading can be replaced by a computerized analysis. Recommends such an analysis for basic writing programs.

1981. Rushton, Christopher, Philip Ramsey, and Roy Rada. "Peer Assessment in a Collaborative Hypermedia Environment: A Case Study." *JCBI* 20 (Summer 1993): 3.

Maintains that although students remained skeptical about peer assessment, their scores were "remarkably similar" to those given by tutors, suggesting a high degree of reliability.

1982. Sacken, Jeannee P. *Alternative Assessment Measures for Nontraditional Students.* Cincinnati, OH: Conference on College Composition and Communication, March 1992. ERIC ED 358 480. 17 pages

Discusses alternatives to the Test of Standard Written English to test the verbal and written communication skills of deaf and hard-of-hearing students.

1983. Scott, Renée S., and Barbara C. Rodgers. "Assessing Communication in Writing: The Development of a Spanish Writing Contest." *FLA* 26 (Fall 1993): 383–92.

Presents a proficiency-oriented writing contest, including topics and rubric-based assessment for four proficiency levels in Spanish.

1984. Sens-Conant, Susan Lynn. "The Cognition of Self-Evaluation: A Descriptive Model of the Writing Process." *MA* 31 (1993): 1489.

Develops a model of evaluation process of 10 first-year composition writers who tape recorded their writing and the evaluation of this writing in two separate sessions.

1985. Sommers, Jeffrey. "Grading Student Writing: An Experiment and a Commentary." *TETYC* 20 (December 1993): 263–74.

Looks at a teacher's struggles with the shifting contextual meaning of grades.

1986. Sommers, Jeffrey, Laurel Black, Donald A. Daiker, and Gail Stygall. "The Challenges of Rating Portfolios: What WPAs Can Expect." *WPA* 17 (Fall/Winter 1993): 7–29.

Continues the conversation about the benefits of portfolio assessment and outlines some "practical methods of gaining reasonable reliability" in scoring.

1987. Sorenson, Ritch, Grant T. Savage, and Larry D. Hartman. "Motivating Students to Improve Business Writing: A Comparison between Goal-Based and Punishment-Based Grading Systems." *JBC* 30 (1993): 113–32.

Examines how instructors may motivate students to improve writing skills; demonstrates the differences between goal- and punishment-based grading systems.

1988. Stahle, Debra L., and Judith P. Mitchell. "Portfolio Assessment in College Methods

Courses: Practicing What We Preach." *JR* 37 (April 1993): 530–42.

Describes how portfolios were used in a preservice reading/language arts methods course. Discusses the development and value of portfolios.

1989. Stern, Caroline. *Student Writers Practicing Self-Assessment*. Cincinnati, OH: Conference on College Composition and Communication, March 1992. ERIC ED 354 509. 11 pages

Advocates students' use of writing portfolios as a means of self-evaluation.

1990. Stricker, Lawrence J., Donald A. Rock, and Nancy W. Burton. "Sex Differences in Predictions of College Grades from Scholastic Aptitude Test Scores." *JEdPsy* 85 (December 1993): 710–18.

The authors appraise two explanations for sex difference in predicting college grades from SAT scores. They find that women's GPA is slightly underpredicted and men's GPA is slightly overpredicted.

1991. Teichmann, Sandra Gail, and Darrell Fike. *Responding to Student Essays*. Gainesville, FL: Florida College English Conference, February 1993. ERIC ED 354 528. 14 pages

Discusses conversational possibilities between teachers and students; underscores the need for teacher encouragement and the belief in students as writers. Sees this as a way for students to begin liking to write.

1992. Terenzini, Patrick T. "Assessment: What It Is and What It Isn't." *ADE* 104 (Spring 1993): 14–17.

Discusses assessment as formative, developmental process designed to enhance learning, not as testing, faculty evaluation, or an administrative activity. Provides eight suggestions for its implementation.

1993. Thompson, Thomas C. *Deprogramming Our Responses: The Effects of Personality on Teacher Responses*. Cincinnati, OH: Conference on College Composition and Communication, March 1992. ERIC ED 353 577. 15 pages

Describes a study that uses scales from the Myers-Briggs Type Indicator to investigate how a teacher's personality influences her/his written responses to student writing.

1994. Townsend, Michael A. R., Lynley Hicks, Jacquilyn D. M. Thompson, Keri M. Wilton, Bryan F. Tuck, and Dennis W. Moore. "Effects of Introductions and Conclusions in Assessment of Student Essays." *JEdPsy* 85 (December 1993): 670–78.

The authors maintain that rhetorical structures, introductions, and conclusions affect the comprehension of texts. They find that the quality of introduction had greater effect on grades than the quality of conclusion.

1995. Valdes, Guadalupe, Paz Haro, and Maria Paz Echevarriarza. "The Development of Writing Abilities in a Foreign Language: Contributions toward a General Theory of L2 Writing." National Center for the Study of Writing and Literacy, 1992. ERIC ED 355 776. 34 pages

Finds that a group of competent English writers writing in Spanish do not appear to follow the developmental sequence implicit in the American Council on the Teaching of Foreign Languages (ACTFL).

1996. Valencia, Shelia W., Elfrieda H. Hiebert, and Peter P. Afflerbach, eds. *Authentic Reading Assessment: Practices and Possibilities.* Newark, DE: International Reading Association, 1993. 328 pages

Presents nine case studies by educators that demonstrate how to meet the challenge of reforming assessment to yield accurate and authentic pictures of students' literacy development at a variety of levels. Each essay is followed by a commentary written by a professional in the literacy field.

Essayists: Afflerbach, Peter P.; Au, Kathryn; Bembridge, Teri; Cambourne, Brian; Collier, Gertrude V.; DeVito, Pasquale J.; Garcia, Mary W.; Hancock, Jan; Hansen, Jane; Hiebert, Elfrieda H.; Kapinus, Barbara A.; Kruglanski, Hannah; Lima, Susan Skawinski; Place, Nancy A.; Snider, Mary Ann; Turbill, Jan; Valencia, Shelia W.; Verville, Kathy; Weiss, Barbara.

1997. Venrick, Reed. "Selective Editing." *LTeacher* 17 (June 1993): 21, 23.

Describes a method of feedback in which editing errors are corrected selectively by category.

1998. Wauters, Joan K., B. Jo Devine, and Christine Hacskaylo. *Uniting Two-Year and Four-Year College Programs through Portfolio Assessment.* Cincinnati, OH: Conference on College Composition and Communication, March 1992. ERIC ED 349 551. 22 pages

Explores the effects of portfolio evaluation on composition students, English faculty, and adminstrators at two- and four-year campuses. Finds that evaluation encouraged revision.

1999. Weppler, Margaret E., and Phillip J. Moore. "The Effects of Cooperative and Individual Writing: Does Choice Make a Difference?" *AJL&L* 16 (May 1993): 149–56.

Describes an investigation of primary school children's writing; explores children's choices between cooperative and individual writing and the effect of this decision on later individual writing.

2000. "What's Wrong with Writing and What Can We Do Right Now?" Office of Educational Research and Improvement in the U.S. Department of Education, Washington, DC. ED 1.302:W 93, April 1993. 4 pages

Argues that high school students will be better prepared for the work force and college if they write more in high school and at home.

2001. Wiggins, Grant. *Assessing Student Performance: Exploring the Purpose and Limits*

of Testing. San Francisco: Jossey-Bass, 1993. 316 pages

Argues that since students are the primary "clients" for assessment, all asssessment is obligated to improve performance, not just measure or comment upon it. Points out that standards have definable characteristics and that real world examples (ranging from Apple Computer to soccer matches) provide models for assessment, for accountability, and for improved education.

2002. Williamson, Michael M., and Brian A. Huot, eds. *Validating Holistic Scoring for Writing Assessment: Theoretical and Empirical Foundations*. Written Language Series, edited by Marcia Farr. Cresskill, NJ: Hampton Press, 1993. 337 pages

The nine contributors treat the history, theory, research, and application of holistic scoring to writing assessment. They discuss contexts for such assessments, issues of validity and reliability, training of raters, and field testing of prompts. *Essayists:* Camp, Roberta; Cherry, Roger D.; Huot, Brian; Janopoulos, Michael; Meyer, Paul R.; Murphy, Sandra; Pula, Judith J.; Ruth, Leo; Smith, William L.; White, Edward M.; Williamson, Michael M.

5.2 EVALUATION OF TEACHERS

2003. Aitken, Joan E. *Empowering Students and Faculty through Portfolio Assessment*. Lexington, KY: Central States Communication Association, April 1993. ERIC ED 355 599. 33 pages

Describes three kinds of portfolios used by the Department of Communication Studies at the University of Missouri-Kansas City for both assessment and insight into the learning process: university-wide portfolio, course portfolio, and student-selected portfolio.

2004. Berns, Laura L. "Teachers' Response to Student Texts within the Growth Model." *DAI* 53 (February 1993): 2719A.

Compares responses of four college writing teachers to seven guidelines established for response to student texts within the growth model.

2005. Burt, Linda Suzanne. "Personal Teaching Efficacy and Ethnic Attributions as Contributors to Caucasian Preservice Teachers' Behavior toward International Children." *DAI* 54 (November 1993): 1762A.

Results show that preservice teachers exhibited more positive than negative behaviors toward both international and United States children.

2006. Creed, Tom. "'The' Seven Principles . . . . Not." *AAHE* 45 (April 1993): 8–9.

Argues that recently published research-based criteria for teaching performance, though neither comprehensive nor prescriptive, offer useful goals for faculty.

2007. Dwinell, Patricia L., and Jeanne L. Higbee. "Students' Perceptions of the Value of Teaching Evaluations." *PMS* 76 (June 1993, Part I): 995–1000.

Points out that most students believe that evaluations alter teacher behavior but do not influence the promotion and tenure process. Looks at studies which suggest examining alternative evaluation methods (observation, for example) based on student input.

2008. Hutchings, Pat. "Introducing Faculty Portfolios." *AAHE* 45 (May 1993): 14–17.

Describes an innovative method of documenting faculty achievement both quantitatively and qualitatively to improve university reward systems.

2009. Murphy, Brian J. "The Role of Community College Faculty in Improving the Learning Environment." *DAI* 53 (May 1993): 3817A.

Examines the relationship between self-reported levels of faculty activities that impact student achievement and faculty development.

2010. Smith, Hoke L., and Barbara E. Walvoord. "Certifying Teaching Excellence: An Alternative Paradigm to the Teaching Award." *AAHE* 46 (October 1993): 3–5, 12.

Proposes that teaching merits, measured by specific national criteria and recorded for transfer among institutions, supplement current awards and directly influence tenure and promotion decisions.

2011. Smittle, Pat. "Computer-Adaptive Testing: A New Era." *JDEd* 17 (Fall 1993): 8–12.

Concludes that computer-adaptive tests are better for entry assignment than traditional paper-and-pencil tests.

2012. Waite, Duncan. "Teachers in Conference: A Qualitative Study of Teacher-Supervisor Face-to-Face Interactions." *AERJ* 30 (Winter 1993): 675–702.

Uses conversation analysis to examine supervisor-teacher conferences. Details how roles—passive, collaborative, adversarial—are constructed.

5.3   EVALUATION OF PROGRAMS

2013. Boren, James L., and Richard L. Stein. " 'Work in Progress': A Dialogue on Curriculum Revision." *ADE* 105 (Fall 1993): 15–19.

Emphasizes the importance of process in changing the English curriculum. Points out the interrelationship of process and product, using the English Department at the University of Oregon as an example.

2014. Dasenbrock, Reed Way. "What Is English Anyway?" *CE* 55 (September 1993): 541–47.

Reviews two books about English departments: *What Is English* by Peter Elbow and *Work Time* by Evan Watkins.

2015. Dickson, Tom, and Lyle Olson. *Journalism Students' Perception of English Composition as a Preparation for News Writing.* Montreal, Quebec, Canada: Association for Education in Journalism and Mass Communication, August 1992. ERIC ED 349 568. 60 pages

Surveys news writing students for their perceptions of first-year composition and its usefulness as preparation for other academic writing, journalistic writing, and the work world.

2016. Harris, Charles B. "Mandated Testing and the Postsecondary English Department." *Profession* 93 (1993): 59–67.

Describes how a state-mandated assessment can lead to a program revitalization, assessment, and review (involving courses, portfolios, and interviews) that benefits students. Argues that mandated testing produces rote learning and leads to reduced budgets for higher education.

2017. Hawkins, Rose. "Classroom Assessment: Who Needs It?" *TETYC* 20 (December 1993): 306–12.

Argues that Classroom Assessment Techniques (CATs) help instructors identify problems with peer editing groups and make those groups more effective.

2018. Holladay, John M., and Sue Zwayer. "Monroe County Community College Writing across the Curriculum. Annual Reports 1990–1991 and 1991–1992." Monroe County Community College, 1993. ERIC ED 353 014. 91 pages

Reports on studies measuring the success of writing across the curriculum programs. Discusses the satisfaction of students, faculty, and fellows in the writing center.

2019. Larson, Richard L. "Competing Paradigms for Research and Evaluation in the Teaching of English." *RTE* 27 (October 1993): 283–92.

Discusses different paradigms for evaluating writing programs. Argues for benefits of a constructivist paradigm.

2020. Laurence, David. "From the Editor." *ADE* 105 (Fall 1993): 1–2.

Explains the background of the MLA-FIPSE English Programs Curriculum Review Project. Identifies seven key questions English Departments should address in planning curricula.

2021. Matthews, Steven Mark. "The Effect of a Summer Bridge Program's Reading Course on the Reading Development of Entering College Freshmen." *DAI* 54 (September 1993): 876A.

Finds that students passively interact with the text. Argues that teachers and students must work together to create a meaningful context for textbooks which encourages active involvement.

2022. McCleary, Bill. "Total Quality Management (TQM) Meets Composition." *CompC* 5 (January 1993): 1–3.

Explains how TQM affects composition instruction and the assessment of writing programs.

2023. Napoli, Anthony R., and George J. Hittner III. "An Evaluation of Developmental Reading Instruction at Suffolk Community College." *JARCC* 1 (Summer 1993): 37–47.

The authors cite two statistics-based studies designed to assist and assess the performance of academically underprepared college entrants. Although the study focuses on developmental reading instruction, the participants demonstrated improvement both in overall grade point average and in performance on standardized tests. They discuss implications for both program evaluation and academic development of students.

2024. Ross, Jeffrey Doyle. "Identifying a Community College English Department's Beliefs about Writing Instruction: A Qualitative Study." *DAI* 54 (September 1993): 798A.

Identifies beliefs about writing instruction held by seven full-time English instructors at a community college campus.

2025. Shook, Belinda Price. "Multicultural Reading and Thinking: Teaching Thinking Skills through the Processes of Reading and Writing." *DAI* 54 (October 1993): 1223A.

Evaluates the multicultural reading and thinking project.

2026. Soven, Margot. "Curriculum-Based Peer Tutoring Programs: A Survey." *WPA* 17 (Fall/Winter 1993): 58–74.

Describes a Brown University survey of curriculum-based peer tutoring programs and claims such programs as among the "most promising activities in WAC."

2027. Spacks, Patricia Meyer. "Prognostications: Concluding Remarks to the November MLA-FIPSE English Programs Curriculum Review Conference." *ADE* 105 (Fall 1993): 3–9.

Discusses effects of pressures from three sources—outside the academy, economics, and ideologies within institutions—and surveys conferees' responses to them.

2028. "Thinking through Writing. Lord Fairfax Community College, 1990–1992." Lord Fairfax Community College, 1992. ERIC ED 353 016. 147 pages

Reports on the "Thinking through Writing" Program for enhancing learning and thinking skills. Includes descriptions of activities provided by 10 faculty.

5.4   OTHER

2029. Crawford, Wayne. *Standards of Performance: Evaluating Grading Standards and Their Role in Student Revision Processes*. San Diego, CA: Conference on College Composition and Communication, March/April 1993. ERIC ED 358 458. 9 pages

Discusses a study of whether student-constructed grading criteria complicate or reduce teacher or programmatic standards, and whether written criteria actually drive students' writing and revision processes.

2030. Cross, Lee. "The Self-Perceived Impact of Peer Evaluation on the Writing of Adult Learners." *DAI* 54 (October 1993): 1196A.

Discusses correlations between adult learners' self-perceptions and their attitudes toward peer evaluation of writing. Points out that most did not perceive peer evaluation as valuable to good writing.

2031. Davis, Kevin. "Assessing Your Composition Course." *ET* 25 (Winter 1993): 6–10.

Assesses the effectivness of a composition course using early and late semester measures of student attitude toward writing and syntactic complexity of their texts.

6
Listservs

2032. *ACW-L (Alliance for Computers and Writing)*
Email:
• listserv@ttuvm1.ttu.edu
with the message
• subscribe ACW-L [your real name]
Contact Person:
Fred Kemp (ykfok@ttacs1.ttu.edu)
Department of English
Texas Tech University
Lubbock, TX 79409-3081

Provides an email discussion list for members of the Alliance for Computers and Writing (ACW) members and anyone interested in computers and writing; presents an informal clearinghouse for information, contacts, and resources on computers and writing.

2033. *CASLL (Canadian Association for the Study of Language and Learning)*
Email:
• listserv@unb.ca
with the message
• subscribe casll [your real name]

Contact Person:
Russel A. Hunt (hunt@StThomasU.ca)
Department of English
St. Thomas University
Fredericton, New Brunswick
E3B 5G3 Canada

Presents an email discussion list for the Canadian Association for the Study of Language and Learning. The organization formed around the annual Inkshed Working Conference and the Inkshed Newsletter.

2034. *C&CD (Computers & Composition Digest)*
Email:
• r0mill01@ulkyvx.louisville.edu
with the message
• subscribe CandCD [your real name]
Contact Person:
Robert Royar
(r0mill01@ulkyvx.louisville.edu)
Department of English
New York Institute of Technology
Old Westbury, NY 11568

Offers a periodical electronic digest for teachers interested in computers and writing. Supplies excerpts of email list MBU-L and USENET list comp.edu.composition. Support for this digest is provided by the University of Louisville.

2035. *CREWRT-L (Creative Writing Pedagogy)*
Email:
• listserv@mizzou1.missouri.edu
with the message
• subscribe crewrt-l [your real name]
Contact Person:
Eric Crump
(lceric@mizzou1.missouri.edu)
Learning Center
231 Arts & Science
University of Missouri
Columbia, MO 65211

Offers email discussion of creative writing pedagogy.

2036. *Ejournal*
Email:
• listserv@albany.bitnet
with the message
• subscribe ejrnl [your real name]
Contact Editors by emailing a message to EJOURNAL@ALBANY.bitnet

This electronic journal for humanists is concerned with the implications of electronic networks and texts.

2037. *Electronic College of Theory*
Email:
• xx124@po.cwru.edu
with the message
• subscribe electronic college of theory [your real name]
Contact:
Society for Critical Exchange
Guilford House
Case Western Reserve University
Cleveland, OH 44106-7117

Provides an email list on literary theory sponsored by the Society for Critical Exchange at Case Western Reserve University. (Membership in SCE required; details available with list signup.)

2038. *H-RHETOR (History of Rhetoric)*
Email:
• listserv@uicvm.uic.edu
with the message
• subcribe h-rhetor [your real name]
Contact Person:
Gary Hatch (gary_hatch@byu.edu)
Brigham Young University
English Department
3146 JKHB
Provo, UT 84602

This email discussion list on the history of rhetoric, writing, and communication includes announcements of conferences, calls for papers, bibliographies of recent books, brief book reviews and notices, notes and queries, and discussion.

2039. *MBU-L (MegaByte University/Computers and Writing)*
Email:
• listserv@ttuvm1.ttu.edu
with the message
• subscribe mbu-l [your real name]
Contact Person:
Fred Kemp (ykfok@ttacs1.ttu.edu)
Department of English
Texas Tech University
Lubbock, TX 79409-3081

Offers email discussion on computers and writing.

2040. *MediaMOO*
To connect, telnet to either of these addresses:
• purple-crayon.media.mit.edu 8888
or
• 18.85.0.48 8888
After entering the address, you'll get a screen that says "Welcome to MediaMOO." There, enter:
    connect guest
You'll be told what guest character you've connected to (Guest or Some-Color Guest), and you'll find yourself in the LEGO Closet. For Help, type
    help
  OR
    help manners

OR
   help purpose
To disconnect, type
   @quit

MediaMoo is an interactive, synchronous online community. It is also the home of "Netoric Complex," a series of real-time discussions, conferences, and workshops for those who use computers in teaching writing. (Netoric project announcements are posted on MBU-L and TNC email lists.)

Problems: MediaMOO is somewhat problematic because of (1) the novelty and rapid development of the technology, and (2) the wide range of activities the community supports.

2041. *National Writing Project Bibliographic Database*
For access details,
email:
• fen00sdw@unccvm.uncc.edu
or write: Dr. Sam Watson, Director
      University Writing Programs
      UNC-Charlotte 28223

Provides gopher access to the National Writing Project's Bibliographic Database.

2042. *PMC/PMC-TALK (PostModern Culture)*
Email:
• pmc-list@unity.ncsu.edu
with the message
• subscribe pmc-list [your real name]
for the journal, and
• subscribe pmc-talk [your real name]
for the discussion list

Offers a quarterly journal and an email discussion list on postmodern culture.

2043. *Project Gutenberg*
FTP sites: think.com in dir /public; quake.think.com in dir directory /pub/etext; mrcnext.cso.uiuc.edu in dir /etext.
Contact Person:
Michael S. Hart (hart@vmd.cso.uiuc.edu)
Illinois Benedictine College
Lisle, IL 60532

Project Gutenberg is a national clearinghouse for machine readable texts, primarily those of literary and historical importance. Aims to encourage the creation and distribution of English language electronic texts. Gutenberg's function is largely as an electronic publishing house, so they span an enormous range of subjects—from classical literature to video on the moonlanding to pi to 100,000 digits.

2044. *PURTOPOI (Rhetoric, Language, and Professional Writing)*
Email:
• listserv@vm.cc.purdue.edu
with message
• subscribe purtopoi [your real name]
Contact Person:
Pat Sullivan (nvo@mace.cc.purdue.edu)
Department of English
Purdue University
West Lafayette, IN 47907-1356

Subscribers to this email list discuss issues in rhetoric, language, and professional writing.

2045. *RHETNT-L*
Email:
• listserv@mizzou1.missouri.edu
with the message
• subscribe rhetnt-l [your real name]
Contact Person:
Eric Crump
(lceric@mizzou1.missouri.edu)
Learning Center
231 Arts & Science
University of Missouri
Columbia, MO 65211

Presents a "cyberjournal" (online journal) for rhetoric and writing

2046. *TECHWR-L (Technical Writing)*
Email:
• listserv@vm1.ucc.okstate.edu
with the message
• subscribe techwr-l [your real name]
Contact Person:
Eric Ray (ejray@kway.okstate.edu)
Technical Information Analyst
OSU Computer Center MS113

Oklahoma State University
Stillwater, OK 74078

Provides an email discussion list for professional technical writers and teachers of technical writing.

2047. *TESL-L (Teaching English as a Second Language)*
Email:
• eslcc@cunyvm.bitnet
with the message
• subscribe tesl-l [your real name]
Contact:
ESLCC@CUNYVM.BITNET

Offers an email discussion list for issues involved in teaching English as a second language.

2048. *TNC (TechNoCulture)*
Email:
• listserv@gtri01.gatech.edu
with the message
• subscribe tnc [your real name]
Contact Person:
Eric Crump
(lceric@mizzou1.missouri.edu)
Learning Center
231 Arts & Science
University of Missouri
Columbia, MO 65211

Subscribers engage in email discussion on technology and culture, particularly from the perspectives of postmodernism and cultural studies.

2049. *UNDERCURRENT*
Email:
• mailserv@oregon.uoregon.edu
with the message
• subscribe undercurrent [your real name]
Contact Person:
UNDERCURRENT
Erick Heroux
Department of English
University of Oregon
Eugene, OR 97403

UNDERCURRENT is an interdisciplinary, applied, accessible, and present-focused free journal available on the Internet.

2050. *WAC-L (Writing across the Curriculum)*
Email:
• listserv@vmd.cso.uiuc.edu
with message
• subscribe wac-l [your real name]
Contact Persons:
Gail E. Hawisher (hawisher@uiuc.edu)
Sibylle Gruber (s-gruber@uiuc.edu)
Department of English
University of Illinois, Urbana-Champaign
608 Wright Street
Urbana, IL 61801

Subscribers discuss issues related to writing across the curriculum.

2051. *WCENTER (Writing Center)*
Email:
• listserv@ttuvm1.ttu.edu
with message
• subscribe wcenter [your real name]
Contact Person:
Lady Falls Brown (ykflb@ttacs.ttu.edu)
Department of English
Texas Tech University
Lubbock, TX 79409-3081

WCENTER is a list devoted to the discussion of writing center theory and practice.

2052. *WHIRL (Women's History—Rhetoric/Language)*
Email:
• listserv@psuvm.bitnet
with the message
• subscribe whirl [your real name]
Contact Person:
Molly Meijer Wertheimer
(mmw9@psuvm.bitnet)
Speech Communication and Women's Studies
Penn State University–Hazleton Campus
Hazleton, PA 18201

This interdisciplinary email discussion list promotes research, scholarship, and quality teaching on women's rhetoric.

2053. *WIOLE-L (Writing-Intensive Online Environments)*
Email:
• listserv@mizzou1.missouri.edu

with the message
• subscribe wiole-l [your real name]
Contact Person:
Eric Crump
(lceric@mizzou1.missouri.edu)
Learning Center
231 Arts & Science
University of Missouri
Columbia, MO 65211

Subscribers to this email list discuss writing-intensive online environments.

2054. *WPA-L (Writing Program Admininistration)*
Email:
• listserv@asuacad.bitnet

with the message
• subscribe wpa-l [your real name]
Contact Person:
David Schwalm
(iacdes@asuvm.inre.asu.edu)
Vice Provost for Academic Programs
Arizona State University West
4701 West Thunderbird
PO Box 37100
Phoenix, AZ 85069-7012

Offers an email list discussing ideas and information on topics of concern to writing program administrators.

Subject Index
Name Index

Subject Index

Numbers in the right-hand column refer to sections and subsections (see Contents). For example, entries containing information on achievement tests appear in Section 5, Subsection 5.1 (Evaluation of Students). When the right-hand column contains only a section number, information on the subject appears in several subsections. Entries addressing assignments in the classroom, for example, appear in several subsections of Section 4, depending on the kind of course for which the assignments are appropriate.

Name Index

This index lists authors of anthologized essays as well as authors and editors of main entries.

Finet, Dayna, 1033
Finke, Laurie, 1034
Fischer, Rick, 629
Fishbain, Janet, 1362
Fishelov, David, 938
Fisher, Edith Maureen, 1093
Fishman, Stephen M., 124
Fitch, Nancy Elizabeth, 1548
Fitz, Chad, 264, 1759
Fitzgerald, Thomas K., 1238
Flammia, Madelyn, 1736
Flanders, Todd, 1548
Flannery, Daniele D., 1839
Flaschenriem, Barbara Lynn, 125
Fleischer, C., 1447
Fleming, David, 1747
Fleming, Susan, 1363
Fletcher, David C., 1364
Fleuriet, Cathy A., 1121
Fliegelman, Jay, 514
Flinders, David J., 126
Flowerdew, John, 1868
Fludernik, Monika, 808, 939
Flynn, Thomas, 1364, 1548
Foa, Lin J., 630
Foltz, Peter William, 631
Fontaine, Sheryl I., 127
Foorman, B. R., 940
Forbes, Cherly Ann, 866
Ford, Cecilia E., 941
Ford, Robert Gilbert, 632
Foreman, J., 1447
Forgacs, David, 106
Forman, Janis, 1665, 1737
Forsberg, H., 910
Forsythe, D. E., 1181
Fortier, M., 1447
Fortune, Ron, 633
Foss, Karen, 128
Foucault, Michel, 106
Fowler, David H., 767
Fowler, Lois Josephs, 767
Fowler, Susan, 375
Fowles, Mary, 591
Fox, Jennifer, 813
Fox, Roy F., 1256
Fox, Tom, 634
Fraisse, Genevive, 129
Fraizer, Daniel T., 1571
Fraker, Charles F., 130
Franan, Jacqueline, 867
France, Alan W., 119, 131, 1427, 1447
Franck, Marion R., 1474

Frank, Robert H., 1087
Frankenberg, Ruth, 132
Franklin, Kay, 127
Franklin, Phyllis, 1365
Fraser, James W., 1531
Fraser, Nancy, 726
Fraser, Norman M., 949
Fraser, Veronica, 428
Frazier, Diedra W., 868
Freebody, Peter, 635
Freed, Richard C., 1666
Freedman, Aviva, 133, 134
Freguson, Delta, 809
Freilech, Pamela, 1268
Freire, Paulo, 1423
Frey, O., 1640
Friedland, Ellen Susan, 869
Friedman, Bonnie, 1035
Friedman, Paul J., 1182
Frisk, Philip, 135
Frisk, Philip Justin, 1607
Frith, Uta, 1036
Fritz, Joyce B., 1069
Fritzman, J. M., 515
Fromkin, Victoria A., 969
Frost, Clare A., 127
Frow, John, 136
Frye, Lowell T., 1419
Fukada, Atsushi, 1878
Fulkerson, Tahita, 1548
Fuller, Hellen, 1357
Fuller, Steve, 137, 138
Fulwiler, T., 1596
Furlong, Peter R., 1037
Futrell, Wiley Michael, 1183

Gabday, D. M., 1230
Gaffney, J. S., 870, 897
Gage, J. T., 1640
Gaillet, Lynée Lewis, 139, 429, 430
Gaines, Brian R., 636, 637
Gale, Frederic G., 140, 1667
Gale, Irene Frances, 141
Gallard, Alejandro J., 1256
Gallas, Karen, 1256
Gallegher, Donald R., 1477
Gallenger, Bruce, 1286
Gamoran, Adam, 1803
Gandell, Terry S., 638
Gantz, Charles R., 1668
Gaonkar, Dilip Parameshwar, 142
Gappa, Judith M., 1315
Gappa, Lavon, 1273